A TROUBLED MARRIAGE

For Barbara,
A brilliant student
of the world and all
around lovely Person!
With Love,
Sean

DIÁLOGOS SERIES   *Kris Lane, Series Editor*

Understanding Latin America demands dialogue, deep exploration, and frank discussion of key topics. Founded by Lyman L. Johnson in 1992 and edited since 2013 by Kris Lane, the Diálogos Series focuses on innovative scholarship in Latin American history and related fields. The series, the most successful of its type, includes specialist works accessible to a wide readership and a variety of thematic titles, all ideally suited for classroom adoption by university and college teachers.

Also available in the Diálogos Series:

From the Galleons to the Highlands: Slave Trade Routes in the Spanish Americas edited by Alex Borucki, David Eltis, and David Wheat

Staging Frontiers: The Making of Modern Popular Culture in Argentina and Brazil by William Garrett Acree Jr.

A Woman, a Man, a Nation: Mariquita Sánchez, Juan Manuel de Rosas, and the Beginnings of Argentina by Jeffrey M. Shumway

The Origins of Macho: Men and Masculinity in Colonial Mexico by Sonya Lipsett-Rivera

Mexico in the Time of Cholera by Donald Fithian Stevens

Tides of Revolution: Information, Insurgencies, and the Crisis of Colonial Rule in Venezuela by Cristina Soriano

Mexico City, 1808: Power, Sovereignty, and Silver in an Age of War and Revolution by John Tutino

Murder in Mérida, 1792: Violence, Factions, and the Law by Mark W. Lentz

Nuns Navigating the Spanish Empire by Sarah E. Owens

The Pursuit of Ruins: Archaeology, History, and the Making of Modern Mexico by Christina Bueno

For additional titles in the Diálogos Series, please visit unmpress.com.

SEAN F. McENROE

A Troubled Marriage

INDIGENOUS

ELITES

OF THE

COLONIAL

AMERICAS

University of New Mexico Press   Albuquerque

ISBN 978-0-8263-6118-9 (cloth)
ISBN 978-0-8263-6119-6 (paper)
ISBN 978-0-8263-6120-2 (electronic)

Library of Congress Cataloging-in-Publication data is on file with the
Library of Congress.

COVER ILLUSTRATIONS

Sequoyah by Henry Inman after Charles Bird King, ca. 1830, oil on canvas,
National Portrait Gallery, Smithsonian Institution.

Atahualpa, Fourteenth Inca, 1 of 14 portraits of Inca kings, probably
mid-eighteenth century, oil on canvas, 23 ⅝ × 21 ¾ in. (60 × 55.2 cm).

Pocahontas by unidentified artist, oil on canvas, after 1616, National
Portrait Gallery, Smithsonian Institution; gift of the A. W. Mellon
Educational and Charitable Trust.

Sebastiana Ynes Josepha de San Agustin by unidentified artist, oil on
canvas, Museo Franz Mayer.

Designed by Mindy Basinger Hill
Composed in Adobe Jenson Pro

CONTENTS

ILLUSTRATIONS

ACKNOWLEDGMENTS

The research for this book took place over many years in archives and libraries in the United States, Mexico, Peru, Canada, and Spain. Consequently, my list of debts is a long one. Though elements of the project were begun at UC Berkeley, Reed College, and Oakland University, the bulk of the work has taken place during my years at Southern Oregon University in the Department of History and Political Science. I am greatly indebted to my past and present department chairs, Paul Pavlich and Dustin Walcher, who have done everything possible to facilitate my research despite an acute scarcity of resources. My SOU colleagues in the neighboring fields of anthropology and Native American studies—especially Jessica Piekielek, Wesley Leonard, Brook Colley, and Mark Tveskov—helped me think about how to address this book to a readership beyond the community of historians.

My past academic writing has focused largely on the early history of Mexico, but in 2012 I began pouring my energies into research on other parts of the colonial Americas. Each time I delved into a new period or region, I was keenly aware of my own inexperience. The help I received from Andean scholars was overwhelming. Vital guidance came from Charles Walker, Zoila Mendoza, Bruce Mannheim, Jean-Jacques Decoster, Kris Lane, Alcira Dueñas, Sara Guengerich, David Garrett, and Ken Mills. For practical advice on work and travel in Peru, I would also like thank Ariadna García-Bryce, Diego Alonso, Ryan Sailor, Hillel Soifer, Smit Caballero, Lidú Pilco, Raúl Dancé, and Isabel Graciela Guerrero Ochoa. My greatest debts while working in the Peruvian archives are to three historians—all at the time graduate students—who knew the collections far better than I, and offered excellent advice: Caroline Garriott, Jeremy Mikecz, and Adrian Masters.

In the world of Mesoamerican studies, I received help and suggestions from William Taylor, Amber Brian, Michele Stephens, Laurent Corbeil, John Pohl, Peter Villella, Brad Benton, Dana Velasco Murillo, José María Portillo Valdés,

Dana Levin Rojo, Karen Melvin, and Linda Arnold. Here in North America, my work was also greatly enriched by the collegial atmosphere at the Library and Archives of Canada in Ottawa and the John Carter Brown Library in Providence. My thanks to Neil Safier, Ken Ward, Barbara Mundy, Michaela Kleber, Juliane Schlag, Carrie Glenn, James Muldoon, Luis Castellví Laucamp, Owen Stanwood, David Orique, Laurent Corbeil, and Daniel Ruck. A number of archaeologists have offered thoughtful suggestions and assistance: Rus Sheptak, Julaine Schlag, Mark Tveskov, Chelsea Rose, Parker Valkenburgh, Sarah Newman, Felipe Rojas Silva, and Hugo Bravo. I have many times vowed to pay as much attention to the physical record as these historical archaeologists pay to the written one.

I am grateful to several people for reading and commenting on early versions of my work: Sylvia Sellers-García, Paul Ramírez, Karen Melvin, Susan Deans-Smith, Jeremy Mumford, David Carrasco, Cynthia Radding, Susan Deeds, and Sara Guengerich. For help with the design of this project and the original proposal, I would like to thank Kate Marshall, Andrés Reséndez, Matthew Restall, and the members of the SOU faculty writing group. I am also indebted to the editors of the University of New Mexico Press—Lyman Johnson, Kris Lane, and Clark Whitehorn, who helped me to think through and improve this project from its inception—to James Ayers, Katherine White, and Alexandra Hoff for help along the way, and to Kirk Perry for skilled line editing.

Funding for this project came from Southern Oregon University, Brown University, and the John Carter Brown Library; and from the Earhart, Fulbright-Hays, Carpenter, and Quinn Foundations. For help with grants and fellowships, my thanks to Joanne Preston.

In the reproduction of maps and artwork, I was aided by Tania Vargas Díaz (Franz Mayer Museum), Gabriela Gamez (San Antonio Museum of Art), Mai Pham (Bridgeman Images), Erin Beasley (Smithsonian), Cédric Lafontaine (Library and Archives of Canada), and Monica Park (Brooklyn Museum of Art). I am especially grateful to the John Carter Brown, Smithsonian, and Newberry Libraries for making their images available free of charge.

No part of this project could have been carried out without the help of librarians and archivists. My thanks to the staff of the SOU library and to all those who helped me in the following collections: Archivo Arzobispal in Lima; Archivo Regional del Cusco; Archivo del Arzobispado de Monterrey; Archivo General de Indias in Seville; Archivo General de la Nación in Mexico City;

Archivo General de Simancas; Archivo General del Estado de Nuevo León; Archivo General de la Nación del Perú in Lima; Archivo Histórico Nacional de España in Madrid; Archivo Municipal de Monterrey in Nuevo León; Bancroft Library in Berkeley; Benson Collection at the University of Texas in Austin; Biblioteca Nacional de Perú in Lima; Biblioteca Nacional de España in Madrid; Centro Bartolomé de las Casas in Cuzco; Escuela de Estudios Hispano-Americanos in Seville; De Golyer Library at Southern Methodist University in Dallas; Instituto Nacional de Antropología e Historia in Mexico City; John Carter Brown Library in Providence; Library and Archives Canada in Ottawa; and Library of Congress in Washington, DC. My own office library has shelves lined with invaluable resources given to me by Mary Karasch and Bill Taylor. I use them every day.

Finally I would like to thank my wife, Moneeka Settles, who accommodates my work in a life already filled with her own academic and professional responsibilities; and my son, Casey McEnroe, who, after years of witnessing this project unfold, still listens intently to my stories about history, no matter how long or obscure—a true act of generosity.

INTRODUCTION

On a green bluff overlooking downtown Portland, Oregon, a bronze sculpture of Sacagawea steps forward toward the edge of a stone block and gestures out over the city. Everyone who grew up in Portland knows that statue. Even as teenagers, we knew that the infant bundled on the woman's back is the young Jean Baptiste Charbonneau, nicknamed "Pompey" by the other members of the Corps of Discovery. As kids, we did not think long or hard about why a Frenchman and a Shoshone woman would be crossing the continent with a baby nicknamed for a Roman consul—it was just a part of the familiar Lewis and Clark story. Each day hundreds of people pass that sculpture and give at least a glance to Jean Baptiste, who is frozen forever in our imagination as a babe. Few are apt to give much thought to Jean Baptiste's later life as a grown man. Fewer still will know his grave site in eastern Oregon. In the high desert of Malheur County, where the population density is less than three human beings per square mile, a lonely historical marker commemorates his burial: "This site marks the final resting place of the youngest member of the Lewis and Clark expedition." A whole lifetime passed by between the events recalled in these two moments—between the fabled infancy of little "Pomp" and his death in 1866. As a child, Jean Baptiste moved to St. Louis and grew to adulthood under the patronage of William Clark, who financed the boy's education. Later, befriended by a traveling German nobleman, Jean Baptiste moved to Stuttgart and lived as a European for six years. He learned new languages, traveled widely, and even fathered a child. But Charbonneau's life was not without tribulations. His son died in infancy, and his place in Europe seems to have been as liminal and insecure as it was in the US. In the end, he returned to the American West, trading on his remarkable range of cultural and practical capabilities. This French-Shoshone man, who lies buried in eastern Oregon, spoke English, French, Spanish, and German; he was a merchant, a miner, a traveler, and a military scout. In the Mexican American War, he guided the Mormon Battalion across the Southwest to California, where he was soon appointed alcalde over occupied San Luis Rey. At the end of a long and fascinating career, he died on his way back home from the California gold mines—headed back to Montana. By the time of his final journey, Western America must have looked very different to Charbonneau than it had in his youth. The landscape and population had been radically transformed during the intervening years. But it was more than that; he himself had also changed.[1]

Every history book has its own history, and this one is no exception. From the time of my first musings over the Sacagawea statue in Washington Park to the present, my research has taken me from Europe to Latin America, to Canada, and even back again to the Pacific Northwest. With every return, home looks a little different. Each time, my perspective on the intermingling of European and Native American experience grows more complex. During most of the thirty years that I have spent studying history, I have also been a teacher. I view this book as a part of that vocation. I offer it to fellow historians with a sense of humility, and to teachers and students in the hopes that it will stimulate new discussions about the psychological complexity of the colonial encounter. This book is partly about literal marriages between European and native people and the families they created. It is also more broadly about marriages between customs, ideas, and institutions. As Charbonneau's story suggests, the colonial encounter was rife with risks, but also pregnant with unexpected opportunities. *A Troubled Marriage* asks students to consider how individual people navigated these risks and opportunities in their daily lives. Jean Baptiste Charbonneau is an unusual historical figure but not a unique one. The pages that follow chronicle the lives of dozens of Indian and mestizo men and women who traveled widely, read widely, crossed cultural boundaries, and found their opportunities in a dangerous world.

The people described in this book—like all people—made choices that were constrained by their environments. To understand their struggles, I have done my best to reconstruct their social and physical surroundings. This goal has taken me into the archives and libraries of Europe and the Americas, but also into the towns, cities, valleys, hill country, and farmlands where my subjects lived. Whenever possible, I have narrated events in relation to a visualized environment built up from layers of firsthand accounts and historical maps, and informed by my travels through today's natural and man-made landscapes.

Even the physical environments of the brick-and-mortar archives themselves have been touchstones for understanding the past.

It is hard to work in Mexico's national archive without being haunted by the place. Reading manuscripts in its dim corridors, I seldom shake off the sense of unease that comes from knowing that this modern repository is a former maximum-security prison built on land that once lay beneath the waters of Lake Texcoco. Many times, I have walked the streets of Mexico City past churches, palaces, and pyramids with copies of colonial-era maps in hand, retracing the daily perambulations of sixteenth-century Nahuas. In Spain, at the castle that houses the Archive of Simancas, I sat for months in the heart of the old Spanish Empire, reading correspondence from the New World. As I did, I pictured Spanish rulers, who themselves never visited the Americas, learning what they could about their Indian subjects from the dispatches that still fill box after box in the building's catacombs. Working in Cuzco, I walked every day from the old center of town, retracing the jaguar shape of the Inca city on my way to the archive. In Providence, I combed through Roger Williams's writings and imagined the plot of land that surrounds the John Carter Brown Library once busy with encounters between Englishmen and Wampanoags. Crossing the Grand River between Detroit and Toronto, digging through the archives in Ottawa, and visiting my alma mater in the Hudson Valley, I looked for the routes and places that tell the story of Mohawk wars, migrations, and resettlements. In the small towns of northern Mexico and the urban barrios of Lima, I searched for the remnants of Indian republics. I tried to keep a low profile as I walked along old boundaries, explored colonial chapels, and chatted with sextons and schoolmasters. On the streets, I was sometimes mistaken for a priest or a missionary—that too was instructive. Even back home in Ashland, Oregon, I keep looking for the shadows of the past. I took my first good look at the Rogue Basin more than twenty-five years ago when crossing the state on foot. I still hike up into the hills and spend time gazing out over the valley. I imagine the Takelma and Shasta villages that were here not so long ago, one nestled by the creek just a few blocks from my home.

An attention to place runs through this book, as does an attention to narrative and biography. This may seem a bit old-fashioned. Admittedly, the book is inspired by old approaches to comparative history and by the even older tradition of comparative biography that has existed since antiquity in the form of "parallel lives." Each chapter explores a set of issues in the marriage between European and native societies, and asks the same questions across multiple environments. How, for instance, was it possible for Europeans to live as Indians and Indians as Europeans? Why did people marry across cultures, and how did their children find a secure place in the world? What happened when complex, multiethnic empires were joined together? How were cities and towns with distinct ethnic communities built into a civic whole? The book concentrates on the lives of influential non-European people living within European empires. It treats them as individuals but also as representatives of emerging social types. To this end, it compares the situation of native writers in Peru and Mexico, the role of native military commanders in North, South, and Central America, and the influence of native religious leaders on emerging Christian societies from Quebec to Bolivia. It asks readers to explore the flexible rules of colonial culture from native and mestizo perspectives.

Teaching and Studying the Colonial Era

This book is addressed primarily to English-speaking readers in the United States who are interested in placing their history within a larger hemispheric context. Perhaps the biggest challenge for all of us is to escape the habit of American exceptionalism—the common tendency in the United States to view Anglo-American history as unique. A second challenge is to wrestle with a fundamental paradox of life within European empires: the colonial encounter was both destructive and creative; indigenous Americans were both the agents and objects of historical change. Thus a fuller retelling of native history means reckoning with the idea of Indians not just as the victims of colonial economies and politics, but also as an integral part of those economies and political systems.

In the United States, two stories dominate the retelling of the indigenous past: the first, the great holocaust of violence, disease, and slavery during the Spanish conquests of the sixteenth century; the second, the tragedy of displacement and genocide on the US frontier during the nineteenth century. This interrupted narrative of Indian history leaves us with great stretches of amnesia between the early sack of the Aztec and Inca Empires, and the much later march of settlers, mines, roads, and rails in the American West. What about those three centuries in between? And what about the times and places that fall outside the US reader's selective view? Our memory of cultural destruction expresses much that is true about the history of colonization, but it also conceals a parallel truth. Amid the casualties of conquest, survivors of a new type emerged: indigenous leaders who seized symbols of authority from the conquerors and blended them with their own. These Indians did not merely survive the conquest; they also turned the political systems, technologies, and customs of the Atlantic empires to their advantage, carving out places of privilege and security in the new colonial order.[2]

To understand how this was possible, we should consider the widely varied attitudes of Europeans toward American peoples. One often reads that European colonizers considered Indians either "noble savages" or cruel barbarians—and both perspectives were indeed common.[3] A third perspective is less familiar: the European notion of the "civilized Indian." In many times and places, colonists encountered Indians who seemed neither innocent nor barbarous; their social organizations, economies, and military prowess marked them as members of civilizations both formidable and familiar. It is true that Columbus deprecated as uncivilized the Caribbean peoples whom he first erroneously called "Indians." However, his judgments reflected the disappointment of a man who sought China's rich marketplaces but found only simply dressed Tainos and Arawaks. When Iberians reached the core areas of America's indigenous empires, they observed a very different reality. In Peru and Mexico, they encountered vast and populous cities, royal courts of unimaginable luxury, complex civil administrations, powerful armies, and markets piled high with dazzling trade goods. The conquering Spaniards incorporated these rich and powerful states into their own empires, co-opting Indian nobles as Habsburg vassals.[4]

Europeans used a familiar vocabulary to describe the leaders among these "civilized Indians." They called them emperors, kings, nobles, and notables. Over time, many Indian elites took on the institutional roles of their European counterparts, holding office as governors, councilmen, military commanders, scribes, and clerks. In Franciscan and Jesuit schools, the children of Indian chroniclers, artists, and artisans grew into a new class of transcultural elites. They wrote in Nahuatl, Quechua, Spanish, and Latin, and they built Baroque churches on the ruins of pre-Columbian temples.

The British and French were latecomers to the project of American empire. Their time of conquest belongs to a different moment in the encounter between the Old World and New. They arrived in lands already transformed by European diseases, technologies, and livestock. Though the French and English never discovered cities on the scale of Cuzco and Tenochtitlan, they did find Indian societies whose power, ingenuity, and sophistication placed them in an altogether different category from the prelapsarian savage or the diabolical barbarian of the European imagination. Though examples of European contempt for indigenous societies abound in the history of North America, there remained many times and places where the colonizers saw indigenous rulers as formidable. From the time of the first wars with the Wampanoags to that of the Anglo-Iroquois alliances, neighboring Indian kingdoms were regarded, depending upon the moment, with fear, respect, or admiration.

Both in Ibero-America and in Anglo-French America, Europeans perceived two kinds of "civilized Indians": those who appeared from the outset civilized on account of their similarities to the invaders; and those who made themselves civilized in European eyes by acculturating to the colonizers. Enterprising Indian elites brandished multiple symbols of authority, proudly asserting their ancient political mandates even as they celebrated traits newly acquired from the conquerors: European language, literacy, dress, customs, political culture, and Christian piety. Thus it was that from Bolivia to Quebec, and from the sixteenth to the nineteenth century, new kinds of transcultural elites emerged: scholars, soldiers, artists, artisans, civil servants, elected officials, and holy men and women.

The goal of this book is to view colonial society through the eyes of these indigenous leaders, asking readers to consider how some communities and individuals weathered the storm of conquest, shaped the structures of empire, and navigated European institutions, turning the tools of the conquerors to their advantage. It also aims to present a more complete picture of the varied ways in which colonizers viewed Indian leadership. Each chapter explores a set of conditions that blended European and indigenous institutions and social elites, producing an improvised marriage of cultures that was both functional and deeply troubled.

The Organization of This Book

Throughout the early history of Atlantic empires, some indigenous Americans entered into European spaces, immersing themselves in European culture. During the same period, Europeans occasionally crossed the cultural boundary in the other direction, living among indigenous peoples and becoming members of their societies. Chapter 1 opens with a series of sixteenth-century stories about these transcultural explorers: a Nahua visit to the Habsburg court; the tale of two Spanish castaways who lived among the Mayas; and the journey of two travelers, one European and one African, who lived for a decade deep in the interior of North America. The chapter considers both the breadth and duration of these cultural exchanges from the time of the first Spanish invasions to the later age of English colonization. In the early eighteenth century, Cherokee diplomats visited the English court, and English negotiators traveled to Cherokee councils. Agents of English and French diplomacy and commerce lived for years among North American Indians and routinely intermarried with them. Later communities of trappers, traders, and settlers continued these transcultural forays. In some respects, this phenomenon never ended. Chapter 1 concludes by describing the social and political environment of Canada's nineteenth-century métis—people who lived at the intersections of nations, languages, and ancestries, and who frequently redefined their identities in relation to changing circumstances. It traces a pattern of family, business, and military alliances that shaped a trade economy, which spread from Lower Canada to the Great Lakes to the Rockies, and ultimately to Oregon Territory.

Chapter 2 explores the history of intermarriage between Europeans and Native Americans as a tool for diplomacy, as an economic and social necessity, and as a broader metaphor for the formation of New World societies. In the early years of conquest, in both Mesoamerica and the Andes, Spanish elites routinely intermarried with the indigenous nobility. These marriages cemented alliances and peace agreements, and joined the fortunes and political privileges of powerful families from both sides of the Atlantic. This chapter describes carefully constructed marriage alliances between Peruvian and Spanish elites, and the intricate diplomacy between the families of indigenous aristocrats inside and outside the colonial system.

Several cultures in the Americas possessed some form of written language prior to European contact, but none had developed a written language with the flexibility and functionality of the European alphabet. Preconquest communities of scribes and scholars survived into the colonial era in the form of Mexico's *tlacuilos* and Peru's *quipucamayocs*. Early missionary efforts to spread the use of the Latin alphabet produced a revolution in indigenous people's abilities to commit spoken language to the page. Chapter 3 describes the spread of alphabetic literacy and the growth of Indian colleges and Indian intellectual communities in Peru and Mexico with particular attention to the writings of indigenous scholars. Formal institutions of higher education arrived much later in English and French North America when seventeenth-century colonial leaders began constructing schools and seminaries for Indian youths. Literacy spread not just through formal, European-style education but also through numerous informal channels, escaping the bounds of colonial oversight and transforming culture far from colonized lands. By the nineteenth century, many educators' dreams for large-scale Indian academic institutions had collapsed. And yet, at same time, significant numbers of indigenous people were now reading and writing in their own languages and in European ones. In the former English colonies, some exceptional Indian intellectuals gained access to leading academic institutions and left their mark as authors and institutional leaders.

Though Latin America's art and architecture were shaped by European aesthetic conventions, the people who actually cut the stones, carved the beams, and put brush to canvas and plaster were often Indians. Chapter 4 describes a Nahua artist who painted church frescoes in Mexico, as well as numerous painters, sculptors, and illustrators from the Andes. It considers how Europeans perceived Indian artists and their artwork, and also how Europeans interpreted these images against the backdrop of the Reformation. Native artists marked their landscape with religious images that anchored living communities to the past. They celebrated their ancestry and political status, emphasizing parallels between European and American narratives of classical and scriptural antiquity.

Throughout the history of the colonial encounter, indigenous leaders have been both the objects and the agents of Christian missionary activity. Since the sixteenth century, Indian converts have accepted and adapted the beliefs, practices, and imagery of the faith, producing novel forms of syncretism in their home communities, and also influencing the evolution of global Christianity. Chapter 5 views Indian communities through the eyes of European clergy and vice versa. Some Indian religious leaders were conscious of their historic role in shaping New World Christianity. Other Indian converts influenced the course of history, not as conscious agents but as symbols of the faith. They became heroes in the narrative of the spiritual conquest: model converts, martyrs for the faith, and even saints. The early Catholic missionaries in Spanish America imagined a special role for Indian leaders and faithfully chronicled their contributions to evangelization. This phenomenon was not limited to the Hispanic world or even to the Catholic one. French Catholics and English Protestants also seized upon Indian Christians as models of pure faith. This artful propaganda aided the conversion of indigenous peoples and also enhanced the credibility of Indian Christianity among Euro-Americans.

Chapter 6 describes daily life in the Indian towns and urban enclaves that existed within European empires. Especially in Spanish America, both the planned and ad hoc development of urban spaces conjoined the social hierarchies of the Americas to those of Europe. Spanish and Indian municipal governments and religious organizations shaped the lives of ethnically distinct communities that lived side by side in early Latin American cities. Over time, however, these social units blended and frayed at their boundaries as Indians and Spaniards passed into each other's environments. Well-positioned mestizo leaders made strategic choices about when and where to acknowledge the different sides of their ancestry. By the eighteenth and the early nineteenth century, Spanish America had departed a great deal from the colonial blueprint in which life was to be organized by membership in an Indian or Spanish republic, and in which individuals belonged to either the commons or nobility of each. In some places, indigenous leaders defended their early compacts with the crown; in others, they changed tactics, sliding between ethnic categories, or advancing their positions within social hierarchies that now favored economic class as much as family and ethnicity. The urban history of English America was different. Despite a few experiments with European-style Indian settlements, the English colonizers sought far more often to displace than to incorporate their indigenous neighbors. Their cities were understood as European spaces. However, just as literacy and material technologies jumped across cultural boundaries, so too did ideas about urbanization and the territorialization of agriculture. Well beyond the bounds of Anglo-American habitation, new indigenous lifeways borrowed from the European model. At the same time, the nucleated farming communities of English settlers borrowed Indian crops and agricultural practices. From the praying towns of early New England to the Cherokee towns of the nineteenth century, Indian citizens assumed social positions modeled on those in European municipalities.

In the sixteenth century, America's imperial wars were fought by multiethnic armies—and ones in which Indians outnumbered Europeans on both sides of the battlefield. Only very late in the history of the colonial Americas did Europeans come to constitute a majority of the soldiers in the field. From the sixteenth-century conquests of Mexico and Peru to the Anglo-French wars of the eighteenth century, military success hinged on Indian recruitment. Even less widely known is the role of indigenous allies in colonizing and governing newly conquered territories on behalf of European empires. Chapter 7 begins by addressing Spain's first important settler-allies in the New World: the Nahua states of central Mexico. These Mesoamerican warriors participated in Spanish military expeditions from Peru to Florida, establishing garrisons, towns, and local governments. On the extreme north and south of New Spain, settling land for the crown was as often an Indian undertaking as a Spanish one. In Central America and in the north of New Spain, the descendants of these Indian soldier-settlers worked for centuries to maintain their privileged position as elite Indian vassals and even noblemen. This chapter also addresses an alternate pattern of indigenous clientage through the example of South America's Guarani republics. There native leaders established armed settlements within their existing homeland that fulfilled missionary aspirations, conformed to Spanish civic norms, and provided allies to fight on the ill-defined boundary with Portuguese Brazil. This chapter traces the successes and setbacks experienced by indigenous client states down to final days of the colonial order.

In the short time from the 1770s to the 1820s, most American colonies achieved independence from their mother countries in Europe. Indigenous leaders and client states often viewed these conflicts from a different perspective than their creole contemporaries, siding with loyalists rather than rebels in the wars of independence. Chapter 8 asks why this was so. It also considers what the subsequent transition from colonial empires to nation-states meant for indigenous leaders. In many cases, new national constitutions nullified longstanding compacts between European monarchies and the native nobility for shared governance. This chapter describes the diplomacy and statecraft of indigenous leaders in Peru, Mexico, the United States, and Canada. It considers the varied outcomes for Indian leadership in the years after these great revolutionary upsets. The chapter concludes by describing the lives of several influential indigenous individuals and families in Canada and the United States, and by explaining how they preserved their authority, property, and cultural capital under legal regimes that rejected old definitions of Indian client states and Indian subjects.

Indigenous America and the Larger World
of Colonial Studies

This book is offered to the reader as part of a much larger discussion of colonial experience. At least since the end of the First World War, the global political community has debated the nature, origins, and aftermath of European colonialism. Students encounter these debates in a variety of academic contexts. Some courses encourage them to consider colonialism in relation to ideologies of cultural superiority and domination. Here the questions often revolve around the history of race, cultural hierarchy, and religious conflict. Other courses draw students into discussions of material history and economic power, as they grapple with the complex social organizations that governed resources, labor, and the distribution of gains. All the while, older questions from philosophy class keep nagging at students of history. We continue to wonder in which respects the conquered found existential freedom, and in which respects owners and rulers—for all their worldly status—found themselves unfree.[5]

The closer one gets to the ground level, the more baffling colonial history becomes. Despite the manifest arrogance of colonial maps and flags, it is far from easy to describe how empires were built, controlled, and bounded. Early modern empires were so vast and so complex that to truly describe them exceeded the capabilities of contemporary observers, not to mention those of subsequent historians. As South Asian and African scholars have discovered, the machinery of empire was constructed as often from the bottom up as from the top down. The victims of empire were numerous and varied, but so were its stakeholders. Colonial history is about European conquerors and their subject peoples, but it is also about the local leaders who inhabited the spaces between them—the non-European vassals, subalterns, and intermediaries who made the economic and political systems of empire work for themselves and for their distant sovereigns.[6]

The encounter between cultures is at the core of colonial history. But naming cultures, finding their edges, and sketching their boundaries on the map is an imperfect science. Early histories of the colonial past used vast analytical categories like race, religion, and nation to construct their narratives. Even today, we are unable to dispense with these categories no matter how insufficient they may be. The colonial studies of the recent past have also added new analytical categories and new ways of thinking about cultural exchange and conflict. Empires are now said to have not just frontiers but also centers and peripheries, borderlands, contact zones, and middle grounds. This broader terminology seeks to express the subtle variations in cultural dominance, negotiation, confusion, and exchange that existed in a world not entirely owned or controlled by any one party.[7]

Geography was once the central organizing principle for these discussions of cultural encounters, but this is no longer always the case. Colonial life came into existence along broad frontiers of conquest, migration, and settlement, but also in more intimate social and institutional spaces: between ethnically defined urban neighborhoods, in marketplaces and trading posts, in military organizations and tradesmen's shops, in marriages and families, and—finally—in the complex psychological lives of individuals of mixed heritage. These places of cooperation, negotiation, and conflict were the crucibles of colonial society, the places of hybridization.[8]

═══

This book aims to introduce new readers to a wider world of American history, and to highlight the universal human capacity for creativity under adverse circumstances. It emphasizes the strange inversions of power that take place in colonial systems, and the ways that the conquered may sometimes conquer. If upon reaching the final pages, readers feel their curiosity not fully gratified—if they feel that they have only begun to understand the complexities of Indian and mestizo life in the colonized Americas—then this book will have served its purpose.

A TROUBLED MARRIAGE

CHAPTER ONE

Crossing the Waters

A Mexican Delegation to the Habsburg Court

In the spring of 1528, a ship made its way from the Caribbean to Europe, leaving behind the shattered vestiges of the Aztec Empire, and carrying with it a remarkable delegation of New World envoys bound for the Spanish court. Under sail in the Atlantic vastness, the ship must have seemed fragile against the forces of nature; but to its most notable passenger, Hernan Cortés, such risks were routine if not trivial. Cortés was a veteran of many such voyages, and his previous decade of experience as an explorer, conqueror, and ruler had left him with a well-deserved reputation for intelligence, resilience, and cruelty. Also aboard the ship was his mestizo son, the young don Martín Cortés, who would soon set foot in Spain for the first time. Though born and raised in the Valley of Mexico, Martín was the product of a worldly childhood. His father was the powerful conquistador and his mother the famed Nahua translator and diplomat, doña Marina. Martín was still a small boy when he boarded the ship for Europe, but he was already well versed in the customs of Spain's ruling classes. He had lived most of his life in the Mexico City palace of Juan Altamirano, in the heart of the new colonial capital where Spanish and Nahua ruling classes rubbed shoulders on a daily basis. His fellow passengers were a formidable bunch. They included the young lords of Tlaxcala and Tenochtitlan, the descendants of Mexico's great rival states. Like don Martín Cortés, the Mexica aristocrats don Pedro Moctezuma and Martín Cortés Nezahualteco-lotl knew well the rocky island capital of Mexico-Tenochtitlan and the wide brackish waters of Lake Texcoco where their grandfathers had ruled. And yet nothing could have prepared them for the thousands of miles of open water that separated New Spain from old. Surely the same was true for the lords of Tlaxcala, don Lorenzo Tianquiztlatohuantzin, don Valeriano Quetzalcoltzin, and don Julián Quaupiltzintli, who bore petitions for royal patronage from their indigenous kingdom to the Habsburg court.[1]

Like some postdiluvian ark or floating museum diorama, the ship carried with it the carefully curated specimens of life in New Spain. Its forty indigenous passengers were drawn from royal families and from the ranks of the commoners; and its holds were filled with exotic plants, animals, and artifacts to delight European eyes. Among the travelers were dancers, athletes, and jugglers, whose performances would soon entertain the emperor and later the pope. For Hernan Cortés, the voyage was a remarkable reenactment of an earlier one. He had first sailed to America in 1504, then a young Spaniard seeking his fortunes in the little-known reaches of the New World. Now he retraced his steps in reverse: back from Tenochtitlan through the Kingdom of Tlaxcala; out the port of Vera Cruz (where he himself had inaugurated Mexico's first European government); across the Atlantic to the port of Palos de la Frontera; onward by river and road to his home estate in Medellín; and finally to his destination, the roving circuit court of Emperor Charles V. Cortés had set out to conquer the New World two decades before; now he returned, an older and more powerful man, acting as the patron for this delegation of young indigenous and mestizo aristocrats whom he would soon present to the crown as new vassals.[2]

Traveling through Spain, these young lords of the New World were quite a sight. Dressed sometimes in the gilded and feathered garb of their homeland, and sometimes in the sumptuous European garments given them by the king, they must have appeared both familiar and exotic to Spanish observers. In either guise, some things remained abundantly clear: they were gentlemen, rulers, and vassals of the empire—but vassals unlike those ever seen before in Europe.[3]

In the 1520s, the Habsburg court was elegant and cosmopolitan; but it was also somewhat elusive. The legions of courtiers that surrounded the king were so great in number and so profligate in lifestyle that the court was forced to remain forever in motion—like a cloud of locusts stripping each region of sustenance as it moved from palace to palace. It usually took a while to reach the court, and even longer to gain an audience. It is not altogether clear where it was that Cortés and the Indian lords finally met with their European sovereign. According to some accounts, the meeting took place in Toledo; according to others, in Barcelona. But regardless of which regional capital received them, one may be sure that the visitors made a powerful impression.[4]

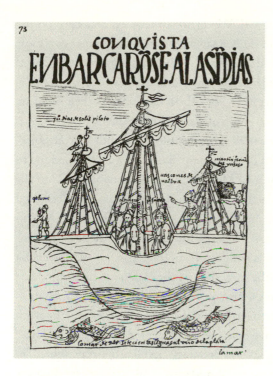

FIGURE I Christopher Columbus, Juan Díaz de Solís, Diego de Almagro, Francisco Pizarro, Vasco Núñez de Balboa, and Martín Fernández de Enciso, 1615/1616. Ink on paper by Felipe Guaman de Ayala (1526–1613). Private Collection / Bridgeman Images. Original in *El primer nueva corónica y buen gobierno*, Royal Library of Denmark, Copenhagen.

Thanks to a fortunate historical accident, we have a pretty good idea how the Nahua lords appeared to European eyes. When the New World visitors reached Emperor Charles V, they found him in the company of Christoph Weiditz, a sculptor, engraver, and painter who produced beautiful and detailed sketches of regional dress and customs as he moved between European capitals.[5] Weiditz captured the appearance and activities of the native Mexicans in meticulous detail. In most of the surviving sketches, the men appear heroic in figure, their skin partly bare, and their limbs thickly muscled. Their faces and ears are pierced with rings and pendants of precious metals. A man dressed only in feathers holds a fletched pinwheel in one hand and a brightly colored parrot in the other. Men step proudly across the pages in great plumed capes; and in one sketch, a woman stands modestly concealed beneath artfully arranged layers of shirt, tunic, and cloak. Several of the images fit comfortably with European notions of masculine competition: a warrior holding a saw-toothed pole arm; two athletes knocking a ball back and forth; a juggler tossing and spinning a log with his feet; and a pair of men locked in a game of chance or skill, staring intently at brightly colored pebbles. These performances of wit and daring were repeated for the emperor and for Pope Clement VII. Weiditz's painterly eye was fixed on the transatlantic visitors, but we can easily imagine the faces of Europe's two most powerful men lit by interest and amusement. Surviving portraits of Charles and Clement, the most famous by Titian and Piombo, show their sharp gazes, suggesting keen powers of observation. For a short time, at least, their arresting eyes were focused on this curious group of visitors from America.[6]

The American envoys had traveled great distances and with specific objectives in mind. They represented three parties, all of whom had something to gain: the Cortés family, the house of Moctezuma, and the nobles of Tlaxcala. The presence of these groups at the great imperial bargaining table reflected several distinct phases of Spanish colonization in Mexico. The young Martín Cortés embodied two elements of the conquest: the contributions of his conquistador father and those of his indigenous mother. The nobles of Tlaxcala could point to their service in the early days of the conquest and in the years since. Without Tlaxcalan armies, provisions, and advice, the early Spanish forces in Mexico would surely have been defeated—and everyone knew it. Finally, the sons of Moctezuma, whom Cortés presented as the "natural lords" of Mexico, arrived with a unique form of social capital. They represented legitimate royal authority in the New World and symbolized Mesoamerica's respectful subordination to Habsburg rule. Many of Spain's early indigenous allies could seek royal preferment based on their military service over the past decade, but the Mexica nobility claimed consideration on the basis of an older and more profound title to the land. They had pledged their fealty to the Habsburg Empire without renouncing their own political mandate.[7]

Several of the petitioners died before they could accomplish their objectives. Nonetheless, within a year, many of the embassy's aspirations were met. Hernan Cortés returned to New Spain as the marquis of the Valley of Oaxaca; his mestizo son Martín remained in Spain to become a page in the royal household and a knight in the Order of Santiago. The Moctezuma family was partially vindicated in its territorial claims, and Isabel Moctezuma, the principal heir of the Aztec emperor, was confirmed in her title as encomendera over Tacuba, with rights to its land and labor.[8]

The Tlaxcalans returned to Mexico with fewer tangible accomplishments. But they were just beginning a diplomatic campaign that would last decades and reap great rewards. Don Lorenzo Tianquiztlatohuantzin died of a sickness contracted in Spain, but don Valeriano Quetzalcoltzin and don Julián

Quaupiltzintli survived their travels, crossed the Atlantic once more, and arrived in Tlaxcala to report on their efforts abroad. The second Tlaxcalan delegation to Spain would prove far more successful than the first. In 1534, a new mission to the crown led by Tlaxcalan nobleman and governor Diego Maxixcatzin Tliquiyahuatzin departed New Spain for Iberia. It was a pregnant moment for indigenous diplomacy. Tlaxcalans were now well informed on the administrative and political contests within the larger empire, and they were ready to respond to changing circumstances. The first delegation had sailed to Spain with Cortés, but it returned to find Mexico under a new political regime, one led by Nuño de Guzmán and the first audiencia. The second expedition was well timed to take full advantage of evolving conditions on both sides of the Atlantic. Maxixcatzin delivered his petition to the emperor and returned to New Spain the following year in the company of Antonio Mendoza, New Spain's first viceroy. The two men were now intimately acquainted with each other, trusted by the king, and in a position to shape the organization of the infant colonial state. Mendoza's orders gave him broad authority to supersede existing administrative arrangements and install a bureaucracy directly responsible to the crown. Maxixcatzin arrived back in Tlaxcala with new titles from the emperor and new privileges for his community. His luggage contained the royal coat of arms for the "loyal city of Tlaxcala," as well as a set of charters protecting Tlaxcala's ancestral lands and granting her citizens freedom from Spanish encomienda.[9] Maxixcatzin and Mendoza no doubt discussed the political affairs of New Spain in the course of their long voyage from Iberia. Mendoza's subsequent comments on Tlaxcalans reflect his great esteem for their republic, as well as their central role in the viceregal state.[10]

Maxixcatzin was one of the many native leaders charged with protecting his community during the perilous and chaotic transition to European rule. Indigenous noblemen of his generation showed a remarkable capacity for political and cultural improvisation in a rapidly changing world. Maxixcatzin was born into an independent Tlaxcalan nation composed of four distinct subpolities, each with its own political and religious center. He returned to his homeland in a more complicated age. Fortunately, Maxixcatzin was now well versed in Spanish political traditions and armed with royal titles. He and his contemporaries were in a position to mitigate the disasters of the conquest era and seize some of the rare opportunities presented by Spanish rule. The church would prove a vital ally in many of their designs. Tlaxcalans formed a close partnership with the Franciscan order and soon set to work constructing a new capital that would symbolize their people's special status as Indian vassals and Christian subjects. By 1536, the walls of a Franciscan college were rising on the hillside, and new municipal buildings arranged around a central plaza rose from the valley floor. The lords of Tlaxcala were, for the time being, exempt from many forms of colonial taxation and service. At the same time, they retained ancestral privileges over their own Indian subjects. It was the Tlaxcalan commoners who cut the stones and carried the burdens for the construction of the new city. The four elements of the Tlaxcalan nation endured, and soon Tepeticpac, Tizatlán, Ocotelulco, and Quiahuiztlán were graced with new churches and palaces built in the Spanish style. In between them, the plazas, town homes, and municipal buildings of the new urban center came to symbolize the wealth and privilege of an emerging Hispano-indigenous elite.[11]

The young men who crossed the waters from Nahua Mexico to Habsburg Europe in the 1520s and 1530s transformed Spaniards' understanding of their infant transatlantic empire. They also returned to Mexico changed men. Their firsthand knowledge of European and American customs, languages, and politics left them uniquely positioned to communicate European ideas to their fellow Nahuas and to influence the terms under which European and indigenous states would be integrated.

But what of the European travelers who crossed the ocean in the other direction? Were they not changed by the experience as well? Several remarkable accounts of early Spanish encounters in the New World suggest that they were. Europeans in the Americas entered Indian worlds, learning their languages, adopting elements of their culture, and sometimes even renouncing their own. The captivating story of early Spanish landings in the Yucatán suggests that the boundary between European and Maya culture could be breached in both directions.

Becoming Indian: A Spaniard among the Sixteenth-Century Mayas

The Spanish conquest of Nahua central Mexico was swift, but the conquest of the Maya Yucatán was not. Though it was one of the first points on the mainland visited by Spaniards, the Yucatán proved a thorny place for the extension of the Habsburg Empire and the Christian faith. In 1536, more than a decade after the fall of the Mexica Empire, and after a long series of battles for the control of Central America, the Maya lands on both sides of today's Mexico-Honduras border still eluded Spanish authority. When the regional leader Ciçumba rallied his countrymen against the Spanish settlement at Buena Esperanza, Pedro de Alvarado, now a veteran of conquests throughout the Americas, came to the aid of his countrymen. Alvarado's troops defeated the local Mayas and captured Ciçumba near the river Ulúa. Afterward, while surveying the battlefield, Alvarado and his men encountered something unsettling. Among the corpses of their fallen enemies lay the body of a bearded European. His face was familiar, but the rest of his appearance was not. He was clothed and painted for battle like a Maya.[12]

Who was this man and what was he doing in the interior of Honduras? Why was he fighting not *for* the Spanish conquest but *against* it? The Spanish settlers thought they knew: he was Gonzalo de Aroca, a Spaniard who had abandoned his countrymen, cast off the trappings of European society, and joined the ranks of their enemies. Historians have long speculated that this fallen rebel was the same man known elsewhere as Gonzalo Guerrero, one of the first Europeans to explore the Mexican mainland, and thereafter a persistent thorn in the side of would-be conquerors. If this is true, the man found dead on the battlefield had been living as a Maya for twenty-five years.

Gonzalo Guerrero was one of two long-term survivors of a 1511 Caribbean shipwreck. In that year he had set out from Vasco Núñez de Balboa's collapsing Panama colony bound for Hispaniola in a ship commanded by Juan de Valdivia. But the vessel struck a reef off the coast of Jamaica, and the survivors, who escaped in a rowboat, were left at the mercy of the currents until they made landfall in the unfamiliar terrain of the Yucatán. Many had perished at sea, and the unfortunate survivors who did make it to dry land were soon taken prisoner by a local lord. In a short time, hard labor, disease, and human sacrifice claimed the lives of all but two: Gonzalo Guerrero and Jerónimo de Aguilar.

The story of what happened to the two men, over the years that followed, offers a fascinating study of the cultural alternatives presented to those on the unstable fringes of colonial society. Aguilar found his way back into the world of the Spaniards and came to play a decisive role in the conquest of Mexico. Guerrero, in contrast, renounced his European identity forever, despite repeated attempts by his former countrymen to return him to the fold.[13]

For almost a decade following the shipwreck, the two men survived without setting eyes on other Europeans, and only faint rumors of their survival reached Spanish ears. In 1517, the expedition of Francisco Hernández de Córdoba traveled much of the coastline of the Yucatán Peninsula. The expedition was a disaster. Unable to pinpoint valuable resources or to venture far inland without provoking the wrath of local people, the whole undertaking came to an ignominious end. The captain himself died of wounds suffered in a battle at Champotón, but much of the crew survived, and with them a curious piece of news. In Campeche, when the ships had stopped to take on fresh water, the men were greeted by local Mayas who called out to them "Castilian! Castilian!"[14] To some of the returning survivors, including the future historian Bernal Díaz del Castillo, the implications were clear: somewhere in the interior, the lost Spaniards had survived.

Two years later, the ship's pilot, Antonio de Alaminos, along with Bernal Díaz and several other veterans of the first expedition, returned to the Yucatán under Hernan Cortés, this time with Maya captives whom they hoped to use as translators. Cortés reached the island of Cozumel in 1519 and soon established friendly relation with the local caciques. Still mulling over Francisco Hernández's strange encounter, Cortés asked the lords of Cozumel (through his Indian interpreter, Melchior) whether they had heard of other bearded men on the mainland. The caciques' response was confident: the bearded men lived two days' journey inland from the coast, where they served the local Maya lords. Delighted by the news, Cortés contrived an elaborate plan to find them. His sailors carried Maya messengers to the mainland bearing letters for the lost Spaniards and gifts for their hosts or captors. The messengers set out as planned with the Castilian notes wrapped tightly in their hair. The whole undertaking suffered some missteps, confusion, and delays, as well as the near sinking of a Spanish vessel. After many days, the ships returned to Cozumel empty-handed. Cortés had nearly given up on the whole enterprise when a great seafaring canoe propelled by many ranks of Indian rowers appeared on the horizon, heading toward Cozumel. In it sat Jerónimo de Aguilar.[15]

Cortés had been seeking a lost Spaniard, but the man who approached Cozumel by canoe was hardly recognizable as such. He wore a loincloth, and his hair was cut in local fashion. Spanish soldier and chronicler Andrés de Tapia recorded the moment of shock and surprise when a man whom he mistook for a Maya trader approached him and, in a voice long unaccustomed to pronouncing Castilian words, cried out: "Dios y Santa María de Sevilla."[16] A few moments later, Cortés, baffled by the man's appearance, asked Tapia: "Where is the Spaniard?" Upon which, Aguilar, kneeling before him in his Maya clothing, replied: "I am he."[17] The remains of his Spanish garments (now scarcely recognizable as such) were wrapped in a bundle protecting his most precious possession, a Book of Hours brought with him from Europe years before.[18] Aguilar's words were still slow and awkward as he recovered his neglected mother tongue; but once he had collected his wits, he began the long and remarkable tale of his shipwreck, captivity, escape, and survival.

Why, we might ask, was so much effort expended on account of these two castaways? After all, Cortés and his men were a hard and ruthless lot, and though they may have had a genuine human concern for the lost Europeans, the scale of the undertaking bespeaks other motives. These were still the early years of exploration when the contours of the Americas were only dimly understood by European cartographers. The continent had yet to be circumnavigated, the interiors were unknown, and the dangers and riches of the new lands belonged largely to the realm of imagination. Without knowledge of the geography, customs, and languages of the mainland, how could the Spanish proceed? The practical value of these two castaways who had lived, worked, and communicated in Maya lands was inestimable. The Spanish desperately needed the help of Aguilar and Guerrero, but only Aguilar had answered their call. For reasons that would soon become clear to all concerned, the Spanish needed Guerrero, but he no longer needed them. A long time had passed since the two men first entered the Maya world. After their narrow escape from the threat of ritual sacrifice, the fates of the two men had diverged.

At first, Guerrero and Aguilar shared the same dire situation. Shortly after the 1511 shipwreck, they were captured, confined to cages, and left to await their deaths as sacrificial victims. But both escaped and quickly sought the protection of other Maya lords. Aguilar saved his skin but ended up consigned to a humble station in indigenous society. His was a life of hard labor under a new Maya protector. Aguilar carried water, chopped wood, and worked in the fields.[19] His relief must have been profound when a messenger from Cozumel unwrapped his hair and produced this note from Cortés: "Gentlemen and brothers, here in Cozumel I have learnt that you are captives in the hands of a Cacique, and I pray that you come here to Cozumel at once, and for this purpose I have sent a ship with soldiers, in case you have need of them, and a ransom to be paid to those Indians with whom you are living. The ship will wait eight days for you. Come in all haste, and you will be welcomed and protected."[20] Aguilar experienced the arrival of Cortés's message as a miracle and as a deliverance from slavery. Guerrero thought otherwise.

In the years since the shipwreck, Guerrero had found his way into the service of Nachan Can, lord of Chactemal. There Guerrero's skill as a soldier and military engineer allowed him to rise through the ranks, ultimately becoming a nobleman and military commander in this Maya city-state.[21] According to Bernal Díaz, Aguilar delivered Cortés's message to Guerrero in person, but his own sad appearance did little to persuade Guerrero. The latter's wife took one look at Aguilar and, noting his humble appearance, remarked: "Look at this slave coming to call upon my husband."[22] Guerrero was married to a noblewoman, he had sired three sons, and he now occupied a position of great honor and influence in one of the region's most powerful states. Why, we might ask, would he wish to return? Aguilar remarked on the man's profound attachment to his wife and child, along with his worldly success. He also hinted at something more: regardless of Guerrero's wishes, it was too late to recross the cultural boundary. His nose and ears were pierced and ornamented, his face and hands tattooed.[23] Guerrero had become a Maya. Later, Franciscan missionary Diego de Landa offered another explanation: "By living as an Indian, he gained a great reputation and married a woman of high quality, by whom he had children, and he made no attempt to escape with Aguilar."[24] Landa believed that in Guerrero the Mayas had found a true convert, not just to their language and customs, but to their religion as well. Fernández de Oviedo agreed. Guerrero, now pierced, tattooed, and married to a Maya woman, was no longer a Spaniard at all; he had "converted into an Indian."[25]

Sixteenth-century Iberians were inspired and obsessed by the possibility of recruiting Indian noblemen into their armies and kingdoms, and by the objective of converting them to the Christian faith. Yet the case of Guerrero shows that not all men who crossed this cultural and religious membrane did so in the same direction. The Spanish reaction to Guerrero suggests a reasonable fear. When Aguilar brought Cortés the news of Guerrero's refusal, he warned the commander that Guerrero was a dangerous man; it was he who had organized an Indian attack against Spanish crews at Cabo Catoche two years before. Whether that was true or not, Cortés was concerned: "I wish I had him in my hands for it will never do to leave him here." If indeed the body found on the battlefield of Río Hondo nine years later was that of Gonzalo Guerrero, then the fears of Cortés were well founded.[26]

As the case of Aguilar and Guerrero suggests, it could be a winning or a losing proposition for a European to cross over into the indigenous world. Success in an unknown cultural environment required sharp wits, a knack for communication, and a great deal of luck and timing. Some who crossed this line were lured by opportunity, but many did so out of desperation and necessity. Such was the case with one of the sixteenth century's most famous travelers and survivors, Álvar Núñez Cabeza de Vaca. His arduous and improbable journey through North America produced one of the first written accounts of the continent's deep interior. For numerous indigenous peoples, Cabeza de Vaca offered the first glimpse of a European; and for his later Spanish readers, he offered the first (and sometimes last) description of the native peoples who lived far beyond the bounds of Nahua civilization. His return to European society began with a fortunate encounter on New Spain's northern frontier.[27]

Soldier to Shaman:
A Spaniard in Native North America

In 1536, Captain Diego de Alcaraz was on the very edge of the world known to Spaniards when he encountered one of the sixteenth century's most interesting travelers. Alcaraz and his underfed troops were exploring and raiding the frontier of today's Sinaloa and Sonora. They were among the first waves of Spanish traders, raiders, and explorers in the extreme north. After the fall of Tenochtitlan in 1521, the victorious Spaniards and their allies had fanned out in all directions, exploring the fringes of the old Mexica Empire and continuing beyond its bounds in search of conquests, captive laborers, and—above all else—veins of gold and silver. Some expeditions had proved lucrative, but most had not. So far, Alcaraz had little to show for his efforts. The Spaniards' reputation for cruelty had preceded them, and they traveled many days through abandoned villages without seeing a single inhabitant. Alcaraz's men, now desperately short on supplies, were in a place that seemed impossibly distant from their fellow Europeans. But their illusion of isolation was suddenly shattered when two unfamiliar men appeared in their midst. One was white, the other black, and they emerged from the wilderness accompanied by eleven Indian companions. Their clothing—what little of it they wore—bore no resemblance to that of Europeans, but from their mouths came perfect Castilian.[28]

The two strange men were taken to Captain Alcaraz, who learned the details of the long and improbable journey that had left them so unusually dressed and so far from home. Their names were Cabeza de Vaca and Esteban, and they had traveled thousands of miles from the site of Spain's early, ill-fated invasion of Florida. They had survived for nine years by grit, intelligence, ruthlessness, and—above all else—their ability to master the languages and customs of North American peoples. So thoroughly had they acculturated themselves to life in indigenous America that one might reasonably ask whether they were still Spaniards. They had endured near endless misfortune by adapting to unfamiliar cultures and by pressing what few advantages they had; they returned transformed. This experience of cultural immersion and adaptation was shared by numerous Europeans in their era, and by even more New World Indians.

Alcaraz must have been greatly surprised by the arrival of the thirteen travelers, and even more so by their companions who appeared soon thereafter. Upon meeting Captain Alcaraz, Cabeza de Vaca explained that his small embassy represented a much larger group. He and Esteban had left behind two more Spaniards and a substantial community of Indians, who were hiding in a secluded mountain valley in order to escape the clutches of Alcaraz's own slave raiders. Esteban now offered to lead Alcaraz's men back to the mountain camp. He returned in a few days with Spaniards Alonso de Castillo and Andrés Dorantes as well as six hundred local Indians.

That the castaways had once been members of the Spanish community there could be no doubt. At least three of the four men had the telltale beards of Europeans, and all four spoke perfect Castilian. Yet judging from Cabeza de Vaca's account, local Indians did not consider them Spaniards at all. Some passages in his narrative make one wonder whether the four men still viewed *themselves* as Spaniards. The castaways had known of Alcaraz's expedition long before he knew of them. When Cabeza de Vaca saw a local Indian wearing a metal belt buckle and iron nail as ornaments, he suspected other Spaniards must already be in the region. When questioned about the buckle, the Indian reported receiving it from bearded men. Clearly, bearded Spaniards in their many guises were already transforming New Spain's northern frontier. The castaways soon came in contact with local Indian bands that had suffered attacks from Spanish raiders. Though the Indian communities were devastated by these encounters, the Spanish fared even worse. Alcaraz's men were on the brink of starvation, and it was Cabeza de Vaca and his Indian allies who came to their aid. He later recalled: "We gave everything else to the Christians so that they could distribute it among themselves . . . and after that we suffered disputes with them because they wanted to enslave the Indians."[29] The phrasing implies that "the Christians" were a community distinct from his own. Likewise, though he often recounted his own amateur missionary activities, he usually used the word "Christian" not to describe himself and his three traveling companions but to describe the armed invaders. In his dealings with Alcaraz, Cabeza de Vaca negotiated on behalf of the hidden Indian refugees who were "fleeing to avoid being killed or made slaves by the Christians," and he later agonized over their fate, noting to his Indian companions that if their new village communities were mistreated, "the Christians" would "be to blame."[30]

Cabeza de Vaca described the community of "Christians" to his Indian friends with some trepidation, and the latter so thoroughly distinguished the castaways from the invaders that they refused to believe the two groups could both be Spaniards, "saying that the Christians were lying because we came from where the sun rose, and they from where it set; and that we cured the sick, and that they killed those who were well; and that we came naked and barefoot, and they went about dressed and on horses."[31] The four wanderers wore buffalo skins, beads, and feathers; they carried ceremonial drinking gourds and indigenous trade goods as they walked barefoot over thousands of miles of inland territory. They spoke a trade language called Primahaitu and learned the customs of trade and diplomacy wherever they went. We are told that Cabeza de Vaca made the sign of the cross to heal the sick and bless food, but also that he considered his God and the indigenous god Aguar to be the same. Though the castaways introduced novel practices wherever they went, it is clear that, after nine years adrift in North America, they had become far more Indian than their Indian companions European.

How Cabeza de Vaca and his three companions came to be living as Indians is a long and interesting story. He began his journey into North America working as a royal treasury official and military officer, and it was in that capacity that he had served the Pánfilo de Narváez expedition to Florida. His companions in the long overland march had joined the expedition by different paths and for different reasons. Esteban, an African from Morocco, who spoke both Arabic and Spanish, began as the slave of Castilian officer Andrés Dorantes.

The fourth survivor of their great journey was Alonso Castillo Maldonado of Salamanca, captain of the ill-fated Florida landing.

Their journey had begun in 1528, in the same springtime that Hernan Cortés set sail for Spain with the young noblemen of Tenochtitlan, Texcoco, and Tlaxcala. Cabeza de Vaca, Alonso de Castillo, Andrés Dorantes, and the slave Esteban set out from Cuba bound for Florida with a vast entourage of mariners, soldiers, and settlers under the command of Pánfilo de Narváez. The expeditionary force endured combat, disease, shipwreck, and slavery. The invasion was a categorical failure; and even the De Soto expedition that followed a decade later was only marginally more successful. It is strangely fitting that Narváez's grand and tragic undertaking was chronicled by Cabeza de Vaca (a European who transformed himself into an Indian) while the De Soto expedition was chronicled by Garcilaso de la Vega, a mestizo Inca nobleman who lived much of his life as a Spanish gentleman.

The Narváez expedition was impressive at the outset. Five ships and four hundred men left Havana and landed on the Florida coast near modern Tampa. Seven years before, Narváez had seen the riches of Mexico. He had played an undistinguished role in the conquest of New Spain through his failed attempt to arrest Cortés in 1520, and through his subsequent defeat and captivity by the more famed conquistador. Narváez, no doubt, dreamed of comparable kingdoms to plunder and tax in Florida. He did ultimately earn his place in history, but as a tragic figure, not a triumphant one. When his men landed on the North American mainland, they encountered skilled and hostile warriors but no rich cities. Guided by Timucuan Indians and tempted by rumors and delusions of gold mines ahead, the expedition worked its way from the Bay of the Cross northward into the land of the Apalachees.

Cabeza de Vaca traveled with this large Spanish force, but it was an expedition that operated as much within an indigenous diplomatic logic as a European one. One of the officers was don Pedro, the Nahua nobleman from Texcoco; he and the rest of the invaders relied on Timucuan scouts to guide them through Florida's densely forested interior. The Spaniards became crueler and more desperate as the mirage of great cities and stone palaces was replaced by the reality of small villages and reed shelters. Unable to sustain themselves on their provisions or trade, the Spanish resorted to theft and extortion, holding hostages in exchange for food. Near today's Tallahassee, they captured an Apalachee chief, which proved a grave diplomatic error. Counterattacks from the enraged local population soon drove the Spanish forces back to the coast. Constructing makeshift rafts, the survivors put out to sea in the hopes of reaching other Spaniards on the Mexican mainland, perhaps those at the Pánuco River hundreds of mile to the southwest.

Only a handful of men reached the Texas coast. Their commander was now dead and the vast majority of their companions lost. The few who made landfall at Galveston Island had no choice but to leave behind the European world and enter into an indigenous one. In the early days of exploration, it was a common Spanish practice to kidnap Indians and use them as laborers or train them as translators. Now, in an unexpected reversal of fortunes, it was the Europeans who found themselves captives. They landed in Texas, malnourished, battered by storms, and almost entirely without equipment or supplies. In this state of desperation, they were taken in by the local Karankawas, first as slaves or servants. Over time, however, the remaining Spaniards were able to adapt to their environment and even thrive in it. While some of the Europeans would experience servitude for the first time, one of their African slaves would emerge from this cultural chaos as a leader and an equal.

The Spaniards had routinely forced their captives to learn Castilian in the past, but the rules were different in Texas. Cabeza de Vaca tells us that he soon learned the language of the "Mareames." As the months and years passed, the castaways' clothes wore away, and they parted with their rusting crossbows and arquebuses, both of which had proved less useful than the Indians' tools and weapons. The Spaniards and Karankawas were remarkably open-minded with respect to each other's appearances, technologies, and beliefs. They healed each other's wounds and diseases with magical utterances, and by blowing on injuries and making the sign of the cross. Over time, the castaways made the most of their ingenuity and their magical skills. They were emancipated from servitude, gained a higher social status, and even achieved positions of political leadership within Indian communities. They navigated between ethnic environments, living among the Karankawas, Avavares, and Arbadaos—societies now almost completely lost from the historical record. Dorantes, Castillo, Esteban, and Cabeza de Vaca mastered several trade languages: that of the Mareames in the East, and of the Primahaitu in the West. They traveled far and wide, proclaiming themselves the "Children of the Sun" and engaging in trade, diplomacy, sorcery, and medicine wherever they went. Cabeza de Vaca seems to have delighted in his reputation as a medicine man, noting with satisfaction that the Indians believed he could inflict sickness by directing his angry thoughts at them. This is the man who emerged from the backcountry of Sinaloa with his three surviving companions and hundreds of Indians to meet Captain Alcaraz in the spring of 1536. His negotiations with Alcaraz suggest a kind of divided identity and divided loyalties after all those years living in the Indian world. Before agreeing to travel south to the new viceregal capital in Mexico City, Cabeza de Vaca exacted a promise: all of his Indian companions would be protected from violence and captivity.

The four travelers were quite a sensation when they arrived in the capital. Their advice was sought by the archbishop and the viceroy, who earnestly consulted them on the prospects for profit, security, and evangelization in the extreme north. Esteban, whose gift for cultural improvisation had already allowed him to live as an African, an Arab, a Spaniard, and an Indian, remained in Mexico City only a short time before returning to the northern frontier. He soon led Fray Marcos de Niza on an enormous, though ultimately unsuccessful, expedition to search for the mythic Cities of Gold in the lands that would later become New Mexico.

Cabeza de Vaca's written narrative, *Relación de los naufragios*, became something of a best seller back in Europe, but Spaniards of the time were principally interested in the book because it provided intelligence on the lands and peoples of North America. Today, the text offers us insight not just into the early cultures and landscapes of North America but also into the minds of sixteenth-century Spanish explorers. It is an unusual tale, but the castaways of the Narváez expedition were neither the first nor the last Spaniards to cross over into indigenous worlds; and not all who did so wished to return again.

Becoming an English Lady: A Powhatan Visit to London

Crossing from the indigenous world to the European one was no small feat. Among Anglo-Americans, by far the best-known early traveler of this sort is Pocahontas. Today she is more a myth, an archetype, and an icon of popular culture than she is a clearly remembered historical figure. The real Pocahontas was forced to reinvent herself multiple times to navigate the violent complexities of the frontier between English and Powhatan Virginia. Born Matoaka, and nicknamed Pocahontas, she would end her life in England as "Lady Rebecca." She was not the first of her people to enter Europeans' cultural spaces or learn their languages, but she *was* one of the most successful. For many years, Spanish and English explorers had captured Indians from her homeland and transported them to Europe in order to use them as informants and translators. Many died as prisoners; some escaped and disappeared from the European record; others broke free and turned against their former captors. The story of Pocahontas is somewhat different. She was not a wandering boy snatched at random from shore but the daughter of the Powhatan ruler Wahunsenacawh, a powerful Algonquian lord acknowledged by the English as the king or emperor of his people.[32]

The earliest Englishmen in Virginia were both brutal and vulnerable. Famously, the first colony at Roanoke disappeared by 1590, its settlers leaving scarcely a trace. Whether they were casualties of hunger, victims of violence, or just desperate people who—like Cabeza de Vaca—merged into the indigenous community remains an unsolved mystery. The feeble Jamestown colony, established by the London Company in 1607, teetered on the brink of extinction for years while settlers struggled to feed themselves. Relief expeditions came and went, their captains chronicling the uncertain prospects of the small beachhead of colonists who remained there. One such expedition was shipwrecked on the shoals near Bermuda, leaving John Rolfe and the other passengers of the *Sea Venture* to struggle on toward Virginia in improvised ships in the year 1610. Those who survived this difficult passage arrived at a settlement whose fate remained uncertain.

The story of Rolfe's subsequent marriage to Pocahontas says much about Englishmen's notions of indigenous leadership, and about the diplomatic strategies employed by all parties in the region. In 1613, Captain Samuel Argall took Pocahontas hostage in the midst of negotiations between the village of Pasptanzie and the English. The practice of seizing or exchanging diplomatic hostages was by no means new to the Europeans or to the Algonquians. Likewise, politically expedient marriages were familiar on both sides of the ocean. Pocahontas's earlier marriage to the warrior Kokoum was probably arranged, in part, to secure the relationship between her father and the leaders of the Patawomecks. They in turn delivered her into the hands of Argall who likely considered her an asset both as a diplomatic go-between and as a hostage. Pocahontas was taken back to the English colony where she became the ward of Thomas Dale, a prominent Virginia settler who endeavored to Christianize and acculturate her. It was during this period that she became acquainted with John Rolfe. The odd courtship that followed culminated in a formal marriage and the birth of a son.

In 1616, John Rolfe and Pocahontas, now known as Lady Rebecca, set sail for England in the company of her one-time captor, Samuel Argall. But her position in the world had changed. Lady Rebecca was not just a valuable go-between for the English and natives in Virginia; she was also a valuable emissary for the Virginia Company back in England, where the directors were carrying out their own domestic diplomacy in an effort to boost financial and political support for the New World colony. Rebecca toured London in style. She was accommodated at the expense of the Virginia Company, dressed regally and guided through polite society. She and her husband attended the theater, aristocratic galas, and dinners with English notables. She was welcomed by the clergy, who took pride in this Christian convert drawn from the ranks of native Virginia's ruling families. In London, she sat for a portrait with the artist and engraver Simon van de Passe, who preserved her likeness for posterity. In his portrait, we see Pocahontas as she would have appeared to London's elite urbanites. She wears a tall, plumed hat, pearl earrings, and a broad lace collar. Her sumptuous blouse is meticulously embroidered with flowing patterns, and her delicate hand clutches a fan of ostrich feathers. Her clothing and her well-orchestrated appearances in London were meant to communicate a message to all concerned: Virginia had a bright future as a colony that would unite native elites and English ones in a shared Christian and European culture.

This dream would not come to pass—at least not in the ways that Rolfe and the Virginia Company imagined. Ongoing epidemics and two waves of warfare between Powhatans and Englishmen in the 1620s and 1640s would deplete the Native Americans' population and leave them dispossessed of their lands and resources. But Pocahontas's visit to England took place at a moment when a different path yet appeared open. Rolfe and Pocahontas traveled to London in the company of several other young Powhatans of high social standing. One young man died in the course of the journey. Two of the young women (whom the English called Mary and Elizabeth) converted to Christianity and learned to read and write. The Virginia Company groomed them as brides for Bermuda colonists and sent them to the island in possession of indentured servants. Clearly, at this formative moment in the English Atlantic, an Algonquian woman of substance could become an English lady in the eyes of metropolitan and colonial society.

FIGURE 2 Portrait of Pocahontas in London, 1616. The inscription reads: "Matoaka Als Rebecca Filia Potentiss. Princ: Powhatani Imp: Virginiae." Black-and-white engraving by Simon Van de Passe (1591–1644), Holland. John Carter Brown Archive of Early American Images, 01508. Courtesy of the John Carter Brown Library, Brown University.

The unhappy fate of Pocahontas herself is well known. The pathogens of London were her undoing. She fell ill in England and died before her return voyage could reach the mouth of the Thames. Nonetheless, an interesting precedent had been set. For a time, Pocahontas held in her grasp a respectability and authority derived both from her birth family and from her cultivated traits as a Christian Englishwoman. Though she did not live long enough to enjoy the fruits of her public relations campaign, her descendants would benefit from her accomplishments. At the end of her short life, Pocahontas gave birth to Thomas Rolfe. Like so many influential postconquest figures in Spanish America, Thomas was the son of a European conqueror and the grandson of an indigenous ruler. He received land titles from his European father, some of which may have been based on customary claims from his mother's family. Thomas served in the colonial militia and maintained a small fortification for Virginia. In the end, it is difficult to know whether we should reckon him among the conquerors or the conquered.

Cherokee Diplomats in Britain

By the time the first English-speaking settlers established colonies in Virginia and Massachusetts, Indians and Spaniards had been crossing the Atlantic in both directions for more than a century. News of European visitors and invaders had already spread among indigenous communities on the Atlantic Coast well before John Smith's arrival at the Jamestown site. The English, likewise, knew a great deal about the Americas before many of them had set foot in the Western Hemisphere. They enjoyed the benefits of secondhand knowledge that emanated from the Spanish colonies in the form of maps, letters, and chronicles. These materials were sometimes coveted as secret documents, and at other times available to a broad reading public, complete with provocative titles and sensational prints. But these early accounts were notoriously inaccurate, and the first sites of English settlement were among people far removed in both geography and culture from the "Indians" of the Spanish kingdoms. Yet, little by little, the same process of mutual discovery long at work among Spaniards and Indians began to take place at higher latitudes. By the eighteenth century, indigenous leaders on the frontiers of British and French North America routinely participated in the sorts of diplomatic missions first undertaken by Nahuas two hundred years before.[33]

One such effort took place in the spring and summer of 1730. In that year, following much preparation and travel, a Cherokee delegation reached England. On the twenty-second of June, seven Cherokee military leaders entered the royal chambers of King George II for a formal audience. They were accompanied by Alexander Cuming, a Scottish adventurer and freelance diplomat. The meeting took place in Windsor Castle, thousands of miles from the Cherokee homeland, and at the center of power for England's expanding global empire. It was an event choreographed to fit the protocols of the day. The visitors bowed, knelt, and exchanged greetings both warm and formal. The cultural encounter was a complicated one, but both the royal hosts and the visitors were accustomed to the complexities of intercultural diplomacy. Language itself was a delicate matter. Cuming was a native English speaker, but the same could not be said for the Cherokees or, for that matter, the king of Britain. George II made his public appearances dressed in French courtly fashion: a powdered wig, white stockings, an ermine collar, and velvet robes stitched with gold thread. Born in Hannover, George was raised first to speak German and French, and only later to use English in preparation for his accession to the British throne. He had reigned for less than three years when he met with the Cherokees, but he was a man raised to rule, and his conception of empire was an expansive and multicultural one.[34]

Though the June meeting was not memorialized with a painting or sketch, records from this and later Cherokee delegations give us some sense of how these visitors from the Carolinas may have appeared to European eyes. Their hair would have been cropped high and short, their faces tattooed, and their garments a mix of traditional leather or fur and English cloth.[35] The Indian emissaries carried no documents of their own—the Cherokee would remain without a written language for nearly a century—but their political commission was clear: they held authority delegated to them by the Cherokee leadership, and they could guarantee the terms of the agreement by attesting to verbal commitments made on both sides of the Atlantic. They represented the larger interregional Cherokee congress that had convened at the urging of Alexander Cuming in the town of Nikwasi a few months before. The site was well chosen. In those days, Cherokee towns were spread over a broad region at the borders of today's Carolinas, Georgia, Alabama, and Tennessee. Politically, the Overhill, Middle, and Lower Towns constituted three distinct confederations. Nikwasi was situated on the banks of the Little Tennessee River, accessible to representatives of all communities and wreathed in an aura of historical authority. The town surrounded a great earthen mound, marking the site as an important urban space since the time of its construction by Mississippian peoples more than seven hundred years before. There, Alexander Cuming had recognized the regional leader, Moytoy of Tellico, as the emperor of the Cherokee people. Cuming gave him gifts in the name of the crown and received Moytoy's ritual gestures of loyalty to Britain. Cuming's memoir describes the meeting at Nikwasi and the later one at Windsor Castle as the crucial moments that joined together English and Cherokee worlds. Cuming saw the British and Cherokee Empires as parallel organizations, and he viewed himself as the brilliant diplomat who drew them together and subordinated the latter to the former. There is some sleight of hand in Cuming's story; and yet the essentials ring true. The structures of Cherokee politics were very different from those of the British Empire, but the meeting at Nikwasi was one

FIGURE 3 *The Three Cherokees came over from the head of the River Savanna to London,*
1762. Engraving on paper by George Bickham the Younger, London. British Museum
1982, u.3745.

in which political elites from the Cherokee community deliberated over the
transatlantic military alliance and trade relationship, then selected representatives to communicate their sentiments to the English crown.[36]

The Cherokee travelers remained in England for several months, finally
concluding an agreement that was committed to writing as "The Articles of
Friendship and Commerce" on September 7, 1730. The Cherokee diplomats are
named in the document: Scayagusta Oukah, Scali Cosken, Ketagusta, Teth-
tone, Clogoillah, Colannah, and Oucounacou. The treaty recognized these
men as the plenipotentiaries of the "whole Nation of the Cherokee Indians"
and memorialized all parties' assent to the agreement sketched out in principle
months before at Nikwasi. Rhetorically, the document is a pact between the
"powerful and great Nation of the Cherokee Indians" and the "Great King" of
the English. The contents make clear that it was not an agreement between
equals. England was to be the hegemonic power and the Cherokee Nation a

dependent ally. At same time, the Cherokees were described as internally sovereign, ruled by their own traditional leadership, and possessing clear title to
their lands and resources. The treaty included a military pact and an exclusive
trade agreement. The British offered status goods, such as belts of wampum
and European broadcloth, but the most important items were tools and weapons: guns, shot, flints, hatchets, and knives. The Cherokees were described as
commercial partners, military allies (against European and Indian enemies),
and, finally, as members of a security compact to protect the institution of
African slavery. The agreement obliged the Cherokees to hunt down and capture fugitive slaves, and offered them in return enormous bounties in the form
of European tools and weapons. The Cherokees were to be legal persons in
the terms of British jurisprudence, and the crown promised that any British
subjects guilty of crimes against the Cherokees would be punished to the full
extent of English law. The treaty stopped short of an equal relationship based
on mutual extradition of criminals, but in other respects this was a document
that regarded Cherokees and Englishmen as equivalent civic actors. This was
a far cry from the place of Africans under English law (or Cherokee law for
that matter) and suggests that indigenous North Americans enjoyed some
early successes in positioning themselves within the ethnic hierarchies of the
empire.[37]

What began as a bit of diplomatic improvisation between Alexander Cuming and a few Cherokee leaders had by the fall of 1730 crystalized in a diplomatic accord that would define the basic framework of English-Cherokee
negotiations for years to come. The crown received the seven emissaries as a
delegation empowered by Moytoy and the Nikwasi congress. When the men
returned to North America, they carried a message addressed to "the whole
Nation of the Cherokees, their Old Men, Young Men, Wives and Children."
The voyage greatly enhanced the authority of the emissaries, cementing their
place as cultural intermediaries and political dealmakers. Moytoy himself become a key contributor to British military efforts in North America, embracing
the mutual-defense compact embedded in the 1730 agreement. A decade later,
he made common cause with the British against Spanish Florida, taking an
army into the field beside Georgia settlers led by James Oglethorpe. Moytoy
was killed in battle, and his death ushered in a new era of Cherokee politics as
competing factions struggled to control succession. In previous eras, the Cherokees had not followed a fixed rule of primogeniture, but Moytoy's teenage

son, Ammonscossittee, seems to have invoked the English practice by seizing leadership upon his father's death, and by touting his family's role as British clients. His tactics worked. Ammonscossittee would rule for more than a decade and leave behind an important precedent: gaining and holding power among the Cherokees would now require both internal support and British imperial patronage.[38]

Three decades later, four Cherokee emissaries led by the influential war chief Ostenaco would follow a similar route. By then the Cherokees knew exactly how to represent themselves in public and private diplomacy among the English. They traveled by way of Williamsburg, visiting with local notables and dining with the president of William and Mary College, then continued on by sea to Plymouth and London. They attended the theater, saw the sights, and received English guests at their local accommodations. The Cherokees' traveling companion, Henry Timberlake, was intent on protecting them from the indignity of contact with the English underclasses; he instructed the servants to admit only "people of fashion" into the Cherokees' company. Finally the emissaries met with the king himself—this time George III—and were received as visiting plenipotentiaries. Ostenaco gave his diplomatic speech in Cherokee, and the Anglo-German king prepared a careful written response that was to be carried back to the New World and read aloud by skilled Cherokee translators. Henry Timberlake had hoped to return with the Cherokees to America and to advance his own economic and political fortunes on both sides of the Atlantic, but he soon found his ambitions frustrated by a lack of royal patronage. Ostenaco and his companions returned to America with greatly enhanced prestige and with a more refined understanding of the opportunities and risks of engaging with the English.[39]

These direct contacts between Cherokee leaders and the crown opened up multiple diplomatic avenues. Now, not only could the Cherokees leverage the British and French against each other, but they could also choose whether it was wisest to negotiate with individual colonies or to work around settler governments and appeal directly to the king. Their later treaty negotiations in the midst of the Seven Years' War show the Cherokees to be well informed and pragmatic as they sought control over the location of forts and the flow of arms and trade goods.[40] The story of Cuming's relationship to Moytoy sheds light on another interesting property of intercultural diplomacy in these years. Prior to his encounter with the Cherokees, Alexander Cuming was not exactly a crown official, and Moytoy was not exactly an emperor—at least not in the sense that these words were currently used in Europe. But both men seized upon their relationship as a form of social capital; and they used this social capital to advance their political status at home. Timberlake and Ostenaco were proceeding on the basis of this example. At the boundaries of English and Cherokee communities, ambitious men were able to renegotiate their social positions and in the process reshape a transatlantic alliance. Perhaps this is how empires are fashioned.

Marriage, Métis, and Ethnogenesis in Western Canada

This view of empire raises a multitude of questions. If Indians and Spaniards could cross from one political universe to another; if they could routinely adopt each other's social traits, exchange technologies and resources, gain new identities, and renounce old ones—if all of this was indeed true—how should historians tell the story of America's colonial era? Our most familiar historical narratives are populated with characters we call "Europeans" and "Indians," but these words seem inadequate to describe the range of cultural identities that really existed in the colonial era. A Spaniard could become a Maya war captain, and a Powhatan could become an English lady. All sorts of native caciques, *principales*, and chiefs chose to live as European gentlemen, and no small number of Indian rulers were actually of European descent. One seems to encounter examples of these successful clients, intermediaries, and culture crossers under every rock. Still, it is fair to ask how widespread and how enduring these experiences were. After all, by concentrating on social elites, this book is by definition a study of exceptional cases, not a description of the average lot. Leaders (both hereditary and self-made) have always constituted a small slice of the human community on both sides of the Atlantic—small, but also very important, and very influential over time. As to the duration of this phenomenon—in which ambitious individuals shifted from one cultural community to another—it seems that it never came to end. As long as there have been powerful political communities defined by heredity and ethnicity, people have been artfully renegotiating their membership in them.[41]

Consider the case of Louis Riel, leader of Western Canada's late nineteenth-century métis rebellion. Remembered today as a founding figure in the history of Saskatchewan and Manitoba, his story illustrates the wide range of cultural improvisations that continued to take place in ethnically complex frontier spaces even centuries after Europeans first arrived in the Americas. Louis Riel was an impressive man. In surviving photographs, he is immediately recognizable by his mane of curling hair, his prodigious whiskers, and his face marked by concentration and resolve.[42] His likeness survives in studio portraits, newspaper prints, and wanted posters, along with written characterizations both hostile and admiring. In his midforties, during the summer of 1885, Riel found himself a prisoner in Regina, Saskatchewan, awaiting trial on charges of high treason. Riel's life story constitutes one of the great mythic narratives of the Canadian West.[43] Descended from generations of explorers, hunters, and trappers, he rose to political prominence as a champion of regional autonomy. He lived in a time of continuous strife among the western tribes, the crown, and the Hudson's Bay Company, and during an era of ever-shifting coalitions among French, English, and Indian settler communities—a time when constructing and maintaining civil society was a matter of political improvisation. His trial, which was followed closely by the press throughout Canada and the United States, raised as many questions about the man and his movement as it answered. Riel was convicted of treason and put to death, but only after leaving behind an astonishing record of his beliefs. The trial transcript shows that his testimony was punctuated by political speeches; mysterious, prophetic utterances; and puzzling dialogues in which Riel performed the roles of both barrister and witness.[44]

At first, the defendant spoke of his political beliefs in artful riddles, but as the trial progressed and other witnesses were called, the central tenets of his movement became clear. Riel described his contemporary Canadian West as a place of poverty, chaos, and exploitation. Indians and French-speaking métis suffered at the hands of trading-company profiteers. Even the white Anglophone settlers struggled to protect their livelihoods and to gain true citizenship. Riel's solutions combined commonsense political reforms with grand constitutional renovations and mysterious millennial visions. He imagined a future Canada as a confederation of regional states, each defined by ethnic identity. His vision was generally Catholic in inspiration but also radically inclusive, aiming ultimately to end the confessional boundaries and institutional conflicts that had defined Christianity since the Protestant Reformation. His revolution, he believed, would bring forth a North American Christian republic with a special historical destiny.

In the trial, Riel referred to all of his plans for new political boundaries and institutions as his "diplomacy," but his use of the word carried an unusually broad meaning. Riel's political designs seem like something borrowed from Aaron Burr, Sam Houston, or Brigham Young. Sometimes his agenda was regional in scale, mirroring these earlier political attempts to build autonomous republics at the instable boundaries of North American empires. At other times, Riel's ambitions appeared global in scope. He foretold the collapse of the British Empire, the end of the Vatican's power, and the rise of a new theocratic capital in North America with himself as prophet. At the trial, his former friend and collaborator Charles Nolin described Riel as a cagey dealmaker and a shrewd politician, who orchestrated his broad cross-caste rebellion through a powerful ad hoc council. Nolan also described a mystical side of Riel's leadership, reporting that Riel had returned to the Red River area with a great book of maps, plans, and prophesies written in Buffalo blood.[45]

Riel's uprising became a five-month insurrection and included three full-fledged battles that cost hundreds of lives. Today it is commonly called the North-West Rebellion, an event that continues to provoke discussion among his admirers and detractors. Riel left behind numerous unsolved questions: Was he a madman? A prophet? Or even a protonationalist? And what was this large regional community for whom Riel claimed to speak? It helps to consider how Riel situated himself among the ethnic groups of the Canadian West. Riel considered his accusers white men, but he thought of himself differently. Addressing the judge and jury he explained: "Yes, you are the pioneers of civilization, the whites are the pioneers of civilization, but they bring among the Indians demoralization." Riel proclaimed himself the leader of a distinct ethnic community born from European and native ancestors—what the English then called half-breeds, the Spanish mestizos, and the French métis. With great pride, Riel announced: "I am glad that the Crown have proved that I am the leader of the half-breeds in the North-West. I will perhaps be one day acknowledged as more than a leader of the half-breeds, and if I am, I will have an opportunity of being acknowledged as a leader of good in this great country." In the course of the trial, the prosecution and the defense sometimes had trouble defining the breadth and nature of the rebellion. Nolin, in a series of responses, finally pinned it down: the rebels were "a constitutional movement [that] took place in the Saskatchewan to redress the grievances," and "the half-breeds of all religions took part." The whites, for their part, sympathized but "did not take direct action in the movement."[46]

One is tempted to think of the so-called half-breeds as a population without a fixed identity that existed at the frontiers of more clearly defined ethnic communities. But to Riel, the métis were a distinct people—one with clearly defined cultural traits and a unique historical destiny. In the midst of the trial, Riel addressed Charles Nolin, his former friend and current hostile witness, as a member of this métis community: "Besides Nolin knows that among his nationality, which is mine, he knows that the half-breeds as hunters can foretell many things, perhaps some of you have a special knowledge of it. I have seen half-breeds who say, my hand is shaking, this part of my hand is shaking you will see such a thing to-day, and it happens. Others will say I feel the flesh on my leg move in such a way, it is a sign of such a thing, and it happens. There are men who know that I speak right."[47]

What should we make of Riel's identity as a spokesman for the métis, and as a self-proclaimed prophet of Canada's nonwhite populations? If we are to believe Riel, his return from the United States to Canada in 1884 was motivated by his concern for the welfare of these people. At trial, he recalled: "When I came into the North West in July, the first of July 1884, I found the Indians suffering. I found the half-breeds eating the rotten pork of the Hudson's Bay Company and getting sick and weak every day. Although a half breed, and having no pretension to help the whites, I also paid attention to them." Here, and elsewhere, Riel calls himself a "half-breed." However, in the strictly hereditary sense, Louis Riel was a white man. Yes, his family tree included an Anishinaabe great-grandmother, but with this one exception, his pedigree was exclusively European. He made no secret of his genealogy while at the same time presenting himself as métis: "I remembered that half-breed meant white and Indian, and while I paid attention to the suffering Indians and the half-breeds I remembered that the greatest part of my heart and blood was white and I have directed my attention to help the Indians, to help the half-breeds and to help the whites to the best of my ability."[48] To a modern reader, Riel's numerous and contradictory statements about his racial identity just do not add up—unless we consider the possibility that *to him* being métis was more about culture than blood. For Riel and his followers, "métis" may have been a political and social condition more than a biological one. He identified himself first and foremost with all of the people who struggled for subsistence on the edges of the English, French, and Indian worlds—men whose markets were global but whose labors and products were local. Their hunt for hides and pelts had, over the centuries, produced a profound convergence of cultures.[49]

The economy and culture of Riel's Red River region had many progenitors—all touched by the opportunities and pressures of the international fur trade. Coureurs de bois (independent French traders) had been working the lakeshores and rivers systems of Canada since the seventeenth century. They lived among native communities and adopted many of their customs. With the French came a stream of trade goods, material technologies, and commercial practices that would also influence native culture. From the very beginning of the French fur trade, intermarriage between European men and native women was exceedingly common. These unions, termed *mariage à la façon du pays*, were generally not church consecrated, but they were widespread, culturally sanctioned, and usually recognized under common law and in company administration. Fur-trader marriages were a crucial element in frontier diplomacy, creating trust and obligations between the European traders and their brides' families. The native wives were vital translators, guides, and instructors who taught languages and customs to their male partners. The households constructed by these marriage were the fundamental economic units of the fur-trade economy. Indigenous women fished, snared animals, cured hides, sewed clothing, and carried burdens. They also mothered generations of children who would combine the experience and capabilities of their parents. After the British conquest of Canada, fur-trade imperialism was more often the work of commercial companies than of traditional political institutions. Chief among these organizations were the North West Company and the Hudson's Bay Company, both of which operated under royal charters. The North West Company had a backbone of French employees while the Hudson's Bay Company was more English in character. Both employed large numbers of Scotsmen, and both relied ultimately on the labor of the many and varied native communities that formed a vast market for the exchange of furs and European trade goods that eventually stretched from Hudson's Bay to the mouth of the Fraser River.[50]

The core of the Red River colony was established in 1812 as part of an ambitious colonization scheme by the Hudson's Bay Company and the Earl of

Selkirk, Thomas Douglas. The colony was intended to serve as the agricultural core for provisioning the HBC's commercial operations in the region. In this complex, multiparty enterprise, Selkirk used Scottish settlers under the aegis of the English company to profit from the French-Canadian fur trade in an area inhabited by Cree, Salteaux, and Assiniboine peoples. This kind of co-colonization was a common practice throughout the colonial Americas, but the Selkirk venture had some distinct advantages: a large community of métis intermediaries and an established custom of intermarriage. The Red River community would have the relationships and the experience it needed to thrive. Unfortunately, commercial rivalries between trading companies in Canada created their own fault lines for regional warfare. The first battles the Selkirk settlers would have to fight were not between nations but between companies. In 1816, a force of métis in the employ of the North West Company attacked the colony's headquarters at Fort Douglas, and the fight for control of the area lasted for several years. In 1821, regional hostilities finally subsided when the North West Company and the Hudson's Bay Company merged. The larger organization now combined the enormous human capital of the region's ethnically diverse population of farmers, trappers, and traders.[51]

Like first-generation conquistadors in Mexico and Peru, the leaders of the fur trade companies used intermarriage with local elites as a tool to cement commercial and political agreements with regional powers. Native women, taking advantage of their family status or their own skills as diplomatic intermediaries, found husbands in the fur trade who could guarantee their safety and comfort in the elite residences of company forts and towns. It appears that the Europeans followed Indian norms of marriage diplomacy more often than their own as they sought partnerships with local rulers. This became a standard practice in the US West, just as it had been in French and English Canada. In the late nineteenth century, the web of colonizers and fur traders—allied to different national governments—converged in the Pacific Northwest.[52]

One of the most influential men in the nineteenth-century Pacific Northwest was Concomly, leader of the Chinook Indians, who controlled trade on the lower Columbia River. Representatives of the British and American trading companies needed his blessing if they hoped to trade goods at the Pacific entry to the vast river system of the Columbia Basin, which covered much of today's Oregon, Washington, and Idaho states. Chinook traders controlled the strategic bottlenecks in the river trade, making themselves indispensable middlemen between native producers and European and American merchants. Theirs was an old economic and political game but not an easy one. It required diplomatic skills, a carefully cultivated image of power, and occasional recourse to violence. On the Columbia River, as was the case elsewhere in the Americas, arranged marriages were vital for establishing trust between communities, sealing agreements, and maintaining channels of communication. Both the Chinooks and the Euro-American traders had practiced this craft for generations. Leaders of the British fur-trading companies who entered the Pacific Northwest in the early nineteenth century and intermarried with influential native families from the Great Lakes and the western interior paved the way for operations that eventually reached the Pacific.[53]

Peter Skene Ogden, who established markets for the HBC throughout Washington, Oregon, and Utah, began his career in Canada. His common-law wife, Julia Rivet, came from a family deeply immersed in the fur trade. She was likely Nez Percé and connected by blood and marriage to the upper Columbia's most competent traders and wayfinders. Julia was Peter's constant companion on inland expeditions that extended over thousands of miles in the American West. During these years, John McLoughlin commanded HBC operations in the region from his post at Fort Vancouver. McLoughlin was a harsh and uncompromising man, but his competence at intercultural diplomacy was impressive. One of the keys to his professional success was his wife, Marguerite Waddens, the métis daughter of early French-Canadian fur trader Jean-Étienne Waddens. John and Marguerite were the first family of Fort Vancouver and as such attended carefully to their relationships with the Chinook traders. They married their sons into Concomly's family, cementing a long-standing pragmatic relationship.[54]

Whether this marriage alliance was first devised by the McLoughlins or the Chinook chief is not clear, but it certainly fit with established practice. Concomly engineered marriages with Europeans and native chiefs, but the fact that so many of his children married leading fur-trade officials suggests that he prioritized these commercial relationships. His daughter Elvamox married Duncan McDougall, one of the founders of Fort Astoria; another, Timee, married Thomas McKay, the son of Marguerite Waddens; a third daughter, Ilchee, married fur trader Alexander McKenzie. Concomly's daughters were often referred to as "princesses" in contemporary documents, giving some sense of the political importance accorded to them by fur traders. Alexander McKenzie and

Ilchee worked closely together, embroiling the company and the tribe in each other's enterprises. In the end, McKenzie was killed by neighboring Klallam Indians during an escalating dispute over trade that involved Salish, Chinook, and company interests.[55]

The terms of marriage, diplomacy, and trade changed radically over the course of the nineteenth century in Western Canada and the Pacific Northwest. On the Columbia, the influx of Anglo-American settlers, and with them the arrival of new epidemics, transformed demographic and political reality. Wave after wave of malaria struck the lower Columbia, starting with an outbreak in 1830 that killed Concomly.[56] The balance of power tipped steadily in favor of Euro-Americans as the new Oregon Trail disgorged its settlers in the Willamette Valley. Elite marriages between fur traders and high-status Chinook women ceased to matter, but everyday marriages between local and settler populations remained important to the survival and prosperity of both groups. At the same time, intermarriage with settlers (especially in an increasingly patrilineal and patronymic context) concealed the indigenous roots of the region's young, mixed-heritage population. Back in Manitoba, the widespread sense of métis identity produced different memories and different ethnic categories. But there, too, the inexorable shift in numbers and power changed the terms of pragmatic intermarriage. Until the late nineteenth century, the leading families of the Red River region included numerous native and métis women. They were married to farmers and voyageurs, but also to clerks, clergymen, and company officials. Slowly, the ground would shift beneath these families. As the old fur trade was replaced with agriculture, and as large numbers of settlers and large numbers of European women arrived, the place of indigenous and métis wives became less secure or, at the very least, less visible.[57]

—————

Definitions of ethnicity and nationality have never been tidy. The long era from the sixteenth to the nineteenth century furnishes seemingly endless examples of people who moved back and forth between indigenous and European cultural spaces, engaged in diplomatic practices that required constant translations and transformations of political symbols and identities. None of this should come as a surprise. The empires of the early modern world were fashioned though pacts among formerly separate ethnic communities. Mohawks were ethnically distinct from Oneidas, Scotsmen from Englishmen, Cañaris from Quechuas, and Basques from Castilians. Across these varied terrains, cultural translation and adaption offered a path to personal advancement for those with sufficient talent. The phenomenon of Europeans transforming themselves into Indians, and of Indians transforming themselves into Europeans, began in the earliest days of transatlantic contact. But shedding one's ethnicity altogether is a rare and difficult feat. More common by far were individuals who retained status traits from their birth communities, even as they appropriated new symbols of power in an adopted culture. With the passage of time, mestizos constituted an ever-larger share of the colonial population. They were uniquely positioned as negotiators between ethnic communities.

CHAPTER TWO
A Marriage of Equals

Dynastic Diplomacy in the Colonial Andes

On June 18, 1565, two powerful men approached the site of
Chuquichaca from different sides of the Urubamba River. Accompanied by
guards, scribes, and retainers, both parties prepared for a delicate diplomatic
encounter. The suspension bridge between them was engineered from native
fibers, and it hung above the frigid waters that marked the boundary between
two parallel Andean worlds. In one direction lay viceregal Peru with its highland
capital of Cuzco; in the other, Vilcabamba, a Quechua kingdom ruled by the
last independent branch of the Inca royal family. The two men were Juan de
Matienzo, a jurist in the employ of the Spanish colony, and Titu Cusi Yupanqui,
emperor of the Vilcabamba Incas.[1]

The meeting had taken years to arrange, and it was not without risks. More
than three decades of conflict and instability within the region's Spanish and
indigenous leadership classes had bred civil wars, conspiracies, and unpredictable cross-cultural alliances. Based on experience, neither man could trust the
other. In the Spanish civil wars, Titu Cusi and his father had intermittently
allied themselves with the Almagro faction against the partisans of Pizarro,
but at other times their agenda was far from clear. Even in moments of relative stability, their men had raided Spanish commerce and encouraged the
Indians under colonial rule to flee to Vilcabamba. The Spanish record was
worse. Though Titu Cusi's father, Manco Inca, had once backed the Spanish
invaders and served as their regional client, he received little reward for it. After
years of Spanish deceit and abuse, Manco finally fled beyond the reach of the
colonial state, first to the site of Vitcos and then to Vilcabamba, the new Inca
capital where Titu Cusi was raised. Even there, the royal family was not safe
from Spanish treachery. In 1544, two Spaniards approached Manco's court

under false pretenses. They described their role in the death of Pizarro and proclaimed themselves friends of the neo-Inca state. Once welcomed into the community, they turned against their hosts, assassinated Manco, and triggered a broader political crisis. Royal succession among the Incas was a complex matter, but the death of Manco came at a moment of especially deep divisions. Over the previous decade, the Spanish had not just pressed against Manco's frontiers; they had also elevated a dynastic rival, legitimating his brother Paullu Inca as emperor within the viceroyalty.[2]

It was this very dynastic breach that had occasioned the meeting at Chuquichaca Bridge. The trauma of the early conquest years had now come to an end on both sides of the Urubamba frontier. Pizarro and Almagro, along with most of their immediate male relatives and followers, lay dead after a civil war that in the end accomplished little more than the extinction of the leading conquistador families. Now Manco and Paullu also lay dead, leaving their patrimonies hotly contested. Manco's younger son, Titu Cusi, remained in Vilcabamba while his elder brother, Sayre Topa, entered the viceroyalty and assumed control of the Inca estates in Yucay, an awkward schism that would leave the Inca aristocracy split into rival states. These divisions at the top of the political hierarchy also meant structural instability at the bottom. For resourceful Andean commoners, this left room for negotiation and improvisation. Humbler indigenous laborers found cracks in the system. Seeking to improve their lot by dodging taxes and labor obligations, many fled across the hard-to-police boundary between viceregal and independent Peru.[3]

Soon both branches of the Inca dynasty, as well as the Spanish viceregal establishment, had a shared interest in healing the political schism. By the early 1560s a plausible solution emerged: a carefully arranged wedding could reunite the branches of the Inca royal family and facilitate the peaceful integration of the Hispanic and neo-Inca political systems. Of course, such a thing was easier said than done. The Spanish governor of Peru, Lope García de Castro, seems to have placed this project high on his list of priorities, sending Diego Rodríguez de Figueroa to meet with Titu Cusi in the spring of 1565. The Vilcabamba emperor was slow to invest his trust in Rodríguez de Figueroa, but after many weeks of patient diplomacy, the latter returned to the viceroyalty with encouraging news. They had reached an agreement in principle that would satisfy the Spanish and also the two rival Inca leaders: the descendants of Titu Cusi and those of Sayre Topa could retain title to the lands and peoples of their current kingdoms provided that their lines of descent were merged. The son of the former would marry the daughter of the latter. The future monarchs, Quispe Titu and his cousin Beatriz Sayre Topa, would hold the lands of Vilcabamba and those in the Valley of Yucay that had been deeded by the Spanish to Inca Sayre Topa a few years before. Other members of the families would be confirmed in their titles of nobility and given annual subsidies. The future Incas would no longer possess categorical sovereignty (inasmuch as all of their lands and peoples would be under the additional supervision of a Spanish corregidor), but this was already the case for the Quechua populations living inside viceregal Peru, and it seemed an acceptable price to pay. These terms would leave most of the political and economic questions resolved, but the synthesis of the two kingdoms also involved profound questions of culture and faith.[4]

Ever since Manco Inca's people fled to Vilcabamba in 1537, Catholic missionaries had dreamed of wooing the breakaway kingdom into the Catholic faith, and of reuniting it with the larger community of Quechua Christians. A few missionaries reached the jungle capital in the years that followed, chronicling and celebrating the small number of baptisms that took place there. But this trickle of elite converts was a far cry from the "spiritual conquest" envisioned by many churchmen. Three decades of steady pressure yielded scant rewards. By the 1560s, Vilcabamba's response to visiting missionaries ranged from lukewarm to openly hostile. Meanwhile, in the core areas of viceregal Peru, a series of unexpected setbacks provoked panic among colonial authorities, both secular and religious. In the very same year that the diplomats met at Chuquichaca Bridge, the Taki Onqoy movement began spreading throughout Peru, shaking the edifice of colonial Christianity to its foundation. Chanting, dancing crowds of Indians cast off church leadership and revived the worship of their traditional huacas, provoking fear and despair among magistrates who had, up until this moment, believed the conversion of the Andes nearly complete.[5]

Titu Cusi's kingdom had received missionaries and adopted elements of Christianity, but it remained, at a deeper level, an Inca theocracy. The buildings of its capital were constructed around natural, geological features that locals regarded as huacas. Traditional religious rituals took place at these sites throughout the year. Plans for political reconciliation with the Hispano-Inca state in Cuzco inched forward, but a total repudiation of traditional native religion seemed unlikely. Missionaries dreamed of a comprehensive conversion to orthodox Christian practices, and they hoped that the proposed dynastic union was a constructive step toward that end. The diplomacy involved some delicate questions since the marriage of the two first cousins violated European incest taboos and contradicted cannon law. Of course, Europe's royal families routinely overcame this problem by securing special papal dispensations, and an exception had already been made in the marriage of the royal siblings Sayre Topa and Cusi Huarcay. When the other fine points of the Cuzco-Vilcabamba negotiations were resolved, the whole pact remained contingent upon the pope's approval, a measure eagerly sought by all parties.[6]

The negotiations of 1565 highlight the limitations of Spanish power over traditional Andean leadership. The viceroy's plan required the support of his Inca client in Cuzco, as well as the cooperation of the independent Inca ruler in Vilcabamba. It was a tough political puzzle to solve but nothing new from the perspective of sixteenth-century Andean statecraft. The existing schism in the Inca royal family was the consequence of a similar, failed diplomatic initiative a decade before. At the time, Philip II was new to the throne. Just a few months into his reign, he could hardly have been expected to grasp the subtleties of intercultural diplomacy in the Andes, but the matter was urgent enough to make it a policy priority. The king appointed the Marques de Cañete as his new viceroy and charged him with resolving the highland leadership crisis. The marques himself was ill-equipped for Inca politics. He needed an expert and a cultural liaison; and he found one in the person of Juan de Betanzos, a man deeply immersed in the languages and customs of the Andes. It was Betanzos, accompanied by Augustinian missionary Martín de Pando, who traveled to Vilcabamba in 1560 with an early version of the plan for dynastic reunification.[7]

Juan de Betanzos possessed enormous political clout in the Spanish and Inca worlds. He is known today primarily for his chronicle of Peruvian history, but he was also a jurist, a businessman, and a valuable servant to the crown. More importantly, he was fluent in Quechua, and his wife was an Inca noblewoman. Betanzos had married Cuxirimay Ocllo (also known as Angelina Yupanqui) in 1541, and in so doing gained the counsel of a woman whose knowledge of Andean political elites—both Spanish and Inca—was unmatched. As a younger woman, she had been the wife of Emperor Atahualpa; but the rapacious Francisco Pizarro killed her husband and took Angelina as his consort. Finally, when Pizarro met his end, Cuxirimay Ocllo married Betanzos, who thus gained a beautiful and able wife, as well as an education in Inca court protocols. Betanzos was undoubtedly the right man for the job: he had married into the family line of Emperor Pachacutec and could enter Vilcabamba on different terms than a normal crown emissary.

The difficulties of Betanzos's 1560 mission were clear from the start. Similar attempts at dynastic synthesis had collapsed upon the death of the Inca client Sayre Topa. In 1557, Sayre Topa agreed to relocate his followers from Vilcabamba to viceregal Peru. They were offered categorical pardon for all previous violence against the colonial state, along with a secure position within it. Sayre Topa brought several hundred followers with him to the Valley of Yucay, where he received a royal title over the lands and dependent laborers that would become the core of the Hispano-indigenous estate of the counts of Oropesa. And yet, something in the Spanish plan went awry. Though Sayre Topa positioned himself as Spain's leading Inca client, his brother Titu Cusi Yupanqui, along with the majority of the Inca aristocracy, stood their ground and remained in the independent kingdom of Vilcabamba. As promised, Sayre Topa resettled in the Valley of Yucay, where his estate and progeny would long survive, but Sayre Topa himself died shortly thereafter in circumstances that bred rumors of assassination. From 1557 to 1558, his followers traveled from Vilcabamba to Lima, and finally to Yucay, only to find themselves leaderless. Fortunately, their best hope for the preservation of the dynasty had been carried with them on this long journey, in the womb of Sayre Topa's royal consort, Cusi Huarcay. In February of 1558, she gave birth to Sayre Topa's only heir: the girl who would later be known as Beatriz Clara Coya Inca.[8] She came into an Inca world just as fragmented as that of her father's generation, and her future life would be caught up in the countless intrigues of contending Spanish and indigenous parties who sought to resolve the Inca schism to their own advantage.

All of these past diplomatic failures must have weighed heavily on the minds of the men who later met in 1565 at the Chuquichaca Bridge. The viceregal colony needed a stable frontier and dependable clients, and the Vilcabamba elites needed security and an end to Spanish-sponsored dynastic competition. For all parties—Spanish and indigenous, clients and rebels—the most significant economic question was who would control the valuable encomiendas of Indian commoners. Everyone had a stake in this fight. It was fueled not just by conflicts between Europeans and Quechuas, but also by competition among Spanish and Inca clans and factions. The discussions at Chuquichaca Bridge were important but not immediately decisive. The negotiations took a year to resolve, and longer to formalize. The final agreement was committed to writing as the Capitulación de Acobamba in August of 1566. In this document, which was subsequently forwarded to the Council of the Indies and the king for approval, the blueprint for the new Inca client state was expressed in full detail. The Vilcabamba Incas would receive missionaries and baptism, they would be granted formal title to vast lands and numerous laborers, they would relinquish independent foreign policy, and they would operate under the general supervision of the corregidores and the viceroys. The key leaders would be pensioned by the state.[9]

This political synthesis might have taken place smoothly were it not for events unforeseen by the negotiators. At the center of the plan for political reconciliation was Beatriz Clara Coya, the surviving heir of Sayre Topa, who was entrusted as a child into the home of Arias Maldonado, the patriarch of Cuzco's powerful Maldonado clan. In the confusion following the death of Sayre Topa (and while the deliberations with Vilcabamba remained inconclusive), Maldonado seized the moment and attempted to force a marriage between Beatriz and his brother Cristóbal, who reportedly raped the child heiress in order to ensure the union. This assault on the Inca family unleashed a scandal that culminated in the arrest of the Maldonados. They were accused of conspiring to overthrow the viceroyalty and replace it with their own carefully engineered mestizo dynasty.

In the 1560s, the Spanish colonial establishment attempted to defend itself against political conspiracies, raids from the Vilcabamba kingdom, and the resurgence of preconquest religion in the form of Taki Onqoy—a threat that missionaries believed was spreading like wildfire. Meanwhile back in Vilcabamba, Titu Cusi Yupanqui was working diligently toward a historical project that would provide him and his descendants with greater cultural and legal legitimacy. With the help of the scribe Martín de Pando and Augustinian missionary Marcos García, he dictated a lengthy history of the conquest and of the postconquest civil wars, chronicling the struggles between Inca factions—all with an eye toward casting his own hereditary line in the best possible light. Not long after the final work was finished and notarized, the emperor fell ill and died.

In the final years of his life, Titu Cusi worked tirelessly toward a stable peace, but the very fact of his death destroyed his well-laid plans. Political assassinations of Inca royalty by Spaniards were so common in the preceding half century that few could believe the near simultaneous deaths of Titu Cusi and his brother Sayre Topa was a mere coincidence. Vilcabamba's reaction was immediate and volatile. Titu Cusi's younger brother, Túpac Amaru, long skeptical about the planned union with Spain, now ascended the Inca throne. His suspicions fell first on the missionaries as the likely agents of Spanish subversion. In this atmosphere of fear and confusion, the Inca leadership accused Martín Pando and Diego Ortiz of assassinating Titu Cusi, and condemned both to death. Túpac Amaru now crossed the Rubicon. With the execution of these Spanish subjects, the treaty of Acobamba was a dead letter, and the window of opportunity for imperial union slammed shut.[10]

The recently appointed viceroy, Francisco Toledo, mobilized an army of Spaniards, Cañaris, and Chachapoyas to invade Vilcabamba. They swept into the remote Inca capital in 1572, running roughshod over the past decade's delicate and ultimately unsuccessful diplomacy. The capital was sacked and burned, and Túpac Amaru fled down the Urubamba River and into the wilderness. The manhunt ended with the capture of Túpac Amaru and a perfunctory show trial. This last independent Inca met his end in a grisly public execution in Cuzco's central plaza in September of 1572. His captor, the highly decorated Basque commander, Martín García de Loyola, would in one sense destroy and in another sense preserve the Inca royal line. García de Loyola married Beatriz Clara Coya Inca.[11]

Hybrid Governance in Peru

The governance of Peru in the late sixteenth century required an inventive combination of European and indigenous institutions. As we have seen, it also demanded a strategic synthesis of privileged families from both sides of the Atlantic. With this in mind, it is worth revisiting some of the most commonly repeated generalizations about the conquest era. Popular retellings of the European conquest of the Americas revolve around a few mythic moments and images: Columbus sights land, Cortés embraces Moctezuma on the causeway over Lake Texcoco, and pilgrims run aground at Plymouth Rock. For the conquest of Peru, we see painted and printed, over and over again, the pregnant moment of first encounter at Cajamarca in 1532: Pizarro stands tense and ready, Friar Vicente de Valverde presents a sacred book, and Atahualpa raises his hand in anger. Revisited and debated from every angle, this scene lingers in our minds. It has sometimes been a set piece in a triumphalist narrative of European supremacy; but now it is more often revisited as the moment of primeval error in the foundation of colonial Peru—the moment at which Europeans took the wrong fork in the road, rejecting the path of peaceful evangelization for that of avaricious and ruthless conquest. Subsequent generations of missionaries and colonial administrators, not to mention indigenous writers, have looked back on this scene as the beginning of a dark chapter in world history, one in which greedy and impatient conquistadors destroyed first the Inca royal family and then each other in a quest for wealth and supremacy that left Peru racked by civil wars for much of the sixteenth century. And there is no small amount of truth in this retelling of events. Yet for all the destruction that ensued, neither the Inca nobility nor the conquerors' ruling families would disappear. Though Atahualpa and Pizarro would both be casualties of the conquest and civil wars that followed, many of the people who surrounded them—both Spanish and indigenous—would ultimately arrive at a series of pragmatic compromises.

Somewhere in the crowd that day at Cajamarca was Francisco de Valverde, the brother of Vicente de Valverde. Also in the crowd were numerous Inca noblemen and military commanders, many of whom would play important roles in the formation of the postconquest state. Vicente de Valverde has been justly criticized for helping to legitimate the conquest. His gesture of presenting the Christian message to Atahualpa fulfilled certain legal obligations for the Spaniards, and Atahualpa's rejection of it allowed them to frame the fighting that followed as a "just war." Valverde's apologists have always pointed to his later role as Peru's first protector of Indians. The office of protector antedates the conquest of Peru, and its role in the defense of indigenous communities was already an important check on the abuses of the invaders. The *protector de indios* was first devised in 1516 in response to the campaigns of Dominican human-rights advocate Bartolomé de las Casas, who sought to improve the treatment of Caribbean islanders in the wake of Columbus's devastating occupation. Vicente Valverde was appointed protector of Peru in 1536 in the midst of the destructive wars between the new Spanish colonial state and the followers of Manco Inca. In the years following the conflict, Valverde would help define the quotidian political and economic relationships between Spaniards and Andean natives. Protectors acted as intermediaries between Indian and Spanish governments. In particular, they were charged with monitoring and mitigating the exactions of goods and labor from the Indian peasantry by both the native nobility and Spanish encomenderos.[12] Among the most

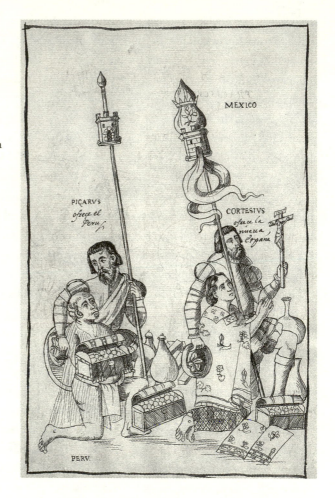

powerful encomenderos of this era was Vicente Valverde's brother, the soldier
Francisco de Valverde.

Francisco's life was in many ways typical among Spaniards of his rank and
experience. He and his peers were military entrepreneurs—men of middling
means who came to Peru with the first wave of invaders, hoping to enrich
themselves with the spoils of conquest.[13] And so they did. After Peru's most
easily accessible and portable wealth had been plundered, conquest took a new
path. With most of the gold and silver melted, weighed, and coined, a more
measured approach to profiteering set in. From this point forward, Spaniards
would have to make their money the way that European aristocrats had for
centuries—and indeed, the same way that Inca gentlemen did—by siphoning

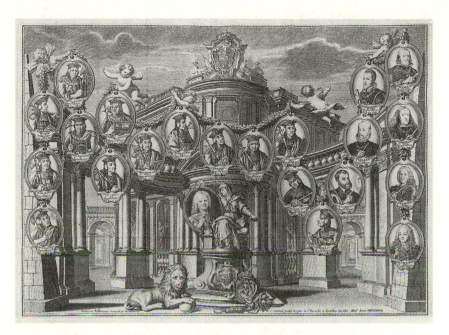

FIGURE 5 The Inca and Spanish rulers of Peru, 1748. Black-and-white engraving by Antonio Marin, Madrid. From Antonio de Ulloa's *Relación histórica del viage a la América meridional* [. . .]. Courtesy of the John Carter Brown Library, Brown University.

off goods and labor from the rural peasantry. Under these conditions, naked theft gave way to conquest by collaboration.

When the Spanish first landed at Tumbes in 1532, Inca princes were themselves ruling over a young multiethnic empire. They had learned to co-opt into their chain of command local clients of other ethnicities by bestowing upon their leaders the rank of "noble by privilege." Now it suited the Spanish to do the same. At first hastily, and later with more deliberation, Spanish military commanders placed the local Indian nobility under the encomiendas of Spanish conquistadors, who were in this way remunerated for their services to the crown. The Indian nobles, in turn, organized the recruitment of labor and the collection of goods, lining their own pockets and those of the encomenderos. Protectors—at least ideally—ensured that the Indians were treated in accordance with royal law, and that disputes among encomenderos, caciques, and commoners were resolved appropriately.[14]

Looking into the affairs of the Valverde family gives us a sense of how this all worked. In the two decades that followed the events at Cajamarca, encomiendas were often won and lost. The powerful Almagro and Pizarro family factions fought tooth and nail to deprive each other of seigniorial powers in a series of civil wars, conspiracies, and assassinations. Finally, when both families and their allies had ground each other into the dust, the exasperated crown officials punished the participants by confiscating their encomiendas and redistributing them to three more trustworthy parties: loyal Spaniards, loyal Indian nobles, and the royal estate itself. Somehow the Valverdes managed to weather the storms. Vicente retained royal favor and received an appointment not only as the protector de indios, but also as the first bishop of Cuzco in 1537. Francisco Valverde received rich encomiendas and sired a line of creole elites that would play an important role in Peruvian politics well into the republican period.[15]

A close examination of the Valverde estates at the beginning of the next century illustrates how the relationship between encomenderos, Indian caciques, and protectors evolved over time.[16] In 1603, Francisco Valverde Montalvo was a second-generation encomendero and fortunate enough to have inherited many of the tributary and usufruct rights to a rich agricultural zone of Parinacochas, which was at the time a dependency of Cuzco. The area had been awarded to his father early in the conquest of the region, and the younger Francisco now found himself in the position of conserving the family's fortunes in a time of demographic and economic decline. Like European elites throughout history, Valverde made his money by drawing manorial obligations from lesser nobles, who in turn exacted goods and labor from the peasantry. In this case, both the immediate clients and the peasants themselves were indigenous Andeans. In 1603, when royal visitor Antonio Quiñones conducted an audit of the region's estates, he described in meticulous detail this hierarchy of obligations and privileges. Valverde held the right to collect tribute from each village. Within the villages, political and economic authority was in the hands of each ayllu (the basic hereditary unit of Andean politics). The hierarchy described by the audit is a lesson on the colonial social order. Valverde controlled seven ayllus, whose inhabitants are listed in the documentary record by order of rank: first the cacique of each ayllu, second all the men of noble rank, third the heads of all property-holding families among the commoners, fourth the widows, and finally the single young men. Ayllus were headed by nobles of a given lineage. Thus, we find the ayllu of Tauna led by cacique and principal don Cristóbal

Tia Tuito Gualpa, who ruled through a local nobility comprised of his male relatives: Felipe Sacaco, don Felipe Tuiro Gualpa, and don Diego Sacaco. It was a social order defined by birth, gender, age, and property. From the perspective of viceregal governance, the most important fact was the individual's capacity to provide tribute and labor—as well as the legal distinctions that obliged some to do so and exempted others. In a community like the ayllu of Tauna, a fully vested household was one headed by a patriarch who possessed a house, an urban garden lot, and agricultural properties. These households offered revenues of all kinds. The households of widows were typically limited to their homes and *solares* (urban lots), while single men's assets might be modest or great depending on their skills, talents, and good fortune. At the apex of this social hierarchy were the reigning caciques (or curacas). The cacique Cristóbal Tia Tuito Gualpa was typical among men of his social type. At fifty-one years of age, he governed his community in the dual roles of indigenous aristocrat and Spanish functionary. He and his wife, doña Luisa Isabella, lived in an urban mansion (a *casona* in regional parlance), one likely surrounded by generous plots for gardens and orchards. In the surrounding countryside, their dependents worked their fields of maize and wheat. Their sons and grandsons formed the backbone of the local elites.[17]

This system joined pre- and postconquest power structures in ways that served the interests of both Spanish and indigenous elites. Of course, it is easier to share profits that are expanding than those in decline. And the harsh reality of colonial life was that the indigenous population of Peru continued to decline well into the eighteenth century, as wave after wave of European epidemics took their toll on human lives and on the agricultural productivity of the highlands.[18] The main purpose of Quiñones's visit was to decide how to adjust tribute demands in light of the shrinking population. The opening of his report to the viceroy is telling. He explained that he wrote "on behalf of the caciques of the repartimiento de Cayautambo" because of the "great decline due to the death of many tributaries" and the heavy burden on the "few that remain in the repartimiento." For the families of both Francisco de Valverde and Cristóbal Tia Tuito Gualpa, this meant dividing the spoils of a shrinking patrimony.

Eventually, the rural population would slowly rebound, and with it the fortunes of some of the families who had survived. The most successful among them formed complex cross-caste alliances that used intermarriage and participation in European institutions to advance their aims. In this dynamic environment, the control of hereditary *cacicazgos* was frequently contested by rival descendants and even outsiders. These conflicts played out in cabildos and courts as dynastic competitors wielded both the traditional language of genealogical legitimacy and the Bourbon-era rhetoric of legality and efficiency. These fights gave rise to high levels of litigation, viceregal intervention in office holding, and even the well-documented phenomenon of "white caciques." The struggles lay bare the mechanics of Spanish-indigenous power sharing and the procedures and tactics used by all concerned.[19]

Native Men, Native Women, and Their Hereditary Estates

The story of eighteenth-century noblewoman doña Juliana Tico Chipana is telling. She saw many things during her tenure as the *cacica* of Urinsaya. For forty years, she governed a region of the high Andes closer to Lake Titicaca than to Cuzco. From her home in the valley of Río Apurimac, she administered her estates, adjudicated disputes, and prospered on the labor of Indian commoners who served as her *mitayos*. Late colonial curacas like doña Juliana were expert political survivors. Their family lines had managed to hold onto property and political privilege, not just through the Spanish conquest of the sixteenth century but also through the evolving administrative regimes of the next two centuries.[20]

Europeans and Andean peoples shared a fundamental expectation that the human community should be divided between the nobility and the commons—and further, that legitimate political leaders could and should combine military, judicial, and administrative functions. In both societies it was a forgone conclusion that the ruling class could exact labor from the peasantry. But the rules governing the transmission of hereditary authority were not identical on the two sides of the Atlantic. Spaniards' official marriages were monogamous, and the inheritance of titles was based on legitimacy, age, and gender. Members of old families gained their positions by birth, but a few fortunate commoners rose in each generation to the lesser nobility on the merits of their service to the crown. Conspicuous in this latter group were the new hidalgos who gained their place in the sun by serving the crown in the reconquest of Iberia or the conquest of the Americas. During the same years in which the Spanish conquest created new nobles, it also confirmed old ones. The Habsburgs favored stability, and one of the swiftest paths to restabilizing recently conquered lands was to confirm large numbers of native nobles as vassals or clients of the crown.[21]

Prior to the conquest, Quechuas had been polygamous; thus their noble lines were based on different notions of legitimacy than those of the Spanish. Furthermore, their aristocracy was defined by membership in *panacas* that descended from each of the past Inca emperors. Polygamy and panaca structures produced many parallel (and often rival) lines of royal descent. Precontact Spanish and Quechua history furnishes endless examples of contested succession. Each system seemed to breed these problems, and because the viceroyalty of Peru was a synthesis of the two, disputes over the transmission of estates and titles were doubly complex. The result was an unstable political terrain in which conflicts among rival family member could be endlessly contested in relation to conflicting laws and customs in both cultures.[22]

Doña Juliana came from a long line of caciques, but successions in her dynasty took a meandering path. He grandfather was a foundational figure in the region: a hacendado, curaca, and recipient of a royal medal from the king of Spain. He transmitted the office to his oldest son, don Joseph Tico Chipana, just as one would in the European tradition. In the next generation, the position passed not to don Joseph's progeny but to his brother's, and not to his brother's son but to his daughter, doña Juliana. Female caciques were not unheard of in eighteenth-century Peru, but they were sufficiently rare as to provoke questions. Doña Juliana's brother noted that his "sister Doña Juliana Tico Chipana found herself in command of the government of this district which I out of fraternal love had relinquished; she in spite of her sex fulfilled with precision and zeal all the responsibilities of the post." The brother, Francisco Javier Tico Chipana, recorded much of the family history in the process of carrying out a legal case against family rivals over the cacicazgo and a variety of hereditary lands. There is an intentional vagueness in the way that the documents treat the years of the Túpac Amaru rebellion. Though doña Juliana is praised for her faithful execution of her public office, one passage also implies that she headed the area under rebel authority. Francisco Javier repeatedly refers to his faithful service during the war and the terrible personal costs he suffered, but he is not at all clear on the details. Doña Juliana's remarkable career is likely attributable to her personal talents and to the flexible rules of succession among indigenous ruling families. If, indeed, she aligned herself with the rebels, her position among them was also not a complete anomaly. These were the years when Micaela Bastidas (wife of Túpac Amaru II) and Tomasa Tito Condemayta (the cacica of Acos), led large-scale military operations.

All of the typical claims about service and heredity weighed heavily in the case of the elderly don Francisco Xavier Tico Chipana who came forward in 1791 with a petition to the viceroyalty. He asked that the government confirm his title to a number of properties and that it ensure his children's future inheritance of the cacicazgo. Though he himself was not the current cacique of Urinsaya, he did have the strongest claim upon the office according to Spanish rules of succession. Don Francisco's arguments were impressive and subtle, though not entirely consistent. His argument for reclaiming the right of succession from his sister's or his uncle's line fit with European practices. But his property disputes against his relative and rival José Pedro Frias all hinged on the property rights of women: those of Francisco Xavier's wife versus those of José Pedro Frias's wife, Isabel Coronel. In this case, Francisco Xavier argued emphatically for the importance of direct lineal descent (though this principle hardly suited his other petition for the cacicazgo). His petition attacked the standing of Isabel Coronel on two grounds: illegitimate birth, and mestizo birth.

This swirling case of intrigue and contested inheritance makes for good reading, but it does not deliver a simple message on the role of gender, birth order, or consanguinity in the transmission of power and property among Peru's leading indigenous families. What it does make clear is that the rules of succession and inheritance, which were already ambiguous in the early colonial period, had become even more so in the years between the Túpac Amaru II uprising and Peruvian independence. The fight for power involved both Spanish and indigenous customs. And those who prevailed needed talent, ruthlessness, and a demonstrable record of family service to the crown.

The position of Indian noblewomen under Spanish rule was somewhat ambiguous. It is clear from testaments, censuses, and litigation records that Indian women (like Spanish women) possessed many of the attributes of adult-male citizenship only when they headed independent households. In practice, property-holding widows could enjoy a high degree of economic and political autonomy. It should be no surprise, then, that widows from the indigenous nobility sometimes assumed the role of curaca.[23] However, their unusual political position made their authority tenuous and susceptible to challenges from male competitors. Even in the 1820s, as Spanish imperial systems neared collapse, many elements of the old multiethnic colonial state remained in place, including the office of cacique and, in some cases, cacica.[24]

In 1823, doña Santosa Olasabal reined as cacica in the small community of Amparaes, having assumed the position upon the death of her husband, don Pedro Ugarte. Amparaes was, at the time, an agricultural community under the jurisdiction of the neighboring town of Challabamba with which it shared a priest. It belonged to the Andean province of Paucartambo, which straddled the high Andes, descending on one side toward the sacred valley, and on the other toward the Amazon. Then, as now, Challabamba was far from Peru's economic and political centers, but this did not mean that its civic affairs were conducted in complete isolation from colonial authorities. Santosa Olasabal's rise to power created a backlash that rippled through the entire chain of authority from Amparaes to Paucartambo to Cuzco.[25]

In 1823, the village priest put pen to paper, setting down his thoughts on women's leadership in general, and on Santosa Olasabal's in particular: "In some places, there have been examples in history of women, on account of their outstanding talents and virtues, having been entrusted with the government of a people. . . . Amparaes, one of the towns in my department, [is] governed entirely by a woman lacking the least qualities to recommend her, accused of losing what little remained of her reason and of her compliance with respect to the governors of the capitals and established laws." This outburst was just the beginning of what would become a concerted campaign against the cacica. The document, which the priest addressed to the region's captain, Juan José Aveno, prompted a formal investigation of the town's misgovernance. In a less stabile community, this leadership dispute might have become a full-blown crisis of legitimacy, but not so in Amparaes. There custom dictated that the local Indian nobility would have a powerful—perhaps even decisive—voice in the decision over Santosa Olasabal's tenure in office. The *justicia mayor*, accompanied by a Quechua interpreter (aptly named Pio Herrera Español) collected affidavits and presented them to the town's Indian cabildo. The five Indian nobles who held the offices of alcaldes and regidores corroborated the alarming tale of a curaca run amok. In a story reminiscent of a Confucian dynastic history, they described an otherwise healthy community cast into anarchy and vice by the succession of a woman ruler, and by the misconduct of her ne'er-do-well son.

They claimed that all virtue had fled the community—so much so that even on the Sabbath the locals no longer set foot in the church, devoting themselves instead to drunkenness and disorder. Satisfied with the evidence presented by the local priest and cabildo, José Villaseñor deposed Santosa Olasabal and replaced her with a new cacique, don Melchor Zamalloa.[26]

Several hundred years later, it is impossible to get to the bottom of a case like this one. Was it truly the story of a mad and incompetent widow dragging the cacicazgo through the mud? Or was all of this just a carefully orchestrated power grab by her opponents, a conspiracy of calculating men who crafted their reports to strike all the right chords of alarm: Anarchy! Impiety! And corruption! Either way, the political process is revealing. Even in this very late colonial era, Peruvians—both Spanish and indigenous—shared a theory of governance in which authority derived from multiple sources. Curacas held a hereditary mandate to rule, but not an unconditional one. Their power was checked on one hand by the Indian cabildo, and on the other by the clergy and the civil magistrates. No single actor, and no single ethnic enclave, could act autonomously without heed to the delicate compromises that distributed obligations and authority across institutions and corporate communities.

Spanish Protectors and Indian Notables

The protector of Indians was a vital office in Spanish America, and one that had a significant effect on the material interests of Spaniards and Indians within its jurisdiction. An honest and zealous protector ensured that work conditions and demands for labor and tribute did not exceed the limits set by royal law; he also provided effective representation for Indians, whether commoners or noblemen, in civil disputes over land or over individual and corporate privileges. Where lax or dishonest protectors held office, Indians could be defrauded of lands, forced to purchase excessive or defective goods (through the *repartimiento de bienes*), or forced into personal service. In frontier areas, the complicity of corrupt protectors sometimes abetted an illegal slave trade.[27]

Events in and around the city of Arequipa in 1763 show that political offices could be fiercely contested, even in the absence of the sort of gender politics that complicated the affairs in Amparaes. On the surface, the dispute in Arequipa was a fight over who would hold the office of protector de indios. The city itself was a Spanish republic, but it also served as the administrative headquarters for the entire region, and it housed the political and civic authorities to whom all surrounding Indian republics reported. The disagreement erupted when Protector don Francisco de Galindo was pushed out of office by Agustín Bedoya y Mogrovejo. Galindo demanded reinstatement, and all interested parties soon entered the fray. Some of the Indian citizens' grievances were personal, but the political battle also involved profound constitutional principles. Mogrovejo and Galindo advocated for themselves in a variety of ways, but the main voices in the dispute were those of the Indian cabildos. The indigenous leaders cited chapter and verse of the *Recopilación de leyes de las Indias* (Compilation of the Laws of the Indies) to resolve the question of whether the dismissal required a hearing before the audiencia. They probed the question of whether protectors could be removed for want of effective representation, and they argued that, at some level, protectors served at the pleasure of the communities they protected. In all of these debates, the cabildos of Santa María and Santa Ana, which were led almost exclusively by Indian nobility, had the strongest voices. Some litigants held that the *Laws of the Indies* permitted the dismissal of protectores de indios only with the approval of the Royal Audiencia; others insisted that the regulation applied only to the office of protector general and not to the more humble local office. Some complained that Bedoya was a protector "only in name" and that he had left "Indian prisoners in public jails without having a protector to defend them or look on their cases with mercy." This lack of effective representation, they suggested, should disbar him from office. Behind all of these arguments was a general consensus among the Indian nobles that protectors served at the pleasure of the cabildos. They complained, "We should not be obliged to have don Francisco Galindo as protector when it is contrary to our will."[28]

In the Spanish Empire, indigenous elites defended their privileges through large, legally defined communities such as Indian republics; they also fought for their interests as individuals and as members of families, clans, and dynasties. They were keenly focused on transmitting their social status and material assets to their descendants. Not surprisingly, colonial archives abound with testaments reciting families' accomplishments and detailing the inheritance of assets and titles. They also describe legacies of goods and status held by religious and civic organizations. Often the custodians of these communities were clerics or the members of religious sodalities; among the latter were many pious women, especially those who were unmarried, widowed, or childless.

These women were highly respected members of their Indian communities, sometimes because of their wealth and patronage, and sometimes because of their service.[29]

María Antonia Montes is a striking example of a woman whose status and influence derived from years of service to the community. She was born into the Indian parish of Santa Ana and ended her life nearby in the neighboring Indian community of Santiago del Cercado on the eastern edge of Lima. Santiago del Cercado was one of the great centers of institutional life for indigenous leadership in the lowlands of Peru. The town was founded as an Indian republic in 1571 by Viceroy Toledo, and it was there that the Jesuits established the Colegio de Caciques, an institution second only to Cuzco's Colegio de San Francisco de Borja for the education of Indians. María Antonia was a community leader of a distinctively colonial type. She was an Indian women without title, without real estate, and without great wealth. She lived in a modest urban home with a small garden and orchard, which she rented from one of the town's landowners. She married three times in the course of her lifetime but had no children. The third husband seems to have abandoned her, though at the time of her final testament, he was still living somewhere—just not with her. Her final accounting of debts and assets suggests that she owed little and was owed little. Her days were spent on religious duties and on the care of her home and fruit trees. But her frugal and quiet life was by no means solitary or thankless. Women like María Antonia Montes had a social status and civic influence disproportionate to their modest wealth.[30]

Her list of personal effects was very short. The only goods she held in abundance were pieces of devotional artwork. Her modest estate included two crucifixes, a print of Nuestra Señora de los Dolores, and two glass display cases containing images of San Salvador and Nuestra Señora de la Asunción. She slept beneath a quilt embroidered with an image of Santa Felipa, an early disciple of Saint Francis. Perhaps her most prized possessions were two inscribed processional sculptures for the annual Christmas observances. María Antonia Montes belonged to two confraternities: Jesús Nazareno and Nuestra Señora de la Piedad. She was also a devotee of the local cult of el Señor de las Maravillas, whose observances centered on a much-venerated image of Christ. In 1801, as Antonia Montes lay on her deathbed, the stones of a new church dedicated to this advocation of Christ were being laid in the center of el Cercado. Her final will and testament left her estate to "el Señor de Maravillas whose sacred effigy and advocation are venerated in this town, and for whom today is being built a new Temple."

Lima's indigenous population included many types of pious women. There were beatas who lived communally, following a lifestyle much like that of nuns.[31] Others, like María Antonia Montes, lived humbly in private homes. But piety and asceticism were not constant companions in colonial Peru. María's more flamboyant contemporary, Rosa Obregon, walked through the streets of el Cercado clad in costly and eye-catching garments. Her wardrobe boasted jewelry of silver and precious stones, blouses from England, a bright yellow skirt, a blue scarf, silk stockings, and a dress embroidered with images of elephants. She had two husbands in the course of her life—both Spaniards—and she enjoyed a status rooted in both wealth and piety. María was childless, but she belonged to two local confraternities. She willed her goods to a faithful servant named María Ramos, and to the confraternity of Nuestra Señora de la Consolación, whose mayordomo, Geronimo Contreras, served as her executor. María Antonia Montes and Rosa Obregon certainly knew each other well. They both belonged to the confraternity of Nuestra Señora de la Piedad. They likely spent many hours caring for the sculpture of the Virgin, attending the same meetings, and participating in the same masses and processions. They belonged to the respectable core of Indian citizens in Santiago del Cercado. Their testaments provide us a glimpse of their public and private lives. Both requested burial in Franciscan habits, and both sought to be remembered for their pious works. They were deeply devoted to their religious practices, but their lives were not cloistered. They had close social ties to nuns and to other lay women, and they had working relationships with the male clerics and male functionaries of local sodalities.

As they walked through the streets, these women were greeted by familiar faces each day—after all, Santiago del Cercado was not such a big place. One could easily pick out its leading citizens seated in the church pews or strolling through the plaza. María Antonia Montes and Rosa Obregon were among the influential women of the town, and they also collaborated with important male leaders like Toribio Dávila and Agustín Miguel Caucho.

In the world of male elites, don Toribio Dávila cast a long shadow. He was captain of the town's Indian militia and an alcalde of the cabildo. He lived in a time when the military and civic systems of the empire were changing; the men most likely to succeed in life were those who stayed actively involved in both. Spain's global empire had been constructed piece by piece as conquered and co-opted kingdoms were incorporated into the larger whole. Early in the colonial history of Peru (as in Mexico), the empire's military forces were largely comprised of Indians, and mostly of Indians who served under their own traditional leaders. But men like Dávila grew up in an era when Bourbon administrators pressed hard for the regularization of military units and commands. In the new administrative language of the era, he was a militia captain and a city councilor; his position was almost indistinguishable from that of equivalent male creole leaders in Peru. Though the titles were new, Santiago del Cercado was not a new place, and men of his type had been around for a long time. When Dávila conducted government business, or conducted legal affairs, he did so with the help of the town's notary, Agustín Miguel Caucho. The documents identify Caucho as an "escribano quipocamayo," a title that captures the bicultural role of these indigenous functionaries. *Escribanos*, or notary-scribes, were found throughout the Hispanic world, but "quipocamayos" were distinctly indigenous in origin.[32] These Quechua scribes had been an important part of colonial administrative practices since the sixteenth century. They were the only ones who could interpret oral testimony encoded in traditional quipus, the knotted strings that were the basis of Inca record keeping. Caucho served two communities; he was a keeper of indigenous memory, and also a Spanish civil functionary.[33]

In the past, the boundaries between Lima and Santiago del Cercado had been quite clear. On one side lay a Spanish republic, on the other an Indian one. Each had its own officials, and each was walled and gated. In theory, the boundaries of citizenship and property titles were once as clear as the towns' fortified perimeters. But all such lines had blurred by the end of the eighteenth century. In the 1680s, Santiago's walls had been breached. By then Lima had become a vast and populous city, much larger, richer, and more powerful than Santiago. The Spanish City of Kings swallowed up its weaker twin, enveloping Santiago within a new and grander ring of walls and fortifications.[34]

The world inhabited by María Antonia Montes and Rosa Obregon was one shaped by generations of indigenous leaders in Santiago del Cercado and Santa Ana. These two neighborhoods, once divided by a wall, would eventually grow together. The same was true of the Indian communities founded separately on the two sides of Lima's Rímac River. In the long run, personal and institutional ties between Lima's multiple indigenous barrios would give birth to a larger community of indigenous *limeños*. The links between once-separate Indian republics were inscribed in the city's sacred geography and constantly commemorated in civic rituals. One of indigenous Lima's foundational moments was the joining together of Indian communities from both sides of the river in 1590. Numerous families resettled to the south around that time, bringing with them an image of the *Virgin of Copacabana*. In the early days of resettlement, the sculpture was carried in procession by no less a personage than Archbishop (and later Saint) Toribio Mogrovejo. From that time forward, a shared devotion to the image cemented the relationships among greater Lima's indigenous communities. Miracles followed. The sculpture wept and sweated, drawing the attention of limeños from every caste community. Soon the sculpture became so important to religious life throughout the city that it was relocated to a place of honor in the Cathedral of Lima. Finally, in the 1670s, devotees of the image—largely Indian women—petitioned for the construction of a new chapel dedicated to the Virgin back in her original neighborhood of San Lazaro. This is the origin of the Beaterio y Ermita de Nuestra Señora de Copacabana that stands north of the river in the neighborhood of Rímac to this day.[35]

The beaterio, which was approved in 1678 and opened in 1691, provided for Indian noblewomen some of the same opportunities afforded to their male counterparts in the prestigious Colegio de Santiago in Cercado. The community's founding leader was doña Francisca Ignacia Carvajal, a woman of solid noble pedigree. Her mother was doña Isabel Quipán and her father don Pedro de Carvajal Manchipula, governor of the Indian republic of Callao. Though the beatas of Nuestra Señora de Copacabana resembled cloistered nuns in certain respects, they were not entirely cut off from the world. In fact, their community had a special role in mediating relationships among all of the Indian towns in the region. Their membership drew from a wide catchment, and their priests gave masses for all of Lima. The sculpture of the Virgin, the history of her travels, and the annual devotions that surrounded her tied together the community biographies of Rímac, Santiago, and Lima. She became the spiritual hub for an indigenous population scattered in pockets throughout the conurbation. The original acts of foundation for the beaterio were issued by the king and the viceroy. Along with the sisters themselves, the institution had a substantial staff including many men. There were facilities to be cared for and lands to be managed. The economic health of the institution required the administration of extensive temporalities, the collection of rents, and the careful accounting of costs and revenues. Along with holy women, this institution employed attorneys and a professional administrator.[36]

Among all the possible images and advocations of Mary, it is no surprise that Our Lady of Copacabana played this special role for Indian limeños. The original *Virgin of Copacabana* was carved in Bolivia (then Upper Peru) in the 1580s by Indian artist don Francisco Tito Yupanqui, himself a descendant of the Inca royal family. Both the story of the original sculpture and the genealogy of its many copies preserved a memory of the vast network of familial ties among the leading groups of Tawantinsuyu. In the 1750s, the head of the beaterio, Catalina de Jesús Huamán-Capac, renewed these ties in a dramatic campaign for the elevation of her institution from beaterio to convent. Her initial proposal was rejected by the Council of the Indies, which cited the beaterio's limited finances, but Huamán-Capac took her appeal for support to the larger community of Tawantinsuyu. In a series of tireless journeys, she crisscrossed Peru, even reaching Copacabana itself on the shores of Lake Titicaca. Huamán-Capac had been born into a family of noble caciques far to the north of Lima in Yungay—a family that once served as regional leaders under the Inca emperors. Her travels retraced an old network of elite ties—ones that clearly still existed under the Spanish imperial order. She returned to Lima in 1753 and died the following year without fulfilling all of her objectives. Her tomb remains beneath the altar of her Rímac chapel.[37]

━━━━

America's postconquest states created both literal and figurative colonial families. The higher echelons of these hybrid societies were constructed from the same kinds of strategic dynastic unions that had been used in Europe for centuries to resolve conflicts between families and advance their political fortunes. Besides these carefully orchestrated alliances among elites, there were multitudes of spontaneous unions between men and women—both church-consecrated marriages and informal relationships. Children came into the world by force, coercion, and rape, but also by planned and unplanned encounters that flourished as love and desire bloomed at the crumbling boundaries between ethnic communities. The variety in these relationships was considerable. The colonial Americas was not Tolstoy's literary world, in which all happy families are alike and all unhappy ones distinct. Both happy and unhappy families existed in new and numerous varieties.

Life in the early modern world was organized not just by biological families but also by family-like organizations—webs of social kinship that joined people in godparentage, religious orders, military organizations, and local sodalities. These figurative families also crossed ethnic boundaries, joining together individuals of distinct social origins. Paradoxically, these organizations both preserved and dissolved older community identities. Confraternities and military units could define themselves both as locally rooted organizations and as parts of global Christendom and the Spanish Empire. Just as members of hereditary families derived pride and power from their ancestors (while harboring grudges and mistrust over past offenses), so too did members of the vast colonial family who constantly revisited their history while advocating for themselves in the present.

CHAPTER THREE

Scribes and Scholars

Antonio Valeriano and Mexico's College for Native Elites

In 1554, the students at the Colegio de Santa Cruz de Tlatelolco were taught by Mexico's leading intellectual lights. Among the most famous was Antonio Valeriano, their renowned instructor of Latin, Castilian, and Nahuatl.[1] Few people so fully embodied the sixteenth-century synthesis of Nahua and Iberian culture as Valeriano. Passing through the streets of Mexico-Tenochtitlan, he went dressed as a Spanish gentleman; but in truth, he was neither a Spaniard nor a noble.[2] Valeriano was born in the 1520s in Azcapot-zalco to parents who were native commoners (or macehualtin).[3] He lived his early days as a student and teacher in an era of both cataclysm and possibility. His childhood took place amid the wreckage and epidemics left by the Spanish conquest, but these were also years when the crown and church permitted remarkable opportunities for talented native youths. For both the church and the state, the creation of an educated indigenous leadership class was the key to the kingdom's future stability and prosperity. Valeriano's Franciscan teachers at the Colegio de Santa Cruz believed they were cultivating a generation of Nahuas who would go on to be priests, scholars, and civic leaders. Later, when Valeriano found himself among the faculty of his alma mater, his students likely expected the same.

Standing before the pupils at the college, Valeriano was both an inspiration and a threat. Coming from outside their city and outside their noble ranks, he was something of an interloper. In other respects, he was one of them. He had passed through the college as an adolescent, training under the great European missionary-linguists of the age; and he had lived and studied beside peers from the noble houses of the Valley of Mexico. As a scholar, translator, administrator, judge, and governor, Valeriano would later become one of the most influential men in Mexico. His contributions were vital to the creation of Bernardino de Sahagún's vast sixteenth-century history and ethnography of Mexico, the *Historia general de las cosas de Nueva España*.[4] Native authors wrote about Valeriano in the *Codex Chimalpahin* and the *Codex Aubin*, where his identity is sketched in traditional glyphs. In the *Codex Aubin*, he is presented as the governor of Mexico-Tenochtitlan, seated on a throne and clothed as a Mexica ruler, but also bearing an Iberian staff of office.[5] Chimalpahin writes of him as a great Latin scholar and a respected judge over the Tenochcas.[6]

Antonio Valeriano inhabited a civic and cultural landscape that was dense, urban, and complex, but his daily routine took place within a fairly small radius from the center of the old Aztec capital. His own birthplace of Azcapotzalco lay close to the shores of Lake Texcoco, facing the waters that divided Tlatelolco and Tenochtitlan. In an urban environment that was both parochial and cosmopolitan, Valeriano made a name for himself. His prestigious marriage to doña Isabel de Alvarado made him the son-in-law of Tenochtitlan's great ruler don Diego de Huanitzin and joined his family to that of the old Aztec imperial line. Nonetheless, these were years when a man like Valeriano needed to hedge his bets. One could easily run afoul of conflicting Spanish and indigenous leaders, and the consequences might be dire.

As a young man, Valeriano witnessed the paranoia and persecution surrounding the trials of Martín Ocelotl and don Carlos Chichimecatecuhtli in the neighboring kingdom of Texcoco. Ocelotl, who descended from a line of indigenous priests, had converted to Christianity, but he was soon dogged by accusations of apostasy. Reports that he practiced ancient forms of divination and sympathetic magic reached the ears of Mexico's first bishop, Juan de Zumárraga, who feared that the project of Mexican evangelization was under attack from crypto-pagan conspirators within the indigenous leadership class. In his 1536 trial, Ocelotl's testimony sketched out a strange parallel world in which the old religion continued to exist beside the new one. Early in 1537, church magistrates found him guilty as charged. Ocelotl was marched through the streets in shame, then banished from the city and spirited away to a European exile. Two years later, the Spaniards' worst fears of religious and political subversion were apparently confirmed by new allegations, this time against don Carlos Chichimecatecuhtli. Don Carlos was a Texcocan aristocrat from the noble line of the famed poet-king Nezahualcoyotl. When his nephew went to the authorities with rumors of don Carlos's religious activities, the colonial church was alarmed. In the trial that followed, witnesses fingered don Carlos for participating in magical rites to control the weather, performing secret rituals to appease ancient idols, and organizing political meetings of traditional indigenous rulers from far and wide. Soon the initial accusations seemed only the tip of the iceberg as new evidence hinted at a widespread plot to restore the preconquest religion and monarchy. In the fall of 1539, don Carlos was burned at the stake in a public ceremony. This grisly scene ushered in a tense and confusing era, one in which the continuing integration of Spanish and indigenous leadership would be accompanied by ongoing fears of Nahua resistance.[7]

Antonio Valeriano experienced these events as a young man, and they must have influenced his pragmatic approach to Spanish and indigenous authority. His later life as a political and intellectual leader was a busy one, as he shuttled back and forth between the centers of Spanish and Nahua culture in Tenochtitlan, Azcapotzalco, and Tlatelolco. In those early days, Spanish Mexico City was a small cluster of urban blocks ringed by a far larger Indian city; both communities were nestled in a valley whose thick constellations of Indian republics constituted the true economic basis of the colonial state. Valeriano must have traveled often in the course of his public and private duties—across the causeways that connected the lakeside republic of Azcapotzalco to the four indigenous quadrants of Tenochtitlan, and from there over the canal to Tlatelolco.[8]

His time at the Colegio de Santa Cruz was a calm between storms. Valeriano witnessed the school's heyday when scores of students from great native houses could demand both the privileges of their ancestors and the keys to the new Spanish kingdom. They claimed the former by descent, and the latter on the basis of education. These young men knew Christian doctrine, European tongues, and the customs of the empire. In the 1560s, a tall cathedral was rising from the rubble of Huitzilopochtli's temple, and a viceregal palace from Moctezuma's royal compound. Indian governments presided over the city's quadrants: Santa María Cuepopan, San Sebastián Atzacoalco, San Juan Moyotlan, and San Pablo Zoquipan. By 1573, Antonio Valeriano would rule over all four, following his appointment as judge and governor. But the 1570s was a troubled time. The decade opened with a great plague that devastated the native population. Soon the missionaries' dreams for Indian universities and Indian clergy faded amid Spanish anxieties over rebellion and apostasy.[9]

As Indian governor of Tenochtitlan from 1573 to 1579, Antonio Valeriano was a judge, administrator, and diplomat. His responsibilities included the organization of labor and tribute, the resolution of legal disputes, and the negotiation of conflicts among the Indian republics and subordinate barrios that constituted indigenous Mexico City. He was also the principal intermediary between the Spanish and Nahua governments. He knew every street and building in the central city, and his frequent travels through European and Indian barrios offered constant reminders of the Spanish conquest and the delicate alliances that followed. It was not much more than a mile from the viceregal palace to Valeriano's alma mater, Santa Cruz de Tlatelolco. Strolling between the two sites, he passed the cathedral (still under construction beside the footprint of a ruined pyramid), passed the first conquistadors' homes (built from the stones of Mexica palaces), passed the Church of San Juan de los Naturales (where Pedro de Gante first taught Nahuas to read and write in Latin script), and navigated through the *tianguis* where Nahuatl-speaking vendors sold everything from maize cakes and pulque to brightly dyed cloth, fresh fish, and botanical medicines. Beyond the vendors, he crossed the plaza called the Quemadero, where the newly formalized Holy Office of the Inquisition turned its ire upon heretics. Finally, he continued to the north, over the canal that separated old Tenochtitlan from the kingdom of Texcoco, and onward to Santa Cruz de Tlatelolco where the chapel and school stood surrounded by the vestiges of ancient temples. This was the site where Valeriano had studied and taught. It was also the site of his most enduring contribution to scholarship, his work with Bernardino de Sahagún. Valeriano was intimately involved in the collection of oral testimony, the transliteration and translation of Nahuatl codices, and the production of the linguistic and illustrated works that were (and still are) part of central Mexico's most significant cultural patrimony.[10]

Like his Spanish mentors, Sahagún and Torquemada, Valeriano was both a preserver and destroyer of the preconquest past. The great missionary texts and chronicles produced at Santa Cruz de Tlatelolco described Nahua culture and religion in order to change them. Valeriano embodied this paradox. He dressed as a Spaniard, but he wrote and spoke in both tongues. His political life was multifaceted: for more than two decades, he was a judge and governor in the eyes of the Spanish, and a *tlatoani* to his native subjects. He was able to escape the limitations of common birth by leveraging Spanish patronage against his indigenous rivals; and he was able to legitimate his political gains by marrying into the highest echelons of the Indian nobility. Antonio Valeriano

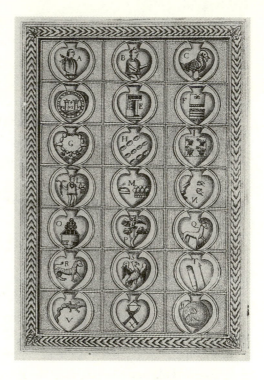

FIGURE 6 The syllabary of Fray Diego Valadés. Engraving from his *Rhetorica christiana*, 1579. Courtesy of the John Carter Brown Library, Brown University.

mastered the complexities of a chaotic era. His success was partly attributable to superior talent and partly to good fortune. Among the Nahuas of his era, Valeriano was not alone. Over time, several thousand students passed through the schools of San José de los Naturales and Santa Cruz de Tlatelolco, and a number of them went on to become scholars, scribes, professors, translators, councilmen, and governors.[11]

Today thousands of tourists and schoolchildren pass by the site of the Colegio de Santa Cruz each day. It stands at the center of a disorienting civic monument called the Plaza de las Tres Culturas—where the sixteenth-century church and the college edifice survive amid partially excavated Aztec temples, surrounded by brutalist apartment blocks. The plaza was constructed in the 1960s to celebrate the Mexican nation's tripartite history as an indigenous, colonial, and modern mestizo society. Today it is more likely to remind Mexicans of the 1968 massacre of student protestors or of the disastrous 1985 earthquake than of the career of Antonio Valeriano. Nonetheless, vestiges of his world remain visible in the old masonry.

Next door to the Church of Santiago, the beautifully restored convent and former school echoes with voices from the colonial past. It was there that young sixteenth-century noblemen from all over the Valley of Mexico faced the rigors of education in three languages. The youngest pupils began their studies at the age of ten, then made their way through an institutional life that was both disciplined and privileged. In the dim predawn hours, they were roused from sleep in the school's vast dormitory. Donning their prestigious blue academic robes and white sashes, they made their way to Lauds Mass, then went on to their lessons in rhetoric, philosophy, and history before rounding out their day with studies in Nahuatl, Latin, and Castilian. The curriculum was rigorous, and the life of resident scholars left them almost entirely isolated from their families and home communities. But the school also afforded luxuries beyond the reach of the average indigenous Mexican. The boys' lessons paused from time to time for well provisioned meals and also for chocolate breaks—a chance to drink that precious cacao beverage that had once been forbidden to commoners and was still prized for its taste and for the status attached to it. When the sun beat down on the Valley of Mexico, the scholars found cool shelter in the college's shaded cloister.[12]

When Valeriano entered the college, he passed through its main stone portal beneath the carved coat of arms that was granted to the school by Emperor Charles V. Like the great universities of Iberia, it was administered by clergymen and operated under the patronage of the crown; and like a European university, the Colegio de Santa Cruz was both a place of instruction and a place for the production of academic knowledge. This was the institution where native and European medical expertise were combined in the so-called *Codex Badianus*, a work produced in Latin and Nahuatl by indigenous scholars Juan Badiano and Martín de la Cruz in the 1550s. Teams of Nahua scholars working with Franciscans composed grammars, prayer books, plays, translations of the gospels, and histories of preconquest Mexico. Most famously, it was here at Tlatelolco that the most talented indigenous scholar-linguists in Mexico conducted the research, compilation, and translations that would yield the monumental *Florentine Codex*, a vast account of indigenous history, religion, politics, and customs that comprised thousands of manuscript pages and thousands of carefully drawn illustrations. Many of the great intellectual projects undertaken in the indigenous Americas sought to influence and inform the leaders of church and state on the other side of the Atlantic. Despite the best efforts of New World authors, their years of hard work frequently disappeared into the libraries and archives of Europe without ever hitting their mark. A few brave souls crossed the sea to carry their messages in person to the halls of power.[13]

Diego Muñoz Camargo: Tlaxcala's Statesman-Historian

In the sixteenth century, a man could spend his whole life waiting for an audience with the king of Spain. Even Hernan Cortés, conqueror of Mexico and marques of the Valley of Oaxaca, spent much of the 1540s hat in hand, unable to gain a meeting with Charles V. Even for the rich, the titled, and the powerful, it took months or years of social networking, palm greasing, and patron-client politics to breach the palace gates with a petition for preferment in hand. And yet, in the 1580s, King Phillip II met repeatedly with an extraordinary mestizo traveler from Mexico: Diego Muñoz Camargo. We might ask why this visitor could pass so easily through the gates of the palace when so many others before him had failed.[14]

Diego Muñoz traveled not on his own behalf (though his efforts would gain him great personal rewards) but as a representative of the Republic of Tlaxcala, an Indian nation whose past and future service to the empire was invaluable to the viceroy and king. Muñoz was a perfect emissary. He was the son of a Tlaxcalan noblewoman and a Spanish conquistador; he was educated by the most famous generation of Franciscan missionaries; he was steeped in the customs of both Tlaxcala and Mexico City; and he enjoyed the confidence of New Spain's most powerful European and Indian leaders. His wife was the Tlaxcalan aristocrat Leonor Vasquez, and his children would one day unite some of the leading indigenous and Spanish lineages of New Spain. When the Indian council of Tlaxcala decided to send an embassy to Spain, they turned to the great houses of the four constituent districts—Tepeticpac, Ocotelulco, Tizatlán, and Quiahuiztlán—asking each to send a representative. But the four ambassadors would also need the help of someone skilled in law, translation, and courtly protocol; for these challenges, the council appointed a fifth emissary: Diego Muñoz Camargo.[15]

Muñoz was born in 1528 or 1529, in the days when Tlaxcala was still tenuously balanced between parties favoring and opposing greater cultural integration with the Spanish. The first missionaries had arrived there about five years before. They selected Tlaxcala as the site for a convent and school, and planned to use it as the center for evangelization in the region. Though many Tlaxcalans welcomed them with open arms, others were more skeptical of Franciscan zeal. In the month leading up to Muñoz's birth, a devastating generational conflict erupted in Tlaxcala. A number of boys and young men educated in the Franciscan college denounced their older relatives for traditional religious practices. Retribution was swift. Some of the boys were killed by traditionalists; others were sheltered by missionaries and fellow converts. Fear and recrimination spread throughout the republic, and the experience traumatized the community. But in the years that followed, Tlaxcalans embraced Christianity with enthusiasm, setting aside their preconquest rituals and celebrating the new faith. In the process, they earned a reputation for orthodoxy and piety that would serve them well in the politics of the colonial state.[16]

Diego Muñoz's generation was the first to be raised Christian from birth. Their republic's royal seal showed hands clasped in prayer, rising from their ancestral mountain and offering the heavenly host that shone like the disk of the sun. Much of Muñoz's youth was spent in Mexico City where his father guided his introduction to polite society. He showed early talent for the mastery of languages and for this reason was appointed tutor to the young Indian captives seized during the Spanish invasion of Florida. Muñoz was shaped by his father's Mexico City, but his ties to his mother's home community were also profound. When the Tlaxcalan cabildo and the alcalde mayor selected Diego Muñoz as an emissary to the crown, they knew that they could trust this distinguished scholar and statesman because he was also a native son.

Muñoz's transatlantic mission to the court of Philip II was undertaken in part to gratify the king's appetite for knowledge about his distant territories and vassals. In 1577, royal messengers had fanned out across Spain's far-flung empire, carrying hundreds of copies of a lengthy questionnaire. It solicited information on the lands, peoples, resources, history, and governance of all the New World's Spanish and indigenous communities. When Diego Muñoz arrived in Spain, he came with maps, illustrations, diagrams, and narratives of the "very loyal and very noble city of Tlaxcala." This encyclopedic collection of documents is to this day among the most valuable records of life in preconquest and early colonial Mexico. The largest portion of these documents has survived in a great tome held by the Glasgow University Library: the *Historia de Tlaxcala*.[17]

The richly illustrated *Historia de Tlaxcala* begins in the deep, mythic past, describing the peregrinations of Tlaxcala's ancient ancestors, who wandered the earth under the protection of their patron god, Camaxtli. It tells how these patriarchs arrived in the center of Mexico and founded the four subkingdoms that comprised Tlaxcala. Like Sahagún's *Florentine Codex*, Muñoz's *Historia* includes lengthy anthropological descriptions of everything from farming and marriage practices to warfare and human sacrifice. Woven throughout the text is a constant celebration of the native nobility with a strategic emphasis on Muñoz's maternal community of Ocotelulco. Despite the sweeping scope of his preconquest narrative, Muñoz reserved roughly half of the manuscript for the dramatic seven decades between the arrival of the Spanish and his current moment. He viewed these years through the lens of local patriotism, and with an eye toward winning the favor of his royal patron. But the voices of dissent were not entirely erased. He recounted the debates between early supporters and opponents of the Spanish, and included the tale of the child martyrs slain by vengeful crypto-pagans at the time of his birth. In this retelling of history, all moments of controversy and human frailty are but brief digressions in a narrative of Christian piety and royal service. Even the account of the child martyrs seems offered more to emphasize the eventual triumph of the His-panophile Christians than to give undue attention to their enemies. Tlaxcala, he concedes, was once overshadowed by sacrificial temples, but their stones were pulled down to build churches. The debates between Spanish allies and enemies gave way to lasting fealty, and the days of crypto-pagans and Christian martyrs ushered in an age of enduring piety.[18]

For Diego Muñoz, Tlaxcalans were the king's greatest conquerors and col-onists, helping to topple the Mexicas, win the wars for the control of Micho-acán and Jalisco, and push the empire deep into Central America. Sometimes honored and sometimes slighted, they persisted in their efforts to serve the crown from generation to generation. At times, the second half of the *Historia* reads like a general chronicle of New Spain, but it is one in which the accom-plishments of the colonizer are constantly associated with the Republic of Tlaxcala. The final part of the *Descripción de la ciudad y provincia de Tlaxcala* extolls the valuable natural resources of Tlaxcala, describing in loving detail the regional flora and its wide range of economic, aesthetic, and medicinal properties. When Muñoz and his four companions delivered this document into the hands of the king, they were giving him an encyclopedia devoted to a kingdom they regarded as a jewel in the crown of empire.

By 1586, Muñoz was back in Tlaxcala and wreathed in royal authority. The delegation had secured a series of decrees from the crown fortifying the position of their republic and protecting the status of its nobility within the larger administrative structures of the viceroyalty. When Muñoz had first sailed from New Spain, he was already an influential man; but when he returned, his power and status were far greater. Muñoz was immediately appointed by Spanish authorities as the procurator for Tlaxcala, a post that he held for the rest of his life and that allowed him to broker many of the economic interactions between the Spanish and his indigenous state.[19]

In the 1560s, Viceroy Luis de Velasco had lobbied Tlaxcala to support his plans for northern conquest and colonization, but the Tlaxcalans declined the offer. Now, in the late 1580s, the proposal was back on the table. No group of Indian allies had proved so valuable in war and peace as the Tlaxcalans; and now the viceroyalty desperately needed their services once again. The northern reaches of New Spain, traumatized by years of licit and illicit slave trading, were peopled by Indians who had proved dangerous and ungovernable to colonial authorities for decades. Again and again, attempts to develop lucrative mining centers had been foiled by the resistance of the local inhabitants. Now the viceroyalty contemplated a more durable and systematic project of settlement, one that called for serial colonization by "civilized" Nahuas who would create the physical and political infrastructure for mining, agriculture, and regional defense. This time the negotiations were fruitful: two hundred Tlaxcalan families agreed to move north as the conquering nobility of a new land. The colonization scheme was a colossal undertaking, and the equipment and provisions were to be financed by the crown. In practice, this meant someone must disburse the funds, requisition the supplies, and enroll the colonists. The most able man for the job was Diego Muñoz Camargo. Once supplied and assembled, the colonists departed from Tlaxcala in 1591, many mounted, armed, and empowered with new charters that ensured their claims to land and resources. They would become the lords of the North, and their descendants would enter the lower ranks of nobility. It was from the hand of Muñoz, in his capacity as royal provisioner and distributor of lands, that aspiring settlers received their goods and titles.[20]

Diego Muñoz amassed great power in the course of his lifetime. In serving Tlaxcala, he also served himself. He obtained a lucrative monopoly on the salt trade in a large territory near his home, he came into possession of extensive

lands and cattle estates, and he dabbled in a variety of other business enterprises. All that remained for a man of his stature was to secure a lasting legacy
for his descendants; and in this, too, he excelled. In the New World, as in the
old, arranging a powerful marriage was a diplomatic art; and the marriage of
his son (also named Diego Muñoz) to Francisca Pimentel Maxixcatzin was a
masterwork. Young Diego, who inherited many of his father's lands and commercial privileges, joined himself to a family of even more venerable lineage
than his own. Francisca traced her maternal ancestry from the famed Maxixcatzin, ruler of Ocotelulco and architect of the Spanish-Tlaxcalan alliance
of 1520. On her father's side, she descended from the house of Pimentel, the
preconquest princes of Texcoco, who had since transformed themselves into
the governors of Texcoco under Spanish rule. From this point forward, the
descendants of Muñoz would conjoin an illustrious line of Spanish conquistadors to the leading houses of two indigenous nations.[21] It is an axiom of
modern politics that to control the outcome of a conflict, one must control the
narrative. This seems to have been just as true in the sixteenth century as it is
today. Diego Muñoz Camargo wrote a history of Tlaxcala that wove together
the glories of an ancient kingdom, the fame of his maternal ancestors, and the
accomplishments of a paternal conqueror. In the end, he wrote himself and his
descendants into a prosperous future.[22]

Native authors in several regions of Spanish America crafted histories that
artfully joined their preconquest pedigrees to chronicles of fealty and service
under the colonial regime. In sixteenth-century Mexico, the College of Santa
Cruz de Tlatelolco groomed several cohorts of native intellectuals for this undertaking. In Peru, colleges for the native nobility came into existence later,
but they also endured for far longer, helping to create a stable institutional
environment for the birth of a cosmopolitan Andean elite.[23]

San Francisco de Borja:
A College for Inca Noblemen

In 1658, church bells rang out across Cuzco's Plaza de Armas,
welcoming thirty-six pupils to the College of San Francisco de Borja and an-
nouncing the beginning of a new academic year. The townspeople watched
as the young men filed across the plaza, past stone spires still rising from the
rubble of the great earthquake just eight years before. At the annual convo-

cation, the young men sat in state as the rector addressed the assembled city councilmen, clergy, and nobility. Across the plaza they strode, marching up the steps and through the gate, rising above the cathedral and city square. Their college overlooked parade grounds where flowing water had once divided the open spaces of Huacaypata and Cusipata in the time of the last Inca emperors. Both the vanished landscape of the preconquest capital and the current glories of the Baroque city were familiar to the students. They were the descendants of governors, curacas, and even Inca emperors.[24] Nor were the illustrious pedigrees of these young men lost on the city's bystanders. The students were scions of the great houses of the Indian nobility, and they wore clothing whose every detail was stipulated by royal decree and which marked them as Peru's leaders. Even at a great distance, this entourage must have dazzled observers. They wore green tunics with matching stockings and the black hats and shoes of Castilian gentlemen. From their right shoulders hung banners bright with the red dye of Mexican cochineal; from their left hung gleaming silver shields inscribed with the heraldic emblems of King Philip and his viceroy. Before disappearing from public sight, they passed below the ornate balcony of the Almirante Palace and beneath the lintel of the college gates where the king's standard was carved in stone.[25]

Inside the school walls, the young men led lives that were both privileged and demanding. San Francisco de Borja was a school for gentlemen in an age that defined education in terms that were at once cultural, spiritual, and intellectual. The full course of studies lasted six years. The boys entered as children but graduated as men. The curriculum began with basic literacy and numeracy, constantly accompanied by instruction in religion. Advanced students studied Latin, classics, and scripture. The daily discipline of the school was not unlike that of a monastery. Students rose early for prayer, and their schedule was punctuated by periodic devotions throughout the day. The graduates of San Francisco de Borja became the caciques and governors of Indian republics. Those who went on to universities became priests, professors, and barristers.[26]

The school's approach to acculturation was subtle and complex. On one hand, its mission was to bring European culture to the indigenous youth; on the other hand, it existed to legitimate and preserve the native nobility. It taught Latin and Castilian, catechism and manners. Students were groomed to become the patriarchs of Christian families and trained to stamp out pagan practices. The rectors took great pains to cleanse the boys of habits that contradicted colonial norms. A kind of abstemious individualism was foisted upon them from the outset as their instructors urged them to reject Quechua customs, such as eating and drinking from common vessels and sleeping in common beds. The students were to reject drunkenness and forsake the company of young women. The institution was governed by a strict code of conduct, and students who violated it faced detention in the college's jail. In some respects, the school resembled a monastery; in others, a finishing school. The institution existed because the sons of caciques needed to be not just good Christians and good scholars but also good courtiers. They studied penmanship, music, and rhetoric; their dress code was that of gentlemen, and their refectory the training ground for a courtly table.

San Francisco de Borja had a broad missionary agenda with respect to custom and belief, but it was not designed to erase all native culture. In fact, the most basic definition of the institution—a school for the sons of caciques—was premised on the idea of political and cultural synthesis between Spanish and indigenous hierarchies. The boys attended the college not just to learn but also to teach. San Francisco de Borja's charter proclaimed its mission to educate Jesuit clergy in the indigenous languages. While the school trained Indians to speak Latin and enter seminaries, it also trained seminarians to speak Quechua and minister to Peru's Indian majority. Over time, the institution shaped generations of missionaries and native noblemen, and had a profound effect on the relationship between native and colonial elites.[27]

Peru's Jesuit colleges belonged to a regional and global network of institutions whose functions were spiritual, economic, academic, and professional. Indian students who entered Jesuit schools could expect opportunities in a wider world beyond the confines of their homes and places of birth.[28] The life of Fray Roderigo de la Cruz illustrates the paths permitted by elite Indian education. He was born the legitimate son of caciques Juan Itache and Luzia Lopez in the coastal town of Colan in Peru's extreme north—though no one later remembered the exact year. Roderigo was born to privilege, and his manifest talents opened up further opportunities. In 1698, Juan de la Concepción brought him to live in the Jesuit mother house in Lima (then called San Pablo and today San Pedro) and invited him to study at the university. Roderigo professed as a member of the Jesuit order in 1708 and was assigned to the college in Cuzco. There, by all accounts, he led an exemplary life of service, collecting alms and caring for the poor. He was both a physician and a priest. When an epidemic claimed his life in 1750s, he was eulogized by Jesuits and Franciscans alike, and praised for his selfless and skillful care for the sick and the destitute.[29]

Obituaries of the period show the ways that Indian clergy and European clergy who ministered to Indians constantly crossed paths. Not only were Jesuits reassigned between Peru's ethnic communities, but many were men with previous experience working among the Indian populations of Mexico and Guatemala. The vast scale of Jesuit operations linked Peruvian clergy not just to the viceregal and Iberian capital, but also to missions throughout the Americas, the Pacific, and Asia. In a town like Cuzco, church institutions connected the lives of Indians who occupied the top and the bottom of the social hierarchy. In the Hospital de los Naturales de Cuzco, one could find the best trained criollo and Indian clergy-physicians working side by side to care for the valley's poorest and least protected Indian residents. The staff included the sons of the nobility who had taken holy orders, as well as service Indians bound by encomienda to provide labor to the facility. Its ornate building was graced with the work of the sculptor and Inca nobleman Juan Tomás Tuiru Rupa.[30] Men like Fray Roderigo fulfilled the dreams of early missionaries who understood elite Indian education as part of a global plan to build Christian institutions on a foundation of stable and universal social hierarchies. Nonetheless, though the education of Indian nobles often consolidated colonial authority, it could also be turned against the conquerors.[31]

Today, the most famous alumnus of San Francisco de Borja is, without a doubt, José Gabriel Condorcanqui, now best remembered as Túpac Amaru II, the rebel leader who nearly brought down the Viceroyalty of Peru in the early 1780s. Condorcanqui exemplifies the strange contradictions that lay beneath the surface of colonial life for the graduates of the school. He claimed political legitimacy on the basis of his descent (actual or supposed) from the last Inca emperor, and he rallied much of the highland Indian nobility and peasantry to his cause. But this Túpac Amaru was very different from his sixteenth-century namesake. He rode on a Spanish horse and wore a brass-buttoned greatcoat; he carried a saber and musket; and his eyes were shaded by a wide-brimmed European hat. Condorcanqui was a man who moved comfortably in multiple worlds. His followers were not just Quechuas and Aymaras but also mestizos and creoles. He spoke and wrote in multiple languages, crafting his most elegant correspondence in Latin. Though Condorcanqui's enemies considered him an existential threat to the colonial order, he himself was very much a product of colonial institutions. His rebellion provoked a profound reversal in viceregal policy and an end to the crown's previously enthusiastic patronage for the native nobility.[32]

The College of San Francisco de Borja belongs to a particular place and a particular time: the hybrid colonial world of the Andes that existed between the execution of Túpac Amaru I in 1572 and the execution of Túpac Amaru II in 1781. In 1572, Viceroy Toledo believed he could bring an end to Inca resistance by drawing the native leadership classes into a closer relationship with the Iberian church and state.[33] Fifty years of conflict had taught European administrators to fear both Inca irredentists and self-serving Spanish conquistadors. Toledo's prescription was comprehensive: he would purge the ranks of dangerous Spanish and Indian elites, rewarding loyal followers and punishing others; he would rebuild the Indian communities shattered and depopulated by war and disease, placing them under reliable Indian nobles and elected officials; and he would act as the patron for new projects of evangelization and education spearheaded by the regular orders (especially the Jesuits). Elite Indian education in the colonial Andes came into existence as a part of this policy. But the world looked a bit different three centuries later when the followers of Túpac Amaru and Tomás Katari threatened to dismantle the viceregal state. From the perspective of the 1780s, elite education began to look more like a cause than a cure for native resistance. José Condorcanqui had studied the texts of Garcilaso de la Vega, learned the tales of his illustrious ancestors, and mastered the skills of the conquerors. He appealed to his followers using sophisticated arguments about law, justice, history, and religion. After the defeat of his movement, the viceroyalty viewed Peru's remaining native nobility with greater suspicion. Some colonial leaders suggested that elite education was itself to blame.[34]

English Colleges for Native Students

Like Peru, English-speaking North America has its own history of ambivalence toward elite education for indigenous students. Colonial education for Indians began later and followed a somewhat different trajectory than that of Spanish America. Yet, in both realms, colleges served as a point of contact between young indigenous leaders and the religious and secular hierarchies of the Euro-American state. In the United States, no institutions are more closely associated with intellectual prestige and cultural capital than the universities of the Ivy League. Chartered in the seventeenth and eighteenth centuries by the British crown, these schools survived US independence and provided the emergent nation with much of its academic, political, and economic leadership. The scattered attempts to bring Indian young men into these institutions says much about the inconsistent attitudes of Anglo-American elites toward their native counterparts.

In the spring of 1912, Henry Roe Cloud crossed the stage and received his diploma from Arthur Twining Hadley, president of Yale University. Cloud was a Winnebago, who grew up in Nebraska, studied in mission schools and trade academies, and ultimately made his way through undergraduate and graduate school at Yale, earning degrees in philosophy, psychology, and anthropology. At Yale, Cloud was known for his erudite lectures in English, but he also spoke the Winnebago language and read classical Greek. He went on to become a well-known intellectual, a Presbyterian minister, the founder of a secondary school, and an influential administrator in the Bureau of Indian Affairs. At Yale, Cloud had no predecessors; he was the first Indian student to graduate from the university, and was a singular political figure in his generation. In the racially stratified society of Henry Roe Cloud's generation, the Ivy League was normally a world closed to Indians. But it could have been otherwise.

A glimpse of Harvard University in the 1660s shows us the ambitious path on which New England's Indian education began. In those years, a visitors strolling across Harvard Yard would have passed a neatly built brick building two stories in height. Behind its glazed and leaded windows, one could see the typical facilities for study, dining, and lodging, but also something rather unexpected: a state-of-the-art printing press. Printing presses were themselves rare, but this one was not just unusual; it was unique. The machine, at first glance, was no different from those in the print shops of London: a heavy wooden frame, a threaded screw, and a heavy plate that stamped out one sheet of paper at a time. But a close look at the wet pages would have revealed to the curious visitor lines of print unlike those anywhere else in the world.

The building was the Harvard Indian College, its printers and translators English-educated polyglots, and the pages pulled from the press were those of the Algonquian Bible. Just a half century after British subjects first beheld the King James Bible printed in their own native English, New England's indigenous peoples first read the Eliot Bible printed in their native Algonquian.[35] Harvard College was originally founded in 1636 to train colonial Englishmen as ministers, teachers, and political leaders. In 1650, the school's charter expanded its mission to include the education of New England's Indian elites. The document proclaimed the institution's desire to advance the study of "good literature, arts, and sciences . . . that may conduce to the education of the English and Indian youth of this country, in knowledge and godliness."[36] To further this end, the Indian school at Harvard was built in 1655, and admitted its first cohort of students in 1661.

The wood-framed machine in the Indian College was one of the first printing presses anywhere in English America. Along with didactic, academic, and inspirational texts, the press produced several thousand copies of the Algonquian Bible. The print shop was often manned by Wowaus, a Nipmuc Indian whose European dress and excellent English (both acquired during his studies with Reverend John Eliot) made him difficult to distinguish from an Anglo-American settler. The building was a vibrant site of interaction for English and indigenous scholars who were devoted to Christian evangelization and intent on the spread of literacy, transliteration, and translation. The remarkable project taking place in the Harvard print shop during the mid-seventeenth century required a striking coordination of efforts. New England in the 1640s comprised a complex collection of civic and cultural bodies. Massachusetts Bay, Plymouth Colony, Rhode Island, and Connecticut Colony were distinct and separately governed political communities, and the spaces between them were—at least until the time of King Philip's War in 1675—sovereign Indian lands ruled by indigenous sachems and councils. The Harvard Indian College and the Algonquian Bible were meant to serve the needs of the English colonies in a time of great religious diversity and complex diplomacy between and among English and Indian polities. The whole project of Indian education had been given additional impetus in 1649 by the formation in London of the Society for the Propagation of the Gospel in New England. This charitable organization gave moral and legal credibility and (more importantly) financial backing to the efforts of New England clergymen to spread Christian belief and European cultural practices among the region's Indians.[37]

The Harvard Indian College was a new kind of institution, and it was created by a distinctive group of innovators: Indians and Englishmen who crossed the cultural and linguistic boundaries that had formerly divided them. The project grew out of a partnership between John Eliot and three indigenous translators: Cockenoe, Job Nesuton, and James Wowaus. John Eliot's partnership with Cockenoe began in the 1630s when he met the young Montauk Indian, a captive from the Pequot Wars who had later arrived as a slave or servant in a private Dorchester household. Cockenoe had been trafficked between different Algonquian-speaking groups and had sharpened his linguistic skills along the way. Both men soon developed a dual fluency and dual literacy. This allowed Eliot to begin preaching in Algonquian languages, and Cockenoe to gain significant influence in diplomatic and legal negotiations between the English and Montauks in his native Long Island.[38] In 1646, while giving sermons among the Massachusetts people in the village of Nonantum, Eliot recruited his second vital collaborator, Job Nesuton. Nesuton would contribute greatly to Eliot's efforts to establish schools and win converts, serving as a preacher, interpreter, and schoolmaster. However, his greatest intellectual contribution was undoubtedly his partnership with Eliot for the translation of the Bible and the composition of didactic texts in Algonquian.

By the middle of the seventeenth century, Indian leaders in New England and the mid-Atlantic were hedging their bets by consolidating their influence inside indigenous polities and simultaneously cultivating alliances with Europeans. A powerful household could now advance its interests by ensuring that some of its members operated within the cultural and linguistic environment of the English. This is how it was that Wowaus (also called James Wowaus and James Printer) came to be educated from an early age among the Englishmen of the Massachusetts Bay Colony. Wowaus's father, Naoas, had consolidated his family's influence as leaders in the inchoate praying towns, communities sponsored by Eliot and the New England Company as sites of conversion and civic acculturation. His sons served on both sides of the porous boundary between English and Indian worlds, leading their communities as headmen and schoolmasters. Wowaus, who was arguably the most successful of the sons, served as a translator and skilled tradesman in English society. He worked with John Eliot and also with Boston printers Samuel Green and Marmaduke Johnson to produce printed editions of Algonquian texts that remain to this day among the most important sources for the region's native cultural patrimony.[39]

While Eliot worked in mainland Massachusetts, his fellow Congregationalist Thomas Mayhew followed a parallel path on the island of Martha's Vineyard. He offered his linguistic expertise to the local Wampanoags, helping them to build over time a community of Indian Christians steeped in a new transatlantic tradition of Christian classicism. His principal ally in this project was Hiacoomes, the man who taught Mayhew to speak Wampanoag even while himself learning English, Latin, and Greek.[40] Hiacoomes was for many years a translator, teacher, and lay preacher before receiving ordination in 1670 from John Eliot. As was the case among the mainland Nipmucs, the Martha's Vineyard Wampanoags quickly grasped the political advantages of multilingualism and of membership in the Christian community. The leading families sought instruction from Mayhew and Hiacoomes in the hopes that their sons might enter English colonial institutions.[41] The first Indian cohort at Harvard University included both Joel Hiacoomes (the son of Mayhew's Indian protégé) and Caleb Cheeshahteaumuck, the son of a leading sachem, and a former student of Mayhew's school.[42]

Thus, the students of Mayhew and the students of Eliot converged in Cambridge as Harvard classmates. Sadly, the visionary ambitions of the Indian school's founders would not be matched with long-term success. Only six Indian students attended the school, and just one, Caleb Cheeshahteaumuck, graduated. In this sense, the project was a failure. Viewed more broadly, though, Harvard Indian College was just one element of a vast social and institutional network of Indians and Englishmen engaged in the activity of translating languages, spreading literacy, producing foundational texts, and integrating English and indigenous political institutions. This broader seventeenth-century cultural project had widespread effects on colonial life.[43]

None of Anglo-America's prominent colleges began with so ambitious a commitment to indigenous education as Dartmouth. The institution's charter described it as a college founded "for the education and instruction of youth of the Indian tribes in this land in reading, writing, and all parts of learning which shall appear necessary and expedient for civilizing and Christianizing children of pagans, as well as in all liberal arts and sciences, and also of English youth and any others." Rather than a school for Englishmen with an ancillary Indian school, Dartmouth was founded as a college for Indians, which also welcomed Englishmen. In practice, Dartmouth fell short of these lofty ambitions, evolving swiftly into a school for Anglo-Americans, but its charter bespeaks an early moment of possibility in the design of higher education.

Conspicuous in the Dartmouth charter is the description of the school's genesis from the collaboration of Indian and English clergymen. Dartmouth was the final incarnation of Moor's Charity School, previously founded in Connecticut by Eleazar Wheelock in 1754. As was so often the case with colonial missionary and educational ventures, the visionaries behind Dartmouth were colonists, but their financial backers were Englishmen. In 1766, the founders crossed the Atlantic looking for deep pockets. In the words of the charter, "Eleazar Wheelock thought it expedient, that endeavors should be used to raise contributions from well-disposed persons in England for the carrying on and extending said undertaking; and for that purpose the said Eleazar Wheelock requested the Rev. Nathaniel Whitaker, now doctor in divinity, to go over to England for that purpose, and sent over with him the Rev. Samson Occom, an Indian minister, who had been educated by the said Wheelock."[44]

Paradoxically, Indian leaders would shape Dartmouth more than Dartmouth would shape Indian life. Occom's efforts raised £11,000 of funding from British benefactors and gave great credibility to the college. Upon his return, Occom and his fellow Indian clergyman William Simons preached to local Indians, English students, and nearby settlers, creating amicable relations between Dartmouth and the wide range of local stakeholders.[45] Though Dartmouth's project of Indian education is usually considered a failure, it was, in retrospect, only a failure relative to its original grand ambitions. Over the course of the long era before the United States' twentieth-century civil-rights movements, when very few Indian students attended any elite colleges, Dartmouth taught nearly a hundred Indian scholars. Still, the project was a grave disappointment to its original architects. A crestfallen Samson Occom, observing the school's loss of commitment to Indian education, soon moved on, turning his attention to the construction of Indian institutions that lay far beyond the centers of Anglo-American authority.[46]

Indian education in colonial North America took many forms, and a comprehensive vision of the subject demands that we consider a wide range of formal and informal educational environments.[47] The vast majority of indigenous young people received their education not in colonial schools but in a traditional setting, developing a practical and intellectual understanding of the world though observation, participation, and instruction in daily activities led by their elders. A fuller understanding of Indian education as a part of colonial culture requires us to consider both the experiences of indigenous students within Anglo-American institutions and the experiences of those in traditional communities who appropriated European ideas, pedagogies, and technologies. Missionaries, both Indian and European, established the social networks that enabled this multidirectional exchange of ideas.

In early nineteenth-century Connecticut, the Foreign Mission School served as a continental hub for this ever-wider world of Indian education. The school was founded in 1817 and funded by the American Board of Commissioners for Foreign Missions. Though located on a modest campus and in a thinly populated region of rural Connecticut, the Foreign Mission School was constructed to serve a global set of objectives: the extension of Christianity, literacy, and Anglo-American customs to all lands touched by the United States. The project was inspired by the remarkable visit of two young Hawaiians who came from the leading families of their Pacific islands all the way to Yale, seeking a formal education. As their story spread, boosters and philanthropists from New Haven, Boston, and London began offering donations to fund a new school in Connecticut. The Foreign Mission School was only in operation for about a decade, but it exerted a profound influence on the cultural and political relationship between white and nonwhite social elites in the expanding empire of the United States. Though inspired by the crusade to Christianize Hawaii, the school went on to enroll North American Indians, Asians, at least one indigenous Mexican, several Europeans, and a dozen Anglo-American young men who were preparing to work on missionary frontiers.[48]

The daily operations of the school were typical of Protestant missionary education, combining prayer and religious instruction with academic and manual training. Its campus on the banks of the Housatonic River featured a church, an academy building, and a dormitory, as well as a workshop for carpentry and mechanics, and the surrounding fields and forests where the scholars operated model farms and lumber operations. Like Latin America's binary communities of Indian and Spanish republics, the township of Cornwall, Connecticut, comprised, during the 1820s, two ethnic enclaves: a community of Anglo-American Congregationalists, and the remarkably ethnically diverse community of the Foreign Mission School students. In this environment, the relationships among individuals of different ethnicities, economic classes, and social statuses were unpredictable and often contested. Though the school sometimes described itself as a project for civilizing "savages" and "heathens," it was also clearly a school for grooming non-European gentlemen. Its presidents and faculty were Anglo-Americans, but so were its cooks and handymen. At the same time, the largely nonwhite student body included the sons of the Hawaiian nobility and those of leading families from the Iroquois North and the Cherokee and Choctaw South.

The distinctive student population created unexpected inversions of status between town and gown, and also between Anglo and Indian, that were much remarked upon at the time. When Cherokee student John Ridge received a visit from his father, the entire town took notice. The elder Ridge arrived in an elegant carriage wearing an officer's dress uniform from the United States Army. Skah-tle-loh-skee, or "Major Ridge" as he was more often called, was not the social equal of the average Connecticut citizen; he was the social superior. Ridge was a wealthy man and the owner of vast acreage, commercial enterprises, and many slaves; he was a decorated veteran and a major in the US Army. Ridge was personally acquainted with President Monroe, and he was a man more accustomed to giving orders than taking them. Ridge was not likely intimidated by anyone in Cornwall, Connecticut. He came there in 1821 to visit his son, who was then convalescing from a long illness in the home of John Prout Northrup. During the major's visit, he was a guest in the palatial home of Colonel Benjamin Gold, one of Cornwall's civic leaders and a founding benefactor of the Foreign Mission School.[49]

Cornwall, Connecticut, was provincial in some respects but quite cosmopolitan in others. The connections among the lives of the Ridges, Golds, and Northrups reveal much about the emerging social networks linking Anglo-Americans and indigenous Americans over distance in the early republic. By the early nineteenth century, leaders among the Cherokees, Choctaws, and Creeks had relationships with Anglo-American elites through business and military service, and increasingly through educational and religious institutions. A few years before his visit to Cornwall, Ridge's son had arrived at the Foreign Mission School in the company of his friend and cousin, Buck Watie (also known as Elias Boudinot). The two Cherokee boys, both from leading families, were first educated by Moravian missionaries at Spring Place, Georgia, before accepting an invitation to attend the Foreign Mission School. Within a few years, all of these families would be connected, in one way or another, by blood or marriage. In 1824, John Ridge married Sarah Bird Northrup, the daughter of Lydia Northrup (the school's nurse and dorm mother) and John Prout Northrup (the school's steward). In 1826, Ridge's cousin Elias Boudinot married Harriet Gold, the daughter of Benjamin Gold.[50] Ridge, like his father, would become a powerful leader among the Cherokees. Boudinot would become the most significant Cherokee writer of his generation and the editor of the *Cherokee Phoenix*.[51]

Though the rhetoric of the Foreign Mission School constantly invoked a crusade to civilize and Christianize the Indians, few Anglo-Americans who met young Boudinot and Ridge on the way to college would have doubted their bona fides as civilized Christians. They traveled comfortably from their homes toward convocation, rubbing shoulders with other well-heeled travelers, visiting the homes of local notables, and stopping to shop for luxury goods in Philadelphia. Foreign Mission School students like Ridge and Boudinot were understood by their teachers more as agents than as recipients of civilization and conversion. Like the Anglo-American seminarians at the school, their role was to bring learning and virtue to distant frontiers.

The daily routine of the Foreign Mission School was designed to train the best and brightest young men for their future endeavors as clergymen, missionaries, and political leaders. In the school's chapel, prayer meetings were held in the English, Hawaiian, and Cherokee languages. The classroom primers and library books included works in many languages and academic disciplines. The curriculum included theology, science, and mathematics, as well as language studies in English, Latin, Greek, and Hebrew. Only in its rigorous approach to indigenous languages did the curriculum differ noticeably from that of traditional elite institutions in England and Anglo-America. The egalitarian accommodations and spare but adequate personal furnishings were not a far cry from elite boarding-school life elsewhere. The students' feather beds and wooden writing desks sat in tidy rooms lit by fireplaces, candles, and oil lamps. Here a Hawaiian prince and an aspiring Greek revolutionary lived beside Anglo–New Englanders and the Cherokee gentry. They all ate at the same tables and sat in the same pews.

But the sense of camaraderie and shared purpose among the white and Indian students on the campus did not always extend to the public at large. The Ridge-Northrup wedding and the Gold-Boudinot wedding were both celebrated in style and consecrated with the approval of the four families. However, these cross-caste unions made others uneasy. The public began to fear a spreading epidemic of courtships between the boys at the Indian school and Cornwall's Anglo-American daughters. The controversy sent ripples from Cornwall to the major cities of the Eastern seaboard, provoking debates in newspapers and mission-board meetings throughout New England.

The marriages were staunchly defended by the college president but roundly criticized by the school's parent organization. In the end, the controversy over interracial courtship was the school's undoing. By 1828, the Cornwall campus was shuttered. The school's short but remarkable history reflects a nineteenth-century United States that was in some respects open to the notion of elite Indian education, and in other respects terrified by its implications.[52] While Anglo-Americans argued over how best to expand and regulate formal, European-style Indian education, Native Americans continued to borrow and transform European knowledge, disseminating it to new frontiers. Literacy was eventually carried to distant lands by the Indians themselves.

Breakaway Literacy: Sequoya and the Cherokee Syllabary

In 1843, a handful of lightly equipped Cherokee travelers crossed the ill-defined border between the Republic of Texas and Mexico. Passing through the hill country, plains, and shallow, winding rivers of Texas and Tamaulipas, this party of a half dozen men must have looked small against the landscape. The modestly dressed travelers were armed with rifles and mounted on horses; behind them trailed a string of pack animals. Their leader, Sequoya, was now in his sixties. He walked with a limp but probably rode with ease and experience as he surveyed the landscape leading toward his destination in Mexico. At a distance, his ethnicity and nationality would have been difficult to discern. As he rode past towns and villages, few if any observers would have recognized him for what he was: one of the great linguists, intellectuals, and cultural leaders of his generation.[53]

Sequoya was older than the United States and older than the Republic of Mexico; he was also well versed in the complex politics of contested frontiers. When he crossed yet another line on the map, he knew what he was doing. Sequoya was born in the 1770s into an emerging Cherokee polity that had already begun the long and difficult fight to protect itself from the expanding Anglo-American states of the eastern seaboard. Cherokees were shrewd pragmatists, appropriating from Englishmen the tools and customs that suited their interests, and rejecting those that did not. Keen on new technologies of warfare, artisanship, and agriculture—but sometimes ambivalent about Christianity and its attendant social conventions—Cherokees charted a careful middle path between acceptance and rejection of Anglo-America practices. They often argued among themselves over the most prudent approach to the future.

Borders, like the one between the US and Mexico, could be a threat or an opportunity for those living on both sides of the line. Cherokees and Creeks had a century of experience living between Spanish and English colonies, learning to minimize risks, maximize trade, and play the colonizers off of each other. During the English colonies' rebellion, the Cherokees tested the prevailing winds. The violence of the American Revolution created an opportunity for them to push back against Georgia settlers, but the subsequent victory of the American rebels imposed terrible costs. During the War of 1812, they bet on a different horse. Anticipating a US victory, the Cherokees turned their fire upon the British, the Spanish, and the allied Creeks. Sequoya saw these events from the inside as a soldier at the Battle of Horseshoe Bend, and as a diplomat for the Cherokees in the years that followed.

In the end, all of Sequoya's previous adventures and accomplishments pale beside his principal intellectual achievement: the invention of the Cherokee written language. By the time Sequoya was dodging bullets at the Battle of Horseshoe Bend, he had probably already begun his most important life's work: a syllabary of simple signs that could quickly express spoken Cherokee words on the printed page.[54] His invention would have important cultural and political implications for Cherokee life forever after. In the early nineteenth century, the great political debates among Cherokees had to do with conversion, religious autonomy, and the defense of cultural tradition—but more than anything, they had to do with land and sovereignty. Sequoya, like many in his nation, agonized over the question of whether to dig in and defend the homeland from colonial incursions or to cut their losses and move far to the west where they might be safe (at least for a while) from the squatters and militias that pushed relentlessly from Georgia into Cherokee lands. Some argued that a western Cherokee settlement might remain an independent nation indefinitely, or even join the US as a new state. Sequoya leaned in one direction and then the other, first agreeing to land cessions but later fighting against them. He even moved his family to the distant Cherokee settlements in Arkansas territory for a time. However, when his new syllabary was completed, Sequoya hoped, above all else, that it would be formally adopted by tribal leaders and become the universal written language of his people.[55]

In 1821, Sequoya appeared before the Cherokee Council with a sheaf of papers in hand, and with his young daughter, Ayoka, beside him. They came to prove beyond a shadow of a doubt that his syllabary was neither a parlor

FIGURE 7 Se-Quo-Yah
and his syllabary. I. T. Bowen's,
Philadelphia. Published by F. W.
Greenough, ca. 1838. Courtesy of
the Library of Congress, Prints
and Photographs Division.

trick nor a mnemonic device but a full written language. No small number of Cherokees had already learned to speak and write English, but their own language had no written form. To English readers, Sequoya's script must have looked at once strange and familiar, like an inscrutable cipher made from fragments of Greek and Cyrillic. But Sequoya himself neither read nor spoke English; he had grasped the phonetic principles behind European writing and then applied them, through his own ingenuity, to the sounds of the Cherokee language. Cherokee leaders responded to his invention with great skepticism. The story of Sequoya's triumph comes to us in several forms, one of the earliest of which is an article from the 1829 *Cherokee Phoenix*, a paper whose very existence owed itself to his ingenuity. The author, an Anglophone scholar named Samuel L. Knapp, had met Sequoya during the latter's diplomatic mission to Washington, DC, in the winter of 1828, and with the aid of an interpreter taken down the dramatic story of the syllabary's invention and adoption. He described Sequoya's triumph over the skeptics on the council thus: "His daughter, who was now his only pupil, was ordered to go out of hearing, while he requested his friends to make a word or statement which he put down, and then she was called in and read it to them; then the father retired, and the daughter wrote, the Indians were wonderstruck." Grasping the potential for this new innovation, but still somewhat doubtful, the council accepted Sequoya's proposal for a further trial: they would select several of the most promising young men from the nation to study his phonetic system for a period of months before making a public demonstration of their literacy. In time the project was declared a success, and Sequoya—lauded by his Anglophone biographers as a Cadmus, a Pythagoras, a philosopher, and a professor—was embraced by his nation as a foundational figure.[56]

=====

Education and intellectual life took on many different forms at the interstices of indigenous and Euro-American culture. Both sides of the Atlantic had long histories of formal and informal leadership and instruction. Oral chroniclers, tlacuilos, and quipucamayocs were important figures in their communities long before Europeans entered their worlds. Yet the arrival of alphabetic literacy was a new and powerful force that eventually touched and transformed most of indigenous America. Knowledge of European written language was a powerful tool in the hands of native people. It unlocked European law, scripture, and communications over distance. The nearly infinite flexibility of the Latin alphabet meant that languages with no previous written form could be rapidly adapted for communication in ink and paper. Thus it was that from Canada to Bolivia the written word spread quickly by multiple means. Missionary schools and colleges trained a class of native leaders in the tradition of European academic life. In these places the roles of indigenous scholar-scribes and those of European pedants and churchmen began to blend, giving rise to a substantial community of transcultural intellectual leaders. Colonial instructors worked diligently to spread dual literacy in European and American languages. But the world of indigenous literacy also extended far beyond these institutions as native people seized hold of the alphabet for their own purposes, putting these adaptable symbols to their own uses and even transforming the script or inventing new ones. A whole universe of narratives, images, and understandings of the world soon collided as documents, books, maps, and eventually newspapers circulated information across ever-greater distances.

CHAPTER FOUR

Artists and Artisans

Juan Gerson's Nahua Renaissance

It was in the final twilight of Michelangelo's old age and on the other side of the world from the Sistine Chapel that in 1562 Juan Gerson began his own magnum opus. Like the Italian master, Gerson's most famous work was a vast narrative of human history and Christian theology; and also like Michelangelo's, his was painted on a church ceiling.

The building still stands in the town of Tecamachalco in Mexico's Puebla state. Imposing and fortress-like, the former Franciscan Convento de Tecamachalco is crowned with stone crenulations and topped with a high tower. One enters through great studded doors twice the height of a man. A few steps farther and one stares down the central aisle toward the altar. Ahead stands a massive stone baptismal font. Above, the vaulting of the choir curves overhead like a tabernacle or the dome of the sky. Its surface is divided by sculptural ribs into chambers like the petals of a flower, and between them luminous painted ovals beckon like portals to an outer world. To the European eye, each painted scene is familiar yet unfamiliar, like pages from a book come to life—and that is what it is. The scenes may be read in a spiral pattern, working outward from a central axis marked by an emblem of the crucifix. The story unwinds around this axis, starting with Old Testament scenes: Cain and Abel, the Great Flood, the construction of the Tower of Babel, Abraham and Isaac. Icons of the four evangelists mark the boundaries between the Biblical past and the prophetic future. As in the Sistine Chapel, the story culminates with the Apocalypse. The image is a shockingly familiar one: four horsemen descend from the clouds wielding a bow, a trident, a sword, and a set of scales. In the right foreground, humans are trampled beneath the hooves; to the left, they are devoured by the jaws of a beast. It is Albrecht Dürer's vision of the scene but infused with new colors.[1]

Juan Gerson was the son and grandson of tlacuilos, the scribes and artists who had chronicled Tecamachalco's history and advised its rulers since long before the arrival of the Spanish. He and his family appear in the Annals of Tecamachalco, which recount the town's political and religious history from 1398 to 1590. It is appropriate that the convent's ceiling should read like a book since Gerson was both a reader and maker of books. In fact, though the scenes appear at first to be frescoes brushed onto the plaster, they are actually painted on paper, which was made from tree bark in the tradition of the tlacuilos, and only later affixed to the surfaces of the church. There can be no doubt that the images are adapted from European art; the resemblance is unmistakable. Gerson clearly spent years of his life studying European prints and printed books only to copy them at a larger scale, breathing new life into their black-and-white forms with the fuller palette of Mexico's bright pigments.[2]

Though Gerson probably never left the region of central Mexico where he was born, his was a well-traveled mind. His Tower of Babel rises on powerful winches and pulleys, driven by an enormous wheel. His Noah's ark looks like a Byzantine church fashioned from quarried stone. Christ in judgment floats enthroned and surrounded by seven flames, partly a visual quotation from Revelation, but in other ways strangely reminiscent of Persian miniatures representing the Prophet Muhammad. Some of the landscapes are from the realm of pure imagination, most from standard iconography, and a few drawn with shocking realism from the existing world. Gerson's holy city of Jerusalem is not a fanciful representation of Solomon's temple, but rather a clear and realistic portrait of the Dome of the Rock—the Abbasid-era mosque that in Gerson's own era loomed over the landscape of Jerusalem. This leaves one wondering: how did an indigenous painter, living in this small town in Mexico, gain such a broad vision of the larger world? The answer is to be found in the rapidly expanding universe of printed books and images that were, in the sixteenth century, pulling readers in Europe and the Americas into a shared intellectual community. These connections may also have had a personal character in central Mexico. Gerson's education was a Franciscan one, and his missionary teachers were Europeans. The Franciscan convent of Tecamachalco shaped Gerson, and was also shaped by him. It was founded in 1541 by Fray Andrés de Olmos, a famed missionary and one of the greatest linguists of his age. The community was probably typical of mission-convents in Nahua Mexico at the time: it was a Franciscan monastery devoted to the conversion and education of Nahua youth, and a place of intellectual exchange between European and indigenous Christians. In this environment, Gerson was the recipient of two literary and artistic traditions: that of his tlacuilo ancestors, and that of the Franciscan fathers. These were also the years when Flemish artistic influences abounded in New Spain. The famed painter and chapel architect Simon Pereyns arrived from Europe in the entourage of Viceroy Gastón de Peralta in 1566. He was preceded by the Iberian painters Francisco de Morales and Francisco de Zumaya, who began painting in New Spain the same year that Gerson began work on the Tecamachalco images. Not only did indigenous painters like Gerson know about the works of famed European painters, they were also sometimes personally acquainted with the artists.[3]

The great indigenous artists and builders of the sixteenth century inhabited an urban world that they themselves had constructed. In his later years, when Juan Gerson approached the portal of the chapel that housed his masterwork, he did so on horseback with the hat, sword, and cape of a Spanish gentlemen. He was descended from Indian nobility, and he had served his pueblo and his king admirably. In 1592, the viceroy granted to him the formal privileges of a gentleman, among them the right to ride on horseback and the right to dress and arm himself as a member of the ruling class.[4]

In these years Tecamachalco was a place of promise that had survived a generation of perdition. Burned over in the great European plagues of the sixteenth century, the region's population was a fraction of what it had been in the preconquest era. Increasingly, the region's indigenous capital of Tlaxcala was overshadowed by the Spanish one at Puebla. Despite this ominous encroachment, the Indian republic of Tecamachalco had many advantages. Surrounded by fresh streams, flowing rivers, and rich farmlands, its urban core now rose to new heights, built stone upon stone at the direction of Nahua lords and Franciscan friars.[5] The Gerson family's grant of royal privilege arrived just months after the final stones of the church tower were mortared into place. An inscription in Nahuatl testifies to the local masons' accomplishment forevermore.[6]

The Book in Native Hands:
Guaman Poma's Andean Chronicle

During the colonial era, viceregal Peru was perhaps the richest region of artistic production in all of the Americas. The remaining vestiges of its New World Renaissance still leave modern viewers mesmerized. Just off the cobblestone streets, painted porticoes teem with images of jousting noblemen, classical specters, and floral excrescences. Church vaults shelter treasuries of levitating saints, vivid crucifixions, winged cherubim, and pious patrons. Lavishly painted panels and canvases retell the genealogies of Peru's great noble houses, both Spanish and Inca.[7] Consequently, some elements of Peru's colonial *imaginaire* are easy for the modern scholar to recover from art: religious life, public pageantry, imperial hierarchies, mines, and riches. But much of the daily life of Peru's indigenous nobles, middling sorts, and hardworking commoners would remain dim in our mind's eye were it not for one remarkable manuscript—a Peruvian document lost for three centuries and recovered in 1908, on the other side of the world, in the Danish Royal Library: Felipe Guaman Poma de Ayala's *El primer nueva corónica y buen gobierno.*[8]

This document, which exceeds a thousand pages in length, contains 398 line drawings that together illustrate virtually every aspect of Peru's history—all from the distinctive perspective of the artist and author, a brilliant, tortured, and idiosyncratic Indian nobleman from the province of Huamanga. His images blend the quotidian with the phantasmagoric, illustrating the woes of daily life against the grand backdrops of the Inca past, the Habsburg Empire, and the sweeping metanarrative of Christian history. The book is at once a chronicle, an almanac of social reality, and an ambitious argument for the renovation of Peru's political system and cultural life.

Guaman Poma was not modest about himself or his accomplishments. By his own account, he was an indigenous prince, a skilled translator and scribe, an intrepid traveler, and a pious member of the laity—and he did not stop there. His enormous book was one long petition that argued for the author's appointment as supreme ruler over the American colonies. It proposed sweeping reforms to the Habsburg king's system of governance, not just in the Andes but throughout the global empire. Guaman Poma proposed that the Spanish crown should govern the world through four viceroys: one ruling over European Christians, another over Turks and Moors, a third over all black Africans, and the final viceroy over all the peoples of the Americas. For this last post, Guaman Poma put forward his own name. He argued that his appointment was justified based on the traditional Spanish criteria for preferment: birth and service. He claimed noble descent through his mother (doña Juana Curi Ocllo Coya) from the preconquest lords of Chinchaysuyu, who had once served the Inca emperors in Cuzco. His conception of a proper ruling elite blended notions of birthright with those of meritocracy. He expected that men like himself, those distinguished by learning and literacy, would one day find themselves seated at the right hand of power.[9]

In one illustration, Guaman Poma shows himself kneeling before the Spanish throne, presenting his book to the monarch. King Philip is dressed as we might expect: he wears a crown, holds a scepter, and is seated on a throne beneath a tasseled canopy. Guaman Poma kneels, reading from an open page and gesturing toward the heavens. He wears a cape, a tunic trimmed with fur, and silk sleeves and leggings with lace around the collar and wrist cuffs. Only one detail reveals his indigenous identity: his hat has been placed carefully on the ground, uncovering the long hair and close-cropped bangs that were at the time typical of acculturated Andean subjects. The accompanying text is a dialogue between king and vassal, the latter gratifying his lord's curiosity about the Inca past and advising him on the problems of the present. This is, we gather, how Guaman Poma hoped his quest would end: with the author's recognition as a faithful vassal, his ascension as a royal advisor, and his triumph over corruption and abuse in Peru.

Though Guaman Poma never actually reached Spain, his extensive travels and experiences within Peru allowed him to write and illustrate with authority. His autobiographical writing shows the ways that literacy spread through both formal and informal channels in the Andes. Guaman Poma's mestizo half brother, Martín de Ayala, was an ordained clergyman. The book presents him as a saintly man who cared for the sick, protected the Indians from abuse, and spread learning and piety to the uneducated. One drawing shows a child Guaman Poma (dressed as a ladino) and his parents (dressed in the garb of the indigenous aristocracy) kneeling before Martín. Martín, as the family's priest, reads the mass and instructs his relations. The image tells us the story of how European literacy and theology spread from the Spanish community to the Andean one through the efforts of mestizo and native clergy and laymen.[10] Guaman Poma was a product of this environment and possessed a

FIGURE 8 Guaman Poma de Ayala kneels before King Philip III. Illustration by Poma de Ayala (1526–1613). Biblioteca del ICI, Madrid, Spain. Bridgeman Images. Original in *El primer nueva corónica y buen gobierno*, Royal Library of Denmark, Copenhagen.

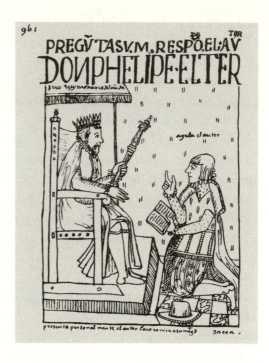

dual literacy in Quechua and Castilian, a skill set that made him valuable to both communities. Beyond his technical fluency, he also had a deep cultural education in both traditions. The titles in *Nueva corónica* are generally written in Spanish (albeit with nonstandard orthography), but many of the captions are in Quechua. The book includes an extensive retelling of Inca history. As if to footnote his scholarship, Guaman Poma tells and shows the reader how he collected his knowledge of the distant past. Several pages illustrate the methods of traditional Quechua scribes and messengers. They show Inca civil servants holding up quipus, the woven and knotted chords used for accounting and record keeping. Guaman Poma tells us that in the course of preparing his manuscript, he consulted with Quipucamayoc centenarians, the oldest trustees of the imperial chronicles. From their accounts he produced his almanac of Inca custom, administration, and political history, explaining the succession of authority from the dynastic founder, Manco Capac, to the tragic Túpac Amaru, whose captivity and execution he illustrates in excruciating detail. Many of his drawings present the deaths of Inca leaders at the hands of Spaniards, a series of events he retells in a style reminiscent of European martyrdom icons.[11]

The whole book draws heavily on European print culture in its contents, its imagery, and even its handwritten imitation of typography, but the author imposed on these forms a distinctly Andean worldview.[12] If Guaman Poma consulted the oldest Andean informants to reconstruct Peruvian history, he seems also to have consulted some of the oldest European sources in order to build his account of global history. The book is explicitly a jeremiad. The opening proclaims: "Jeremiah tells us we should repent and change our lives as Christians. The prophet King David tells us the same." Guaman Poma was presenting himself both as a traditional courtly petitioner and as a prophetic advisor, attacking vice and corruption in the kingdom. The text is peppered with Biblical quotations and illustrated with heraldic emblems and religious icons that demonstrate his mastery of European symbols of authority.[13] The book also shows his literacy in the classics. The front matter includes a series of forewords, letters, and introductions. Conspicuous among them is a letter from the author's father, don Martín Guaman Mallqui de Ayala, "Lord of the provinces of the Lucanas, Andamarcas, Circamarcas, and Soras," who introduces the book as a contribution to arts and letters in the tradition of Herodotus: "In addition to the service to Your Majesty that will result from publishing this history, it will begin to celebrate and immortalize the memory and the name of the former great ancestor lords, our grandparents, as their deeds deserve."[14] The book that follows these introductory remarks is partly in the Greco-Roman tradition, chronicling heroic and tragic events, and partly in the prophetic Biblical tradition, enumerating the moral shortcomings of leaders and the divine judgment that will fall upon them. Guaman Poma makes no categorical distinction between European and New World societies. His universal history begins with Adam and Eve, and grafts the peoples of the New World onto the genealogy of the sons of Noah. History on both sides of the Atlantic, he suggests, was always dictated by God, his divine favor and punishment doled out over time in proportion to human vices and virtues. Guaman Poma offers a corollary to Biblical history by adding narratives from the New World not heretofore present in Christian scripture. He affirms that the plagues, invasions, and cataclysms of Mosaic and Davidic history were matched by floods, earthquakes, volcanic eruptions, and epidemics in the New World. Just as he makes no sharp distinction between Old World and New World history, he sees no sharp distinction between Biblical history, the recent past, and his historical present. The Spanish conquest, the great epidemics of the sixteenth century, and the horrors of the wars between Almagrists and

Pizarrists are just as much a part of the story of sin and divine wrath as the Exodus from Egypt and the fall of the Davidic monarchy.[15]

To modern eyes, much of the *Nueva corónica* reads like a grim graphic novel. Hundreds of images testify to the corruption, cupidity, and avarice of Peru's leading classes. We see Indian servants and mitayos beaten and abused, clapped in chains, trodden underfoot, and bent beneath unsupportable burdens. Indian women appear at some points victimized and at others points corrupted. In one scene an indigenous woman lies in bed, stripped of her clothing, while a Spanish corregidor and his lieutenant leer down upon her, candles in hand, contemplating a sexual assault. Guaman Poma singles out local priests in Indian districts as among the most corrupt and abusive Spaniards. He illustrates their gluttonous excesses and describes their households as compounds where dependent Indians are treated as slaves and worse than slaves. The priests keep young servants for sexual exploitation, probing, raping, and sodomizing them. The scandalous resulting pregnancies bring forth a large and unfortunate population of mestizos.[16] The corrupt clergymen's dependent workers and tributaries suffer in the fields and workshops, generating a steady flow of profit for clerical estates. The merchants, miners, and soldiers come off no better than the priests. Indian mitayos labor to the point of collapse while their exploiters demand more sweat and toil. So great is the Spanish greed for gold that one early conquistador is shown asking whether he and his fellows can eat the precious metal in place of food.[17] Amid these many villains, Guaman Poma presents a handful of heroic individuals who rise to the defense of the Indians but find themselves opposed at every turn.

The *Nueva corónica* shows the ravages of the conquest and the failure of enlightened colonial government. It also gives us a glimpse of a multiethnic society in which the middle ranks of the social hierarchy were largely non-European. In one drawing a native scribe works in his study. The man sits before a bookcase filled with leather-bound volumes in a nicely furnished room. On his desk sit a rosary, a book, a blotter, and an inkwell. The room could be easily mistaken for one in contemporary Italy or Spain, but the man's clothing and his floral headdress identify him as person of some standing in the indigenous world. The caption identifies him as a cabildo *quilcaycamayoc*—an Indian municipal scribe in the tradition of quipucamayocs, but literate in Latin script.[18] Clearly, despite widespread abuses in public administration, some Indians held positions of authority in Guaman Poma's day, not just his esteemed brother (whom we see teaching, praying, and receiving a wreath of laurels from an angel) but also the scribes, the councilmen, and the native aristocracy. Guaman Poma describes the power of indigenous lords (whom he calls *apos* and caciques) within the Spanish imperial system. They are sovereign within their own realm: "Anyone who enters one of these lords' jurisdictions, whether he be a Spaniard, a gentleman, an hidalgo, an encomendero, or a mestizo, a mulatto, a black, a slave, or an Indian who has recently arrived in that province, is the lord's subject and must obey him."[19] Guaman Poma describes a wide range of indigenous leaders: some embody virtuous traditional governance, while others pad their wallets at the expense of the poor. In one drawing, a feasting corregidor lifts his glass to make a toast. His guests include a traditionally dressed curaca along with prosperous and well-fed mestizo and mulatto gentlemen, who raise their glasses in agreement. Meanwhile, a tiny Indian laborer waits on them hand and foot.[20] The variety in the dress is revealing: some are clothed like European courtiers; others in traditional tunics and headdresses. *Nueva corónica* shows us Indians and Spaniards of all stations. Indian elites are sometimes shown lording over Peru in partnership with the European conquerors. We also see poor Spanish drifters, cruel and prosperous mulattos, and mestizos of every sort. One page offers a Dantean image of eternal punishments for Peruvian sinners: Andeans of all castes devoured by the mouth of Satan.

Guaman Poma expected his grievances to be heard and his efforts to be rewarded. He wrote with a sense of authority born of experience and direct observation. He had served the church and the crown and had seen Spanish and indigenous worlds from the inside. Long before composing his great work, Guaman Poma had been contributing to royal administration. In the 1570s, when the ecstasies of the Taki Onqoy movement were seducing Indians away from the Catholic Church and back into the arms of traditional religion, Guaman Poma worked hand in glove with the clergy in their efforts to stamp out the religious revival and root out its idols. Guaman Poma supported Cristóbal de Albornoz in the latter's investigation of heterodoxy, serving as his assistant and translator. Albornoz appears in a manuscript illustration looking dignified and erect; he carries a rosary and punishes evildoers. The accompanying passages describe the cleric as tireless and incorruptible in his mission to destroy idols and eliminate sorcery. When Guaman Poma wrote about native religion and about the virtues and shortcomings of the Catholic Church, he did so from a perspective that was well informed by experience.[21]

By the time Guaman Poma wrote the *Nueva corónica*, he had already spent years of his life working for church officials, participating in local administration, and fighting on behalf of his interests in colonial courts.[22] The book was not his first historical project. Sometime in the 1580s or 1590s, he contributed to the most extensive Spanish account of Inca history yet written. Though *Nueva corónica* heaps abuse on the Augustinian scholar-priest Martín de Murúa, it is clear that the two men collaborated closely in the research and production of Murúa's *Historia general del Piru*.[23] The contents of the two books overlap, and Guaman Poma's distinctive illustrations grace both books. The result is a pair of academic projects that combine native and European scholarship in ways that are difficult to disentangle. Much like Bernardino de Sahagún's *Florentine Codex*, these works retell preconquest, conquest, and colonial history through multiple cultural lenses. They reveal an early Hispano-indigenous intellectual community whose relationship with the Spanish colonial establishment was sometimes symbiotic and sometimes antagonistic.

Scattered throughout the pages of the *Nueva corónica*, we see glimpses of the author himself. He comes across at times as arrogant and bold, trumpeting his privileged birth and his imperial service. At other times, he seems wounded and resentful, indignant at the treatment of indigenous Peruvians, and angry at the slights he has suffered from priests and scholars who should be his peers. His life exemplifies many of the contradictions of indigenous leadership in the colonial Americas, as does his persistent faith that the distant Habsburg king will act in good faith to set the world right again. More than 1100 pages into his vast manuscript, we see this hopeful notion illustrated in a self-portrait. Guaman Poma and his young son, Francisco, dressed as pilgrims and framed by the Andean peaks, lead their dogs and packhorse down the Inca roads toward the new capital, the City of Kings, bearing their message to Philip II. Somewhere in the horse's cargo, or in the bundle tied to the author's shoulder, is his own life's work: a literary and political treatise intended to transform his homeland forever.[24]

Andean Artists and Transatlantic Intellectual Life

Guaman Poma de Ayala was a trailblazing writer and illustrator who expressed the indigenous past and present using artistic techniques borrowed from the European tradition. In the two centuries that followed, this phenomenon of aesthetic synthesis would blossom into a full-fledged Andean Renaissance of painters who are now often described as members of the Cuzco School.[25] In 1753, Marcos Zapata, an Inca nobleman and one of the most famous Andean artists of his day, completed his most important commission: a large, richly colored canvas of the Last Supper that would soon grace the walls of Cuzco's Church of the Triumph. It was a Biblical scene already painted hundreds if not thousands of times by other artists, the definitive version produced by Leonardo da Vinci more than a hundred years before. Zapata was a master painter, and one who had spent years studying prints, sketches, and canvases transported from Europe. Still, he must have wondered what, if anything, his gifts might add to a scene so often and skillfully painted by others. In the end, his painting was a triumph. The finished work is ingeniously conceived so as to join the image to its architectural surroundings. Through the frame and canvas, the wall of the chapel seems to open into a painted space. In this second room—a clever trompe l'oeil—we enter the scene of the feasting apostles. This room, in turn, opens into other spaces and visions: a window beyond the illuminated head of Christ reveals the starry night sky; another opens on a vision of the crucifixion. Much of the painting matches precisely its European prototypes. Christ holds bread in one hand, and a chalice sits before him. The table is heavy with food, and a basin and cloth for washing the feet of weary travelers sits on the floor beneath it. The apostles lean toward Christ in expectation as Judas surreptitiously clutches his sack of silver coins and gazes toward the viewer. However, it is not these familiar features of the painting that most delight art historians and modern travelers but rather the menu on the table of this particular Last Supper. The guests have decanters of wine at their elbows but also a great feast of fruits and multihued potatoes. Two golden platters contain European fruits, such as grapes and peaches, as well as a dazzling variety of Andean delicacies. At the center of the table sits a roasted *cuy* (or guinea pig) in place of the expected paschal lamb.[26]

Zapata's *The Last Supper* is a magical window that opens from the back wall of the chapel into an ancient scene in Jerusalem—but it is a vision of Jerusalem imagined in distinctly Andean terms. In the eighteenth century, most Mediterranean artists knew little about the material culture of the Andes, but the reverse was not true. Zapata was the product of an artistic community that had been studying and emulating European artwork for more than a century. Men like Zapata could—if they chose—reproduce the works of European masters in such a way as to make the copy indistinguishable from the original. This roasted cuy is not incidental to the painting, nor is it a mistake like some error of transcription in a hastily copied text. It sits front and center before Jesus. It is this meat that he offers to his apostles, saying, "Take and eat; this is my body."[27]

The location of the painting also matters. Zapata's *Last Supper* was commissioned to hang in the Church of the Triumph (el Triunfo), a structure built atop the rubble of Inca Sunturhuasi, a royal edifice seized by the Spanish during their final desperate attempts to survive Manco Inca's 1536 attack on Cuzco. El Triunfo was built to commemorate the miraculous battlefield intervention of the Virgin, whose supernatural aid saved the Spanish cause from ruin. This imposing stone church was surrounded by a cluster of related Spanish construction projects (the adjacent cathedral, the Plaza de Armas, and the soaring Jesuit church). Together, these colonial structures had by the seventeenth century largely erased the most recognizable features of the Inca ceremonial and imperial precinct. Despite this apparent act of cultural erasure, the interior splendor of the new buildings was largely the work of Quechua artists and artisans. The hands of Marcos Zapata and his contemporaries breathed life into the cold stone walls of viceregal Cuzco. He produced a series of fifty canvases for the cathedral that illustrated the verses of the *Letanía Lauretana*, celebrating the virtues of the Virgin mother. He painted a twenty-four-canvas series representing the life of Saint Francis. In the Jesuit church, whenever priests donned their vestments and prepared for mass, they did so beneath Zapata's enormous paintings—great instructive works for the edification of the clergy.

Whoever sets foot in Cuzco's most important religious buildings sees theology, Biblical history, and hagiography through Zapata's mind's eye. But Zapata's voice—that is, his words—is largely lost to history. Unlike Guaman Poma or Garcilaso de la Vega, Zapata left us no written transcript of his thoughts. A tantalizing line appears beneath his images of San Ignatius Loyola and San Francisco Xavier, along with the date of composition: "Marcos Zapata me fecit y aiudo Sipriano Gutierres"—I made it and Sipriano Gutierres helped.[28] Apparently Zapata was not just a master artist, but also a master teacher, and perhaps the head of a large workshop where others, such as the man named here, contributed to his artistic production. Hundreds of paintings have been attributed to Zapata, and even in his own time, they graced the walls of churches from Cuzco to Lima to Santiago, but his influence extended farther still—to a vast community of artists shaped by his Quechua-inflected vision of Dutch, Spanish, and Italian traditions.

Though Cuzco looms large in our understanding of colonial arts, this Andean Renaissance was much bigger than Cuzco or even Peru. Quito was also a center for artistic production and for the exchange of techniques brought to the Americas by European artists. Church commissions provided an economic engine for the development of a fine-arts tradition that flourished in parish communities and was transmitted through family lines. Like Cuzco and greater Lima, Quito had distinct native parishes, a native leadership class, and a college designed for the education of indigenous leaders. From the 1550s onward, the Colegio de San Juan Evangelista and its successor institution, the Colegio de San Andrés, educated large numbers of Indian and mestizo students, many from the ranks of the caciques. There, as in Mexico City and Cuzco, a cross-cultural institution run by Franciscans trained students in fine arts, languages, humanities, and even artisanal skills. The school was a key ingredient in the growth of a substantial community of literate artists who were concentrated in the city's native parishes of San Roque and San Blas but who executed important artistic commissions throughout the city.[29]

The Andean Renaissance—if we may call it that—was at least as expansive as the old Inca Empire, stretching from Ecuador to Bolivia. Perhaps no single work of art from the colonial era has had such a powerful cultural influence as the *Virgin of Copacabana*. Even more than paintings, Latin America's early devotional sculptures capture the complex relationship between artists—both Indian and European—and the generations of parishioners and pilgrims of all types who have adored them.[30] Some early colonial sculptures are artistic masterworks, but others appear quite ordinary. Outsiders to Latin American Catholicism may find themselves staring at these santos, scrutinizing them for some physical characteristic that might explain their cultural importance. When one gazes at images of the Virgin Mary, this search is confounded by the typical concealment of the sculpture itself. In most cases, only the face and hands of Mary are visible. One knows that somewhere, buried beneath the layers of fabric, is a simple wooden form crafted long in the past. The wigs, crowns, and garments—even the paint that defines the faces—are often accretions added over time, right down to the present. These layers of paint, plaster, garments, and jewelry are an apt metaphor for the cultural meanings of devotional art in the context of a living and constantly evolving tradition.[31]

Our Lady of Copacabana is an image that confounds the viewer in this way. The sixteenth-century sculpture is shaped from wood but topped with a wig, dressed in robes, and adorned with paint, gold leaf, jewels, and a crown. She stands atop a rising crescent moon of gold and carries in her arms an infant Jesus. She is somewhat less than life-sized, but her commanding position, high in a sculptural niche, lends a sense of majesty to the diminutive figure. Since 1583, Our Lady of Copacabana has been enshrined on the shores of Lake Titicaca, first in the local church, then in an Augustinian chapel, and finally in a dedicated basilica built under viceregal patronage. She is the patron saint of Bolivia but receives devoted pilgrims from all over the Andes and, indeed, from all over the world. She is also a key to understanding how people in the Viceroyalty of Peru understood the meanings of religious art, the social position of indigenous artists, and the multicultural qualities of Latin American Catholicism.

The sculpture itself was shaped in the early 1580s by Francisco Tito Yupanqui. He was a Quechua nobleman, educated and literate, and tied by family and social networks to the curacas of the highlands. His project was an arduous one. Learning the craft of image making, producing the sculpture, and overcoming opposition from innumerable local factions and authorities was exceedingly difficult, but Tito Yupanqui was ultimately successful. In the end, the sculpture was venerated by the church, embraced by Indian political leaders, and seized upon as the inspiration for new religious sodalities in Copacabana.[32]

How are we to interpret Tito Yupanqui's quest? Some four decades after the creation of the *Virgin of Copacabana*, the Augustinian friar Alonso Ramos Gavilán sought to answer this question in a book titled *Historia del santuario de Nuestra Señora de Copacabana*.[33] This is a complex work whose long narrative of the site describes the ancient indigenous past, the conquest era, the story of the sculpture's creation, the miracles attributed to it, the institutions built around it, and the pilgrimage traditions that followed. It also includes the testimony of the artist, Tito Yupanqui. Ramos Gavilán makes clear from the outset that the story of Tito Yupanqui should be understood as an allegory of the human quest for spiritual knowledge. In order to make sense of this allegory, modern readers must immerse themselves in both the landscape of the colonial Andes and the theological writings that shaped Gavilán's worldview. In many respects, the real, living, breathing artist was reshaped by Gavilán as a character in his book; but the character was also a real man, and one who spoke for himself.

Tito Yupanqui's own account of how he made the famed image of the Virgin

FIGURE 9 *Virgin of Copacabana.* Engraving by F. F. Bexarano. From Fernando de Valverde's *Santuario de N. Señora de Copacabana* (Lima: Luis de Lyra, 1641). Courtesy of the John Carter Brown Library, Brown University.

Mary occupies only a few pages of *Historia del santuario*, but it has received more attention from scholars than the much larger work that surrounds it.[34] To go beyond a simple reading, one must examine the sculpture in relation to the artist, and examine the artist's narrative in relation to Gavilán's theology. *Historia del santuario* is divided into three books, the first describing the religious and political history of the Copacabana region prior to Spanish conquest, the second describing the creation of Our Lady of Copacabana and the miracles attributed to her, and the third describing a novena (a nine-day cycle of reflection and prayers) intended for pilgrims to the site. The tripartite organization seems to mirror the three stages of human history described by Augustine's *Enchiridion*: life before the law of God, under the law of God, and finally under a state of grace.[35] Here we are witnessing an Augustinian integrating the history of the Andes into a global eschatology. The first book describes Andeans initially untouched by God, then later visited by magically transported apostles of Christ, and finally lured from the true path by the wiles of Satan and the snares of a false religion.[36] During the age that followed, images of the cross and signs of the Virgin abounded, but the distortions of the devil prevented the Andeans from grasping their true meaning.[37] The author repeatedly compares the preconquest Andes to the age of classical antiquity when philosophers struggled toward the light without the benefits of direct revelation. Book 2 opens with a word to the wise: "Christ our Lord wished to say that the lazy sinner did not deserve to understand the secrets of the faith" and was left in confusion and darkness.[38] Ramos Gavilán likens Inca temples to the Temple of Solomon, and to those of the Greeks and Romans. In all these ages, men struggled to discern divine truth through "hieroglyphics, symbols, and figures wrapped in confusing emblems."[39] The author implies that human history is divisible into stages of understanding, and that his book likewise reveals its message in distinct stages. Patient readers who study the book, go on pilgrimage to Copacabana, and pray the novena will arrive at a true knowledge of the Virgin. The 1621 edition of the book opens and closes with poems by the author and by some of his admirers that attest to this very process of spiritual edification.[40]

At the center of the work is the story of the fashioning and reception of the *Virgin of Copacabana*. It is presented in two versions: the first in the authorial voice of Ramos Gavilán; the second in the voice of the sculptor, Tito Yupanqui.[41] Ramos Gavilán introduces the writing of the Indian artist with a preamble on philosophy: "The desire to know is so fundamental in man that the prince of philosophy, in his *Metaphysics*, distinguished it as almost his true nature. . . . All men are naturally inclined to want to know; and thus it is that many authors—keen to appeal to this passion—have tirelessly investigated many mysterious things, unsatisfied until they have brought to light whatever lay buried, unscrutinized, in perpetual silence."[42] The reference to Aristotle's *Metaphysics* is explicit, but the reader soon encounters implicit references to Plato as well.[43] Clearly, Tito Yupanqui's narrative is not to be read on its own but rather interpreted in connection to classical works of philosophy.[44]

For Aristotle, the role of the artist was to produce from transitory and specific physical materials representations of forms that are immaterial and eternal. In Gavilán's words, great artists, like great intellectuals, "brought to light" truths unseen. Like the hypothetical traveler in Plato's *Republic*, these truth seekers struggled out of the shadow realm of earthly confusion and toward a more perfect apprehension of light and truth.[45] Gavilán's frequent association of light, truth, and Platonic logos would, of course, ring true for his readers. It is the language of the Gospel of John.[46] But these associations also had a deep local resonance in Copacabana where pilgrims once stopped on their journeys to the Isla de Sol and to its temple, which at the time promoted the association between Inca unity, the natural order, and the solar creator god, Viracocha.[47] Ramos Gavilán himself devotes numerous chapters to the sun cult, describing its religious and political qualities.[48]

The philosophical message of *Historia del santuario* is best expressed in the chapters that describe the fashioning and reception of the image of Our Lady of Copacabana. The main narrative appears in the form of a text reportedly written by the artist, Francisco Tito Yupanqui, and transmitted to Ramos Gavilán by the former's brother, don Felipe de León.[49] The narrative and frame story closely resemble those found in Plato's *Republic* and later in More's *Utopia*—both of which were widely read by New World churchmen of the day.[50] Ramos Gavilán seems to be reminding us to consult the classics before pressing on. The *Republic* begins with Socrates and Polemarchus walking home from a religious ritual. Their conversation on law and justice wanders broadly until they reach Polemarchus's family home, where they begin discussing the relationship between earthly and spiritual things. At the heart of the *Republic*, one finds the powerful and oft revisited allegory on truth seeking and political life, in which a benighted cave dweller struggles upward into the light of the sun.

Tito Yupanqui's quest is presented to us as part of a work of philosophy in the tradition of Plato, Aristotle, and More. The meaning of the *Virgin of Copacabana* comes to us in a layered frame story: Tito Yupanqui's memoir of its creation, wrapped in Ramos Gavilán's larger history of the shrine and the region. Ramos Gavilán follows his reflection on Aristotle's quest for truth with his introduction to the Tito Yupanqui document: "Wanting to play my part in so universal a quest, amid all that this kingdom offers, I wanted to know of the beginnings and true origin, of the holy image of Copacabana. . . . While looking into things, I met the very brother of the sculptor who made her, and he handed me an account which the deceased had left."[51] Beneath all these layers of the story, how are we to find the true message of the text? Like the statue itself, which at first appears all wig, crown, and robes, the "true" philosophical meaning of the *Virgin of Copacabana* is difficult to reach. Fortunately, Ramos Gavilán's references to Aristotle's *Metaphysics* offer us the right heuristic.

In the Aristotelian tradition, when an artist fashions an image, there is both a tangible and intangible outcome, the latter being more important. Human hands may create multitudes of imperfect images, but the accumulated experience brings humanity closer to understanding the ultimate spiritual forms they are meant to imitate. Aristotle has a lot to say about the proper role of art in the human search for wisdom. In *Poetics* he remarks, "The instinct of imitation is implanted in man from childhood, one difference between him and other animals being that he is the most imitative of living creatures, and through imitation, he learns his earliest lessons. . . . Thus the reason why men enjoy seeing a likeness is, that in contemplating it they find themselves learning or inferring."[52] Viewed in this light, it is the understanding produced by the *Virgin of Copacabana*, not the aesthetic object itself, that matters most. Gavilán endorses a series of experiences and reflections linked to the sculpture, which, like the Stations of the Cross or the *Spiritual Exercises* of Saint Ignatius Loyola, offer a terrestrial path toward transcendent understanding.[53]

Ramos Gavilán first tells us that his writing is part of a quest for truth; he then presents Tito Yupanqui's quest for a truer image of the Virgin. The latter is clearly told in service of the former. Tito Yupanqui and his brother begin their great undertaking by studying with one of the region's master artists, Diego de Ortiz. It is the brother, Felipe de León, who comes up with a method of refining their vision. He suggests that, guided by prayer, they and other Indians should study the existing images of the Virgin before making this new image.[54] The brothers follow the same path that Aristotle attributes to great artists: the systematic observation and comparison of flawed earthly instanti-ations in order to arrive at a nearer apprehension of the underlying universal form.[55] The brothers' subsequent efforts to sculpt the image are plagued by recurrent setbacks: three attempts to construct a model end in failure. After earnest prayers and a dedicated mass, a final attempt succeeds. But even after the rough shape of the Virgin is cast, it must be painted, gilded, and clothed, then duly accepted by the local authorities. At each step, the brothers are met with opposition: the bishop of Chuquisaca refuses them a license to sculpt and paint; Spaniards mock their image as the work of Indian primitives; and even their fellow Indians in Copacabana initially scorn their efforts.[56]

The story of the two brothers fits a classical script for describing the in-quiries of a philosophical pilgrim. In the *Apology*, Plato describes Socrates's exhaustive search for wisdom as a tireless exercise. The philosopher wanders the earth seeking to find one man who is truly wise. He tells his listeners, "I want you to think of my adventures as a kind of pilgrimage." He interrogates politicians, poets, and craftsmen but finds them all lacking. Along the way, though, he remarks on the variety of ways in which artists touch upon truth. The poets and artists, he notes, could not explain their transcendent work but seemed to have produced it from "instinct or inspiration." After provoking the anger of all sectors of local society, he concludes: "The truth of the matter, gentlemen, is pretty certainly this: that real wisdom is the property of God and this oracle is his way of telling us that human wisdom has little or no value."[57] The story of Tito Yupanqui is not so different. In his quest to produce the perfect statue, he consults virtually every kind of local authority, secular and religious, Indian and Spanish. They all prove themselves unworthy, but like Socrates, Tito Yupanqui never presents himself as the final arbiter of truth. In fact, the artist scarcely claims credit for the image. It is represented as a miracle.

What Plato's and Ramos Gavilán's writings express though dialogue and narrative, Aristotle's *Metaphysics* spells out more directly: "The man of experi-ence is thought to be wiser than the possessors of any sense-perception what-ever, the artist wiser than the men of experience, the masterworker than the mechanic, and the theoretical kinds of knowledge to be more of the nature of Wisdom than the productive."[58] Aristotle is here speaking of artists and build-ers, though they are not the ultimate subject of his inquiry. Rather, he aims to show by analogy that just as the imperfect may derive from the perfect or the built from the builder, all things must originate from God.[59] By asking his readers to consider the *Virgin of Copacabana* in relation to Aristotle, Ramos Gavilán is encouraging them to consider the relationship between a physical image and its spiritual prototype.

Ramos Gavilán offers us Tito Yupanqui's story as part of a larger discussion with the reader about the search for truth. This is a rational journey that starts with sense, then proceeds to speech, and ultimately to understanding. Socrates explains this process in Plato's *Republic*. He begins by comparing the qualities of visible things but then suggests we must reach beyond them: "You won't be able to follow me any farther. . . . You would no longer see an image of what we are describing, but the truth itself." This is, of course, the most important aspect of Plato that Augustinian Christianity seizes upon. The perceptible object, such as Tito Yupanqui's sculpture, is not the ultimate objective of the artist or the intellectual. As Socrates says in the culmination of his argument, "Then isn't this at last . . . the theme itself that dialectical discussion sings? It itself is intelligible. But the power of sight imitates it."[60]

It certainly appears that the narrative of the quest for the *Virgin of Copacabana* was composed as part of a discussion about Christian Neoplatonism and the Aristotelian search for universals. But why would this discussion emerge in the 1580s and in relation to an Indian community in the high Andes? To answer this question, we need to consider the ways in which the religious life of the Andes—however geographically distant from Europe—still belonged to the same cultural moment and drew from many of the same sources. The mythic story of the *Virgin of Copacabana* should be considered both in reference to the early 1580s when the sculpture was made and to the 1620s when the official story was penned.

Andean Art, Native Religion, and the Counter-Reformation

The final session of the Council of Trent adjourned just two decades before the creation of the *Virgin of Copacabana*. It drew the bishops of western Christendom together amid the great conflicts of the Reformation. The council was summoned both to answer the accusations of Lutherans and to more clearly define the boundaries of orthodoxy. One of its objectives was to refute the Protestant accusation that Catholic devotional images of saints were a form of idolatry. The defense of devotional imagery drew heavily on

Platonic and Aristotelian arguments about the relationship between objects of perception and ultimate spiritual reality. The Council of Trent insisted that "the images of Christ, of the Virgin Mother of God, and of the other saints, are to be had and retained particularly in temples, and that due honor and veneration are to be given them; not that any divinity, or virtue, is believed to be in them, on account of which they are to be worshipped; or that anything is to be asked of them; or, that trust is to be reposed in images, as was of old done by the Gentiles who placed their hope in idols."[61] In Europe, Catholic leaders were keenly aware of the need to defend their use of art and to distinguish it from idolatry even while constantly celebrating the early church's struggle against classical idolatry in the Mediterranean. At the same moment, the Andean church was both exalting exemplary devotional art and rooting out "ancient idols," in this case the huacas associated with the indigenous past.[62]

In the very same year that Francisco Tito Yupanqui approached the bishop of Chuquisaca, churchmen from the entire region convened for the Third Provincial Council of Lima. The council had many charges, but its most pressing policy questions treated the position of indigenous Andeans within the church. The council urged a fuller inclusion of Indians in Christian ritual and institutional life, placing a particular emphasis on education in the faith. At the same time, the council renewed the call for the suppression of Indian idolatry—that is, the use of indigenous images in traditional religious practices.[63] In other words, Francisco Tito Yupanqui shaped his image of Mary at the very moment that Andean clergy were intently focused on teaching the indigenous population to renounce their traditional images and to regard Christian images in precisely the right way.

If these issues were in play when the image was shaped, they were even more pressing when the story of the object was committed to writing. In 1620 or 1621 when *Historia del santuario* was written, the Andean church was engaged in the first major campaign to suppress indigenous religious practices. This campaign for the extirpation of idolatry devoured the energies of the church from 1609 to 1622 under the direction of Archbishop Bartolomé Lobo Guerrero. It had begun with the discovery of secret unorthodox practices in the province of Huarochirí, but soon snowballed into a vast regional investigation.[64] Though the most vigorous investigations took place within the archdiocese of Lima, reactions to the event continued to shape church policy throughout South America for the following century. In the same year that Alonso Ramos

Gavilán published his history of Copacabana, Jesuit leader Pablo José de Arriaga published *Extirpación de la idolatría del Perú*, a guide to investigations of Indian apostasy. Together, the two works encapsulated the Andean church's position on licit and illicit images.[65]

Both Ramos Gavilán and Arriaga took a subtle position on the Indian practice of Christianity. Though church policy of the era was heavily focused on rooting out surviving vestiges of indigenous religion, and though both men had a stake in this project, neither disparaged the role of Indians in the church—far from it. In fact, Arriaga was both a leading figure in investigations of Indian religious apostasy *and* a seminal figure in the education of a new indigenous elite for the Andean church. Just three years before the publication of *Extirpación de idolatría*, Arriaga threw his weight behind Jesuit efforts to create a new generation of indigenous leaders by founding two new colleges for the sons of caciques, one in Cuzco and the other in Lima. These institutions drew from ruling families throughout the region and aimed to send the young noblemen back to their home communities as exemplars of Christian orthodoxy and leaders within the local church and state apparatus.[66] Along with their fellow Jesuits and Augustinians, Ramos Gavilán and Arriaga sought to destroy the traces of pre-Christian idolatry and rebuild in their place a new indigenous Christian society—a society without pagan idols, but also free of the Protestant iconoclasm then ravaging Europe.

Many of the most venerated images in Latin American Catholicism date from the late sixteenth and early seventeenth centuries, an era when European religious culture was redefined by resurgent Renaissance classicism, the evangelization of the Americas, and the great theological debates of the Reformation. It was a time when the value and meaning of religious art were hotly contested. We should never assume that American missionaries and indigenous intellectuals were untouched by these debates in the global Christian community. These years witnessed a rapid expansion in print culture, in the global social networks of missionary orders, and in the transcultural educational opportunities afforded to indigenous elites. For all of these reasons, it is just as important to place the story of the *Virgin of Copacabana* in a global intellectual context as it is to understand her within the specific ethnographic context of the town and region.[67]

In the end, the clothes she is wrapped in, the story of her origins, the landscape that surrounds her, and the miracles attributed to her mean far more than the simple figure itself. She is at the center of a symbolic system with multiple authors: Our Lady of Copacabana is in some ways a maternal goddess reinhabiting a sacred pilgrimage landscape from the preconquest era: she ties Aymaras to Quechuas, and both to Europeans. She signifies the Christian triumph over indigenous religions but at the same time celebrates indigenous cultural survival. Her sculptor, both humble and triumphant, vindicates the role of Indian spiritual leadership within Andean Christianity, and her biographer, Ramos Gavilán, makes her an allegory for the triumph of Neoplatonic philosophy and of Tridentine orthodoxy amid the dangers of resurgent Indian paganism and Lutheran iconoclasm.

Sculpture, History, and Syncretism in Native Mexico

The phenomenon of indigenous artists and colonial interpreters wrapping devotional objects in layers of meaning is as common in Mexico as it is in Peru. Though less well known than the *Virgin of Copacabana*, Mexico's corn-paste sculptures of Jesus (*Cristos de caña*) tell similar stories about the interactions of European and native Christianity. Their secrets have been unlocked bit by bit since the time of a surprising discovery in 1946. In that year, art historian Abelardo Carrillo y Gariel and his colleagues entered the shuttered and collapsing church of San Mateo de Mexicaltzingo to assess the state of the building and its artwork. The history of Mexicaltzingo goes back beyond the era of the Spanish conquest to the time of Emperor Axayacatl, and the origins of its first chapel go back to the mid-sixteenth century.[68] Time, weather, and seismic shocks had taken their toll on the town's oldest art and architecture. The visitors found that the chapel's famed sculpture of Christ had fallen to the floor and split open. The sculpture, it turned out, was not carved from wood but built from layers of paper and paste. Since then, numerous sculptures from the same era have been reexamined, revealing unexpected discoveries about Mexico's indigenous arts.

The Cristos de caña tell a complex story. Many have their origins in the Purépecha regions of Michoacán.[69] Others come from the Nahua center of Mexico or from places colonized by Nahuas. Most scholarly observers, whether art historians, anthropologists, or historians, are first struck by the same aspects of these enigmatic sculptures: crafted by indigenous peoples who subsisted on maize—and whose rituals had once ensured terrestrial fertility by sacrifice and bloodletting—these sculptures were themselves made from corn stalks and corn paste. The image of the redemptive, self-sacrificing Christian God mirrors perfectly the earlier ritual cycle of agricultural renewal. Clearly, these corn-paste Christs were a vital link between precolonial and colonial cosmology. They were among the Christian symbols most immediately and intuitively comprehensible to Mesoamerican people. But the Cristos are not just a bridge between the Christian and pre-Christian worlds; they also reveal their own distinctive moment in the religious life of the sixteenth century.[70]

In addition to corn and paste, the Cristos were sculpted from paper, and often from paper inscribed with writing. The paper's function was structural, as it is in other forms of papier-mâché; and this fact, coupled with the high cost of paper at the time, has led many to suppose that the writing on these hidden pages is of no particular import. According to this logic, the sculptors are thought to have used whatever paper was on hand—and perhaps this is so, but there are good reasons to delve deeper and consider the contents of these hidden texts. Abelardo Carrillo y Gariel's early description of the construction of the *Cristo de Mexicaltzingo* was published with photographs, transcriptions, and translations of the santo's contents (from Nahuatl to Spanish). The writings buried in the sculpture are of two types: tribute lists and sermons. The tribute lists are the work of indigenous scribes and include pictographic accounting. The sermons are in Nahuatl, and one of the largest extant fragments begins thus: "And in chapter 14 it says that our Savior Jesus Christ resolved to cast out all those that were selling in the Temple of Jerusalem." The combination of elements is striking. In this Christian temple of San Mateo Mexicaltzingo stood an image of the sacrificed Christ. It, like the region's sculptures of pre-Columbian gods, was made from maize; and the mystery of its nearly weightless body was ensured by hollow chambers—chambers built from paper lists of tribute crops, tucked into place beside a scathing sermon that included the scriptural jeremiad "but you have made his house a house of thieves."[71]

This one object of art and devotion appears to contain, wrapped in its skin, memories of a pre-Christian world, the experience of conversion, and the struggles between the higher aims of the faith and the quotidian demands of the empire. This image, with all of its hidden contradictions, proclaims survival and victory in an age of conquest and defeat, and it turns the authority of Christ and scripture against earthly leaders.[72]

It turns out that the *Christ of Mexicaltzingo* is just one of many corn-paste images of the crucifixion. In northeastern Mexico, three such images remain at the center of important local devotions in towns founded by Tlaxcalan settlers in the sixteenth and seventeenth centuries: *El Señor de la Capilla* in Saltillo, *El Señor de la Expiración* in Guadalupe de Monterrey, and *El Señor de Tlaxcala* in Bustamante. It is likely that all three of these images were transported to their current sites by Tlaxcalan leaders who founded the towns under royal charters during New Spain's first great push to the north. The three images share a number of things in common: their construction from paste and paper, their nearly identical iconographic representation, their association with local festivals and cofradías, and their connection to the foundational stories of Tlaxcalan communities.[73]

The local stories describing the origins of *El Señor de la Expiración* and *El Señor de la Capilla* are nearly identical. In the early years of Saltillo (then San Esteban de Saltillo) and Bustamante (then San Miguel de Aguayo), townspeople were surprised to hear the bells of their simple chapels tolling loudly at an unaccountable time. When they arrived on the spot, they found an unaccompanied pack animal tugging the bell chord. When the beast was unburdened of its cargo (usually described as lumber or planks), the locals discovered a miraculous image of Christ hidden in the bundle. In both cases, the images were placed first in existing chapels and later in newer and grander churches.[74] The more ordinary provenance of *El Señor de Tlaxcala* is described in early accounts of Bustamante's institutional foundations. There a Tlaxcalan noblewoman, by then the widow of a prosperous Tlaxcalan miner, bequeathed a finely made image of Christ to the town. In 1700, a visiting bishop accredited the image as the focus of local devotions and recognized the widow Ana María as its patron. Her final arrangements with the town's cabildo (council) charged the community with the responsibility for housing and maintaining the image in perpetuity.

Local cofradías and hermandades have served these Christ images for over three hundred years. In many towns, images like these remain today the focus of annual celebrations accompanied by masses, feasts, and dances. The Cristos of Guadalupe and Bustamante have a long history of traveling in annual processions and of serving in times of civic emergency to summon supernatural aid for the town. Each year the Hermandad de Nuestro Padre Jesús carries *El Señor de la Expiración* from its home in Nuestra Señora de Guadalupe to the cathedral in Monterrey. Likewise, in Bustamante, the image is carried through the streets of the town amid the Dances of the Matachines.[75]

These Tlaxcalan Christs are both pilgrims and conquerors. They mark the sites of Tlaxcalan colonization from Gran Tlaxcala to Saltillo, Bustamante, and Guadalupe de Monterrey. The Matachines Dances at Bustamante belong to the well-known phenomenon of the Dances of Christians and Moors that take place throughout Mexico. The dances have their origins in Iberia as a commemoration of the reconquest of the Muslim South. In Mexico they became a commemoration of the Christian conquest of pagan America. Later, in the context of the Tlaxcalan diaspora, they evolved into a celebration of Tlaxcalans as conquerors of frontier lands. Just as the image of the crucifixion transforms defeat into triumph and death into resurrection, this inversion of the conquest story transforms conquered into conqueror.

The physical location of the Tlaxcalan Christs sketches across the landscape a map of colonization. Between the late sixteenth century and mid-eighteenth century, Tlaxcalan settlers—often in groups of either fifty or two hundred families—detached themselves from their communities of origin and established new colonies under royal charter farther to the north. The three crosses just mentioned mark the transit of settlers from Tlaxcala to Saltillo / San Esteban, and finally to San Miguel de la Nueva Tlaxcala (Bustamante) and Guadalupe de Monterrey.[76] These objects linked the foundation of churches and towns in a genealogical hierarchy going back to the mother country of Tlaxcala. Just as European missionaries inscribed the map with a sacred geography of genealogically connected missions, shrines, and artifacts, so too did Latin America's Indian colonists.

———

America's native artists have a long history of recording their own peoples' histories using objects borrowed from European culture: the book, the church, the devotional image of a saint. Native authors, sculptors, and painters blended the symbolic vocabulary of Europe and of the Americas. In this way, they produced things of beauty while at the same time promoting their own interests, arguing on behalf of their communities, and preserving a collective memory of the preconquest past. In the process, they contributed to new transatlantic forms of Christianity that were emerging in the context of Counter-Reformation thought.

CHAPTER FIVE

Saints, Martyrs, and Missionaries

Native Peru through a Bishop's Eyes

When Toribio Alfonso de Mogrovejo sailed for Peru as a newly appointed bishop in 1581, he carried with him a powerful mandate for institutional reform.[1] At the time, King Philip II had two priorities for the Americas: extending royal authority and improving conditions for evangelization. After many decades of violence, Peru's civil wars had come to an end, and the viceroyalty had finally subdued the rival factions of conquistador-encomenderos who had bled the colony of its wealth and manpower. The last bastion of Inca resistance was overcome with the Spanish conquest of Vilcabamba and the execution of Túpac Amaru in 1572. As peace returned to the Andes, it appeared that men like Viceroy Francisco de Toledo and Archbishop Toribio de Mogrovejo would have a free hand to organize a more perfect New World kingdom and New World church.

By the time of his death in 1606, Toribio probably knew more about Peru than any man of his generation. His endless travels to visit each parish and *doctrina* in the vast and inaccessible viceroyalty were so legendary that his itineraries were later offered as evidence for his canonization as a saint. In five extended journeys from 1581 to 1605, he covered the map of his archdiocese, traveling by foot and burro more than twenty thousand miles. The archbishop did not survive his last journey, but he continued to record his meticulous observations about the towns, haciendas, and parishes he visited right down to the end of his life.[2]

For Father Toribio, the educated and pious Indian nobleman was a crucial element of the new colonial state; consequently, descriptions of native leaders figure prominently in his writings. At the time, Spanish leaders debated what positions traditional native elites should have in the evolving hierarchies of church and state. On the one hand, the crown was committed to the Hispanicization of Peruvian culture and to the suppression of indigenous religion. On the other hand, the empire desperately needed the collaboration of Indian leaders. In the wake of the great sixteenth-century wars among conquistadors, royal officials often viewed native noblemen as allies who could help defend royal administration against the corrosive influences of corrupt and self-serving Spanish settlers. Native Catholic priests and pious laymen promised a bulwark against resurgent paganism.

In December of 1605, near the end of his days, Toribio recorded a final glimpse of his relationship to the Indian nobility. His last reported visit was to the lands of Jerónimo Mina Quispi, the cacique of Umbral. Fray Toribio described the estate and the neighboring Indian pueblo and doctrina in good economic and social order, but he had hard words of criticism for the local priest. He complained that the *cura* "does not know the evangelizing language of these Indians . . . or even the general language of the Incas and only ministers to them in that of Castile." This tone of contempt for poorly educated European priests is a refrain that runs throughout Toribio's book of episcopal visits. In his judgment, among the most important characteristics of competent and effective clergymen were their mastery of indigenous languages and their close ties to the native population. Toribio was himself a devoted student of Peruvian languages and a great promoter of polyglot education. Toribio's notes do not mention what language he spoke when meeting with Jerónimo Mina Quispi to discuss local affairs, but we can guess that the two men felt very much at home in each other's company. Toribio was a confident man. He was born a gentleman, he studied in Spain's most prestigious universities, and he earned appointments as a professor of canon law at the University of Salamanca, and as Grand Inquisitor for Spain. He lived simply and traveled simply, but for all his Christian humility, he was a firm believer in social hierarchy and institutional authority. When Toribio toured the estate at Umbral, he noted with approval its fields of cotton and wheat, and its vast vineyard of five thousand vines. It was not so different from his own family home in Mayorga de Campos, where his father had been governor. The cacique, Jerónimo Mina Quispi, lived in a comfortable home surrounded by fertile lands. Six families lived on his own estate, and his manorial rights extended to hundreds of tributaries in the neighboring Indian community. Father Toribio took an interest in all of the cacique's affairs. In contrast, he had little to say about the local priest. He recorded a visit to the Spanish *cura doctrinero*, but the man was uneducated and unremarkable. Toribio did not even write down his name.[3]

Bishop Toribio's long journeys were interrupted by a series of church councils. The most important of these was the Third Council of Lima over which he presided in 1582 and 1583. The decrees of the council are a blueprint for the Hispano-indigenous church that Toribio helped to create. The council argued that the best strategy for destroying pagan religion was not to wantonly attack all native customs, but rather to integrate indigenous customs and leadership. The participants envisioned seminaries that would educate European priests in native languages, and native priests in European ones. Toward this end, they promulgated a new catechism for Peru written in Spanish, Quechua, and Aymara. Through a variety of reforms, the council sought to soften the confrontation between cultures, and to build an Andean church that was pluralistic with respect to custom and language but orthodox with respect to belief. In the long run, the results were mixed. Neither traditional indigenous religious revivals nor the persecutions they provoked would come to an end any time soon. And though a slow trickle of Indians and mestizos joined the priesthood, their entry into the vocation was often contested. The Andean church imagined by the delegates to the Third Provincial Council was never fully realized. And yet the dream was never entirely abandoned either.[4]

The Christianization of Peru began in fits and starts, and its slow progress in the sixteenth century was a cause of great concern to churchmen. In comparison, New Spain was trumpeted as a miraculous success. To this day, popular and institutional Catholicism constantly revisit and celebrate the ways that Mexico's indigenous communities have embraced and enriched the practice of the faith. Nowhere is this truer than in the Nahua heartland, where half a millennium of Christianity has allowed words, images, and devotions to circulate freely among Indian, European, and mestizo populations.

New Spain's Miracles and Martyrs

Pope John Paul II arrived in Mexico City in July of 2002 on a historic and much-publicized visit to Tepeyac Hill. Tepeyac draws over fifteen million pilgrims each year, the most devout among them making the final phase of the journey on their knees. The visitors wish to see with their own eyes the miraculous image of the Virgin of Guadalupe, a symbol as central to Mexican identity as the nation's flag—perhaps more so. The old Basilica of Guadalupe, constructed more than three centuries ago, still stands on the hill, but the scale of modern devotions has long since exceeded the building's capacity. When John Paul ascended the dais to view the image in 2002, he did so in the new basilica, a vast 1970s edifice meant to accommodate the ceaseless flow of modern visitors. The scene was carefully staged for the press and public. The Mexican flag behind the pope was draped low in order to reveal the image of Our Lady, ascending on her crescent moon. Indian women in traditional dress fanned the smoke from copal braziers, and male dancers clad in feathered Nahua costumes flanked the pontiff. A song composed for the occasion exalted the local advocation of Mary as "Tonantzin la Morenita," the small, dark, indigenous Virgin whose name is now bound up with that of Tonantzin, the preconquest mother goddess.[5] John Paul had come to the site to mark the canonization of Juan Diego Cuauhtlatoatzin and the beatification of the Child Martyrs of Tlaxcala, all central figures in Mexico's retelling of the sixteenth-century conversion.[6]

The historicity of the Juan Diego story is very much in doubt, but the vast influence of his legend is not.[7] His miraculous visitation by the Virgin of Guadalupe is said to have taken place in 1531, though documentary evidence from the sixteenth century has proved hard to come by. Nonetheless, two accounts, published in Spanish and Nahuatl in 1648 and 1649 respectively, fixed the essentials of the Juan Diego story in the collective imagination from at least the mid-seventeenth century onward.[8] In the traditional version, the recent Nahua convert Juan Diego Cuauhtlatoatzin was on his way to mass when the Virgin Mary appeared miraculously. She entrusted him with a special mission to Mexico's first bishop, Juan de Zumárraga. The bishop, she insisted, must build a shrine on Tepeyac Hill. Juan Diego followed her instructions to the letter, but the bishop doubted the Indian's story. Zumárraga asked for some proof or sign, and Juan Diego soon produced one. In a second apparition, the Virgin instructed him to travel to Tepeyac Hill and collect roses that would bloom miraculously in the depth of winter. He did as instructed and returned to town carrying a bundle of blossoms wrapped in his garments. When Juan Diego poured forth the contents of his cloak at the feet of the startled bishop, the fabric revealed a perfect likeness of the Virgin printed on its surface. Ac-

FIGURE 10 Our Lady
of Guadalupe appears
to Juan Diego. From
José López de Avilés's
*Veridicum admodum
anagramma* [...] (Mexico
City: Ex Typographia
Vidue Bernardi Calderon,
1669). Courtesy of the
John Carter Brown
Library, Brown University.

cording to tradition, this is the very same cloak and same image that now hangs
in a gilded frame in the Tepeyac basilica.

Several decades of close academic scrutiny have cast doubt not just on
the magical image itself (it is, in fact, a painting on canvas, not an Indian
cloak), but also on the historical existence of Juan Diego. Even the question of
whether Mexico's Guadalupan devotions arose first in the Indian community
or in the Spanish one has been difficult to resolve.[9] It now appears more likely
that the cult of Mexico's Virgin of Guadalupe began first among creoles, and
that the image only later emerged as a symbol of Mexico's indigenous and
mestizo identity. Even if the popular story of Juan Diego is more myth than
historical reality, it is nonetheless a myth that speaks powerfully to a collective
memory of the nation's indigenous Christian origins.

Just a decade after the mysterious events at Tepeyac, the Virgin Mary appeared once again—this time in the nearby Kingdom of Tlaxcala, and at a site

with marked similarities to Tepeyac. On the hill of Ocotlán where the goddess Xochiquetzalli was once worshiped, Mary communicated her message to yet another pious Nahua convert who was also named Juan Diego. There, at the mouth of a rushing spring, she spoke to the man who would be her emissary to the community in the valley below. Just as at Tepeyac, the story inspired a tradition of pilgrimage to the Ocotlán hill that has endured to the present.[10]

Of course, these dreams and visions belong more to the realm of myth and memory than to that of demonstrable historical events. The characters that populate these stories are shadowy figures, but they reflect a worldview born from a very real indigenous encounter with Christianity. At other times the religious encounter took place in the full light of history. The story of the Virgin of Ocotlán eventually became an important part of the Tlaxcalan people's narrative of their alliance with the Spanish, their fealty to the Habsburg emperor, and their conversion experience. This story, told in a variety of forms (written chronicles, dramatic reenactments, and programmatic artwork), highlights Tlaxcala's trials on the path to piety. European chroniclers also cast Tlaxcala in a starring role when recounting the spiritual conquest of New Spain.[11]

In the year 1520, when the combined armies of Spain and Tlaxcala stood poised to attack the core of the Mexica Empire, the lords of Tlaxcala accepted baptism. For missionary chroniclers, it is a moment that prefigured the miraculous conversions that would follow the arrival of twelve Franciscan missionaries under the leadership of Martín de Valencia in 1524. The Franciscan visitors left their mark on the customs, beliefs, and language of the community. Coyolchiuhqui, a Tlaxcalan nobleman and political leader, took the baptismal name of his new spiritual patron, becoming Martín de Valencia. And Coyolchiuhqui was not alone.[12] Numerous Indian and European leaders gave and received new names marking their entry into each other's world. Among the twelve Franciscans was Fray Toribio de Benavente, whom the Tlaxcalans called Motolinía (the poor one) in admiration of his rigorous asceticism.

Traditional Christian writers have retold a history of the world in which new communities entered the faith despite doubt, suffering, and martyrdom. Tlaxcala's first Christian martyrs appeared in the 1520s and early 1530s.[13] At the time, the great houses of Tlaxcala were the patrons of missionaries. The Franciscan visitors lived in the palaces of the local nobility and worked closely with leading families as they built churches and monasteries amid the sites of ancient temples. Tlaxcala's Franciscan guardian, Fray García de Cisneros, lived during the mid-1520s in the palace of Maxixcatzin, where he helped to educate a generation of young noblemen as future Christian leaders. His students soon became the vanguard of a movement to stamp out the preconquest religion.

Until this moment, the seasoned leaders of Tlaxcala had charted a pragmatic middle course between the two religious traditions. Prominent among these cultural pragmatists was the son-in-law of Maxixcatzin, don Gonzalo Acxotécatl, lord of Atlihuetzia. Acxotécatl had a long and intimate relationship with the Spanish. He had fought shoulder to shoulder with Cortés in the first joint campaigns against rival Nahua city-states. For his bravery and fidelity, Cortés gave Acxotécatl an image of the Virgin Mary brought from Spain. Acxotécatl educated his sons under the Franciscans, and he touted his years of service to the crown, but he did not wholly abandon the religious practices of his ancestors. Even as Martín de Valencia attacked the vestiges of the old religion, doggedly toppling images of the war god Camaxtli and replacing them with the crucifix, Acxotécatl and many of his noble peers continued to practice traditional religious rites behind closed doors. Acxotécatl's son Cristóbal was different. Young Cristóbal took Martín de Valencia's words to heart, making himself a missionary among his own people. He soon discovered, however, that crypto-paganism was as widespread in his own household as it was in the larger society. When Gonzalo encountered old sacred objects concealed at his family estates, he destroyed them. Acxotécatl, filled with wrath, put the boy to death.

The reverberations from this event spread conflict throughout Tlaxcala for several years. Church-sponsored investigations sought to root out remaining pre-Christian artifacts in the face of ongoing resistance. Acxotécatl and three of his noble peers lost their lives, and two more young noblemen educated in the missionary college were killed in retaliation for their Christian zeal and iconoclasm. One of the young martyrs, Juan, was the grandson of Lord Xicoténcatl and heir to much of the family's remaining titles, wealth, and political power.[14] Both the casualties and the survivors of this intergenerational conflict over religion came to define Tlaxcala's story of conversion.[15]

Pope John Paul II's invocation of Juan Diego and the Child Martyrs of Tlaxcala was surely meant to recall them as key figures in the creation of a transcultural Catholic order. But both stories also recall an era of uneasy tensions both between European and indigenous authorities, and between distinct generations of Indian elites. In the rapidly changing cultural and political conditions of the sixteenth century, native leaders faced difficult decisions about whether to reject, preserve, or adapt elements of traditional religion within the context of a Catholic community that offered distinct opportunities to favored converts.

Indigenous Mexico through the Eyes of a Mestizo Churchman

As European missionaries learned native languages and indigenous converts learned European ones, a new world of shared literacy was born. The first published book written by a Mexican-born author was *Rhetorica christiana*. Diego Valadés composed his book in Latin, but he was equally at home speaking Tarascan, Otomi, and his own native languages: Castilian and Nahuatl. His breadth of vision was at least partly attributable to the circumstances of his birth. Valadés was the son of a prominent conquistador father and a Tlaxcalan mother. He was educated by the greatest intellectuals in New Spain's missionary orders, and he was ordained as a Franciscan friar. His professional experiences crossed the domains of many liberal arts: he worked as a writer, an illustrator, a teacher, a confessor, and a linguist. His ministry and his intellectual life led him from Tlaxcala to Mexico-Tenochtitlan, to the northern frontier, and ultimately across the sea to Spain, France, and Italy.[16]

Ordinarily, the inner thoughts of sixteenth-century Mexicans remain inaccessible to us. But this is not the case with Valadés. In his 1579 magnum opus, the Tlaxcalan literatus left us a thought-provoking diagram of his own mind. He offered it as part of a chapter devoted to memory and the art of rhetoric. Valadés sketched the inner architecture of his brain with labels marking the organs of perception and the regions charged with memory, imagination, and analysis. In the diagram, his head is flanked by two great triton-like man-beasts whose tails—distinctly like those of sea horses—call to mind the writings of Valadés's contemporary Julius Caesar Aranzi, who had just a decade before named and described the hippocampus, the strange sea-horse-shaped region of the brain associated ever since with the faculties of memory. This vivisection of Valadés's head yawns open, the profile of the author still visible, his eyes alive and awake, the contents of his mind exposed to view and coldly labeled for the reader. Above this arresting image, the serene head of a lion floats between great rolls of acanthus leaves, framing the title: "F. D. Valadés Inventor."[17]

FIGURE 11 The mind of Fray Diego Valadés. Engraving from his *Rhetorica christiana*, 1579. Courtesy of the John Carter Brown Library, Brown University.

The chapter is rich with classical allusions. The author especially admired the work of Cicero, and the captivating copper-plate print of the human head seems offered as part of a great Ciceronian memory palace. Valadés's twenty-fourth chapter, titled "On Memory, the Treasure of the Sciences," overwhelms the reader with its dizzying procession of literary and historical references. Valadés presents his own project as the continuation of a great cultural undertaking begun by Pliny, Quintilian, and Cicero. His heroes of ancient history triumphed as much by intellect as by physical strength. Cyrus the Great, he avers, could muster his tens of thousands of soldiers and recall each man's name.

But the great undertaking to which Valadés dedicated his book was not the military conquest of empires but the spiritual conquest of the New World. His instructions for disciplining one's memory were intended to train readers as evangelists. As part of this education, Valadés presented his philosophy of cognition and communication. He explained that written words summon speech, and that the sound of speech then reaches the ear, conjuring images in the mind. He implies that, even more than spoken words, visual arts communicate directly to the observer. Pictures are the mind's own language. Valadés reproduced and then adapted the work of Lodovico Dolce, whose illuminated alphabet functions like a Ciceronian memory palace, the letters signifying sounds, shapes, and ideas. In the hand of Valadés, the Dolce alphabet takes on a new life. It becomes a series of mnemonic symbols carefully selected to speak to his New World audience. The letters are distinctly Mesoamerican figures of men and beasts, each inscribed within a sort of canopic heart. They recall images, and the images recall words. The words, in turn, dissolve into acrostic codes, leading the reader deeper into Valadés's schema of carefully ordered sacred knowledge. The alphabet is followed by even more intricate illustrations: concentric rings of symbols and numbers seem to spin before the reader's eyes, demonstrating how the Mesoamerican calendar corresponds to the Julian one. *Rhetorica christiana* is a complex puzzle that when solved unveils a vast and integrated system of perception, memory, translation, analysis, and communication.

Valadés presents artwork not as a secondary mode of communication or as a stopgap measure for reaching the illiterate, but as the sublime language of the human spirit. One of his most richly drawn pages shows an Indian congregation in rapt attention as a friar speaks from the pulpit. With a pointer in hand, he gestures toward a complex artistic program painted on the walls of the church as he explains its scriptural meaning. Once again, the illustration is glossed with captions; in this case, they describe both the members of the congregation and the pedagogy of the missionary. The men in the first row are identified as leaders of the Indian state: "Those that are seated in this part and which have the rods in their hands are those that discharge the office of judges among our natives, and to them has been entrusted the government of the entire republic."[18] Valadés's illustrations are dense with detail, and with images nested inside other images. These embedded drawings sometimes show the ideas that bloom in the minds of readers and listeners—as texts, sermons, and conversations pass information from mind to mind.

Diego Valadés, much like Garcilaso de la Vega, arrived in Europe late in life as a scholar and a visiting dignitary. Traveling from his native New Spain, he reached Seville in 1571 before continuing on to France and ultimately to Rome where he completed his masterwork, *Rhetorica christiana*. As a spokesman for the New World church, his résumé and ancestry were impressive. Valadés was born scarcely a decade after the initial Spanish invasion of Mexico. His European father (also named Diego Valadés) had once crossed the Atlantic in

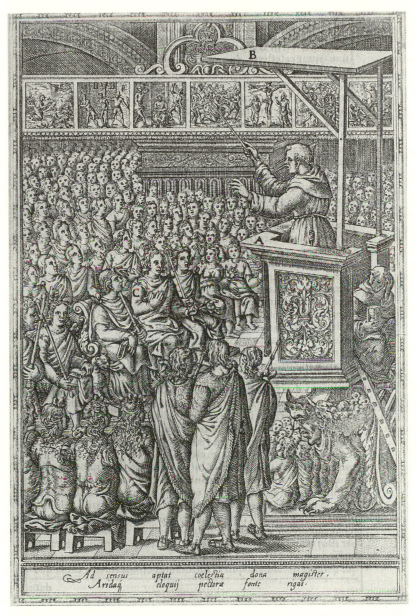

Ad sensus aptat coelestia dona magister,
Aridaq́ eloquij pectora fonte rigat.

FIGURE 12 A friar preaches to the Indian noblemen. Engraving from Fray Diego Valadés's *Rhetorica christiana*, 1579. Courtesy of the John Carter Brown Library, Brown University.

the other direction, and had played a crucial role in the conquest of Mexico. The elder Valadés embarked from Cuba in 1520 under the command of Pánfilo de Narváez on a mission to apprehend Hernan Cortés and return him to Cuba at the behest of the governor. But Cortés, using an artful combination of force and diplomacy, won over his would-be captors. The roles of captor and captive were reversed as Cortés co-opted the members of the punitive expedition and took Narváez into custody. So it was that the elder Valadés entered the ranks of Cortés's forces. He marched through the Aztec Empire and saw it in its full glory, the land and people not yet ravaged by European disease and subordination to Spanish rule. He entered the Aztec capital of Tenochtitlan while Nahua multitudes still thronged the marketplaces, ferried goods down canals, and walked in plazas beneath the imposing facades of their great stepped temples. Valadés survived the much-mythologized "Noche Triste," when the infuriated inhabitants drove the Spanish from their city; he was sheltered by the Kingdom of Tlaxcala with the wounded remnants of the Spanish forces, and he fought his way back into the city a year later, supported on all sides by thousands of Tlaxcalan warriors. His son and namesake was born to a Tlaxcalan woman. The boy was groomed from birth to lead.[19]

In the years when the Spanish City of Mexico was rising from the remains of Tenochtitlan, the father's home and business stood on Calle Donceles, a street that ran just a few feet from the tumbled ruins of the Temple of Huitzilopochtli. The elder Valadés built his mercantile house there in the years before the first stone was laid for the cathedral. Already Pedro de Gante had established the Convento de San Francisco and the School of San José de los Naturales. It was there, just a short walk from his father's home, that the younger Valadés began his rigorous education in the humanities. Valadés studied among the greatest linguists and humanists of his generation. His mentors were the first Franciscan friars to arrive in Mexico, the architects of Mexico's earliest Hispano-indigenous institutions. He joined the Franciscans as a novice in his teenage years and was ordained in 1550 while still in his early twenties.[20]

The pages of the *Rhetorica* illustrate the workings of a highly trained mind, one formed by an intellectual and aesthetic heritage that was at once Mesoamerican, classical, and Christian. As the book's title suggests, the idea of language unified all of the author's religious and academic aspirations. One plate shows muse-like personifications of the liberal arts: these goddesses in classical draperies, surrounded by growing wreathes and blossoms, are attended by floating cherubim. At the base of the page, grammar personified arranges the letters of the Roman alphabet on a table while a cherub bows before her, embracing a great leather codex. Valadés explains that of all the liberal arts, "The first is grammar, which is like the key and the mother of the other arts. The second, rhetoric, ornaments the other sciences by scattered blossoms and hands extended below." On another page, the figure of theology personified as a friar stands on a mound of books, whose spines are labeled with the names of the seven liberal arts. From these texts, leaves and flowers burst, rising skyward while the priestly figure ascends through an arc of flames, his hand pointed upward in a Socratic gesture toward the heavenly host and the cloud-borne trinity. Throughout the book, classical and Christian references are constantly intermingled in both the composition and the illustrations. *Rhetorica* references more than 150 authors, from Greek philosophers to medieval saints, along with a profusion of texts: the resolutions of church councils, works of classical literature, and the compositions of Renaissance humanists. The *Rhetorica* is not just an argument on education and faith; it is an entire curriculum.

Diego Valadés's arrival in Tlaxcala in 1570 must have occasioned tremendous local pride. In that year, he returned to the place of his birth to assume leadership of the republic's religious life. As the new guardian of the Convento de San Francisco, Valadés became the leader of one of Mexico's most famed spiritual institutions. It was there in Tlaxcala in 1524 that twelve Franciscan missionaries arrived with their message for the leaders of New Spain's most powerful indigenous state. They carried out mass baptisms and laid the foundations for the first diocese in Mexico. Their leader, Fray Toribio de Benavente, baptized and renamed countless Tlaxcalans, but he was also renamed by them and known forever after by the epithet "Motolinía," or "the Poor One." The successes of the early Tlaxcalan Church were legendary in the contemporary Catholic world, and its convent and school created one of the most cosmopolitan and privileged groups of indigenous people in the colonial Americas. However, though the government of Tlaxcala was headed by an elected Indian cabildo, the convent (which provided sacraments, education, and social welfare in the community) was for decades led by Europeans.[21] When Diego Valadés took the reins, he did so as a native son. His leadership typifies the dual personality of Tlaxcalan elites, who touted both their preconquest glory and their pivotal role as co-conquerors of the Mexicas. Valadés represented two powerful genealogies and embodied a new notion of colonial meritocracy, in which Renaissance education, literacy, and social grace lifted talented men even beyond the conditions of their birth.

Valadés helps us to visualize what the world of elite indigenous education, scholarship, and religious observance looked like. In a series of prints, he shows us idealized representations of instruction and worship in the Indian republics of his day.[22] He show us a preaching friar lecturing to assembled Indian noblemen within the church; he also shows us the larger community of Christian Indians in a complex illustration of the open-air chapel that stood beside the Franciscan missionary college. To this day, visitors to the former Franciscan convent in Tlaxcala are struck by the four beautifully constructed stone *posas* that mark the corners of the verdant atrium. Valadés shows us how to experience this space, both as a physical environment for community activities and as a great programmatic allegory. His illustration renders the Holy Spirit as a radiant dove in the center of the courtyard, with beams of light reaching out toward the four posas, dividing the space into quadrants. The dove is framed by a massive model of the church carried on the shoulders of Franciscan friars in a procession led by Saint Francis himself. Holy Week and Corpus Christi celebrations around the world carry processional images of this kind, but in Valadés's illustration, the whole scene is both a description of physical reality and a carefully interpreted allegory. His four posas are labeled "men," "women," "girls," and "boys." Groups of Indians populate the atrium, each faced a by spiritual leader. The groups correspond both to stages in spiritual education and to each of the sacraments. Baptisms, marriages, and funerals are taking place, while at other spots students cluster around their teachers. The lessons include teachings on creation, doctrine, and penitence. Friars take confession and examine their students. In one corner, Pedro de Gante—the famed teacher and missionary so instrumental in the conversion of Tlaxcala and the education of Valadés himself—addresses a group of students. With a pointer, he directs their attention to a series of pictograms.

When Valadés returned to the Republic of Tlaxcala as the new Franciscan guardian, he must have imagined himself building the idealized Christian society that he described in his book. One wonders what the other members the community thought of him: Did they see him as a native son? A returning missionary? A great translator and scholar? At the same time, one wonders how he was perceived in Europe: Was this visitor from America seen first and foremost as a clergyman? An Indian? A diplomat? In the end, Valadés was both a missionary *to* indigenous America and a representative *of* indigenous America. Like the Tlaxcalan emissaries to the crown who traveled across the sea in 1528 and 1534, Valadés embodied a new sort of transatlantic leadership.

Writing about Native Christianity in Spanish and French America

The lives of colonial women were more tightly constrained than those of their male counterparts. However, for a few exceptional women, religious life opened paths to new experiences beyond the bounds of family. Nuns and pious laywomen created their own social networks, engaging in ritual and service activities that bridged creole and native communities. In the 1670s, two women who are now celebrated figures in colonial history were still in their twenties: New Spain's Sor Juana Inés de la Cruz and New France's Catherine Tekakwitha. Both emerged as cultural leaders at the intersection of European and indigenous life—but they were leaders of very different sorts.[23]

Sor Juana was perhaps Mexico's greatest seventeenth-century writer. Her interests were wide-ranging, and her writings included everything from classical philosophy and natural sciences to love poetry, Dantesque dreams, and pointed commentaries on gender and institutional life. She was a creole and an urbanite. The privileged social circle of her youth included Spanish aristocrats, governors, and learned churchmen. Sor Juana's Mexico City was one rich with indigenous history and inhabited by a vast Indian population. Juana's own family line was entirely Spanish, but she spoke and wrote in Nahuatl, as well as in the classical and living languages expected of European scholars. Her most enigmatic work, *The Divine Narcissus*, was composed as a mystery play for religious celebrations in Indian republics. In it, a series of allegorical characters (Occident, America, Zeal, etc.) describe Mexico's preconquest religion, the arrival of Christianity, and the miracle of the Eucharist. The audience beholds first a great pagan festival to the "God of Seeds," next a contest between East and West, then the unveiling of the Eucharist as the sign of Christian truth, and finally a moment of reconciliation in which the Host is revealed. The words ring out: "Blessed the day I came to know the great God of Seeds." Sor Juana wrote from the confines of her Hieronymite convent, but her perspective was global. She imagined that her writing might spark a deep memory of shared religious truth buried in the minds of her Indian audience.[24]

In Sor Juana's day, Mexico's first missionary encounters were already two centuries past, but in French Canada the age of evangelization had just begun. Montreal had its start in 1642 as a colony called Ville Marie on a freshwater island midway between the Great Lakes and the sea. At first, the French settlers numbered only a few dozen, giving little cause for alarm among the area's Mohawk inhabitants. But the Europeans' diseases created a crisis disproportionate to their numbers. The first epidemics reached the area before the Frenchmen themselves. By the mid-seventeenth century, the demographic catastrophe that had hit Mexico the century before had ravaged Canada from the Atlantic to the Great Lakes. Smallpox swept through the Mohawk community in the 1620s and again in the 1660s. In the 1640s, Mohawks lashed out at unwelcome missionaries and settlers, and the Europeans clung precariously to small beachheads. It was into this contested environment that Catherine Tekakwitha was born in 1656, in Gandaouagué, a village on the Mohawk River near the site of modern Auriesville, New York. Catherine's childhood community was soon unraveling around her. The smallpox epidemic of 1660 killed her mother and left Catherine scarred for life. Paradoxically, while Europeans and their diseases devastated her homeland, it was a new European religion that lent purpose to her life.[25]

Catherine's conversion to Christianity, her faith, and her famed austerities would make her widely admired by Jesuit missionaries and by French and native laypeople. Her example inspired an informal following among Europeans and Indians in the region, and led ultimately to her canonization as a saint.[26] Catherine belonged to a time and place when religious improvisation was a part of everyday life. Jesuit missionaries were working feverishly, even facing martyrdom, to spread Christianity into indigenous Canada. But while they did so, new converts were imagining and reimagining Catholicism in their own ways. In Haudenosaunee mission communities, some young women spontaneously embraced Catholic notions of asceticism, forming their own convent-like organizations. Jesuit missionary Claude Chauchetière, who chronicled these years, described groups of women converts banding together in unsanctioned convents, devoted to prayer, asceticism, and shared work.[27] The women embraced chastity, thereby removing themselves from the kinship systems of their birth communities. But Catherine was not among them—or not exactly. Hers was a more solitary anchorite faith. At her baptism on Easter Day 1676, she took the name Catherine after Catherine of Siena, the Italian saint famed for her learning, her virginity, and her spiritual marriage to Christ. But Catherine Tekakwitha's world was very different from that of her namesake.

Mohawks lived in the broad swath of territory along today's New York–Quebec border. They traded with the Dutch at Fort Orange (now Albany), with the French at Ville Marie (now Montreal), and with other Haudenosaunee nations and Algonquians throughout the region. In Catherine's time, the attitude of the Mohawk community toward Christianity was uncertain; missionaries were sometimes welcomed and sometimes attacked. The most important Mohawk social structures were clan based. When Catherine converted, accepted baptism, and renounced a traditional life of marriage and family, she placed herself outside of her kinship group and, in some respects, outside of her nation. But by stepping into the cultural universe of intentional Christian communities, she entered an environment based on different relationships, and one in which status was measured differently. There, neither wealth nor family was the measure of her accomplishments—just the opposite, in fact. Her virginity, her poverty, and even her physical infirmities became a source of prestige. In a short time, a surprising inversion of status took place between her and her spiritual mentor, Claude Chauchetière, as the later came to regard her less as a student and more as a model for Christian piety.[28]

The story in some ways upends the expected hierarchies of gender and social station; in other respects, it conforms to seventeenth-century Catholic culture. Reversals of status are standard tropes in hagiographies. Catholic literature venerates saints who appeared from humble circumstances and instructed the powerful. This may explain why some non-European women were first attracted to the faith. The story of Catherine Tekakwitha in some ways reinforced and in other ways challenged European authority. Pierre Cholenec, who was present at her death, described Catherine's miraculous transfiguration as she drew her last breath: her smallpox scars were erased and here skin turned "beautiful and white." The wording speaks to a paradox in European understandings of Catherine Tekakwitha's legacy. Her indigenous identity is at the core of the story and is crucial to her eventual canonization. Viewed through this lens, her sanctity arose from her innocence, her status as an outsider, and her role as a handmaiden of conversion. At the same time, the hagiographies celebrate the ways in which she *shed* her Indian identify. Both dimensions of her personality are present in the historical record. Catherine and some of her native contemporaries were building their own Christian spaces and communities loosely modeled on the European practices they had observed.[29] Catherine fashioned her own wooden crucifixes and built her own simple outdoor chapels. She invented her own fasts and austerities. She learned from the missionaries, but she also taught them.[30] The devotions surrounding Catherine Tekakwitha began shortly after her death. Her bones were carefully preserved, guarded by the faithful, and later reinterred at a new church of Saint Francis Xavier in Kahnawake. Her grave site consoled mothers who had lost children, and her relics healed the sick. One of her teeth was regarded as a sacred object and was steeped in hot water to produce curative teas. Catherine's following spread through Indian and settler communities, and it helped to define a regional identity for Christianity that crossed ethnic boundaries.

In 1724, four years after the foundation of the church that would house Catherine's earthly remains, the first full-length biography of this folk saint was published. The book was printed not in Montreal or in Paris, but in Mexico City in a shop on Espiritu Santo Street, just a few blocks from the Hieronymite convent where Sor Juana's life had come to an end three decades before.[31] The biography, written by Cholenec and translated by a Jesuit peer, includes a forward explaining the author's notion of Catherine Tekakwitha's place in world history. It describes her life as one element in a series of miraculous events advancing the faith from Latin America to China. The message is clear: the Catholic missionary project was global in scope and it transcended all categories of language, birth, and ethnicity. The church revered not just Europeans who suffered martyrdom as missionaries, but also newly converted non-Europeans like Catherine Tekakwitha and Juan Diego Cuauhtlatoatzin. Cholenec believed that new converts around the world were having experiences much like those of Sor Juana's literary characters who glimpsed a Christian truth buried in the rites of the God of Seeds.

In Protestant Anglo-America, education in missions and schools allowed some native women to navigate colonial social environments and win recognition from the colonizers. Conspicuous among these women was the famed Cherokee convert, Catharine Brown. In the first years of the nineteenth century, the Cherokee nation was under intense pressure from neighboring white settlers and from increasingly hostile and avaricious state governments. Despite these external threats, the Cherokees had enjoyed remarkable success over the previous half century: they had developed advantageous commercial relationships with indigenous and European trade partners, and they had borrowed shrewdly and selectively from the technologies, commercial practices, and labor organizations of the Anglo-Americans. Still, their position in the world was tenuous. White populations from Georgia and from the newly formed states of Tennessee and Alabama pushed into Cherokee territory, dominating the region by violence and weight of numbers.[32]

It was into this environment around the year 1800 that Catharine Brown was born. Though she did not live past young adulthood, Brown had a significant impact both inside and outside her community. To Protestant, Anglo-American readers, she was the most widely known Cherokee woman of the era. Had she been Catholic, Brown might well have been canonized for her renowned purity, piety, and Christian learning. But her education was under Protestant missionaries; and Protestants would make Catharine into their own kind of informal saint: a symbol of the embattled Indians' capacity for Christian civilization, and a hero for religious reformers who were fighting to protect the Cherokee people and transform their culture. Yet the surviving story of Catharine Brown is not simply a myth crafted by her admirers. Brown learned to read and write the English language with great skill and elegance. Unlike Catherine Tekakwitha, Catharine Brown left for posterity an extensive record of her thoughts in the form of personal correspondence written in her own neat hand.[33]

Indian Heroes for Protestant America

In the spring of 1817, Catharine Brown set out on the long journey from her home in Wills Valley (now in the state of Alabama) through the thickly forested Appalachian Mountains to the site near modern Chattanooga where the new Brainerd Mission was still rising one plank at a time from the site selected by the American Board of Commissioners for Foreign Missions. This multidenominational organization from New England planned to build a network of economically self-sufficient mission schools that would train their students in academics, skilled trades, and theology. The graduates would become emissaries for Christianity and for European language and culture. In short, the schools were imagined as small colleges run by Anglo-American missionaries for the purpose of training indigenous-American missionaries. Catharine Brown become the inspirational human face of this project.[34]

The official story of Catharine Brown was crafted immediately after her death by Congregationalist minister Rufus Anderson. It was published in 1825 as a brief didactic biography, which aimed to celebrate and justify the project of Indian education. Representatives of the American Board had met with the Cherokee Council in 1816 and received enthusiastic support for the creation of the Brainerd School in the Cherokee village of Chickamauga. A year later, Catharine Brown was among the first Cherokees to accept the opportunity to study there. She arrived at the school speaking Cherokee and a few words of English. She could neither read nor write in either language—in fact, the invention of Cherokee script was still a few years off. In the months that followed, the teachers described her exceptional talent and rapid academic progress. A year later, she read and wrote beautifully in the English language, and was already serving as a teacher and translator for younger students. Anglo-American visitors to the school remarked on her beauty, grace, and academic education. She was the first Indian baptized at the mission, and her education was the school's proudest achievement.

Even as the Brainerd project was thriving, the surrounding Cherokee nation was fighting for its life. Brown's own parents, Yau-nu-gung-yah-ski and Tsa-lu (known to Anglophones as John and Sarah), came to the mission in November of 1818 with distressing news: bands of invading settlers had ransacked their lands, stealing their draft animals and cattle. Believing their dispossession inevitable, they decided to move west to Arkansas Territory with their remaining assets. The parents' fears were well placed. In Alabama, Georgia, and Tennessee, every inch of Cherokee land was at risk. Squatters and state governments continued to seize territory, and the federal government did little to stand in their way.[35]

John and Sarah soon departed from the school and from their home, but Catharine did not go with them. Already her life's path was diverging from that of a traditional wife and mother. She remained among the Cherokees, serving now as a missionary, teacher, and caregiver. The American Board was building a new school at Mission Creek, about fifty miles from the Browns' original home, and Catharine would be among its first teachers. Sadly, her career was cut short by the tragic appearance of disease in her family. Tuberculosis destroyed her brother's health, and then her own, leading ultimately to Catharine's death in 1823. The final two years of her life are beautifully documented in her extant correspondence. This intimate record of communications among the members of the Brown family presents some surprises. It appears that the real lives of the Browns were very different from those in the stories told by her eulogizers and repeated for the benefit of mission-board benefactors.

To her biographer, Rufus Anderson, Catharine Brown symbolized every aspect of the encounter between Indian and European, pagan and Christian, wilderness and civilization. She was rescued from the stultifying environment of her family and brought into the Christian community where her God-given talents thrived. Anderson tells us that she began her life as a vain and ignorant child who came to the mission dressed in jewelry and ornaments, never having heard the name of Jesus. Soon she was transformed by missionary hands, shedding the jewelry, embracing the English language, acculturating to European norms of modest humility, and experiencing a sudden and powerful religious conversion. Anderson tells us that Brown's parents were "half-breeds who never learned to speak English." Her people lived in darkness: "Not a book existed in the language: the language was unwritten. The fountains of knowledge were sealed: the mind made no progress."

While missionaries often extolled the virtues of civilization in contrast to Cherokee culture, they also exploited the rhetorical inversion of this idea, celebrating the Indians' innocence and virtue in contrast to the corruption of the white community. According to Anderson, the Cherokees were among the "Indians of North America who [had] not incorporated the worst vices of civilized life into their own."[36] Like Mexico's sixteenth-century Franciscans, the American Board missionaries hoped to inculcate the Indians with the virtues of the European faith while protecting them from the evils of white society. Anderson's outlook on the Cherokees was hopeful, but he described Catharine and her countrymen as currently surrounded by the "dangers of some irreligious white people" who "endeavored to perplex her mind by objections against scripture."

The contents of Catharine Brown's correspondence call into question much that Anderson had to say about her childhood and her family. The letters do reflect the traits of kindness, patience, and sincere religious sentiment that others attributed to her. But her writing describes a Cherokee community very different from that of Anderson's book. The Anderson biography describes Catharine's family and community as a place of primeval innocence (and ignorance) now further endangered by new Anglo-American vices and the pernicious influences of freethinkers. And yet, anyone who reads the Brown family letters will be struck by their literacy and fluency in the English language.

Catharine's own writing is so elegant that it is nearly impossible to believe she entered school with no previous education or literacy. In the summer of 1822, John and Sarah Brown wrote to their children in nicely composed English. The sentences reflect not just skill but comfort with this medium of communication. The letters discuss religion, family, and the affairs of the world. The Browns were far from destitute: John reported that his wife had grown so fat that she could no longer walk very far and instead enjoyed traveling to town by horse. And it wasn't just the Browns who seemed literate and comfortable, but a broader community of respected Cherokees who sent their children to the mission schools. Like any proud middle-class parents, the Browns wrote to their son David about his cohort at school: "We have heard that all the Cherokee youth are coming home next fall and hope you will too." In fact, David was such an academic success that by fall he was enrolled at Andover Theological Seminary.[37]

The Browns enjoyed access to some of the advantages of both the Anglo-American and Cherokee worlds, but their situation was tenuous, and they were all too aware of the fact that their fortunate circumstances might soon come crashing down around them. In 1822, all was well: their daughter was a teacher in Alabama and their son was advancing his education in New England. Still, the Browns were perceptive people, and they knew which way the wind was blowing. Even as they discussed their family's good fortune, the parents were making concrete plans to flee westward.

The Browns were in some ways typical of the more privileged members of the Cherokee nation. They were (despite Anderson's assertions to the contrary) quite knowledgeable about Euro-American life and experienced in the cross-cultural commercial and political negotiations that the era demanded. Their new (or perhaps renewed) Christian faith informed their understanding of this hybrid colonial world. Catharine, after caring for her ailing brother, John, over many months, wrote her parents to inform them of his death. The letter's prose is lovely, and the contents indicate the depth of cultural exchange in Catharine's day. The composition could easily be mistaken for that of any educated New England Protestant as it comments on adversity, faith, and death. It also gives us a glimpse of her family's affluence and comfort. In the letter, she recounts to David the last words of their brother, John: "You should remember to keep the Lord's Day. You are too much engaged in the kitchen on the Sabbath days. You should keep the blacks from work, and take them with you to meetings; when you return, keep them still in the house, and not let them play on this day." Clearly, the life of Catharine Brown involved not just teaching Cherokee youth and caring for her ailing brother, but also overseeing a group of slaves. Privileged Cherokees such as the Browns were deeply involved in the economic and social structures of Anglo-American society. Far from being untouched by modern society or innocent of its vices, Indians like Catharine Brown were as immersed in Euro-American culture and economics as they were in traditional lifeways.[38]

Missionaries sometimes capitalized on urban readers' ill-informed notions about Indian frontier life when drumming up support for the mission school. And Anderson may have capitalized on his readers' expectation that Indians were either holy innocents or savages. But just because some Anglo-Americans were ignorant of Cherokee life does not mean the reverse was true. By the early nineteenth century, Cherokees were well versed in Euro-American practices and had, in fact, adopted many of them. Their most privileged families lived in wood-framed houses, bustled about the kitchen, read books, and corresponded with their children. Their farms were full of draft animals, cattle, and hogs; and they rode their horses on errands into town. They owned African slaves, purchased directly or indirectly from Anglo-American sellers. If the mission board was hoping to save untouched pagan idolaters or rustic Indians living in Edenic simplicity, they had clearly missed their moment. But if they were looking for an Indian to serve as a symbol of ascending American Protestantism, they had found her in the person of Catharine Brown.[39]

═══

Indigenous leadership shaped virtually every aspect of early Christianity in the Americas. In some cases Indian converts fit into narratives predetermined by Christian traditions. Missionaries who believed they were experiencing one of the great moments in theological history expected that new Christians would relive the experiences of the early church.[40] In this they were not disappointed. Native converts demonstrated exemplary faith and suffered admirably in the face of persecution. Some were inspirational visionaries, some martyrs, and others themselves became missionaries. Clearly, some of these celebrated Indian figures are as much myth as flesh and blood, but many led lives well documented by historians. Though a few exceptional individuals became saints or national heroes, Indian religious leadership was not limited to these larger-than-life figures. Countless indigenous and mestizo people helped to create the culture and aesthetics of New World Christianity through their work as artists, teachers, writers, and clergy. Entry into the institutional life of Christianity was a way for traditional elites to preserve their social standing, and for talented Indians of more humble origins to advance their own.

CHAPTER SIX

An Evolving Urban Hierarchy

New Spain and Old Tenochtitlan

During the sixteenth century, Europe devoured itself in the endless wars of the Reformation. Mobs of iconoclasts smashed stained-glass windows and inquisitors hunted heretics. But on the other side of the Atlantic, new church spires, civic buildings, and apartment blocks lined the streets as hopeful missionaries, converts, and settlers created a new kind of American city.[1] The leaders of New Spain, now thousands of miles from the shores of old Spain, did their best to erect a respectable simulacrum of the mother country. The first bishops and viceroys supervised the construction of a cathedral and a viceregal palace, laying the stones over the center of the Mexicas' island capital. The audiencia heard cases, the Holy Office sniffed out heterodoxy, and artisans ran their workshops while merchants traveled the commercial routes that linked Mexico City like the hub of a great wheel to distant mines, fields, and frontiers. But whether this was a city in bloom or a city in ruins was very much in the eye of the beholder. The core of Mexico City was a dense *spolia* of new buildings wrought from old. The cathedral rose from the roots of the temple complex of Huitzilopochtli, and the viceregal palace was assembled from the tumbled stones of the palace of Moctezuma. Even the city's basic infrastructure was like a rickety machine—broken, patched, stitched, and improvised to keep the wounded leviathan's food and water circulating.[2]

If one could look down from Mexico's then-clear skies upon the vast basin of Lake Texcoco, the valley would betray signs of both chaos and vitality. The hydrological engineering of the triple alliance had been savaged by the Spanish conquest. The invading armies breached dikes, smashed bridges, and backfilled canals. But all was not lost. The invaders set about restoring the city in their own way. Water still flowed from Chapultepec to Mexico-Tenochtitlan, and the Spanish soon rebuilt old pipelines, adding new aqueducts and fountains. The core of the Aztec city was a natural island, crisscrossed by a network of canals and surrounded by an archipelago of man-made islands, green with Nahua gardens. The Spanish planners were more Castilian than Venetian in temperament; they plugged the urban waterways with earth and slowly expanded the city over marshes and shallow lake beds. But on all sides, the island gardens survived, and the marketplaces of Tenochtitlan and Tlatelolco still overbrimmed with produce carried to the busy plazas each day by Indian vendors.

For many years, Spanish Mexico City remained smaller than Tenochtitlan had been. European diseases devastated the population during the conquest era, and more epidemics followed. Still, despite all these deaths, and despite all the newcomers, the island remained a Nahua city. In many places, the language and customs of the marketplace did not change; Indian vendors hawked their goods in Nahuatl, and they wore clothing more Mesoamerican than Iberian. The new city was half brick-and-mortar and half mirage. Maps and drawings showed the aspirations of the colonizers as much as physical reality. A given place was often known by more than one name and spoken of in more than one language.[3]

The indigenous leadership in urban New Spain emerged from two distinct historical experiences: that of native states who had backed the Spanish invasion of Mexico, and that of conquered states who managed to retain some power and autonomy after their defeat. Tlaxcala as a former ally, and Tenochtitlan as a former adversary, typify this phenomenon. Seventeen thousand feet above sea level, the smoldering, snowcapped volcanoes of Popocatépetl and Iztaccíhuatl loomed over both. To the west lay Mexico City in the great bowl of Lake Texcoco. To the east lay the valley of Tlaxcala, flanked on one side by the no-less-impressive Mount Matlalcuéyetl. Though Tlaxcala lacked Tenochtitlan's inland sea, it was graced with fertile soil and a confluence of gently flowing streams and rivers. The inhabitants were as skilled in hydrology as their Mexica neighbors, though they built their fields by bringing water to soil rather than soil to water. Before the arrival of the Spanish, Tlaxcala had long coexisted with the Aztec state. These twin societies had been perpetual rivals, speaking the same language, observing the same customs, and fighting against each other in

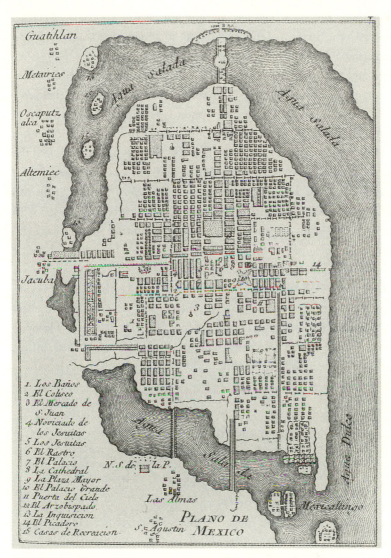

FIGURE 13 Map of Mexico City, 1758. From Tomás López de Vargas Machuca's *Atlas geographico de la America septentrional y meridional* (Madrid: Antonio Sanz Plazuela de la Calle de Paz, 1758).

the same fashion, but their fortunes changed abruptly in 1521 when Tlaxcala cast its lot with the Spanish. Tenochtitlan was soon occupied and looted by a combined army of European and Tlaxcalan enemies.

By the sixteenth century, both societies had survived and evolved in unexpected ways as indigenous leaders—one set victorious, the other defeated—ingratiated themselves with the Spanish invaders. The people and resources of the two kingdoms now became the basis of Christian Indian republics within a larger Habsburg Empire. Tlaxcala was home to the first archdiocese and the first great Franciscan institution in New Spain; and it became the exemplar for Spanish diplomatic and evangelical efforts in the New World. In the fifteenth century, Tlaxcala had been composed of four powerful subpolities, each with its own identity based on geography and clan. Under European tutelage, Tlaxcalans now constructed their first urban capital. Soon Tlaxcala's aristocratic elites moved to this brick-and-stone city, pragmatically positioned between their old seigniorial estates. Some powerful lineages, like the Salazar family, enjoyed great institutional success as clergymen, public servants, and intellectuals.[4] The leading families of Tlaxcala, Texcoco, Tenochtitlan, and Tlacopan did not disappear, but they did have to adapt. By the late sixteenth century, their homes, neighborhoods, and public buildings looked very much like those of Spain.

Tawantinsuyu and the City of Kings

Urban life for Peru's native leadership class had much in common with that of New Spain. Indigenous elites could be found throughout rural areas and regional capitals, but it was in Lima and Cuzco that they inhabited metropolitan environments most like those of Mexico City. In these twin capitals of highland and lowland Peru, leading indigenous families exercised their influence though political councils, church organizations, and commercial guilds. As already noted, the young men of these families were educated in institutions meant to perpetuate native authority. In Cuzco, the words "Colegio San Francisco de Borja" and the school's old coat of arms are still proudly displayed on the façade of a handsome yellow school building that rises prominently above the Plaza de Armas. Some *cuzqueños* still know the story of its origins. Things turned out differently in Lima, where the Colegio de Santiago del Cercado and the once-great Indian republic that surrounded it are all but erased from the urban map and from popular memory. The Church of Santiago el Apóstol stands among the last remaining colonial buildings on a small plaza surrounded by a sea of collapsed modern structures and the shadows of a new light-rail viaduct. Over the centuries, earthquakes have shaken the church walls and brought down the vaulted ceiling, but after each disaster the church has been lovingly rebuilt, restored, and repainted. The church shares its eastern wall with a venerable stone building that conceals behind its plain exterior a shady arcaded courtyard. For most of the twentieth century, this structure housed a police academy named for Túpac Amaru II. In the nineteenth century it was an insane asylum, the Manicomio del Cercado; but before that, it was the Colegio de Caciques, an institution at the center of the intellectual and political life of Lima's indigenous leadership.[5]

A few blocks from the church, one can yet see a fragment of Lima's old city walls, and a hint of the fortifications that gave their name to the Cercado neighborhood. Santiago was once an Indian republic in its own right, founded at a time when the center of power in Peru was beginning to shift from Cuzco to Lima, and from the Indian nobility to Spanish and creole elites. Lima is located near the mouth of the Rímac River, not far from the preconquest city of Pachacamac. This coastal zone was a valuable but peripheral part of Tawantinsuyu, whose center of wealth and political power was Cuzco. Over the course of the colonial era, the relationship between center and periphery was inverted, with Lima becoming the headquarters of imperial administration and Cuzco persisting as a regional capital.

Lima, once called "City of Kings," was founded on the banks of the Rímac in 1535 on the eve of an uprising that nearly swept the Spanish off the map. For a time, it appeared that forces loyal to Manco Inca might succeed in their attack on the new capital, but the siege was lifted and the Inca irredentists were defeated. Still, Lima long remained more fragile and less prosperous than its founders had hoped. The Spanish city was surrounded on all sides by Indian communities, each with its own nobility, and each burdened by the tribute and labor demands of the invaders. The native gentry built their casonas, squares, and churches, and planned to sire great aristocratic lines, but they were painfully aware of the forces eroding their patrimony. The Indian population around Lima was collapsing in the face of European diseases, just as it was everywhere else in Peru and Mexico. This was a crisis, not just for the conquered but also for the conquerors. Most of the inhabitants of Peru

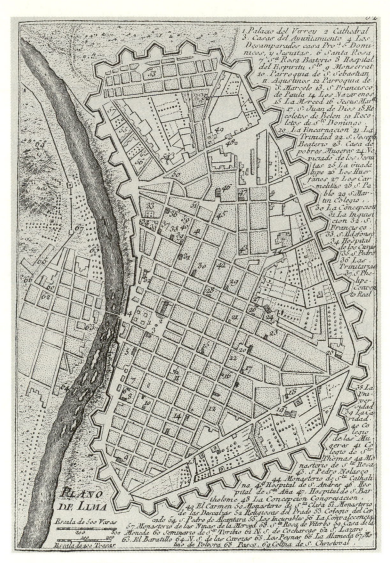

FIGURE 14 Map of Lima with Santiago del Cercado visible, 1758. From
Tomás López de Vargas Machuca's *Atlas geographico de la America
septentrional y meridional* (Madrid: Antonio Sanz Plazuela de la Calle de
Paz, 1758).

had submitted to Spanish rule, and most had embraced Christianity, but the much-hoped-for community of Indian Christian subjects, both numerous and prosperous, was not materializing.

In the 1570s, Viceroy Toledo had to confront the crisis of falling population, declining revenues, and social fragmentation. He set to work addressing these problems on both the regional and local levels. Toledo ordered the relocation of several communities of Indians from the Rímac valley to a new community just east of Lima. This new town—soon to be called Santiago del Cercado— reflected many of Toledo's policy initiatives: *reducción* of Indian populations to concentrate their numbers, extension of Spanish modes of governance into Indian republics, improved religious education, and protection of the Indians from other castes. In all of these undertakings, Toledo worked closely with the Jesuit order. Santiago was to be an Indian republic, planned with a grid of urban streets, a central plaza, and a surrounding cluster of homes, orchards, and fields. From the beginning, it was gated and ringed with high walls. Fearing that the inhabitants would be exploited by Spaniards or subjected to the supposedly deleterious influences of Afro-Peruvians, mestizos, and mulattos, the founders of the town built it as a sanctuary for a pure and self-governing Indian population. Members of other castes were forbidden to own property there, and the gates were to be locked at night to keep out miscreants of all sorts.[6]

In the decades that followed, Santiago grew, even as the general population of Indians in Peru shrank. The citizenry combined the progeny of the original founders with new populations. Some were drawn to the community by opportunity; others were pushed there by force or desperation. In 1590, the alcalde of Lima, Juan de Barrios, working with the archbishop and the local corregidor, transferred seven hundred more Indians from San Lorenzo. Here and elsewhere in Spanish America, Indian towns were built in order to cobble together viable economic and political units in a time when traditional communities were decimated by disease, flight, and migration.

Santiago del Cercado was one of the places in Peru where one could find a firmly established indigenous elite. It was a site where Indian scholars, governors, and aristocrats had their urban homes. Visitors to the town in the mid-seventeenth century observed rows of prosperous and elegant homes in this community of nearly a thousand inhabitants. Many of the Indian gentleman of el Cercado prospered from their hereditary claims to native labor. No small number also held African slaves within the city limits despite the town's original policy of excluding all non-Indian people.

The history of the town's college for indigenous nobility closely parallels that of its sister institution in Cuzco. During the 1610s, Spanish fears of resurgent Andean religions were stoked by the discovery (or supposed discovery) of crypto-idolatry, first in Huamanga Province and then throughout Peru. The viceroyalty responded with two strategies: the first inquisitorial and the second educational. The key to the second approach was the development of a much larger community of highly educated caciques to serve the church and local Indian governments. The ultimate objective was to create among the Indian population of Peru the same sort of faithful lay piety that the Council of Trent had promoted among the humbler classes in Europe. King Philip III issued two charters to create new schools for Andean nobility: one for San Francisco de Borja in 1618 and one for Santiago del Cercado in 1621.[7]

The curriculum of Santiago del Cercado was much like that of San Francisco de Borja, and young noblemen came from all over Peru to attend. The youngest enrolled at the age of ten and remained there until adulthood, studying arts and letters in Castilian and Latin. The school's endowment portfolio included properties like the vast sugar plantation of Vilcahuara. The revenues of these estates ensured that students enjoyed the privileges appropriate to their birth and to their membership in an elite academic institution.[8] The founders created a system of education to strengthen Peru's Indian republics. However, the urban landscape that surrounded Santiago del Cercado soon changed in ways that subverted this goal.

In the 1680s, the walls between el Cercado and Lima came down. After a century of cohabiting the banks of the Rímac, the relative size of the two cities had changed dramatically. Lima had become a major viceregal capital inhabited by Spaniards, Indians, mestizos, and mulattos; Santiago was now, in contrast, just a small satellite of the expanding metropolis.[9] Don Melchor de Navarra oversaw the construction of Lima's new fortifications in the 1680s, and his decision to encircle Santiago and Lima in one set of walls formalized a merger of two communities that was already a reality in daily life.

All over Hispanic America, something similar was taking place: the theoretical boundary between the Republic of Indians and the Republic of Spaniards was contradicted by the quotidian realities of demography and commerce. By the eighteenth century, the mobility of populations, intermarriage between castes, and exchange of goods and labor made it nearly impossible to enforce old rules that had segregated residential and political communities. For Indian elites, this trend presented both risks and opportunities. They were forced to weigh the merits of defending old privileges against the risks of grasping for new ones. Was it better to retain control of exclusively Indian institutions or to fight for inclusion in Spanish ones?[10] In the 1750s, traditional indigenous elites in Lima considered both options and decided to gamble on the second strategy. Their spokesmen were two highly respected churchmen of mestizo origins: Fray Calixto de San José and Fray Isidoro de Cala y Ortega. The former bore their message first to the king and later to the pope. All of the documents carried by the two friars expressed the same set of concerns. The indigenous limeños argued that the labor demands of the mita system were cruel and excessive, and asked that the system be abolished. Furthermore, they warned that Peru's public administration was rife with incompetence and corruption. The petitioners proposed that the scarcity of talent and virtue among Spaniards could be dealt with by purging the ranks of church and government, and opening more offices to Indian and mestizo functionaries. San Francisco de Borja and Santiago del Cercado had for years been turning out highly qualified graduates fit to serve the empire in these capacities. It seemed only logical that the crown should make better use of them.[11]

Fray Calixto apparently drafted and redrafted his memo as he met with Indian nobles in Lima, Jauja, and Cuzco, each time improving the document in order to win their approval. After traveling a lengthy circuit to meet with the stakeholders, he set out for Buenos Aires, then continued on to the royal court in Spain. Fray Calixto was an impressive choice for the job. The son of Pedro Montes and doña Dominga Estefanía Túpac Inca, he could claim a noble pedigree on his mother's side. He was also the product of the finest education. He spoke Spanish, Latin, and Quechua, and wrote elegantly. Fray Calixto was diligent and persistent in his attempts to gain the ear of the king. He arrived in Spain in 1748 and soon joined the Order of the Santo Espíritu del Monte in Valencia while awaiting a response from the king. But he never gained a royal audience. Calixto returned to Lima for a time before traveling back to Spain and living out the rest of his days as a Franciscan brother. The story of Fray Calixto's mission and of the interregional body of Indian elites whom he represented says a great deal about the uncertain position of native leaders in the Andes. They were on one hand powerful and well organized, but on the other hand vulnerable to Spanish administrative misconduct and often restricted in their political and professional ambitions.[12]

The story of Lima and Santiago del Cercado also says a lot about the negotiations between Spanish and native leaders when confronted by their shared and conflicting interests. In the sixteenth century, Santiago was a reducción designed to pull together scattered and declining Indian populations and bind them to the colonial state; it was both an Indian republic and the site of a Jesuit mission. In the seventeenth century, it became a college town and an intellectual capital for Hispanicized Indian elites, but it was also a walled city and a garrison, a key component in the viceroyalty's strategy for regional defense. The walls of Santiago del Cercado (and the later circumvallation of Cercado and Lima) were there to protect the Indian population, but they were also built to serve the Spanish. In a military emergency, this pueblo de indios was expected to come to Lima's defense. The founders of Santiago and their descendants enjoyed privileges based on both nobility and royal service. Even after Santiago merged into greater Lima, some of these old privileges survived and were jealously guarded by the locals. So attractive were the terms of this special citizenship that outsiders sometimes disguised themselves as Indian *vecinos*. This phenomenon also cropped up in central Mexico where non-Tlaxcalans tried to pass themselves off as members of the community and as trusted crown vassals.

In 1796, just such a case of contested identity became a local controversy in Lima and Santiago del Cercado. Juan de Dios Chumbiraico Casahuaringa, a resident of el Cercado, refused to pay the type of Indian tribute that was customarily exacted from Peru's commoners. He claimed exemption from the tax on account of his status as a fully vested Indian citizen and a member of the militia. His detractors claimed that he was in fact Juan de Dios Quispe—and not a hereditary member of the community, but rather a migrant from the neighboring province of Huarochirí and a member of the Ayumpuya ayllu in the town of Langa. Since the case involved both a question of fact and a question of law, the magistrates had a choice: they could either issue a narrow ruling by simply determining the man's identity, or they could issue a broad ruling by clarifying the relevant principles of Indian citizenship and corporate privilege. Conscious of the instable political situation that surrounded them, they chose the latter. The judges were careful to avoid a precedent that would further erode the boundaries between the two republics or blur the lines between distinct Indian populations. They worried that permitting outsiders to represent themselves as vecinos of Cercado would invite "considerable fraud" and trigger the "grave inconvenience of tributary Indians pouring out of the districts around this capital." The document listed all the legitimate grounds for relief from tribute. Indians who spent the season laboring on behalf of the church or who suffered a year of crop failures could be granted a temporary exemption based on service or hardship. But all such measures were temporary. After the stipulated time period expired, the people in question had to return to their normal tributary status "in recognition of their vassalage because it is important to conserve the Indian nation." The magistrates picked over all the details of Chumbiraico's biography. Ultimately, his classification hinged more on the census category of his ancestors than on his own place of birth, work, or residence: "Despite the fact that the petitioner accredited himself . . . as being born in this city and being a militiaman, none of this is enough for him to be taken out of this category of tributary of said district." Chumbiraico was unable to produce any proof that he was descended from the families listed in the town's original charter. Consequently, the court shot down his pretensions of membership in Cercado's hereditary elite. At the same time, the magistrates did everything possible to protect the legal status of the republic and to reassert the authority of its legitimate leaders. The final summary of the case carefully articulates the special standing of the town's vecinos: "Your excellency may know that Indians of the pueblo of Cercado and others in the vicinity of the capital have not been subject to tribute." According to the court, Chumbiraico was right about the status of Cercado elites—he just wasn't one of them.[13]

Perhaps the most privileged residents of Santiago del Cercado were the young men at the Colegio del Príncipe. Admission to the institution required a thorough vetting of the applicants' genealogy. Several principles were involved. Students must be Indians (though many were in fact mestizos), they must be nobles, and their families must be free of the ancestral taint of Judaism. Just as Spaniards in Iberia seeking admission to high office or elite institutions needed to demonstrate their limpieza de sangre, so too did the applicants for the New World's indigenous colleges. Eugenio de Chumpitasí was one of the leaders (or principales) of the pueblo of Chilca about twenty miles south of the old city of Pachacamac. Enrolling his descendants in the Colegio del Príncipe was an important sign of privilege. But to gain admission, the applicant's pedigree had to be unimpugnable. In 1799 the Chumpitasí family submitted an extensive dossier describing generations of family history, authenticating it with testimony from priests, godparents, and respected witnesses drawn from the Spanish and indigenous nobility. The Chumpitasís boasted about their descent from loyal caciques, principales, and governors over many generations. Chilca was a very old community—far older than the Inca Empire. Long ago the region had weathered the Inca conquest and become an important client state within Tawantinsuyu. When it was conquered and incorporated into Spanish Peru, Chilca (now within the province of Cañete) retained its own local elites who continued to exercise power through colonial institutions. When the first families of Chilca sent their children to the Colegio del Príncipe, it further legitimated their standing as traditional leaders who operated within Spanish colonial norms.[14]

For the sons of the Chumpitasí family, attending the Colegio del Príncipe was an important source of social capital, but it also meant access to a high-quality Jesuit education. From the students' perspective, school life was difficult and intellectually demanding, but it was luxurious compared to the lives of average residents of Peru—or, for that matter, compared to the lives of the average inhabitants of the world during the seventeenth and eighteenth centuries. In the 1790s, the student boarders could look forward to an excellent menu. They ate meat every day but Friday—when piety dictated otherwise— and they sipped chocolate sweetened with sugar for lunch. The dining-room tables were provisioned with the finest foods of the New World and Old: beef and fowl, shrimp and quinoa, potatoes and yams of every description, tamales and yucca, garbanzos and spinach, and fresh fruits of all kinds. The students wore fine clothes, tailored neatly and laundered regularly. Though the young pupils were only boys, they were always referred to as lords or caciques. When ill, they were tended around the clock, fed soups and sweetened porridges, warmed with charcoal braziers, and protected from evil by finely wrought scapulars.[15]

The boys slept in a dormitory beside a courtyard and fountain. The building stood across from a green plaza, and surrounded by the gardens of convents and neighboring estates. Though the institution was monastic in inspiration, it also afforded plenty of diversions for its adolescent wards. The bold and the reckless among them could reach the vices of central Lima in a two-mile walk. Lima had always been a good place for a young man to squander his family fortunes. When the first Indian colleges were built, the vice and profligacy of the young native lords was a source of great concern for churchmen. In fact, the founders of the College of San Francisco in Cuzco (built before its sister institution in the lowlands) argued that the school was desperately needed, in part, as a means to draw the young lords away from the evils of the viceregal capital. In the end, native colleges were established in both cities. With the foundation of the College of Santiago del Cercado, young nobles could have their cake and eat it too. The school offered great prestige and the finest education along with an enviable quality of life and a tantalizing proximity to the sorts of urban adventures not easily found in the provinces.[16]

The Kingdom on Parade

The lives of native students give us a glimpse of what life was like for one privileged subgroup in colonial Latin America. But reconstructing the whole social hierarchy for urban Indians is a more complex matter. Perhaps the best illustration of the place of Indian elites in Catholic colonies is to be found in descriptions of religious organizations and festivals. Feast days and the processions that accompanied them were like the cities themselves: exuberant, multicultural, and multilingual.[17] In a strange civic paradox, parades and feasts expressed both conflict and order, as the city remade itself each year in a public performance of imperial harmony and shared Catholic faith. On the surface, respectable citizens marched in carefully orchestrated ranks, carrying banners, crosses, and holy images atop great gilded litters. They pulled carts with ornately crafted dioramas, filled the air with music, and danced through the streets. And yet, if we are to believe contemporary paintings, this choreographed utopia was also vexed by tricksters, drunks, and ne'er-do-wells—not to mention costumed demons, serpents, and devils that flitted about among the celestial floats. The rowdy rabble of the city danced, drank, and hollered at the margins. But the processions and follies in the streets are only part of the story. It took all year to raise the money for these events, and it took many months to practice the steps, paint and clothe the images, and build the floats and litters. Judging from the legal records, it also took much of the year for the sponsoring sodalities to elect officers, purge their membership rolls, and litigate over the confraternities' lands and revenues. As much as the brotherhoods fought over concrete resources, they fought even more over status. On a city's most important feast days, virtually the entire population was represented, marching in groups whose membership was defined by birth, ethnicity, trade, and neighborhood. A bird's-eye view of a Corpus Christi procession would have looked like the unfurling of a vast, living map, charting out all the communities and hierarchies of the metropolis. Where a person stood on this moving map said a great deal about his power in the community. Consequently small points of etiquette and precedence were worth fighting about.[18]

For Lima in the 1680s, the symbolic focus of the annual Corpus Christi celebration was a procession involving more than eighty cofradías. This enormous honor guard for the consecrated Host twisted its way through miles of narrow urban streets, cheered on by fashionable limeños who lined the balconies of elegant homes, and by the humble rabble who clung to the stoops and storefronts. In previous decades, conflicts over ritual precedence had become so acute that the episcopal leadership and even the Holy Office of the Inquisition were eventually drawn into the thorny question of who would take the lead and who would follow as the parade marched through town. The procession included twenty-four Spanish confraternities, nineteen Indian confraternities, and thirty-nine organizations with black and mulatto members. A radiant golden monstrance containing the sanctified Host was the focus of the entire event, and proximity to this object defined one's status in the city. The most venerable of Spanish brotherhoods came first: the members of Santo Domingo marching on the left, and those of Nuestra Señora de la Limpia Concepción on the right; a chain of twenty-two other Spanish organizations followed. Next came the Indian leaders of the Cofradía of Santiago del Surco, followed by eighteen groups of pious Indians. Finally, the Cofradía de Rosario de los Negros de Santo Domingo and the thirty-eight other black and mulatto confraternities took up the rear, representing the largest share of Lima's population.

The membership of the Indian confraternities gives us a sense of the social stations occupied by native people in Lima. A seventeenth-century mayordomo of Our Lady of Loreto in Santa Ana was an untitled Indian mat weaver.[19] A few decades later, when his organization became embroiled in a squabble with the cofradía of San Joachim, it was opposed by Captain Juan de Barzana, the Indian master of a shoemakers' guild, an affluent man who spoke Castilian fluently. The question of whose patron saint should be carried first through the streets was a sensitive one, not just for the opposing mayordomos but also for the members of their respective communities. Confraternities like theirs held property, collected revenues, and organized vast amounts of labor. Though their rituals centered on particular shrines and sculptures in Lima's cathedral and parish churches, their web of members and assets was surprisingly broad, and their sources of status drew from the deep preconquest past.

In the early eighteenth century, the black confraternity of Santa Cruz de la Trinidad was considered Congolese; its patron church in the San Lazaro district stood on the other side of the Rímac River from Spanish Lima. Like most confraternities, it accumulated lands and other assets as bequests, building an endowment for its annual operations. Its land claims in Pachacamac—more than twenty miles from the home church—soon became a point of dispute, as they were within the bounds of the region governed by the patrimonial estate of don Francisco Taullichumbi Sava Capac Inga. This Inca lord claimed descent from the ruling house of the region's old Inca capital. Even two centuries after the Spanish conquest, he wielded power as governor, cacique, and principal.[20]

That an African organization in a Spanish metropolis was struggling with an Inca lord for the usufruct rights to a distant estate speaks volumes about the ways that the Spanish colonial system contained and negotiated conflicting interests. Many cofradías were still identified in public records as ayllus—or noble Inca kinship groups.[21] But by the late eighteenth century, alliances between interest groups crossed ethnic and kinship boundaries in unexpected ways. For instance, doña Josefa Astocuri, an enigmatic figure in the age of the Túpac Amaru rebellion, was an Indian noblewoman who acted as patron and administrator for a number of Spanish and indigenous cofradías.[22] When Corpus Christi was celebrated in the viceregal capital, the whole population and social hierarchy became legible to the viewer through this elaborately staged parade. Lima was a city whose public life demanded the constant coordination of African, European, and indigenous populations, and Corpus Christi manifested the strengths and tensions inherent to this system.

Some five hundred miles away, up winding Andean paths and eleven thousand feet above the sea, a different Corpus Christi procession snaked through the streets of Cuzco. To visualize this annual event requires no great feat of imagination; eyewitnesses preserved a rich visual record of it. Cuzco's famed seventeenth-century artists painted the street scenes of Corpus Christi in loving detail. Individual churches, parishes, and cofradías commissioned their own paintings of the event, each providing a distinct perspective and self-representation. Such is the case with a series of paintings that now hangs in Cuzco's Palacio Arzobispal. Each canvas opens like a window in the wall, revealing the streets as they appeared four centuries ago.[23]

These paintings once adorned the walls of Santa Ana church, which stands in the barrio of Carmenca on the bluff above the Plaza Regocijo—the Plaza of Joy. In the colonial era, Carmenca was the gateway to Cuzco for those traveling the long route from Lima. And it was a gateway guarded both literally and symbolically by its proud Chachapoya and Cañari citizens. Perched beside its high plaza, Santa Ana's stout tower rose even above that of the city's cathedral. Below its portico, a steep central street led down the rocky slope toward the center of town and the home of Garcilaso de la Vega. The vecinos and parishioners of Santa Ana were deeply rooted in the history of this district. They were the descendants of the soldiers who served as the bodyguards and honor guards to the royal Incas and later to the Spanish conquerors.[24]

The Chachapoyas had come to Cuzco first. Half a century before the Spanish conquest, Inca armies under the command of Túpac Inca Yupanqui pushed the bounds of empire into the subtropical forests far to the north, and into the upper reaches of the Amazon Basin. In the process, they conquered and absorbed the Chachapoyas, but the peace that followed was an uneasy one. The Chachapoyas rose in rebellion during the reign of Huayna Capac. In order to put down the rebellion and create a lasting peace, the Incas co-opted the Chachapoyas, integrating them into the political fabric of their society. Using a time-tested tool of empire, the Inca royal family distributed the Chachapoya population throughout Tawantinsuyu as *mitmaes*: soldier-settlers who now served the interests of their Inca lords. It was in this capacity that the Chachapoyas traveled more than a thousand miles from their ancestral homeland to settle in Cuzco. The Cañaris came to the city in more or less the same way. Half conquerors, half conquered, they fought first as partisans in the Inca civil wars before casting their lot with Pizarro. They fought in battle after battle, and in numbers far greater than the Spaniards themselves. In the hard-fought struggles between the Spanish and Manco Inca, the Cañaris served as a praetorian guard: elite troops who became a hallmark of the Andean Hispanic order, contributing to the empire as combat troops, urban security forces, and ritual honor guards. Some colonial-era accounts recall thousands of Cañaris and Chachapoyas guarding the Inca palaces in the years before the conquest. Fifty years after the Spanish conquest, the leaders of the Santa Ana community described themselves as the "guards of the justices of Cusco."[25]

The public events of the Santa Ana barrio were performances that high-lighted the residents' piety, loyalty, and history. They fit neatly with the feast-day culture of the early modern Catholic world. The rituals of Baroque Cathol-icism celebrated the display of effort, wealth, and beauty. Few places surpassed Cuzco as a venue for these events. In the seventeenth century, it was a city where one could commission processional sculptures, carriages, and clothing from the finest artists and artisans in the Americas. The events were commem-orated after the fact by Peru's greatest painters, those now widely referred to as the members of the Cuzco School. The surviving paintings—and there are many—suggest a beautiful symmetry between Spanish and indigenous social hierarchies: the viceregal officials march in gowns that bear the insignias of the Knights of Santiago and the Knights of Malta; indigenous leaders march in their own ceremonial garments, those of Carmenca in distinctive tunics, and those of the Inca ayllus in imperial regalia.

In one of the Santa Ana canvases, a life-sized sculpture of Saint Christopher (a figure associated with Columbus, Spanish maritime expeditions, and the missionary project) is conducted through the streets by an Inca nobleman in full regalia. The man wears a royal tunic and crown with a golden solar disk strung from his neck. Beneath his feet, a caption identifies this impressive fig-ure as don Carlos Guainacapac, the royal standard bearer for the crown.[26] In another canvas, the Inca standard bearer, similarly attired in crown and *uncu*, leads forward a parade float whose gilded columns support a sculpture of Saint Sebastian, pierced with arrows and bound to a tropical tree, the branches teem-ing with brightly feathered songbirds. The two paintings, observed together, seem to tell the story of the sixteenth century. The ancestral indigenous author-ities of the Andes welcomed the missionaries and conquerors. These Indians survived the ravages of European diseases under the protection of Saint Se-bastian, whose painful wounds symbolized plagues, and whose compassionate intercession was the best defense against them.

In many of these Corpus Christi paintings, we see not just the participants in the parades but also the spectators and bystanders. The official ranks of the processions are made up largely of Indian elites, but the margins of the paintings are packed with other figures. We see the balconies of Cuzco's af-fluent homes bedecked with fine cloth, and the doors flung open to reveal the well-dressed gentry. On the fringes of the street, and often conspicuous in the painted foreground, we see cuzqueños of other types: Africans with turbans, mestizos in fashionable cloaks, and drunken revelers of all castes. Some stand, hands clasped in poses of piety, others revel in the festive atmosphere, and a few stare straight toward the paintings' viewers, as though we too stand in the street, participating in the events of the day. This artwork was painted for the enjoyment of the urban Indians who commissioned it. It was also created as a visual argument that celebrated the presence of indigenous subpolities within the larger Spanish Empire.[27]

A Place at the Table: Confession and Community

Not all religious experiences took place in public view or with the noise and fanfare of Semana Santa and Corpus Christi. The quiet, intimate ritual of confession was at the heart of the Catholic experience, and it took place in the shaded privacy of the church interior. Yet the practices of confession also defined the Indian Christian's place within a city's multiethnic social hierarchy. To be a Catholic was to be the citizen of a parish. Sin, confession, penance, absolution, and communion are words that described in theological terms a social process by which the individual was first excluded *from* and then reunited *with* the community.[28] Since the parish (or the doctrina) was the most universally intelligible small political community in colonial Latin America, the process of excluding sinners from communion and then brokering their return to the Eucharistic table was, in effect, a procedure for describing and regulating spiritual citizenship.[29]

The contents of parishioners' confessions are lost to history. But clergymen wrote extensively about the experience of taking confessions in Latin American cities. Their written guides for training confessors describe the full range of ethnic communities that existed in urban parishes.[30] One of the striking features of early confession manuals is that they were so often written in the form of a script.[31] The authors provided general counsel to confessors accompanied by extensive examples of typical confessional dialogue for different groups of penitents, as defined by ethnicity, gender, class, and profession. They trained priests to take confessions by improvising on the basis of the models. The manuals, then, offer us a kind of social taxonomy.[32] And the changing contents of confession manuals over time record the changing status of urban Indians as seen through the eyes of priests—men who knew the public and private lives of their fellow urbanites better than anyone.[33]

FIGURE 15 A holy man gives his belt to a pregnant woman. From Mateo Ximénez's *Colección de estampas* [...] (Rome: Pedro Bombelli, 1789). Courtesy of the John Carter Brown Library, Brown University.

The first confession guides for Latin America were focused on the Indian population and on the project of conversion. Often bilingual or trilingual, these manuals sought to translate Christian beliefs across languages and cultures. They also reflected the differences between the concerns of missionary confessors in the New World and those on the other side of the Atlantic. European priests of the sixteenth century were deeply concerned with Protestant heresies, while their contemporaries in the Americas were concerned with instructing and persuading penitents to avoid pre-Christian religious practices. In early New Spain, the clergy feared indigenous religious revival above all else, and they consequently organized the confession manuals around the distinctly different spiritual dangers faced by Indians and Spaniards.[34]

In 1632, don Bartolomé de Alva, a mestizo priest of elite Nahua ancestry (and brother of the more famous Fernando Ixtlilxochitl) wrote two guides to confession in parallel Latin, Spanish, and Nahuatl scripts. These pages are a snapshot of how the church understood Mexico's multiethnic society after a century of missionary efforts.[35] The *Confesionario mayor* divides colonial society into Spanish and Indian spheres, then further divides the Indian community by gender, station, and calling. The guide's model dialogue opens with the expected question: "How long has it been since your last confession?" But the second and third questions are different from those that might be heard in a modern confessional. They are attempts by the cleric to place the penitent in a social category that will shape the rest of the inquiry. He asks: "What is your job? How do you make your living?" The manual furnishes the likely possibilities: "I am a governor, I am a councilman, etc. / I am a painter, a carpenter, a stone mason, I work the land, etc." The next strand of questioning addresses gender and marital status, soliciting answers like "I am married / I am a widow / I am single / I am a maiden." Finally, the questioner tries to determine the penitent's education in the faith: "Do you know spiritual things? The four [prayers] and [14] articles of faith?"[36]

The manuals indicate a clear expectation that people of the same social type would be guilty of the same transgressions. While the 1634 manual makes quick work of sins like murder and theft, offering little in the way of exemplary dialogue, its attention to sexual transgressions and pagan religious practice is meticulous. The voice of the priest hammers away relentlessly at idolatrous practices. In one such passage, it warns:

> Your neighbors the Spaniards who greatly exceed you in spiritual and earthly goods, whom none of you equal, do they walk around warming idols, dolls and little creatures . . . ? Do you believe that they [the *ahuaques*] come and go from the mountain Tlaloc and from other high and lofty mountains; [that] when the rainy season begins they become overcast and touch the clouds, and so by the heat of the sun and the moisture of the earth vaporize and condense into clouds and water, etc.? And are you very convinced that this does not happen except through ahuaques, and that they produce the rain storms?[37]

This exhaustive (and exhausting) line of questioning forces the Indian listener to survive a rather precise litmus test for sin and heterodoxy. The voice of the priest is that of both inquisitor and pedant. It reflects an obsession with rooting out crypto-paganism and with educating imperfect Christians into orthodox ones.

Early on, the missionary church in Mexico had a conflicting set of attitudes toward its new Indian members. As John Leddy Phelan famously pointed out, early Franciscans often saw a special role for Indians in the unfolding of Christian history and in the final conversion of the earth's people. Sixteenth-century missionaries like Gerónimo de Mendieta found Indians especially receptive to the divine word.[38] And yet, the psychology at work in the seventeenth-century *Confesionario* and in a later eighteenth-century confessional, *Advertencias para los nuevos confesores*, seems closer to Inga Clendinnen's portrait of Diego de Landa than to Phelan's portrait of Mendieta.[39] Landa was a man desperate to save the souls of his Indian charges; but he was also obsessed with the idea that their transgressions were shaped by the wiles of Satan, and he expected that their sins would conform to his expectations about idolatry and blasphemy. In Landa's thinking, Indians had a kind of tragic flaw that dictated a particular script of transgression and redemption.[40] Colonial confessional manuals reflect the same worldview. Like early works of criminology, the manuals posit something like a "criminal type." Once the type is identified, the moral failings of the penitent are easily guessed.[41]

The methods of confessional interrogation employed by Mexico's colonial church were rooted in its early strategies for winning converts and a rooting out crypto-paganism. Over time, clergymen's attitudes toward Indian converts were transposed onto a wide variety of other groups whom the church regarded with concern or distrust. The persistent interrogation modeled in *Advertencias para los nuevos confesores* seems less about determining the truth than about forcing the penitent to disclose a truth already known by the questioner. In this way, it resembles the investigations of Diego de Landa or those of the Holy Office of the Inquisition. The manual seems to have been written for use in Valladolid (today's Morelia), and it helps to fill in the details of this late colonial milieu. Each social type is expected to manifest a predictable moral flaw and to present distinct challenges in the course of questioning: merchants tend to avarice, servants to theft, mulattos to drunkenness and violence, farm workers to sloth; teenagers have wandering wits, whereas Indians stumble over language and are prone to dishonesty. The manual's sample dialogues present a cultural taxonomy, a pedagogy for spiritual education, and an instrument for social control in a highly diverse population.[42]

In both confession manuals (*Advertencias* and *Confesionario*) there is an assumption that penitents will misunderstand questions or dissemble in predictable ways. The seventeenth-century manual cautions that Indians, when asked how many times they have engaged in a sexual sin, always answer "two or three times" even if they have engaged in the sin persistently for years. This type of answer seems an intentional obfuscation, but the manual attributes other misleading answers to the Indians' poor command of language or muddled thinking. In the eighteenth-century guide, readers are cautioned that Indian penitents are unable to follow a long chain of questions. If one asks three questions in a row, the Indian is apt to answer only the last one. While the two guides have similar expectations about Indian penitents, the eighteenth-century guide dwells on the limitations of other social groups as well. The section on "Gente ruda e ignorante," includes some of the same instructions as those given for Indians: "With gente ruda, one should not ask them questions that have two or three clauses; because either they will not respond, or respond only to the last clause."[43]

Later we learn what sorts of people fall into the category of gente ruda: "This class includes the teenagers, Indians, many gente ruin, and various others known for their little talent, crude ingenuity, and without necessary education."[44] The instructions for dealing with these groups suggest using simple language, presenting multiple iterations of the same idea, and using devotional images to communicate theological concepts to the unlettered. Clearly, the broad distinction between Indians and Spaniards was less important to the author than the distinction between the more and less enlightened members of each caste community.[45]

In the century and a half that separates the two manuals, there was a striking change in clerical writers' understandings of the social origins of confusion and dishonesty. Perhaps the most detailed discussion of the topic in Advertencias occurs in the section on "gente ruin," or vile people. This much maligned group included "peddlers, mulattos, blacks, porridge eaters, millworkers, lazy people of bad upbringing, vagrants, lepers, and the despicable."[46] This is an interesting set of social descriptors that mixes traits of ethnicity, class, and calling. We are told that the members of this heterogeneous and benighted group tell stories like those of blind men and rarely confess. The line of questioning for such people features a strong attention to drinking, fighting, and wife beating, and it requires the confessor to acquire a specialized pornographic lexicon for discussions of sexual vice. Notably, the first section on "gente ruin" does not address itself to Indians, though a subsequent passage gives instructions for speaking to "gente ruin and also to the Indians."[47] Like early missionary explanations of Indian transgression, the Advertencias document at times presents a sympathetic attitude toward the innocent transgressions of the uneducated and at other times takes a hard line with respect to their moral defects.

The changes to urban demography in the eighteenth century required a general reorganization of clerical notions of social hierarchy. By the 1790s, a place like Valladolid was no longer intelligible merely as a point of contact between the European and Indian worlds—the two republics still existed on paper, but they were less and less real in daily practice. The city was thronged with people of all shades and extractions. The clergy were fully aware of this new reality; and yet their confessional practices remained marked by habits acquired in the long colonial history of separate Spanish and Indian republics.[48]

The contents of the 1792 manual suggest that very old habits and attitudes for dealing with Indian penitents were now transposed on new social groups. The 1790s was a time when education, literacy, and class were overtaking language and caste as the principal markers of social status. Whereas the 1632 *Confesionario* struggled to reach out across the cultural gap that separated Spaniards from Indians, the 1792 *Advertencias para los nuevos confesores* struggled to reach out across the gulf that divided the respectable classes of late colonial Mexican cities from the much larger and more ethnically complex underclass.

It was more in urban life than in any other realm of colonial experience that the Iberian model differed from that of the English and French. Whenever possible, Spain's colonial capitals were built on the foundations of preconquest cities; and it was in these cities that the interests of European and indigenous elites were most carefully negotiated. Client states of various kinds existed throughout the Western Hemisphere, but the notion of a city as a planned community with clearly defined spaces and parallel institutions for Indians and Europeans was a special trait of Habsburg administration rooted both in Iberian history and in the history of Mexica and Inca practices of conquest, clientage, and colonization. The Spanish colonial city was organized by a fully elaborated legal and political system for the two republics. Both were supported by religious organizations that likewise reflected the theory of parallel Indian and Spanish communities. Early colonial cities were largely indigenous by population, and the colonizers' vision of the Spanish republic was originally more aspirational than substantive. Over time, however, the cities changed, and power shifted increasingly into the hands of the growing population of creoles. And yet, by the time that independence movements swept through the Americas, even this state of affairs had come to an end. The political system of the two republics was based on a set of assumptions about demography, culture, and residence patterns that was no longer true. While Spaniards and Indians fought to defend the rules of the old republics—especially the Indian elites who benefitted from them most—it was increasingly clear that the city was turning into something different: a competitive and dynamic environment in which new wealth and power could be leveraged against the old rules of ethnicity and birth.

CHAPTER SEVEN

Captains, Conquerors, and New Frontiers

Two Conquests of Florida

In the years following the War of 1812, it seems that Florida was on everyone's mind. It was a strange, liminal space: a final retreat for Creeks and Seminoles, a sanctuary for escaped slaves, a lawless borderland for arms dealers and rum runners, and a contested territory for the English, the Spanish, and the emerging United States. It was a time when claims and counterclaims about the nature and character of Indian political life were hotly debated and constantly modified to suit changing political circumstances and material interests. For Anglo-Americans, Florida is remembered in these years as a new frontier, and as the site of Andrew Jackson's reckless and unsanctioned invasion of 1818. Jackson, then a major general, was deployed to the area ostensibly to defend Anglo-Americans from attacks by the Seminoles, who routinely moved back and forth across the border and refused to heed the authority of colonial governments. Though the boundary appeared clear on US and Spanish maps of the time, the cartographers' line was actually of recent and dubious provenance from the perspective of most of the region's inhabitants. If the Seminoles ignored the border, it was partly because they had no hand in drawing it. In the end, Jackson's campaign would involve not just attacks on the Seminoles but also the conquest of Spanish towns, the occupation of Pensacola, and the negotiation of a settlement with Spain that paved the way for the annexation of Florida as a new US state.

Andrew Jackson was only slightly more compliant with orders from Washington than the Seminoles were. He invaded Florida first and asked permission afterward. Upon his return, Jackson had a tough political case to make. He had attacked a neighboring country in peacetime without authorization from his own government. In the months that followed, the retroactive political logic went something like this: Spain, lacking effective control over Florida, was permitting Seminole bandits to attack the US with impunity; the only way for America to protect its "civilized" communities was to subdue the stateless Indian enemies operating within Spanish territory. The US attack on Florida infuriated the Spanish government, but it was welcome news to some of the Lower Creeks who inhabited adjacent territory and had allied themselves to the US against the British in the War of 1812.

During the invasion of Spanish Florida, supreme military authority over Lower Creek forces was in the hands of William McIntosh. McIntosh (whose birth name was Taskanugi Hatke) had long been an influential figure in Creek politics and business; he also held the rank of brigadier general in the US Army and commanded more than a thousand troops. He was a hard man, and one experienced at seizing power and influence in ambiguous cultural spaces. McIntosh's father was a Scottish merchant; his mother was a Creek and a high-born member of the politically influential Wind Clan. McIntosh himself was eager to lay claim to the cultural capital that he inherited from both sides of his family. He had three wives, many children, and excellent connections—all of which contributed to his success in negotiating alliances among the kinship-based political groups in the region. He executed complex agreements among the members of the Lower Creek Confederacy and also represented them in negotiations with Thomas Jefferson. McIntosh held plantation lands worked by numerous African slaves, and he controlled two important points of transit and transshipment as a merchant and ferry operator. For him, prosperity and security demanded constant vigilance with respect to Creek politics, intra-Indian diplomacy, and negotiations with European powers.[1]

Once back in the US, Andrew Jackson had to narrate the story of his Florida invasion very artfully in order to justify his actions. Many American statesman were skeptical of his one-man foreign policy, but Jackson ultimately prevailed in domestic politics just as he had on the battlefield. His occupation of Spanish territory created facts on the ground that forced the hands of diplomats and legislators. In 1821, the terms of the resulting Adams-Onís Treaty went into effect, and three centuries of tenuous Spanish rule in Florida came to an end. Jackson is rightly criticized for his long career of mistreating Native America. And yet, the alliances that won this undeclared war in Florida demonstrate just how varied his relationships with Indian nations were. McIntosh (a brigadier general from the Lower Creek nation) and Jackson (a major general from Tennessee) defeated a force of Seminoles, occupied Spanish towns, and conquered a Spanish territory. For Anglo-America, this war is part of a larger story of advancing frontiers. The old patriotic version of the narrative is familiar: soldiers and statesmen excused the conquest of Indian lands by arguing that they were spreading civilization, agriculture, literacy, and Christianity. Of course, this set of justifications was in no way unique to Anglo-Americans. All of these explanations for conquest had been offered by the Spanish for centuries. In fact, the United States was so late to this game that any argument presenting North American frontiers as virgin lands appears ridiculous in retrospect.

The first European invasion of Florida took place in 1539, three centuries before Andrew Jackson's impetuous raid. The most widely read early history of the event was first published in 1605 and written not by a Spaniard, or even by a participant, but by the eminently civilized, surpassingly literate, and enthusiastically Christian Inca nobleman Garcilaso de la Vega. Who better to tell the story of this New World conquest than a scholar whose father was among Peru's Spanish conquerors, and whose mother was among the conquered? Garcilaso was a multifaceted writer. Depending on the moment, he wrote in the style of a historian, a journalist, or an ethnographer. Half a century after De Soto's landing in Florida, Garcilaso pieced together disparate scraps of information about the invasion: material from official histories, an account by the dimly known "Fidalgo de Elvas," and his own conversations with an elderly "noble Spaniard" who goes unnamed in the text but is identifiable to historians as Gonzalo Silvestre, a contemporary of Garcilaso's father and an officer in the expedition.[2]

One can easily imagine the sorts of conversations that took place between Garcilaso and the aged Silvestre. One man was an Inca-Castilian nobleman, the other a widely traveled Spanish officer; both were veterans of imperial wars, Silvestre having fought in the conquests of Peru and Florida, and Garcilaso having served in wars against the Muslim rebels of the Alpujarras Revolt in the South of Spain. Garcilaso himself was no longer a young man when he composed his chronicle of the Florida expedition, and the Americas had already changed radically from the time of his birth. It was an era when the past was fading swiftly from collective memory. Fortunately, Garcilaso's efforts as a scholar of North and South America preserved two gifts for readers of later generations: knowledge about the preconquest Americas, and a complex, multicultural account of the conquest itself.

Garcilaso's monumental work on the Florida expedition is presented in six books. It opens with a dedication to the Duke of Braganza, a nod to Silvestre, and an invocation of Herodotus: "Conversing over a long period of time and in different places with a great and noble friend of mine, who accompanied this expedition to Florida, and hearing him recount the numerous very illustrious deeds that both the Spaniards and Indians performed in the process of the conquest, I became convinced that when such heroic actions as these had been performed in this world, it was unworthy and regrettable that they should remain in perpetual oblivion." The entire book is composed in the most elegant prose. Garcilaso was already a respected author and widely known for his translation of León Hebreo's *Dialoghi d'amore*. Thus, when he concluded his preface by asking to be "pardoned for its errors" because "Indians are a people who are ignorant and uninstructed in the arts and sciences," he did so not just with false modesty but also with intentional irony.[3]

Garcilaso's was not the first written narrative of the invasion of Florida, but it was the best. Like Alonso de Ercilla, who in the 1550s transformed South America's inconclusive frontier conflicts into the epic *Araucana*, Garcilaso transformed the fragmented record of scant Spanish successes and great suffering into a Florida epic—not just a simple report of events but a story of tragedy and perseverance on the scale of Xenophon's *Anabasis*. He described the pageantry of De Soto's armada of 1538 as it embarked from Spain through the port of Sanlúcar de Barrameda, sailing first for Cuba—where the thirty ships and nine hundred men were joined by additional soldiers, fortune hunters, and opportunists—and then onward to the mainland. They reached the shores of Florida, but soon the great expedition began to unravel one thread at a time. Garcilaso's story fills the reader with mounting dread. Like Thucydides's account of the "ill-fated Sicilian expedition," dreams of vast conquests and plunder dissolve before the reader's eyes into a seemingly endless succession of forays and flights without tangible gains. The Europeans were for a time guests of the exotic Lady of Cofachiqui, and captors of the Curaca Tascaluza, but they soon found themselves confused, betrayed, and surrounded by a population that was enraged by their abuses. The would-be conquerors fought an increasingly desperate rearguard action through the forests and hill country back to the Gulf Coast. With all hope of victory lost, the survivors

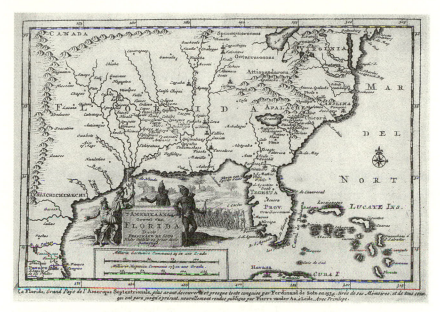

FIGURE 16 Florida in the age of De Soto. Engraved map in Garcilaso de la Vega's *Histoire de la conquete de la Floride* (Leiden: Chez Pierre van der Aa, 1731). Courtesy of the John Carter Brown Library, Brown University.

built hastily improvised ships that would carry them on a fifty-five-day journey to the mouth of the Pánuco River, the northernmost outpost of the Spanish mainland. Remnants of the original force returned to safety with nothing to show for all their efforts. Their commander, Hernando de Soto, who died of fever in 1542, never set foot on Spanish territory again.

Despite Garcilaso's tantalizing accounts of rich lands, gold, and populous Apalachee towns, the Spanish survivors returned to New Spain more refugees than conquistadors. Why, we might ask, did he devote hundreds of pages to this tale of epic failure? It seems that Garcilaso was as much a moralist and literary writer as a chronicler. Like Herodotus, who sought to preserve "great and marvelous deeds—some displayed by Greeks, and some by barbarians," Garcilaso was keen to present history as a study of human traits and capacities, not just a record of events. In his own words, he was recording the "numerous very illustrious deeds that both Spaniards and Indians performed in the process of the conquest," saving their memory "from perpetual oblivion." Of course, Garcilaso was especially qualified to view this tale from both sides. He tells his readers that he is "under obligation to two races" since he is "the son of a Spanish father and an Indian mother." Scattering references to his own family throughout the book, Garcilaso reminds us that *La Florida* belongs to a much larger hemispheric story of conquest and cultural synthesis, and that his scholarship (as well as his own family) is a marriage of cultures and continents.[4]

La Florida describes an epic war between Spaniards and Indians as told by an author who belonged to both Atlantic communities. Along with the larger-than-life deeds of conquerors and Apalachees, Garcilaso's writing shows us the individuals who, at the ground level, facilitated the synthesis of cultures. He emphasizes the role of indigenous guides and translators, considering their work a hopeful sign of things to come. Early in the expedition, the invaders relied heavily on the help of an Indian whom they called Pedro. After describing Pedro's service to the expedition and his struggle to find religious truth among the voices of evangelists and demons, Garcilaso concludes: "By what we have related concerning the Indian Pedro, one can see how easy it was to convert these Indians and all of the others of the New World to the Catholic Faith, and I as a native of Peru and an eyewitness of the Indians of that land venture to remark that just Pedro's preaching of what he had seen would have been sufficient to convert all of the people of this province and to make them ask as he did for baptism."[5]

La Florida is both a literary tragedy and tribute to the heroism of Indians and Spaniards, but it is also a call for further exploration and settlement in North America. It presents the region as ripe for conquest, rich in material resources, and peopled by Indians yearning for spiritual salvation. The book is a cautionary tale of human vices and frailties—one that reflects poorly on both the Spaniards and the indigenous Floridians. There is real ambivalence in this text. Garcilaso cheers on the efforts of conquest and conversion; and yet he laments the unnecessary suffering of the Apalachees and describes them as part of a hemispheric human community that includes Mesoamericans and Andeans like himself. Again and again, he reminds the reader that he too is an Indian. In this respect, *La Florida* embodies an emerging notion among indigenous intellectuals that a shared identity connected all native New World peoples, no matter how geographically distant or how distinct from each other in language and culture.

Indian and Mestizo Conquistadors on Mexico's Frontiers

While Garcilaso de la Vega was crafting his vision of multi-ethnic empire for a rarified transatlantic readership, other indigenous leaders were making it a reality through warfare, commerce, and settlement.[6] We need look no farther than New Spain's northern frontier to see this process of state formation in action during the same years. In the late sixteenth century, it was hard for viceregal Mexico to accomplish much of anything in the North without the help of men like Miguel Caldera. From his estate of Monte Caldera on the slopes above San Luis Potosí, Caldera held sway over a vast region of northern settlements as the *justicia mayor de la paz Chichimeca*, the man who concluded alliances, resolved disputes, and distributed resources to a multitude of Indian communities in a region that was only then, for the first time, becoming a part of the Spanish Empire. Caldera was a soldier, a diplomat, and a businessman. The documents of the day identify him as a "mestizo chichimec," which made him unlike the other men of mixed ancestry who wielded great power in the colonial order. Most of the influential cultural intermediaries of the sixteenth century in Mexico and Peru shared the same background: they were the children or grandchildren of conquerors from Spain and noblewomen from preconquest empires. In New Spain the sons and grandsons from the leading lineages of Tlaxcala, Texcoco, and Tenochtitlan remained major players in the viceroyalty's economic, political, and intellectual life. But Miguel Caldera was different. His father, Pedro Caldera, was a Spanish soldier of some means and reputation, but he was not among the rich and famous conquistadors who established great houses in Mexico. His mother, whose identity remains largely unknown, was an Indian woman not from the palaces of the Valley of Mexico but from the chaotic frontier region around Zacatecas. She was probably Guachichil, which meant that Caldera's maternal line was not among the Indian conquistadors but rather among the humbler northern nations regarded by Mexicas and Spaniards alike (with no small amount of condescension) as Chichimecs.[7]

Raised on the frontier and educated by the Franciscan friars of Zacatecas, Caldera witnessed and shaped the early years of Spanish colonial expansion into the region of silver mines and cattle ranches that would become an economic engine for the viceroyalty. Just as Cortés's early conquest of central Mexico had demanded a series of shrewd alliances with native Nahua leaders, the conquest and settlement in the North required intricate diplomatic connections joining Spaniards to Nahuas and Nahuas to Chichimecs. A handful of people had the ability to engineer these kinds of alliances, and Caldera was one of them.

At the time of Miguel Caldera's birth, Spain was just beginning to subdue and colonize the North. All such efforts were premised on the idea that the region's indigenous inhabitants could be governed from Guadalajara and unified under the jurisdiction of New Galicia. Nuño de Guzmán's brutal early conquests were accompanied by widespread slave raiding, triggering spasms of resistance. In the 1540s, numerous northern nations rose against the Spanish and their Nahua allies in what came to be known as the Mixtón War, a conflict named for the great fortress of the Cazcanes on the Santiago River. The war was hard fought and the subsequent peace uncertain. For the Spanish, the price of the conquest was increasingly difficult to justify. This all changed in 1548 with discovery of silver at Zacatecas. The initial discovery was soon followed by others at Guanajuato and San Miguel. Overnight, the northern frontier, once a peripheral concern for the viceroyalty, became a top economic and military priority. A steady stream of people, livestock, and supplies—not to mention silver—now moved on the roads between Zacatecas and Mexico City, provoking near continuous raids from the local Indian populations. Meanwhile, the labor demands of the mining economy created markets hungry for new slaves and wage laborers. Consequently, both Spanish travelers and northern Indians were subject to constant attack. Persistent low-level violence soon snowballed into the vast forty-year conflict known as the Chichimec War.[8]

Miguel Caldera entered into the fray as a young man in the early 1570s. His personal experience and cultural expertise made him a natural broker between Spanish soldiers, "civilized" Indians, missionaries, and the region's Zacatecos and Guachichiles. He lived and worked in a time when punitive raids could earn rich rewards for the soldiers. The invaders seized local Indians, charged them with the crime of rebellion—a thin legal fiction—and by this judicial mechanism transformed captives into chattel. In the 1580s, European epidemic diseases once again swept through the region, worsening conditions of life in an area already ravaged by decades of intra-Indian disputes, Spanish slave raiding, and counterattacks on colonial outposts. As the conflict escalated, Spanish jurists and churchmen agonized over the enormous human cost of the conflict, asking whether these condition of seemingly endless violence and judicial servitude could possibly meet the legal requirements of "just war." Northern commanders were often criticized for their cruelty during these campaigns of "fire and blood," but in the end, the audiencia and viceroys determined that the violence was necessary and legitimate.

Throughout the 1570s and 1580s, Miguel Caldera was one of the key leaders of the frontier state, waging war, building alliances, negotiating peace agreements, and founding new settler communities. With the rank of lieutenant general, he commanded a body of troops that included Nahuas and Europeans, as well as allied Chichimec auxiliaries. The Mixtón War had taught viceregal forces that over time northern enemies could be co-opted into the colonial establishment, forming a bulwark against hostile groups on the outside. The Cazcanes, who had been formidable enemies during the days of Miguel Caldera's father, now became valuable soldiers for the colonial state. Both diplomacy and field commands required linguistic and cultural expertise, and in these respects Caldera had an ace up his sleeve: he was deeply familiar with the cultural practices of the region, and he was probably a native speaker of the Guachichil language. His efforts along with those of contemporary military commander Francisco Urdiñola helped to transform the Guachichiles from enemies into friends of the colonial state, paving the way for a new era of multiethnic settlement in the North.

In the late sixteenth century, the fringes of New Spain were loosely governed, to say the least. In this unstable environment, a man like Miguel Caldera could become not just an agent of royal policy but its author. When the worst of the Chichimec wars subsided, it was partly because his carefully wrought program of regional diplomacy was so successful. Early in 1590, having already concluded a complex series of verbal agreements with northern Indian leaders, Caldera laid out a blueprint for peace and sought formal approval for his plan from the viceroyalty. Only a handful of people could expect access to the viceroy of New Spain, but Miguel Caldera was one of them. Early in 1590, Caldera and the selected representatives of several northern nations followed the long route from Zacatecas to the capital in order to meet with Viceroy Luis de Velasco II. It was an unusual pairing of statesmen that sat down to the table that day in March of 1590: on one side was Luis de Velasco, viceroy, son of a celebrated viceroy, and member of King Phillip II's inner circle; on the other was Miguel Caldera, a mestizo Guachichil who had begun his career with little more than arms and mount. Velasco had only been in New Spain a short time, but in Miguel Caldera he had already found a seasoned expert to advise him on northern affairs. Caldera left this meeting with new resources, political support, and broad authority to engage in regional diplomacy as the newly titled "general protector and defender of all the Chichimeca Indians."[9]

The truth was that for all the pomp and pageantry of the viceregal court, its powers diminished sharply with distance. For the king and viceroy, a settled frontier with productive mines, safe roads, and secure revenues was an urgent objective. But it was clear to all concerned that the Spanish populace—small in numbers, concentrated in a few urban centers, and incapable of sustaining a large standing military force—was far from ready to conquer, occupy, and develop the lands and resources of the North. If the colonial state was to expand and prosper, the main engine of northern settlement would have to be the king's indigenous subjects. It was a project so complex as to require a tripartite political pact among the empire's Spaniards, its traditional allies from the Nahua heartland, and new leaders in the North. The viceroy could deliver one part of the bargain; men like Miguel Caldera and Tlaxcala's Diego Muñoz Camargo would deliver the rest.

By the 1580s, co-colonization by the Spanish and their Indian allies was already a time-honored practice. And though Nahua, Otomi, and Maya vassals of all stripes had participated in Spanish conquests to the north and south of New Spain since the 1520s, no group had been so central to Spanish designs as the Tlaxcalans.[10] Given this history, Caldera and Velasco could expect valuable Tlaxcalan assistance, but their hopes had to be tempered with realism. Decades of European diseases had weakened Tlaxcalan society; and year-by-year changes in demography had shifted political and economic power in favor of the Spanish. Tlaxcala was no longer the great power that it had been at the beginning of the sixteenth century, but it was still a force to be reckoned with. In the 1560s, Velasco's father, Viceroy Luis Velasco I, had lobbied the Tlaxcalans to launch a major settlement of the North, but they rejected the offer. Now the younger Velasco made a second bid for their support.

His timing was fortunate. One of the leading cultural figures in Tlaxcala was Diego Muñoz, a man perfectly situated to broker deals between the Indian republic and the viceroyalty. Like Miguel Caldera, Muñoz was the son of a cross-cultural union.[11] His Spanish father and Tlaxcalan mother brought Muñoz into the world at a moment when his talents would be much in demand. He became a great scholar, and in 1585 he completed his magisterial history of Tlaxcala, a text that chronicled his people's preconquest glories and their faithful service to the young Spanish Empire. The time was ripe for the Tlaxcalans, whose fortunes had been waning, to reassert themselves as New Spain's most indispensable allies—and that is precisely what they did. Following a series of agreements with the crown, the Indian republic launched an ambitious and systematic colonization of the North. By 1591, both Diego Muñoz Camargo and Miguel Caldera were hard at work on the northern frontier, helping to construct a new social order for New Spain. Negotiating the particulars with the Tlaxcalan cabildo took some time. The Tlaxcalans were capable of undertaking the project that the viceroy dreamed of, and they were willing to do so, but their participation would come at a price: they demanded land grants, supplies, arms, mounts, and special political and legal status for their descendants in perpetuity. More than a year after Velasco's meeting with Caldera, the viceroy had agreed to the proposal, and the plan was underway.[12]

In June 1591, Viceroy Velasco appeared before a crowd of more than a thousand Tlaxcalan colonists who had assembled themselves, fully equipped and ready, in a great caravan poised to depart on their northward journey. The project was organized around the efforts of two hundred Tlaxcalan families. Together they set out along the royal road, then fanned out in smaller groups to establish new settlements. The colonies would be part village, part garrison, and part cultural and religious mission—all spread out across hundreds of miles of the Gran Chichimeca. Miguel Caldera and Diego Muñoz Camargo appear to have exercised broad influence over this program of settlement, and they worked closely with each other to construct one colony in particular: San Miguel de Mexquitic de la Nueva Tlaxcala. The composition of the leadership team that governed this town says much about the alliances that produced the colonial order in the North. Diego Muñoz Camargo spoke for the Tlaxcalan settlers from Tepeticpac, who set to work surveying the home sites and fields. Miguel Caldera, as royal protector of Indians, brokered a joint settlement agreement with the area's Guachichiles; Juan Tenzo spoke for the Guachichiles themselves. At the founding ceremonies, skilled interpreters translated the words of these leaders for all to hear. San Miguel de Mexquitic was a complex multiethnic settlement, and it came into being through the efforts of two mestizo leaders who employed a wealth of experience and social capital.[13]

Miguel Caldera was richly rewarded for his successes. As provisioner for the colonists, he controlled the flow of goods and money in and out of the region; and as the community's justicia mayor, he held his thumb on the scales of justice. The security of Mexquitic required continuous diplomatic engagement with the mobile Indian bands in the area. Their ambiguous relationship to the colonial state constituted a threat and an opportunity. Caldera—with his mastery of military force, negotiation, and persuasion—prospered in this environment. He soon owned a mine, cattle herds, ranches, and the title to his own settlement. In time, Mexquitic would be overshadowed by the great mining city of San Luis Potosí that sprang from its roots, but the influence of the Tlaxcalan colony that Muñoz Camargo and Caldera designed would persist long beyond their days.[14] This story of Spanish-indigenous co-colonization is not unique to northern New Spain. Similar partnerships were formed for the colonization of Central America with lasting cultural and political effects.

Commemorating Conquest

Memories of America's early colonial conquests have been told and retold, erased, altered, and augmented through the centuries. Throughout Latin America, these foundational stories are often expressed through dance. Every December in the Honduran community of Gracias a Dios, a beloved sculpture of Santa Lucía comes out through the church doors to meet her public; and every summer, in the northern Mexican town of Bustamante, the Lord of Tlaxcala emerges from his church and into the adoring crowds on the surrounding streets. These are small towns whose streets are often empty, but on the annual days of celebration when venerated images are carried on the shoulders of the faithful, the streets are full. The distance between the two sites stretches more than a thousand miles from Honduras in the south to the US Mexican borderlands in the north—but the histories of these two communities are closely linked. Both were once frontier towns that guarded the boundaries between the colonial Ibero-Indian empire and the unincorporated peoples beyond them.[15]

Santa Lucía's home is the Mexicapa barrio of Gracias a Dios. There her annual celebration includes an elaborately staged *guancasco*—a dance that re-enacts the history of Spanish conquest and Christian conversion. Santa Lucía goes forth into the streets, protected by the members of a local religious brotherhood. There she witnesses the confrontation between Indians and Spaniards and gives her blessing to the pact between Europeans and Mexicans to rule over Central America. The musicians' songs narrate the arrival of the Mejicanos. The cast of performers includes actors dressed as sixteenth-century Spanish and Indian conquerors, accompanied by their modern progeny: the current alcalde and mayordomo, who flank the saint and are followed by the townspeople. The lengthy festival includes interactions between European, African, and Indian characters, as well as an encounter between Santa Lucía and San Sebastián, the patron of a neighboring community. This guancasco is a late echo of the early compact between the Spanish crown and its Indian allies; but it is merely one of many such performances that commemorate early co-conquests in Latin America.[16] Far to the north near today's us-Mexico border, the Lord of Tlaxcala is carried each year through the streets of Bustamante Nuevo León by an equally devoted crowd. In popular memory, this figure of Christ has defended the town from catastrophe for more than three centuries. The object itself is an artifact from the earliest days of Hispano-Nahua settlement: a devotional image carried to the North in the seventeenth century by one of the town's Tlaxcalan founders.[17]

Correlating these mythic reenactments with the chronology and geography of documentary history is difficult, and the story of Santa Lucía and Mexicapa is even harder to follow than that of the Lord of Tlaxcala. There are, in fact, two Mexicapas in the region, one a largely forgotten barrio of Comayagua, the other a still thriving barrio of the smaller city of Gracias. To further complicate matters, there are also two celebrated sculptures of Santa Lucía: the seventeenth-century image from Mexicapa de Gracias, and a mid-sixteenth-century one in Comayagua. The older sculpture once stood in Comayagua's Iglesia de Santa Lucía de Jeto in a chapel beside an open-air church for Indian worshippers. When fire destroyed the church, the precious sculpture was removed to the Iglesia de la Caridad, where she remains today. The Jeto community (now called Suyapa) was originally inhabited by Indians subjected to encomienda, but it was soon fused with Spanish and Indian communities, including Mexicapa, whose inhabitants claimed a very different set of political and economic privileges.[18] The stories of the two Mexicapas and the two Santa Lucías are at times impossible to disentangle in the documentary record. It is clear from both, however, that the history of central Honduras is marked in a variety of ways by indigenous conquerors from Mexico whose political status was staked on their preservation and elaboration of a historical conquest narrative.

The two festivals are in fact part of the same deep story of Nahua conquests.

Though historic reenactments featuring patron saints, processions, mystery plays, and historic dances of all kinds are commonplace throughout Latin America, these two celebrations in Bustamante and Mexicapa mark a specific and distinctive shared heritage.[19] A century after the first colonial settlements in Honduras, both Spanish and Indian conquerors were keen to retain the spoils of victory. The conquest of Central America won both land and local Indian labor for the crown's Mexica, Tlaxcalan, Otomi, Mixtec, and Zapotec allies. The labor and wealth exacted from the locals was heavy, and all the more so over time as the population collapsed under the pressure of disease, warfare, and material deprivation.[20] The town of San Miguel de Aguayo (known today as Bustamante) was founded more than a century after Mexicapa. Both communities were once on the extreme periphery of a hub-and-spoke network of colonies built by Spain's central Mexican allies. Both were Indian republics that governed themselves under imperial charters, and both struggled over time to preserve their legal status as autonomous municipalities. The two stories, taken together, reveal a substructure of colonial conquest and government that accounts for much of the Spanish New World's cultural geography and multiethnic political system.[21]

The tale begins in the chaotic conditions that followed the collapse of Tenochtitlan. From 1519 to 1521, both the Tenochcas' long-term enemies and their erstwhile friends had seized upon the Spanish invasion as an opportunity to turn against the imperial capital. Foremost among the Spanish allies was Tlaxcala, whose soldiers (probably numbering in the tens of thousands) were decisive in the battles for control of the Valley of Mexico. While Hernán Cortés consolidated his position in central Mexico, Pedro de Alvarado turned toward the Maya South, bringing with him an army that included a variety of Nahuatl-speaking allies: Cholulans and Tlaxcalans as well as new Mexica forces who offered their services in the aftermath of defeat. In this period of rapidly changing diplomacy and patronage, the conflicts among Maya states created an opening for Spanish intervention far to the south in Chiapas and Guatemala. In 1524, Pedro de Alvarado's irregular army of Spaniards and Nahuas began the conquest of Guatemala, now accompanied by Kaqchikel Mayas who leveraged a Spanish alliance against their Quiché neighbors. Santiago de Guatemala became the main hub for regional colonization in Central America—though a somewhat tenuous one.[22] For the Spanish, nearby Honduras remained for years a vexing zone of indigenous resistance. In the 1530s, European and Indian forces under the authority of Francisco de Montejo built the regional capital of Comayagua and its affiliated Indian republic of Mexicapa during their struggles against the powerful indigenous leader Lempira (now mythologized as a great national hero in Honduras). In the years that followed, Mexicapa's Nahua colonists, living first in a vulnerable garrison camp, then in a proper town, and ultimately in the two communities of the same name, continued to assert their distinctive conqueror privileges.[23]

The early history of northern New Spain was not so different. A century after the first Spanish forays into Central America, multiethnic forces loyal to the viceroyalty established carefully planned garrison communities throughout the modern states of San Luis Potosí, Coahuila, Tamaulipas, and Nuevo León. Both in the 1560s and in the 1590s, the viceroyalty of New Spain sought the services of Tlaxcalans to conquer and settle the region. On the first occasion, Tlaxcala declined the invitation; on the second occasion, it accepted. Spanish commander Francisco de Urdiñola, working with Tlaxcalan leaders and Franciscan missionaries, planned Saltillo and its twin Indian republic of San Esteban as a regional hub from which Tlaxcalans would send out generations of settlers to farther frontiers. Their efforts would, over time, transform the region's agriculture, commerce, and military organization. In the 1680s, Tlaxcalan expeditions seeking sites for mining and settlement led to the foundation of San Miguel de Aguayo. With the aid of Franciscan missionaries from the College of Santa Cruz in Queretaro, the settlers built a prosperous town among the Alasapas. On the edge of a region controlled at various times by Tobosos, Apaches, and Comanches, they established a garrison town to defend the empire. Theirs was a Tlaxcalan republic under cabildo governance that incrementally incorporated local Indians of other ethnic origins. Today it is called Bustamante Nuevo Leon and is protected by the Lord of Tlaxcala.[24]

Indian Vassals in the Colonial Hierarchy

In the desperate pragmatism of the sixteenth century, there were several ways to snatch victory from the jaws of defeat. For native leaders, a shrewd alliance at the right moment could be the difference between subjugation and security. The wars for Central America were fought by armies cobbled together from combinations of European irregulars, early indigenous allies, and former enemies now co-opted into the imperial forces. Some of the soldiers were European and Nahua veterans of the victory at Tenochtitlan; others were drawn from the defeated Tenochcas themselves—former enemies turned to the Spanish side.[25] Whether in Mexico or Central America, these indigenous allies clung to their narratives of victory. As Octavio Paz reminds us, most people prefer to imagine themselves victors rather than vanquished. In colonial Spanish America, there was more than simple pride at stake when communities retold their histories of the conquest. Being on the winning side of history meant greater wealth, security, and political status.[26]

The Spanish labor regime placed Indians in three broad categories: (1) the conquered whose descendants were bound to provide tribute; (2) the elite indigenous allies and conquerors who were rewarded with the tributary labor of other Indians; and (3) the many Indians in the middle. The members of this third category—whether humble and unrecognized participants in the conquest or later migrants—lacked patrimonial rights but could escape tributary demands from Spanish and Indian elites. Colonial archives are full to bursting with the records of Spaniards, Indians, and mestizos who presented testimony to defend their membership in an advantageous legal category or alternately to escape membership in a disadvantageous one.[27] For three centuries the descendants of the Spanish Empire's Indian conquerors and co-colonizers staked their claims to property, status, and self-governance on the story of their service to the crown.[28] These political arguments appear in the archival record in the form of *probanzas de méritos* (records of loyal service), litigation, testaments, *relaciones geográficas*, primordial titles, and pictorial codices and *lienzos*. Researchers who dig into this record cannot help but be struck by the concentration of documentation at certain moments, and by the paucity of documentation at others.[29] Though the records reflect a variety of changing local conditions, the overall pattern seems to have been dictated by shifts in royal policy. Any changes in royal policy that affected the chartered status of *pueblos de indios* (Indian municipalities) by threatening their land rights, symbolic status, political autonomy, or their exemptions from tax and labor obligations inevitably stimulated a flurry of legal and political activity. Indian co-colonist communities on the extreme north and extreme south of New Spain remained linked not just by their shared origins and traditions but also by their parallel and often synchronized responses to threatening royal policies.[30]

The most prominent Indian settlers on New Spain's frontiers were Tlaxcalan and Mexica, but numerous Otomis, Mixtecs, Zapotecs, and Mayas also contributed to the colonies. The original rationale for these communities was more or less the same throughout the empire, but the long-term outcomes varied considerably. Some of the colonies were ephemeral, and many lost their character as independent conqueror republics, but a significant number survived through the centuries with their special status intact. Many Nahua colonists based their alliances on those of the 1520s, recalling how Spanish invaders gained the help of armies from Tlaxcala, first to topple Tenochtitlan and later to extend the power of the emerging Hispano-indigenous empire farther to the north and south.[31]

For Europeans, the initial blueprint for conquest and administration was a feudal one. The young Indian republics provided the empire with ongoing military aid in return for local autonomy. This state of affairs was compatible with sixteenth-century Habsburg practices in Europe. However, the global Spanish Empire was not a static organization. Changes in its military, legal, and tributary systems in the coming centuries presented both threats and opportunities to these Indian republics. After the initial conquest era, renegotiations of the colonial compact were triggered by shifts in royal policy: the New Laws of the 1540s, the administrative reforms of Juan de Ovando in the 1570s, the attempted fiscal and military reforms of the Duke of Olivares in the 1620s and 1630s, and finally the Bourbon Reforms of the 1770s and 1780s. At all of these junctures, the crown sought to alter its earlier agreements with local nobility (both Spanish and Indian), to reduce or eliminate heritable privileges based on service during the conquest, and to impose a more uniform system of taxation and military organization. Each transition created winners and losers; and yet, a remarkable number of Latin America's indigenous corporate communities preserved their identities and safeguarded their privileges through much of the colonial era. Many of the social and political organizations of Spain's inchoate colonial states were, in the 1520s and 1530s, shaped by the Spanish conquerors' military systems and by the compacts between these conquerors and their indigenous allies. Consequently, the political geography of frontier spaces featured Spanish and indigenous-ally garrisons surrounded by conquered populations; the later were heavily encumbered by tributary demands from both. Attempts to reform this state of affairs and to protect conquered Indians were codified in the New Laws of 1542, a document that at once protected subject Indians and at the same time diminished the authority of Spanish encomenderos and allied Indian nobility. This attempt to revise the early colonial compacts would continue through the period of Juan de Ovando's reforms in the 1560s and 1570s, provoking resistance from Spanish encomenderos and relentless petitioning from Indian nobles and cabildos.[32]

History became its own battlefield as rival conquerors used their stories from the past as legal weapons in the present. Numerous visual and written chronicles of this type have survived in some form. Perhaps the best known are those from Tlaxcala and Quauhquechollan. Though the two *altepeme* (indigenous city-states) were little more than fifty miles apart, and both located in the core area of Nahua civilization, their inhabitants participated in conquests spanning the entire length and breadth of the expanding Hispano-Indian state. The famed *Lienzo de Tlaxcala* and *Lienzo de Quauhquechollan* recounted the invasions of the Gran Chichimeca to the north and the invasion of the Maya South respectively.[33] Many details about the production and provenance of these lienzos (narrative images on cloth) remain obscure; what is certain, though, is that both capture a distinctly sixteenth-century conception of Spanish-indigenous co-conquest. These visual narratives meld the imperial iconography of the Habsburg court with native symbols of sovereignty. They tell a story of military service in the foundation of the new transatlantic empire, and they foreground the role of Nahua soldiers. These images promoted the Indian allies' claims to land, status, autonomous governance, and authority over conquered Indians. Their implicit message is rooted in the political logic of the Iberian Reconquista and the New World Conquista—one in which feudal service to the crown was rewarded with wealth, title, and local authority. The two visual documents find their written analog in Mexico in the form of Diego Muñoz Camargo's *Historia de Tlaxcala*, and in Central America in the form of lengthy petitions begun in the 1540s and continued through the end of the century.[34]

Sixteenth-century reformers (both fiscal and humanitarian) were eager to end encomienda, or at least to sunset the institution by preventing its intergenerational transmission. For humble native subjects under the thumb of Spanish or Indian encomenderos, this moment promised emancipation from compulsory labor. Among Indian lords who held encomiendas, the call for reform was less welcome.[35] Other native elites saw an opportunity to settle scores, reclaim lost privileges, or renegotiate their positions in the colonial pecking order. In 1547, numerous Indian conquistadors from Central America joined together to defend their status as encomenderos. They presented them-

FIGURE 17 Tlaxcalan armies conquer Michoacán. Illustration from a facsimile of *Lienzo de Tlaxcala*, ca. 1550; color lithograph, 1892, Mexican School. Private Collection Archives Charmet / Bridgeman Images.

selves once again as the conquerors rather than the conquered. The petition recounted their meritorious service in battles against local peoples, their poor treatment by military commanders, and their own entitlement to lands and labor: "After the land was settled, we rested a little bit from the wrongdoings and mistreatments. . . . To make us settle in the area they made us great promises of giving our leaders allotments of Indians."[36] The petitioners described their tragic loss of status as they fell from the ranks of conquering nobles to that of commoners and tributary Indians. In some Central American communities, as late as the 1570s, the descendants of conquering Indians fought not just for freedom *from* tribute labor but also for their rights *to* tribute labor in the form of encomiendas over the local Indian population.[37]

The end of the century was a time of declining fortunes for many of the Indian kingdoms that had bound themselves early to the Habsburg Empire. A second and third wave of catastrophic diseases in the 1540s and 1570s weakened the military power of native states and made the delivery of adequate tribute from their subject populations difficult.[38] Spain's once-indispensable

Indian allies had less to offer once the age of great and lucrative conquests came to a close. Yet the settler populations of the Tlaxcalan diaspora did not disappear from history. In several locations, the seventeenth century occasioned a renewal of the old colonial compact as indigenous leaders offered their services for new imperial projects. In the North of New Spain, the renewal of the Spanish-Tlaxcalan alliance is largely attributable to the new mining discoveries at Zacatecas in the late 1540s and at San Luis Potosí in the early 1590s. The resulting agreement between the crown and the soldier-settlers of Tlaxcala was by then a familiar arrangement, but the project also drew on other populations. The expeditions of Miguel Caldera and Spanish commander Francisco de Urdiñola opened the region to conquest and set in motion a procedure for civic formation that would long thereafter shape northern society. They seeded binary settlements of Indian and Spanish towns at key sites for mining and military security. In the Northeast, Spanish San Luis Potosí was paired with Tlaxcalan Mexquitic, and Spanish Saltillo with Tlaxcalan San Esteban. The responsibilities of these Tlaxcalan settlers were both military and economic. They were to seize lands from local peoples, defend the settled valleys from intruders, and draw the region's Indians into a colonial system of agriculture and commerce.[39]

The proliferation of military threats from northern tribes lent urgency to the formation of new Tlaxcalan settlements—among them San Miguel de Aguayo, a military and agricultural pueblo established in the 1680s to guard and supply recently discovered mines at nearby Villaldama. If a swift and decisive conquest had yielded lasting peace, Tlaxcalan claims of ongoing military value (and to related legal privileges) would soon have lost credibility; but in the North the relatively secure conditions so common in central Mexico eluded the colonial state for centuries. The role of the settler-soldiers became a permanent one. In the early eighteenth century, the whole network of Tlaxcalan settlements was expanded and formalized under the leadership of royal visitor Francisco Barbadillo. An old sixteenth-century alliance was given new life.[40]

Defending the Empire from Land and Sea

Early Habsburg alliances in the Americas were designed to wage wars against native states; a century later, the world around them had changed. By the seventeenth century, the Spanish perceived European competitors to be as great a threat to the colonial order as the unassimilated natives of America's internal frontiers were. This threat was sometimes more imagined than real, but it helps to account for a resurgence of arguments for political preferment from the members of surviving Indian settler colonies. Whereas early Indian settlers in Honduras had typically touted their service in the conquest of the valleys of Ulúa and Comayagua, or their aid against Ciçumba and Lempira, later vecinos of the settler towns had less to commend them. A new opportunity for royal service arrived in 1604 when foreign privateers threatened Central America. The Captaincy of Guatemala soon called upon Honduran Indian republics to man coastal lookouts and defenses. The native troops stood watch against European privateers and also captured contraband cargos.[41] This allowed some Indian soldiers to claim military *fueros* and conquistador privileges that were not just inherited from their ancestors but also earned by ongoing service. In New Spain, a few groups of indigenous forces were also deployed against European threats. Tlaxcalans from San Miguel aided Alonso de León in his attempts to locate and destroy French settlements in Texas and Louisiana between 1686 and 1690. Tlaxcalans also helped create the constellation of settlements that would eventually become San Antonio, Texas. At the time, the threat from the French settlers was minor, but the danger from European corsairs on the coast and from skilled plains warriors in the interior was significant.[42] Beginning in 1749, the settler community of Altamira was charged with guarding the mouth of the Río Pánuco north of Tampico. The town's free black and Indian settler-vecinos claimed autonomy and privileges based on military service; but as in Texas, the real threats came more often from the land than from the water. Their enduring work would be to guard the pass of Metate and to secure the road between coast and interior.[43]

Much of Central America was brought into the Spanish Empire through the chaotic expeditions launched from the Valley of Mexico in the first years after the fall of Tenochtitlan. The conquests were scattered, poorly coordinated, and plagued by intra-European conflicts. More of the conquerors came from the New World than from the old, and these Indian co-colonists left a distinctive pattern on the demographic and political map in the centuries that followed. From Chiapas to Nicaragua, Nahua and Maya soldiers serving with the Spanish put down roots, carrying with them practices from their motherlands and blending them with the cultural and political practices of the Spanish. In northern New Spain, Indian soldiers and settlers outnumbered Spanish ones in the first days of conquest, but the balance would shift over time as the nuclei of early colonial settlements were gradually surrounded by larger mixed-caste populations. In some cases, ethnically Spanish towns subsisted side by side with Indian ones; in other cases, the Spanish municipalities incorporated them as semiautonomous barrios.[44]

Some Indian garrison towns were on the remote edges of European empire, but others were established on internal frontiers—on islands of colonial spaces surrounded by zones whose inhabitants lived outside colonial authority. The settlers brokered communications with these extracolonial peoples and policed the corridors of transit and commerce most vital to the empire. These routes and archipelagos have, in some cases, a history that reaches back into the pre-Columbian past when the long commercial and tributary tentacles of Mesoamerican empires reached deep into ethnically and politically distinct regions. Both the preconquest and colonial-era political geography are distinct from that of modern nation-states and should be understood on their own terms.[45] Envisioning the position of Comayagua's Mexicapa community within seventeenth-century Honduras is a good way to understand this world of attenuated colonial spaces and internal frontiers.

In 1629, the leading citizens and elected officials of the town of Mexicapa submitted a thick petition to the king. The petitioners were Indians, but Indians quite different in origin from their Kaqchikel neighbors. Like most legal correspondence of this type, the letter placed the petitioners within the vast systems of the empire, describing their location at the end of a great chain of communications and of a great social hierarchy reaching upward and outward from their remote corner of the empire toward the court and king. Just describing the king's territorial holdings consumes pages of these documents. They wrote to the King "of Aragon of the two Sicilies of Jerusalem . . . of Navarre of Granada of Toledo of Valencia of the Island of Majorca of Sicily of Cordoba of the court of Murcia . . . of the Algarves of Algeria and Gibraltar and the Canary Islands and the western and eastern Indies and Terra Firma of the ocean sea, Archduke of Austria Duke of Aragon . . . of Milan . . . of Barcelona . . . and to you governor of the province of Honduras." Farther down the great chain of being one finds "alcaldes ordinarios of the city of Comayagua and San Pedro," and finally the writers themselves, "the Indians of the pueblo of Mexicapa in the valley next to the city of Comayagua."[46] At the humble base of the great

FIGURE 18 Central America in the seventeenth century. Engraving by R. R. Donnelly. From John Ogilby and Arnoldus Montanus's *America: Being the Latest, and Most Accurate Description of the New World* [...] (London: John Ogilby, 1671). Courtesy of the John Carter Brown Library, Brown University.

imperial pyramid, we find the king's vassals, both Spanish and Indian, in the small towns of Central America.[47]

This long chain of colonial authority left considerable room for political negotiation at the local, regional, and imperial scale. Especially in the years following the promulgation of the New Laws of 1542, local fights throughout Spanish America over labor, land, and taxation pitted rival claimants against each other in the New World audiencias and in the Spanish court. Often, the root of the problem was an early history of ambiguous or conflicting conquest grants. In Central America, the clients of Cristóbal de Olid, the Alvarados, and Francisco de Montejo issued conflicting grants of encomienda.[48] Consequently, the exemptions, titles, and privileges of their Indian allies were far from clear, as was the status of the local subject peoples. Finally, efforts by the crown to sunset intergenerational encomiendas, regularize administration, and defend Indians from abuse tended to pit all of these privileged early stakeholders against later colonial administrators.[49]

From Vassals to Militiamen

Central America's local leaders cared most about status, land, and labor in their own backyards. But from the bird's-eye view of the imperial court, revenue and defense were the issues that really mattered. In the court of Philip III, all policy was driven by the financial demands of war against the English and Dutch. The state had faced bankruptcy in 1627, the capture of the royal treasure fleet in 1628, and the spiraling costs of near continuous campaigns by land and sea. To the king's chief minister, the Duke of Olivares, victory could only be achieved by squeezing new fiscal and administrative efficiencies from a global empire whose structures had resulted more from historical accident than from rational design. His grand scheme for imperial reorganization included the Union of Arms, a universal regime of taxation and military systems that was to encompass all the dominions of Philip III.[50] The correspondence of the Audiencia of Guatemala shows what this meant for royal subjects heretofore untouched by the European wars.[51] Documents from 1629 indicate that the jurisdiction of Guatemala was ordered to raise 250,000 ducats for the Union of Arms.[52] Viewed from the center of the imperial system in Spain, this quota was part of a rational redistribution of burdens among imperial subjects. But from the perspective of Indian elites on the colonial periphery, levying this type of tax on old Indian garrison towns violated time-honored agreements that exempted Indian allies and militiamen from military taxes.

As the Council of the Indies demanded new revenues from the Audiencia of Guatemala, and as the audiencia in turn demanded more revenues from the province of Honduras, the local power brokers began to squabble among themselves. Honduras was a place of layered conquests. Its Lenca inhabitants had been subdued—and only with great difficulty—by Spaniards and their Indian allies in the 1530s and 1540s. Spanish Comayagua (or Valladolid) grew up beside a community of Nahua co-colonists in Mexicapa. In the years that followed, the descendants of the Spanish encomenderos, the descendants of Nahua colonists in Mexicapa, and the cabildo of Valladolid-Comayagua would all jealously guard their historical claims in contradistinction to each other's, and often to the detriment of the local Lencas. Later (if we are to trust the story as told by the vecinos of Mexicapa), something went wrong. In an age of falling Indian populations and mounting demands for revenue, encomenderos and municipalities began demanding tribute labor, not just from the conquered Indians but also from the Indian conquerors.

The old Nahua settler communities pushed back forcefully when their status was threatened. The Mexicapa petitioners fired their first salvo, describing themselves as the "Indians of the pueblo of Mexicapa in the valley beside the city of Comayagua," who represented the town's principales and the rest of the "Conqueror and settler Mexica Indians." They spoke as high-born royal vassals and with the authority of legally elected officials. Their argument was simple: They had conquered the valley for the crown a century beforehand and had been granted self-government, land titles, and freedom from ordinary labor tribute. Now they were faced with illegal demands both from encomendero Alonso Rodriguez Gallegos and from the valley's main municipal government. They turned to the Audiencia of Guatemala for relief, insisting that "in conformity with the royal provision, one must declare that they should not owe service Indians to the city of Comayagua nor carry out orders of that government, [and they should be] free from Alonso Rodriguez Gallegos."

While Tlaxcalan and Mexica allies established roots in Guatemala and Honduras, another part of the Nahua diaspora spread northward. They fought in the Mixtón War, in the Chichimec wars, and in the various frontier conflicts that would last until the end of the colonial period.[53] In the North, the Nahua invaders conquered, co-opted, and slowly integrated with the region's indigenous population. The stories of Central American and northern colonization have much in common, but they are also distinct. Southern co-colonization took place largely in the initial phase of conquest. Mexica, Tlaxcalan, Mixtec, and Zapotec settlers entered the Maya sphere, and then reached beyond it during the first Spanish invasions of the early sixteenth century. Their influence was greatest in this early period, whether judged by wealth, population, or military power; and their status was greatest as judged by legal privileges, exemptions, and autonomy from Spanish oversight. In contrast, northern colonization only began in earnest after the compact between the Kingdom of Tlaxcala and the Spanish viceroyalty in 1590.[54] Tlaxcalans continued to establish new colonies in the North as late as the early eighteenth century. Consequently, it was in the time of Gálvez and the Bourbon Reforms (the 1770s and

1780s), rather than in the time of Olivares and the Union of Arms (the 1630s and 1640s), that the ancestral privileges of the northern settlers were put to the test.

Central America and Mexico's northern frontier faced many of the same challenges and political tensions. In the North, Spanish and Tlaxcalan conquerors gained early land grants and charters of self-government; and both groups sometimes dealt in captive labor, either in the form of early de jure Spanish encomiendas or, more commonly, in the form of de facto judicial slavery, corvée, or *congregas* of seminomadic northern Indians. The region weathered wars and rebellions, changing administrative oversight, and a general reorganization of mission and labor rules in the 1710s. Through all these transitions, Tlaxcalans held onto their privileges tenaciously.[55] Then came the Bourbon Reforms. Though Olivares's attempts at a Union of Arms for Philip III collapsed by the middle of the seventeenth century, a similar aspiration gripped Charles III in the eighteenth. Confronted with yet another cataclysmic threat from England, the Spanish monarchy sought all possible means to squeeze from its far-flung empire the revenues and military resources needed to turn the tide. In New Spain this meant new taxes and new tax administration. A system of intendants now oversaw a vastly expanded system for regulating mining, collecting sales taxes, and administering royal monopolies. As in the time of Olivares, the goal was both to mobilize physical resources and to train and mobilize men. The crown sought to replace old quasi-feudal military obligations with a regularized system of militias that would cover Spanish America from sea to sea.[56]

Before the new militias could form, stakeholders of the old settler colonies stepped forward to defend important elements of the existing system. In the 1780s, the governor of Nuevo León, Vicente Gonzáles de Santianes, was stuck with the difficult task of explaining the region's administrative practices to his superiors while applying new Bourbon practices to a region quite distinct from Iberia. Any attempt to levy new taxes on the region's settler communities raised a hue and cry from the old chartered Tlaxcalan towns. Their pact with the crown had always been a simple one. They served the viceroyalty by conquering territory, suppressing local resistance, defending against outside threats, and bringing new mines and agricultural lands into the colonial economy. In return, their leaders (and no small number of followers) received titles of lesser nobility, ceremonial honors, land, charters of self-government, and relief from most forms of taxation and tributary labor. Like Europe's early elites, their obligation to the crown was discharged on the battlefield. The governor described many of the Tlaxcalan towns in ways that would have been familiar to the governors of the conquest era. Their obligations for taxation and service varied in relation to the functions they fulfilled within the empire. In some areas, Tlaxcalans functioned as part of a missionary program, living beside recently settled northern Indians. In others, they lived apart from the northern Indians but still served as members of garrison communities. In a third category, the governor placed Tlaxcalans who served in partnership with assimilated northern Indian communities that now held a kind of Tlaxcalan legal status. Such was the value of these settlements that, despite many waves of administrative reform, their colonial pacts survived until the era of Mexican independence. Governor Gonzáles was precise in describing the rationale behind these communities' privileges: "There still persist in the two villages and in San Miguel de Aguayo the frontier conditions of territories through which barbarous Indians still enter to carry out hostilities, to the remedy of which it [San Miguel] contributes a small company of horsemen which the aforementioned Tlaxcalans formed there and another of archers from the *antiguos borrados*."[57]

New Spain benefitted from native allies on all of its frontiers, but it was in the North that it needed them most. It was a region of persistent violent frontier conditions and great mineral wealth. Whereas the Spanish colonial project in Honduras desperately needed its Nahua garrisons in the time of the Lempira Revolt, this was no longer the case a century later. Though many indigenous spaces in the interior of Honduras remained outside the effective control of the colonial government for centuries, the province experienced nothing analogous to the endless wars against Apaches and Comanches, adversaries whose mobility, military prowess, and resistance to colonial acculturation made them an insoluble problem. For this reason, the Tlaxcalans of the North were indispensable to the state. At the same time, their numbers were finite, and their survival required the serial recruitment of new indigenous groups to aid their efforts.

In the North, military and religious leaders spoke of Tlaxcalan communities as existing in a land of *guerra viva* and *viva conversión*—the language betrays their sense of urgency. These conditions permitted Tlaxcalans to make two successful arguments in defense of community privileges: they constantly reinvoked their ancestors' faithful service in the age of Cortés and Alvarado, *and* their current contributions to wars against frontier enemies in the North. In contrast, the descendants of the indigenous soldier-settlers of Honduras could hope only that the crown's gratitude toward their conquistador ancestors would protect them from the economic and administrative overreach of their Spanish neighbors. Often, it did not.[58]

An Alternate Path: Guarani Towns on Contested Borders

Across the Americas, native leaders capitalized on their nations' early histories as European allies, retelling their ancestors' roles as co-conquerors and co-colonists. Other peoples were not so fortunate. Their ancestors were among the conquered, and their patriotic narratives had to wrestle with this misfortune, atone for their opposition to conquest, bury the past, or transform it. The Guaranis, who inhabited the region of modern Paraguay as well as the borderlands of Uruguay, Brazil, and Argentina, embodied a third political experience—one based on a different early-contact narrative. In the sixteenth century, the Guaranis founded new towns on their own lands, and they entered into the empire on their own terms. Theirs was a different kind of vassal state on the colonial frontier.

When Jesuit missionaries first arrived in the area of the upper Parana and Paraguay Rivers, they encountered no cities and no empires, but the land was already densely populated, at least by New World standards. Jesuit efforts began in the first decade of the seventeenth century, following many years of intermittent contact between Guarani communities and other Europeans. Goods from the other side of the Atlantic were already known to the Guaranis, as were the risks of interacting with invaders who sought slaves or encomienda labor. The Jesuits brought a compelling religious message, but they also offered tangible advantages: access to European goods and technologies, and the help of trusted intermediaries for negotiations with the growing Spanish settlement at Buenos Aires. Following the Jesuit model, the Guaranis soon became town dwellers, Christians, and Spanish vassals. Judging from their own accounts, the Guaranis considered themselves neither conquerors nor the victims of conquest. They were the founders of their own kingdom.[59]

In the eighteenth century, the Guarani towns in the Paraná, Paraguay, and Uruguay river basins had a combined population of more than one hundred thousand individuals. In cooperation with the Jesuit missionaries, the local people had constructed towns that conformed to the Spanish ideal. In most, a church of quarried stone adorned with fine carvings stood beside an open courtyard and central plaza. A neatly planned grid of longhouses partitioned into individual family dwellings housed the Christian Guaranis, who attended weekly masses and studied catechism. Soon, local militias drilled in the plazas, armed with European weapons supplied by the Jesuits. The towns boasted blacksmiths' forges, pottery wheels, looms, mills, and bakery ovens—and in a few cases printing presses. Well-trained musicians and choirs performed works for voice, organ, and stringed instruments. These communities provided for their own subsistence but also produced a surplus of goods for the larger colonial economy, chief among them cattle hides and yerba mate. Though external threats, disease, and out-migration created volatility in the population and the economy, the Guarani towns were a remarkable success story judged against the standards of the seventeenth and eighteenth centuries.[60]

In the mid-eighteenth century, the Guaranis found themselves in the middle of a territorial dispute between the Spanish and Portuguese Empires. Their response to the crisis highlights local understandings of their history as frontier vassals. The Jesuit-Guarani missions functioned almost as an independent state—or, more precisely, as a constellation of affiliated local republics—through much of the colonial era. Their security was constantly threatened by slave raids from Brazil's Portuguese, African, native, and mixed-race *bandeirantes*, but the Guaranis were able to hold their own. For the better part of two centuries, the Guaranis protected themselves while siding with the Spanish Empire and their Jesuit patrons in regional conflicts. After more than a century of alliance to Spain, the eastern Guaranis were blindsided and betrayed by the terms of the 1750 Treaty of Madrid. Spain and Portugal had resolved their territorial conflicts at the expense of the local population. The following year, Jesuit missionaries informed Guarani leaders that the populations of seven large mission towns would be relocated west of the Uruguay River in order to vacate the lands now ceded to Portugal. In 1753, the Guarani corregidor and cabildo of San Juan Batista, dismayed by the order to abandon their homes, petitioned King Ferdinand VI to reconsider the plan. They described the origin of their land titles not as contingent on the conquest era but as eternal and divine: "God himself has given these lands to our poor ancestors: after this, God himself sent from heaven his Vassal San Miguel who made our ancestors know God's will." At all points, the petitioners described themselves as the creators of their own polity, and the Jesuit missionaries as their advisors: "Our ancestors complied with what the saint had asked: three caciques spoke and in the company of some of their vassals, and after a great deal of work, they went to Buenos Aires with great hopes of finding a priest and our ancestors brought him to this land, and showed him to his vassals with great jubilation." Thus, the Jesuits came by invitation, and the Guaranis served the crown by their own free will.[61]

These claims were not far from the truth. Indeed, Spanish armies had never really conquered the Guarani lands. Moreover, Guarani armies had themselves several times defended the frontier against Portuguese intrusions. These Indian republics had received Jesuit guidance and Spanish arms, but the battles were won with their own sweat and blood. The Jesuit-Guarani kingdom—or something like a kingdom—had been in existence a century and a half by the time of the border crisis, and the Guaranis had long memories. The Treaty of Madrid gave them four years to vacate their lands. In that time, Guarani leaders mobilized a defense that was both diplomatic and military. The San Juan Bautista petitioners reminded European rulers that they had defended their lands many times before: "We do not ask for help here. Remember, remember well Portuguese, we made ashes out of your fathers at Colonia, only a few fled, three thousand of us went because of the great love we had for our good Holy King and the Priests." In the end, both their appeals for justice and their recitations of past service left the European monarchs unmoved. In the spring of 1752, representatives of the Jesuit order and the Spanish and Portuguese courts arrived in South America with clear marching orders: the seven mission complexes east of the Uruguay River must be abandoned. Some of the inhabitants complied, but most did not. By 1754, all diplomatic avenues had been exhausted, and further attempts by outsiders to occupy sites in Guarani territory were met with force.[62]

What made the Guaranis believe they could prevail in a war against the combined might of Spain and Portugal? Perhaps it was the experience of the past century. The Guaranis had suffered terribly at the hands of Portuguese slave raiders, but they had also prevailed against them in several spectacular victories. In 1639 at Caazapá Guazú, and in 1641 at Mbororé, Guarani soldiers defeated thousands of invaders who attacked from Brazilian territory. A hundred years later, the capabilities of the Guarani were formidable. Their tactics were informed by generations of European training and by even more generations of experience fighting in the densely forested, twisting waterways of the local terrain. They were well armed and highly capable.[63]

By the 1750s, the Guaranis also enjoyed the advantages of literacy and large-scale political organizations, which allowed them to advance long-term strategies over vast areas. Even before the first shots were fired, Guarani leaders fought for hearts and minds, and prepared their communities for battle in pamphleting campaigns and correspondence between cabildos. Important diplomatic efforts were spearheaded by Nicolás Ñeenguirú, corregidor of the Indian republic of Concepcíon. Nicolás Ñeenguirú spoke on behalf of the Guaranis throughout the region. His authority to do so was rooted partly in his local office, but more broadly in the status that his ancestry conferred. His father enjoyed great esteem as a commander of native troops who were victorious over the Portuguese at the Colonia do Sacramento in 1704. His ancestor and namesake, Nicolás Ñeenguirú, was a key figure in the early pact between the Guaranis and founding Jesuit missionary Roque González. Protesting the displacement of mission-town populations, Ñeenguirú reminded Spanish officials of how his people had entered the empire and the faith: "They say that a long time ago our good, holy saint called Roque González de Santa Cruz, after he came to our land, and instructed us about God and also what it is to be a Christian. There was not even a Spaniard here in this land. Of our own will, we agreed that God comes first, and of course, then our King, who would always be our protector." As war with the Iberian powers approached, the Guaranis were certain that they were in the right: they had joined the empire freely, they had negotiated the terms, and the Spaniards had now violated them.[64]

When a crown delegation arrived at Mission San Gabriel to impose the treaty terms, they were confronted by Captain Sepé Tiarajú and his Guarani troops. The war that followed lasted for two years and was, in the end, a disaster for the Guaranis. But it also demonstrated their capabilities and their resolve. If the Guarani War was a failure for the native inhabitants, the plot to remove them from their homes was also a failure for its European architects. The battles were long and costly; the relocation was messy and incomplete; and the economic costs for all concerned were significant. Though the seven towns were formally dissolved, and though the Jesuits themselves were soon expelled from the Spanish and Portuguese Americas, the Guaranis persevered. In 1761 the Spanish repudiated the Treaty of Madrid, and in 1777 Portugal formally acknowledged the return of the lands to Spain. The seven towns were legally and actually reborn.[65]

The seven mission sites east of the Uruguay River are within the modern boundaries of Argentina's Misiones Province, while the majority of the Jesuit-founded Guarani towns lie within modern Paraguay. In both places, the early Indian republics are central to collective memory and to the origins of modern civic life. They are celebrated as the birthplace of the region's distinctive culture. Three quarters of Paraguayans are Guarani speakers, and thousands of Guarani speakers remain on the other side of the border in Misiones.[66] The Guaranis, as individuals and as whole communities, played important roles in the independence era and in the tumultuous border conflicts between Brazil, Argentina, Uruguay, and Paraguay. In 2015, the Argentine government proclaimed independence-era Guarani military commander Andrés Guacurarí a national hero, thus tidily connecting memories of cultural synthesis, state formation, and patriotism.[67] And yet, though memories of the colonial Guarani communities are celebrated and redeployed for political purposes, the truth remains that they did in fact constitute a remarkable example of native success in negotiating the terms of membership in Atlantic empires.

=====

In Santa Fe, New Mexico, curious tourists occasionally pause to examine a sign that stands beside San Miguel de Analco: "Oldest Church structure in the U. S. A. The original walls and altar were built by Tlaxcalan Indians from Mexico under the direction of Franciscan Padres, ca. 1610." No such plaque greets the millions of Texas tourists who visit the Alamo historic site each year. There visitors encounter a Franciscan mission so thoroughly transformed into a monument of American nationalism as to all but obscure its origins. Yet, beneath a layer of modern restoration and blurred recollection, the two sites share something in common. Both places were settled (at least in part) by Spain's Nahua vassals who colonized the land of today's southwestern United States from the South.[68] To Apaches and Pueblo Indians, the Tlaxcalans and Mexicas were likely viewed as invaders; to the Spaniards, they were allies.

Across the Americas, the conquest of indigenous spaces and the expansion of colonial frontiers has taken place not in a single era of warfare and settlement, but over the course of half a millennium. Most Indians and mestizos have been the victims of this long historical process, but some number among them has also been its beneficiaries. Strategic alliances helped these individuals (and sometimes their entire communities) to triumph over competing indigenous states, advance claims of nobility and legitimacy, secure military resources and commands, and gain legal titles over traditional and newly conquered lands. Most importantly, strategic alliances offered native people the greatest prospects for individual and community survival. History is written by the victors, and many indigenous allies and client states sought to write themselves into the winning side of history. It was a shrewd strategy, and one that often averted disaster. In the long run, however, the gratitude of the European empires proved fleeting. In practice, most Indian clients were able to defend their privileges only as long as their services remained indispensable to the colonial state.

CHAPTER EIGHT

The End of an Age
Indians and Independence

The Many Meanings of Independence

In the United States, the phrases "American Independence" and "American Revolution" are often used interchangeably to describe the period of protest, war, and state formation that took place between 1775 and 1789. There is some confusion in our national myth between the original grievances of the settlers, the later objective of secession, and the final aims and ideologies of the Constitutional Convention. Even our use of the word "independence" suggests a muddled memory of the era. In much of the world, "national independence" describes literal decolonization: a region's original inhabitants expelling European colonizers and seizing control of the state. This is what one typically means by "independence" in Kenya, India, or Vietnam. But Americans mean something very different when they say that the US declared independence in 1776. After independence, the thirteen American states were ruled not by liberated Iroquois or Algonquians—but by the descendants of the conquerors themselves.

North Americans are not the only ones to describe independence in this peculiar way; the same notion is common all over the Western Hemisphere. Between 1810 and 1825, wars of "independence" produced new republics ruled by European settler populations throughout Spanish America—this is what historians generally call "creole independence." At the end of the colonial period, the New World's population had three main components: indigenous Americans, Europeans, and Africans. Consequently, rebellions by these groups against imperial authority might have produced very different kinds of post-colonial states: New-World African republics, revanchist indigenous states, racialized creole republics, or multiethnic republics. Haiti is the singular example of successful African-led independence, but the possibility that slaves and their descendants might form independent nations existed from Brazil to the Carolinas. The revival of indigenous leadership was also a distinct possibility in Mexico and Peru, though it never came to pass. Despite the possibility and opportunity for other kinds of revolutions, Latin America's independence movements generally followed the same path as the United States': toward a creole-dominated nation-state modeled on European political practices. And yet, though Euro-Americans would control most of the postrevolutionary successor states, Indian leaders were intimately involved in the military contests that produced them. Sometimes native communities sided with European empires; at other times they cast their lot with the emerging creole states. The diplomacy of indigenous Americans was informed by a long history of colonial contact; and their varied alignments in the wars of independence were based on significant ground-level differences in the treatment of Indian subjects and allies among European empires.

Between a Rock and a Hard Place:
Iroquois Leaders and the American Revolution

In Anglo-America, perhaps the most famous Indian loyalist of all time was Joseph Brant. Brant was a Mohawk and a British subject, a politician and diplomat, a businessman and a lay missionary, a scholar, a translator, and an interpreter. Depending on the occasion, he wore a European dress uniform or a feathered headdress. He was a Christian and a Freemason. He attended school in Connecticut, served in diplomatic missions to London, and brokered negotiations among the Six Nations of the Iroquois Confederacy. Like George Washington and so many revolutionary leaders of his generation, Brant also served as a British military officer in the Seven Years' War. But in the end, he remained loyal to the crown. Washington's politics turned in one direction, Brant's in the other. Some thirty years later, as Joseph Brant lay on his deathbed, in exile from his New York homeland, perhaps he wondered whether he had made the right choice. His decision to side with England had not been an impulsive one. No one had seen the conflict between Britain and the Thirteen Colonies from more angles than Brant. He chose carefully, and despite finding himself on the losing side of the war, subsequent events seem to have vindicated his decision.

Joseph Brant died at home in his estate near the shores of Lake Ontario in 1807. His land stood only about fifty miles from Niagara Falls, where turbulent waters separate Canada from the United States—an apt metaphor for the life of a man whose actions in an era of revolutionary violence so extensively shaped the history of two future nations. To any European visitor, Brant's Georgian-style manor with its gleaming white exterior and imposing columns was immediately recognizable as the home of a gentleman. Though his Mohawk people now lived in exile from their homeland, on the other side of a newly formalized international border, their relative good fortune—when compared to the fate of Indian nations south of the border—owed much to Brant's shrewd decision-making.[1]

The Six Nations of the Iroquois Confederacy were circumspect in their deliberations over the War of Independence. Throughout previous colonial history, the Iroquois had been a formidable military presence in the Old Northwest. Though highly autonomous in their domestic policies, the Six Nations (Haudenosaunee) carefully coordinated their military and diplomatic policy. During the Seven Years' War, an alliance with Britain against the French and neighboring Algonquians served the Iroquois well. A generation later, they sized up the expanding conflict between the English crown and rebellious settlers, and tested the prevailing winds once more. When push came to shove and neutrality was no longer possible, nearly all of the Haudenosaunee nations remained loyal to Britain—with one notable exception: the Oneidas. The Oneidas broke with the rest of the confederacy and sided with the American revolutionaries. They predicted a rebel victory, and that is exactly what came to pass. However, the Oneida statesmen, who expected the gratitude of the new republic, were in the end sorely disappointed. When peace arrived, the United States pushed the Oneidas from upstate New York to Wisconsin and ultimately to Oklahoma and Canada. These native allies received scant thanks for their service to the American Revolution.[2]

In the years that followed, the Iroquois nations suffered terrible setbacks, but the Mohawks faired far better than other tribes, owing partly to the efforts of Joseph Brant. Upon achieving independence, the US turned against its former enemies and allies alike. But the British, though they lost the war, did not forget their friends among the native states. When the conflict came to an end, Brant's people were given desirable lands on the shores of Lake Ontario, aided

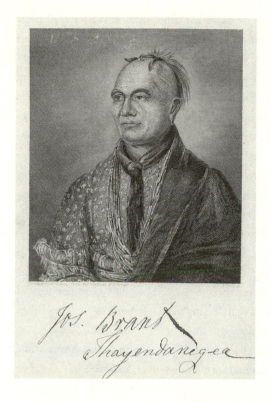

in relocation, and permitted to keep their slaves. It was a sentence of perpetual exile, but on the best possible terms.

British gratitude toward the Mohawks was well earned. During the war, royalist, rebel, and Indian armies fought their way back and forth across Mohawk lands, imposing great hardships on the inhabitants. During this period, Brant worked as a field commander, a translator, and an emissary to the London government. At the zenith of royalist fortunes, he was in Manhattan working for British general William Howe. In the final phases of the war, when the tide turned against England, the Iroquois and British forces were pushed ever farther to the north and west. So it was that in 1779, many of the Iroquois forces retreated past Niagara—that no-man's-land that would one day harden into an international boundary.

The Iroquois nations made many sacrifices for the loyalist cause in the course of this war. One might ask why they did it. What did they have to gain or lose from the outcome? The Iroquois were skilled diplomats, and they had been interacting with Europeans for almost two centuries by the time the American rebellion broke out, so we can be sure that their decision to ally with the British was informed by experience. Joseph Brant's biography illustrates the many avenues by which native leaders could study imperial politics and chart their plans. Brant crossed between European and Indian worlds countless times, as did his sister Molly Brant and their father, Tehonwaghkwangeraghkwa, before them. Molly was a significant political and religious leader among the Mohawks in her own right; and her influence was enhanced by her marriage to William Johnson, the British superintendent for Indian affairs. From their regal home in the Mohawk Valley, this influential couple played a vital role in English-Iroquois diplomacy in the years leading up to the war.

During the eighteenth century, Iroquois diplomatic strategies were not so different from those of European nations. Their priorities were security, the defense of territory, and the maintenance of trade. They had a long history of working with both the French and British, and of playing one against the other when it suited their interests. The best possible future for the Iroquois was one in which they could maintain internal political and economic autonomy while monopolizing access to European markets, trade goods, and technologies. For the Iroquois, European merchants and missionaries were an asset; European settlers were a problem.[3]

To understand why the Iroquois supported the crown in the Revolutionary War, we need to consider the history of their participation in the Seven Years' War. In the 1750s, the British alliance with the Iroquois Confederacy was a vital factor in their victory over the French. The Iroquois wanted something in return: legal protection of their lands against intrusions by Anglo-American settlers—and that is precisely what they got when the war came to an end in 1763. In that year, King George III issued a proclamation defining the boundary between European provinces and Indian lands, creating a border that ran the length of the Appalachian Divide from Georgia to Maine. The British government saw the maintenance of this boundary as crucial to North American peace, but Anglo-American colonists considered it an unreasonable obstacle to western settlement—so much so that the issue is highlighted in the Declaration of Independence. The document complains that the king "has endeavoured to prevent the population of these States; for that purpose obstructing the Laws for Naturalization of Foreigners; refusing to pass others to encourage their mi-

grations hither, and raising the conditions of new Appropriations of Lands";
and further that the king "has excited domestic insurrections amongst us, and
has endeavoured to bring on the inhabitants of our frontiers, the merciless Indian Savages, whose known rule of warfare, is an undistinguished destruction
of all ages, sexes and conditions." In other words, the American rebels were
fighting the war in part to seize and settle Indian territory that had been under
crown protection. By siding with the British, the Mohawks, Onondagas, Senecas, Cayugas, and Tuscaroras were fighting to save their own land. Though the
Mohawk-British alliance was rooted in a long history of cultural, religious, and
economic contacts, this was the heart of the issue.

Loyalty, Rebellion, and Dreams of Inca Restoration

In North America, the year 1780 ended with an especially harsh
winter. On New Year's Eve, George Washington and the Continental Army
were stuck in Morristown, New Jersey, enduring deep snow and frigid tempera-
tures. It was a dismal time for the snowbound army, but the new year would
deliver a decisive victory to the creole rebels and their French allies. Far to the
north, Joseph Brant and his troops were at their winter camp in Fort Niagara
at the beginning of what would prove to be a permanent exile from their New
York homeland.

Four thousand miles to the south, in the Peruvian Andes, two armies were
locked in a fight to control the city of Cuzco. One army was royalist and the
other rebel, but both commanders were Incas. High above the elegant city, the
armies of rebel commander Túpac Amaru clung to their strategic redoubts. In
the town, protected by Inca stonework and Spanish fortifications, the army of
Mateo Pumacahua was poised to strike back. Here, more than anywhere else
in the Americas, one could see how the fabric the Spanish Empire was woven
from its client states. This war for control of the Andes lasted from 1780 to
1782, and though it ended with a crown victory, the conflict exposed deep fis-
sures in regional politics that would reemerge during the independence era.[4]

Peru was late among Spanish American nations to achieve independence.
During the surrounding period, indigenous leaders played very important roles
in its military and political history. At the time, the chaos of war, occupation,
and revolution in Europe cast all parts of the Spanish Empire into confusion—
to such an extent that even applying the labels "loyalist" and "rebel" to armed

indigenous groups can be misleading. And though the Napoleonic era was the ultimate undoing of Spanish America, this crisis of authority in Peru went back farther than the French Revolution, at least to the time of Túpac Amaru.

A close look at the leaders fighting for control of Cuzco in 1780 highlights the difficulties of defining loyalty and rebellion. Today, José Condorcanqui (or Túpac Amaru II) and Mateo Pumacahua are constantly evoked in Peru's patriotic imagery, but neither their conflict with each other nor their relationships to the viceregal government and Spanish crown can be easily packed into a tidy narrative of rebellion and decolonization. Both are to this day regarded as great indigenous heroes in Peru—and yet, they fought more often than not on opposing sides of civil wars. Taking a close look at their political decisions reveals much about the complex diplomatic calculus of Quechua communities in their time.[5]

Mateo Pumacahua and José Condorcanqui were both men of great influence in the world of Andean politics. Condorcanqui was the hereditary ruler of Pampamarca, Surimana, and Tungasuca. He was raised in comfort and groomed for leadership. Educated in Cuzco's Jesuit college for Inca nobility, and literate in several languages, Condorcanqui was a worldly man. His genealogy was blue-blooded, to say the least. When he traveled to Lima in 1777, he arrived with documentation attesting to his legitimacy as the Count of Oropesa and claiming descent from the Inca royal family. Pumacahua was the curaca of Chinchero and lord of rich farmlands. Through his father he claimed local privileges, and through his mother he claimed descent from Emperor Huayna Capac. On the strength of these pedigrees, Condorcanqui called himself Túpac Amaru II and Pumacahua called himself Mateo Pumacahua Ynga.[6]

How did these two men end up pitted against each other?[7] It started in the town of Tinta in 1780 when a particularly unpleasant Spanish corregidor touched off a series of local conflicts that soon engulfed the entire colony. In colonial Peru, local government usually had three main forces: corregidores (royal administrators), bishops, and caciques. Caciques were the heads of indigenous noble families, empowered to collect and distribute resources from their own communities and to act as the arbiters of relations between indigenous and European populations. When the Spanish corregidor of Tinta, Antonio de Arriaga, stepped on the toes of local cacique José Condorcanqui, the latter rose up and proclaimed himself to be Túpac Amaru II, the final descendant of Peru's last Inca emperor and the rightful leader of the Andes.[8]

The choice of dynastic titles was telling. Peru was conquered by Spaniards in the 1530s in the midst of an Inca civil war. In those early years, Europeans worked with one Inca pretender after another in the hopes of reducing the royal family to clientage. But the Spanish rarely made good on their promises and soon antagonized their own clients. In 1536, Manco Inca Yupanqui rose up against the Spanish and nearly succeeded in driving them out of Peru. Eventually, though, the tide turned against him, and Manco was forced to retreat into the forested seclusion of Vilcabamba, where he established a break-away kingdom that would remain unconquered by the Spanish for thirty years. The last of the Vilcabamba emperors, Túpac Amaru I, was captured by the Spanish in 1571. He was taken from Vilcabamba to Cuzco where he was tried, convicted, and then finally drawn and quartered in a public plaza built on the site of the old Inca capital.

This is the man whom José Condorcanqui invoked when he took the name Túpac Amaru II. The genealogy that connected the two men was important to Condorcanqui's claims. A decade before the outbreak of hostilities in Tinta, he had traveled from the highlands to Lima carrying a thick bundle of documents in an unsuccessful attempt to prove his ancestry and claim his patrimony.[9] Though Condorcanqui did not persuade the magistrates about his lineage, he did persuade his followers. As Túpac Amaru II, he celebrated his Inca ancestry and identity. However, despite the strong strains of cultural nationalism in his rhetoric, the revolutionary program announced by Condorcanqui was decidedly Spanish in inspiration. He described the blueprint for a reformed viceregal state that merged Inca and Spanish conceptions of good government and placed the resulting Peruvian subpolity within a global Spanish Empire.[10]

Túpac Amaru II called himself both a supreme Inca and a loyal vassal of the king of Spain. To modern readers this may at first appear a contradiction in terms. How could Condorcanqui be both a rebel and a loyal subject? Quite easily, it turns out, in an era when audiencias and viceroys were frequently vilified even while the crown was exalted. Túpac Amaru's proclamations describing his followers as both servants of the crown and agents of reform fit the revolutionary discourse that existed throughout Latin America in the late colonial era. Indigenous rebels sought to cast out corrupt alcaldes, bishops, and viceroys, and to restore enlightened royal authority.

When José Condorcanqui executed Tinta's rogue corregidor, he did so at least nominally on behalf of the crown. Condorcanqui's ties to Europe were not superficial. His notions about politics, religion, and social justice were deeply rooted in the Spanish tradition. Though the preconquest Incas were theocratic leaders who presided over the temple of the sun god in Cuzco, Túpac Amaru II was an ardent Christian. He called himself not just the king's loyal vassal but also "defender of the faith." He had his disagreements with the church over the fine points of local administration, but his political manifestos called for an official Catholic state and for the suppression of all unorthodox practices.

Crucial to all of Túpac Amaru's military and diplomatic initiatives was his wife, Micaela Bastidas. She had been raised in the town of Abancay, the daughter of an African father and a Quechua mother. At the height of the rebellion, she and Condorcanqui commanded separate battalions in two distinct military theaters.[11] The core of Túpac Amaru's supporters was composed of Quechua-speaking highland Indians, but his movement was not just rooted in one caste community. The diversity within his movement is apparent in contemporary descriptions of his followers and in the royalist legal records that recorded the ethnicity of prisoners of war.[12] At its apogee, the rebellion counted significant numbers of mestizos, mulattos, and even creole Europeans in its ranks. Clearly, Túpac Amaru's agenda of faith, fidelity, and administrative reform resonated with large numbers of Peruvians. Within his movement for regional autonomy, there was also a revolutionary economic agenda. He called for an end to state-sponsored forced labor and to the repartimiento de bienes, a system under which compulsory purchases of goods enriched corregidores at the expense of the populace. His followers envisioned a Christian Peru loyal to the Spanish king but governed at the roots by indigenous noblemen and civil functionaries.

It was not just Túpac Amaru's army that drew from all castes and classes; so did the viceroy's. When loyalist commander Mateo Pumacahua mobilized his forces against Túpac Amaru, he brought thousands of indigenous soldiers. But he was also aided by European soldiers and by a substantial body of free blacks from Lima. The further one digs into the historical record, the harder it becomes to tidily characterize the conflict in simple terms of ethnicity, race, caste, or class. Pumacahua's authority was both political and military. He commanded in the field, but he also served the state as the president of the Junta de Guerra in Cuzco, which made him the emergency leader of the entire region. He recruited his army in cooperation with the colonial state, but its structure was also built around the leadership of the indigenous noblemen that he rallied to the cause.

The war against Túpac Amaru would last for more than a year, but Pumacahua and the viceroy were ultimately victorious. On May 18, 1781, the defeated Túpac Amaru II was taken to Cuzco's Plaza de Armas where he drawn, quartered, and decapitated in the same square as his illustrious ancestor. For all its brutality, Spanish colonial governance was punctilious in its attention to legality. Condorcanqui was convicted in a trial that followed the standard legal protocols of the day, leaving a rich record of the event for future historians. He maintained to the moment of death that he was loyal to the Spanish crown—and there are good reasons to believe him. Condorcanqui and the many native noblemen like him had a stake in Peru's colonial system. They had spent nearly three centuries navigating Spanish imperial institutions to secure their lands, titles, and traditions under the new laws of the land. In some ways we might categorize José Condorcanqui as a conservative rebel—one fighting for his position within an established colonial system and resisting new administrative reforms that threatened it.[13]

This type of conservative indigenous rebellion was a logical outgrowth of changing conditions throughout Spanish America. We might reasonably ask whether the same phenomenon existed in French and English North America during these years. There is, of course, a glaring distinction between the Iberian conception of indigenous lands and citizenship and those of the French and English. French and English statesmen generally understood native allies and clients as external to the state. The English might view neighboring Indian nations as allies or as enemies, but rarely as citizens or members of English society. In contrast, the Spanish crown had long understood Indian kingdoms and republics to be integral elements of its large multiethnic empire. However, in the half century between the Seven Years' War and the era of independence, this multiethnic structure was threatened by changes to the population of the New World and changes to the administrative practices in the Bourbon state. In the sixteenth century, the Spanish had designed their New World empire as the union of two parallel republics, one Spanish and the other indigenous—each with its own lands, courts, and elected and hereditary leaders. But over time, this system frayed around the edges as intermarriage across ethnic divides created an ever-larger population of mestizos—nowhere more so than in New Spain.[14]

Conservative Rebels: Mexico's Indians and Mestizos in the Napoleonic Era

Mexico's collective memory of indigenous experience during the years of independence is as fallible as our popular memory in the United States. And yet, flawed though it may be, the Mexican tradition does assign a place of pride to the large non-European army that made a failed attempt to overthrow the Mexico City government in 1810. To this day, the most important civic holiday in Mexico is not the anniversary of national independence in 1821—nor is it the relatively minor military event that took place half a century later on Cinco de Mayo—but instead July 16, the day in 1810 when Miguel Hidalgo, the parish priest in the town of Dolores, ascended his church spire in the last moments before dawn and tolled the bells, summoning his parishioners to war.

The viceregal government of Mexico was very nearly overthrown by Hidalgo's spontaneously recruited army. By October 30, 1810, roughly eighty thousand of his Indian and mestizo soldiers were massed in a narrow pass above the Valley of Mexico, poised on the brink of victory. At that moment, Mexico City was the richest and most populous metropolitan area in the Western Hemisphere. It must have been hard to imagine that its power could be challenged by such an undistinguished group of adversaries. The army menacing the capital was enormous, but its men were un-uniformed, poorly equipped, and not all properly trained. Among them were only a few thousand members of organized militias who had the benefit of regular drills and command structures. Despite these manifest weaknesses, it seemed that victory was almost in the rebels' grasp. In the preceding months, this legion of irregulars, its nucleus formed in the town of Dolores, had already conquered Guanajuato, Mexico's greatest mining town; Valladolid, a proud regional capital; and many of the smaller towns and villages along the way. Some communities resisted the rebels but most opened their gates and sent volunteers to flood the ranks of the rebellion.[15]

Miguel Hidalgo is among the most famous faces in Mexico, appearing on textbook covers, public murals, and even on the front of the 1000-peso bill. Despite the familiarity of his name and face, Hidalgo remains a great enigma. He was a scholar and seminarian, an amateur agronomist, a manufacturer, and a playwright. He was also a ceaseless conspirator. The narrative of the Hidalgo rebellion is fairly well known, but historians have struggled to answer a crucial question about it: what were his tens of thousands of poor rural Indian and mestizo followers fighting for? The exact wording of Hidalgo's predawn message at the Dolores church is lost, and contemporary characterizations of his movement varied a great deal at the time, just as they have ever since. However, eyewitnesses to the rebellion agreed about one thing: the slogans chanted by Hidalgo's followers. As they marched thousands of miles through New Spain, they chanted "Long live Fernando VII and the Virgin of Guadalupe" and "Long live the Virgin of Guadalupe and death to the Spanish." Their battle standard was a flag that mixed patriotic images from the New World and Old. It featured a regional advocation of the Virgin Mary (the Virgin of Guadalupe) and the heraldic symbols of Castile and Leon.

The slogans and images of the rebellion seem oddly mismatched to the biography of the movement's architect. Miguel Hidalgo was an erudite man, deeply involved in the philosophical debates of the day, and intimately familiar with the ideologies of the US and French Revolutions. He likely saw his movement as the first step toward a modern and enlightened political system. This leaves us to wonder not just what Hidalgo was thinking, but also what his indigenous and mestizo followers were thinking when they launched this risky political movement. Their slogans suggest a paradox: How could "Long live King Fernando VII" and "Death to the Spaniards" come from the same lips? And what should we make of their invocation of the Virgin of Guadalupe?

The broader context is worth considering. By the time Hidalgo's crowds were on the march in the fall of 1810, both Spain and most of the Spanish New World had been in political chaos for two years. It was a crisis of authority that began with the Napoleonic invasion of Iberia. In 1808, King Carlos IV made an agreement with Napoleon allowing the French to pass freely through Spain and invade Portugal. He hoped this arrangement would spare Spain from attack, cost nothing, and perhaps benefit his kingdom. Soon, however, Spain learned the risks of riding on the tiger's back. Once France was firmly in control of Portugal, more French armies poured over the Pyrenees—this time bound for Madrid. A desperate and humiliated King Carlos IV, now reviled by urban mobs, abdicated in favor of his son Fernando VII. But he acted too late. In no time, both father and son were taken prisoner, and Spain was left in the hands of the French emperor's brother, Joseph Napoleon.

It was this young captive king whom Miguel Hidalgo's soldiers invoked when they shouted "Long Live Fernando VII and the Virgin of Guadalupe!"

In effect, these chanting mobs were demanding the restoration of the prince, the expulsion of the French, and the death of Spanish collaborators. In Mexico they wanted corrupt and incompetent Spaniards expelled, and they wanted for themselves a safe, secure, and prosperous position under the crown. But what of the Virgin of Guadalupe? What did she signify to Hidalgo's followers? This image from Tepeyac was a miraculous copy of the medieval Virgin of Guadalupe from Castile, which appeared in the sixteenth century to a Nahua Indian in central Mexico. In selecting this symbol to represent the rebellion, Hidalgo's followers were sending a clear message: they were Christians and Spanish subjects, but also Indians and Mexicans.

There is much yet to be said about the vagaries of Miguel Hidalgo's program and the political complexities of this worldview; and his followers may have been animated by a variety of concerns. However, one thing seems clear: they weren't fighting against the Spanish crown—they were fighting for it! These men were pious Catholics and loyal subjects of the king. They may have had their grievance against local mine owners, landlords, and tax collectors, but when push came to shove, they were Bourbon vassals and the humble back-bone of a great empire that was rooted in a multicultural pact going back three centuries. Their goal was to expel corrupt Spanish bureaucrats and restore the moral fabric of the old monarchy.[16]

It turns out that the battles waged in 1810 and commemorated annually by Mexican schoolchildren were *not* fought for the glorious cause of independence. Mexican independence arrived a decade later and for somewhat different reasons. In the ten years following Hidalgo's famous rallying cry, Spain experienced a series of political reversals that left the constitutional relationship between colony and mother country up in the air. Between 1808 and 1820, the dynasty was disrupted then restored; and a constitution was adopted, then repudiated, then adopted again. This made the question of loyalty in the New World a complicated one. Depending on which way the wind was blowing in Spain, rebellion against the standing government in Mexico City could be led by republicans or absolutists, Bourbon vassals or secessionists.

Spain in the 1790s was a typical eighteenth-century European state: a layer of royal bureaucracy superimposed on traditional feudal structures. The whole system was maintained through a pragmatic mix of local patronage and centralized oversight. In 1808 when the king found himself a captive of the French, the leaders of Spanish towns fled to Cádiz where they remained safe under

British protection. There they created the blueprint for a new constitutional monarchy. The exiles in Cádiz, just like Hidalgo's armies in Mexico, awaited the return of Fernando VII and prayed for Spain's delivery from the godless armies of Napoleon. They also wrote a new constitution for the empire. The Cádiz Constitution of 1812 conceived of Spanish citizenship on a global scale: it created formal equality between American and European subjects and granted representation for both groups in the new legislative council. Unfortunately, by the time a finished draft of the constitution arrived in Mexico, Miguel Hidalgo had already been defeated, captured, and executed.

The new constitution, if fully implemented, might well have satisfied Hidalgo's followers, but its fate was uncertain from the very beginning. The authors of the document controlled little of Spain at the time of its composition, and Spanish officials in the Americas did not know how best to proceed. In 1815, a massive European coalition defeated the Napoleonic regime, and in Spain the long-awaited Fernando VII ("el Deseado") returned to the throne. To the dismay of the longsuffering Cádiz statesmen, King Fernando soon tore up the constitution and reinstated the old absolutist model of governance. Meanwhile, in New Spain the war continued. New recruits joined the remnants of Hidalgo's forces, fighting on under the leadership of Vicente Guerrero. Guerrero was a merchant and soldier of African, Spanish, and Indian ancestry, whose mixed-race and mixed-class followers continued to resist and harass viceregal forces for the next five years. Back in Spain, another constitutional crisis struck in 1820. General Rafael del Riego, who was mobilizing an army to confront revolutionaries in South America, surprised the king by turning his forces against Madrid and demanding the restoration of the constitution of 1812.[17]

So it was that in 1820, Mexican conservatives (not liberals) began to see the appeal of independence. Hoping desperately to preserve tradition in the face of Spain's leftward turn, Mexico's General Agustín de Iturbide came up with a novel solution: he marched out to meet Vicente Guerrero, and the two men arrived at an agreement to overthrow the viceregal government and establish an independent Mexican nation. The resulting Plan of Iguala had three main elements: national independence, Catholicism, and government by a king (preferably Fernando VII himself). In essence, they planned to reconstruct in Mexico the kind of traditional monarchy that had now been destroyed in Spain. The convoluted story of Mexican independence involved conflicts among liberals, constitutionalists, and republicans, but these ideological debates were relatively new. This period of warfare and political confusion is part of a much longer story. Mexicans (and especially indigenous Mexicans) were generally fighting to defend, not destroy, the old colonial system. The independent Mexico that was born from this moment was Catholic and, at least initially, monarchist. Within a year of the agreement at Iguala, Iturbide proclaimed himself the emperor of a new Mexican nation.

The Cost of Independence

By the time Mexico emerged as a sovereign state, much of Spanish America had already achieved independence. Peru was a notable exception. Though Peru was harried by revolutionaries on all sides, it remained one of the strongest centers of loyalism in the continent—especial in the indigenous highlands. Why, we might ask, did Peruvians have such a different outlook from the neighboring populations in Argentina and Venezuela, which flocked early to the cause of independence? The French occupation of Spain created the same crisis in South America as in Mexico: with their king held prisoner, South American capitals were left to find their own way forward. The creole leaders of La Paz and Quito formed emergency juntas and proclaimed themselves legitimate leaders of their domains. In Lima, the viceroy attempted to hold together the colonial hierarchy even as it crumbled around him. Cuzco stood between these points. This former capital of the Inca Empire and current regional capital of highland Peru was a rich prize for the contending factions.

Surrounded by rivals and menaced by revolutionaries from Venezuela and Argentina, Lima's viceroy, José Fernando de Abascal, found himself in a tight spot. Trustworthy allies were in short supply. In the highlands, he could rely on one man above all others—the man who had saved his life on the battlefield in 1781, the same man who had defeated Túpac Amaru II: Mateo Pumacahua. Responding to the viceroy's call, Pumacahua and fellow Inca nobleman Manuel Choquehuanca de Azángaro raised thousands of troops and marched for La Paz. Brigadier General Pumacahua was now an old man, but he served with distinction in the fight against the junta of La Paz. When he returned to Cuzco, he was appointed president of the audiencia and governor of the valley of Cuzco. And yet, by the summer of 1814, Pumacahua was having second thoughts about his allegiances. The new 1812 Spanish constitution was changing the structure of the empire and the king of Spain remained a French prisoner. In November of 1814, when local Cuzco leader José Angulo and his two brothers proclaimed regional independence, Pumacahua turned away from the viceroy and joined the movement. After years of loyal devotion to the crown and viceroyalty, one wonders why he had this change of heart. It was a risky decision, and in the end he paid dearly for it. In the spring of 1815, he was defeated, captured, and executed in the same plaza where Túpac Amaru I and Túpac Amaru II had met their ends.

To this day, Pumacahua is memorialized as a rebel and as a martyr to the cause of Peruvian independence. But is that really what he was? Was his decision to turn against the Lima government some kind of ideological conversion? The evidence from his long political career points in the opposite direction. From the time of the Túpac Amaru rebellion to the end of his life, Pumacahua was steadfast in his defense of a consistent set of beliefs. He was an Inca nobleman first, a Spanish vassal second, and always a convinced defender of the old hybrid Inca-Spanish state. When Túpac Amaru II threatened Cuzco, he sided with the crown; when French revolutionaries and creole rebels threated the empire, he again sided with the crown; even when the king was made prisoner, he kept the faith. Only when Spanish liberals acting putatively in the name of the absent king began to rewrite the rules of empire did he cease to support the viceroyalty. More than anything, Mateo Pumacahua was a defender of Cuzco and of the traditional Hispano-Inca state that he was raised in.

Looking across the Americas in the years of revolutionary upset that spanned from 1775 to 1825, common patterns in indigenous politics emerge. Native leaders made their decisions in light of considerable experience. Three centuries of European conquest and settlement had not been kind to New World peoples. And yet, over time shrewd Indian leaders had seized whatever opportunities were available to create stable relationships with the colonizers. By the 1770s, Indian leaders from Quebec to Bolivia could invoke longstanding agreements with the Spanish and British crowns whenever threatened by creole attacks on their land, livelihood, or political status. In many cases, European kings and parliaments acted as arbiters in conflicts between native and settler populations. Without royal patronage, native communities were especially vulnerable to expanding creole colonies.

When independence arrived in the Americas, it usually came in the same form: the new polities were defined by notions of territorial sovereignty and liberal citizenship. This was a radically different political landscape for Indian leaders. Europe's American empires had once preserved spaces of native autonomy both within and beside the settler states. Up until the revolutionary era in Latin America, governance was organized around two parallel structures: Spanish republics and Indian republics. Towns were often built in pairs, or split down the middle. Each community elected its own leaders, and both were subjects of the crown. Indians in Mexico and Peru had their own churches, schools, municipal governments, and village lands. They were led by their traditional nobility and represented by their elected leaders. For Latin America, independence and the triumph of liberal republicanism spelled the end of traditional Indian citizenship. The constitutions of the 1820s made all the inhabitants of Mexico into Mexican citizens, and all the inhabitants of Peru into Peruvian citizens—without regard to language, ethnicity, family, or birth. Not only did all citizens become legally identical, but all property became legally identical. Nobility was abolished. Consequently Indian leaders were soon stripped of their hereditary privileges, Indian towns of their governors and councilmen, and Indian villages of their shared land. This was a consequence not just of independence but also of the political ideologies that had first emerged with the Constitution of Cádiz and subsequently shaped new national constitutions. When Indian leaders fought against Spanish viceroys in 1813, 1814, and 1815, they knew exactly what they were doing: fighting against the liberal republican conception of citizenship, and fighting to preserve the old multiethnic empire. When King Fernando repudiated the Cádiz Constitution in 1815, the implications for the New World were clear: creole leadership could be contained and controlled only if the king's power were preserved.

In the long run, Indian leaders' worst suspicions were confirmed. Liberal republican states would triumph throughout the Americas, and they would ultimately strip the Indians in Mexico and Peru of their village lands and their traditional authority. In North America, as we have seen, Indians were usually external to the colonial state. They possessed few of the political and economic privileges held by corporate Indian communities in Latin America. Pushed outside areas of European settlement, they had made the best use of military, commercial, and diplomatic strategies to protect their boundaries from expanding creole settler states. Joseph Brant's mistrust of the American revolutionaries was based on sound judgment. The success of the American independence movement would have disastrous consequences for North America's Indian nations.[18]

The largest political organizations among North American Indians during these years were those of the Iroquois, Cherokees, and Creeks. Their confederations were large and diverse organizations, and their diplomatic choices illustrate the costs and benefits of alignment with Europeans and Euro-Americans. Most of these populations fought on the side of the British and were subsequently punished by the United States. But the US was no kinder to its friends than to its enemies. In the case of the Oneidas, we have an example of a nation—the only one among the Iroquois—that allied itself to the creole rebels. Cherokees sided with the British Empire, as did many Creeks, among them McGillivray's followers. Other Creek towns chose neutrality, hoping to maintain profitable trade agreements with England while staying out of the war. But regardless of these decisions, the long-term consequences for Indian nations under US authority were very similar. The American Revolution was bad for indigenous states. The Creeks would be driven farther and farther from their lands. They fled deeper into the forest and swamp country of the Florida and Louisiana borderlands, accepting escaped African slaves to bolster their numbers. For the Creeks, the most devastating wars would be with the United States, beginning in 1786 after the British troops had gone home.[19]

After the American Revolution, Cherokees and Creeks were subjected to relentless intrusions and attacks by neighboring Georgia settlers. Without the British crown to mediate disputes or defend their borders, the Cherokees' only recourse was to appeal to the government of the United States. For the next forty years, the federal government proved itself first unable and later unwilling to defend the territorial sovereignty of Indian nations in the Southeast. Abandoned by the British and betrayed by the United States, much of the region's native population faced forced deportation to the Indian Territory that later became Oklahoma and western Arkansas. Viewed from a bird's-eye perspective, our small American Revolution here in the United States was part and parcel of a much larger hemispheric war and revolution. The wars of independence severed the political ties between settler populations and their mother countries and at the same time radically transformed the political relationship between indigenous America and settler America. Indian leaders across North and South America were stuck between the horns of a dilemma—there were no good options available to them. In the end, most chose the lesser of two evils. They fought to preserve their place within an older colonial system, and to preserve the alliances that had served their interest over the previous three centuries.[20]

Defending a Northern Refuge: Indian Allies on the Great Lakes

North of the US border, the history of the British Empire continued uninterrupted. The decades immediately following the Revolutionary War reveal sharp distinctions between British attitudes toward native communities and those in the US. For indigenous statesmen in the Great Lakes region, these years required new strategies for war and diplomacy. The War of 1812 highlights the difficulties involved. The conflict arose from unresolved issues of land and sovereignty in the Great Lakes region in the years after US independence. Though it is now usually described as a war between the US and Britain, it was also very much a war between settler states and native states. During the American Revolution, the Iroquois Confederacy had been the greatest Indian military force in North America, but twenty years later, Iroquois power had declined. Now Shawnee leader Tecumseh and his charismatic brother, Tenskwatawa, built a vast coalition of tribes that would fill the vacuum. For a time, this revived Indian confederation would become a major power in the region, but it was ultimately short lived. After William Henry Harrison's surprise attack on the ad hoc Prophetstown capital, the position of the British-allied tribal confederation weakened. This conflict on the border of the US and British Canada soon expanded into a full-scale war. Commander Perry's victory over the British fleet on Lake Eerie permitted a US reconquest of Detroit. From this point forward, US aggression was no longer just a regional crisis; it became an existential threat to British Canada.[21]

Getting a US army from Detroit to the capital of Upper Canada at York was mostly a matter of marching down the road. Protecting the route from invasion was Joseph Brant's colony on the Grand River. US forces reached the Grand River in November of 1814 and approached the established crossing at Brant's Ford. They were met in battle by the local militia, which fought hard to defend the town. The US force was commanded by General Duncan McArthur. His invasion of Canada was a scorched-earth campaign, which sought not just to defeat the British and occupy territory but also to destroy the Canadians' ability to feed and equip their troops. Brant's Crossing was a strategic point along the route, but it was also one of McArthur's objectives. The young town had a lumber mill and a grist mill, and it was well situated as a point of supply: the Grand River flowed into Lake Eerie, but was also a short

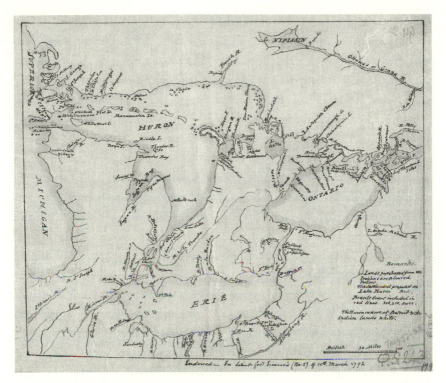

FIGURE 20 Map of the land grant negotiated by Joseph Brant. Plan showing lands purchased from the Indians, proposed settlements on Lake Huron, grant to Joseph Brant, etc., 1792. "Endorsed. In Lieut.-Govr. Simcoe's (No. 5) of 10th March 1792." Courtesy of the Library and Archives Canada.

portage from Lake Ontario. The militias of the Grand River region reflected the pattern of multiethnic settlement engineered by Joseph Brant two decades before. McArthur's troops were opposed by a combination of soldiers from the new, largely European villages and from the Six Nations. Conspicuous on the militia rolls were Tuscaroras and Mohawks, the latter group counting among its members the young and soon-to-be-influential John Smoke Johnson of the Bear Clan. The multiethnic composition of the British forces would have been familiar to US commanders, whose troops included a large number of Ohio militiamen who had come with seventy Indian auxiliaries.[22]

McArthur's men reached Brant's Ford on November 5, 1814, only to discover that their arrival had been anticipated far in advance. Haudenosaunee and English militiamen had sunk the ferry to prevent US soldiers from crossing the river, and they were now entrenched on the other shore ready to defend the ford. Faced with high water and a row of sharpshooters, the Americans withdrew, turning their wrath upon other nearby communities, and seizing the supplies and destroying the infrastructure that would otherwise aid the English forces. It was a cruel and effective strategy. The following day, the Americans were opposed once again by Canada's multiethnic militias at the Battle of Malcolm's Mills. It was a defeat for the Canadians, and one that imposed real costs on the local population. The invaders devastated the area: five mills were burned to the ground, a number of Canadians were killed, and even more were taken prisoner. The Grand River forces had stopped the Americans at Brant's Ford only to be bested at Malcolm's Mills. For McArthur, it was a Pyrrhic victory. The fight for control of the Grand River region demonstrated the depth of Canadian resistance and the strength of its combined forces of settlers and Indians. Unbeknownst to any of the participants, events elsewhere in North America would soon render their efforts irrelevant. The War of 1812 was coming to an end, and the future of North America would be worked out from this point forward not on the battlefield but at the bargaining table.[23]

John Smoke Johnson survived the battle, and his military service was a point of pride in subsequent years. Johnson was born in the early days of the Iroquois resettlement, and his experiences reflected those of the second generation of Mohawk leaders. He was raised in the Grand River valley, grew up speaking English and Mohawk, served in the militia, and became influential in politics. Like many of the powerful people in the region, he was closely connected to the Johnson-Brant family. Though John Smoke Johnson was entirely Mohawk by ancestry, he had received the name Johnson at the time of his baptism. His godfather was Sir William Johnson.[24]

One usually thinks of the War of 1812 as a fight between the emerging United States and England—and so it was—but the Grand River region that General McArthur invaded in 1812 was its own distinctive cultural space. It was a proud part of the British Empire, but not entirely English. It was an uneasy meeting point where local Mississaugas, the Iroquois nations, and a variety of English and Scottish settlers formed a new society. Thirty years beforehand, the British Empire's defeat by American colonists in the Revolutionary War had created a hemispheric refugee crisis. A good fifty miles up the river from Brantford—or a bit more if one followed its winding course—stood the village of Waterloo. The town was first settled by Germans, many of whom had sided with the British in the Revolutionary War (like the Haudenosaunee), or fled from the conflict as Mennonite pacifists. The Haudenosaunee were vital allies of the British in the Seven Years' War and again in the American Revolution. They were in some respects a subordinate kingdom within the British Empire; in other respects, they remained independent. When the American Revolution erupted, the leaders of the Iroquois Confederacy still considered themselves the representatives of sovereign peoples, and they still charted an independent foreign policy. This is the heritage of the Haudenosaunee settlers who established themselves in the Grand River region and later fought in the War of 1812.[25]

The Six Nations forces at Brant's Ford were likely fighting for two reasons: first and foremost to defend their homes and families, but second to fulfill a compact that had been carefully negotiated over many years. In the fall of 1811, Major General Isaac Brock had come to the Grand River seeking a solid alliance against the United States. The Six Nations council at first took a cautious approach to his offer. A number of individuals voluntarily enlisted with the imperial forces, but the tribal leaders did not immediately commit themselves. First, they wanted to see whether the English would be able to deliver on their promises. When British and Shawnee forces captured Detroit in August of 1812, they were finally convinced. The Haudenosaunee cast their lot decisively with England, and it was they (among others) who held the line in 1814.[26]

General McArthur's forces were turned back just a few hundred feet from Brantford by Canada's Euro-American and Native American militiamen. If the US soldiers had crossed the river, entered the town, and reached the core of the Six Nations district, they would have seen exactly how the political structures of British Canada operated at the ground level. Brant's Ford was a complex place. Here an enclave of white settlers lived right beside a Mohawk village and not far from Tuscarora, Seneca, and Onondaga villages.[27] These communities were all, in one way or another, integrated into Canada's legal and commercial systems: many of the indigenous inhabitants held private-property deeds and participated in a cash economy; and they engaged in the same forms of agriculture and skilled trades that one would find anywhere in Anglo-America. In other respects, the Iroquois communities differed from those of their white neighbors. They preserved political structure that they had carried with them into exile after the American Revolutionary War. Their leadership was based on clans and nations. Each of the Iroquois nations had its own council house where civic matters were first discussed internally before being submitted to the sachems of the League Council. The old political geography of the Iroquois had taken root in a new land. In truth, though, neither the Iroquois political system nor its economy was static. Brantford had mills, shops, and artisans of all kinds. In the years after the War of 1812, the town and its hinterlands were increasingly connected to the larger economy by roads, barges, and canals. In the coming decades, the Brantford-to-Hamilton stagecoach line and the Niagara-to-Detroit toll road would keep the Six Nations in close communication with the rest of North America.[28]

Leading Nations in Exile: The Haudenosaunee of the Grand River

Today not much remains of the earliest structures in the Grand River Reserve. One conspicuous exception is the Mohawk Chapel that still stands on the east side of town. Joseph Brant lies buried beside its wall, his tomb a fitting resting place for the man who planned and patronized its construction. The first stones were laid in 1788, making it the oldest Anglican church in Ontario. It dates from an age in which Mohawk and Christian beliefs were mingling and new forms of religious life emerging. The schoolhouse and the church were the first public buildings in Brant's settlement. The architecture was fundamentally European, but despite its outward appearance, these European institutions and buildings were in the hands of Indian leaders. Many young Iroquois were educated at the school, though the wealthiest families sometimes sent their children east for an elite education. This was certainly the case for Joseph Brant's sons, Isaac and Jacob, who were educated at Dartmouth. But formal education was not just for the richest among them; the Six Nations leaders placed a premium on education for the larger community as well.[29]

Joseph Brant planned the construction of the school immediately upon founding the settlement, and it soon became a focus for Mohawk community life. It is not easy to recapture the daily lives of schoolchildren from this era, but contemporary textbooks provide us some glimpses of what went on inside the schoolhouse. A 1786 textbook titled *A Primer for the Use of Mohawk Children* includes an illustration showing the interior of a Mohawk school. The schoolroom is an open hall with massive wooden beams above and broad plank flooring below; the walls are plastered and the space is well lit. Architecturally

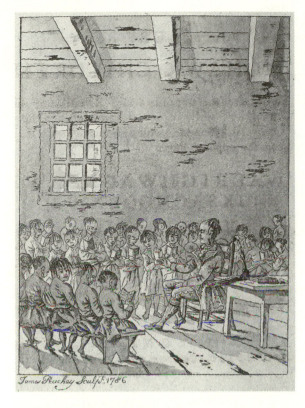

FIGURE 21 A Mohawk schoolroom. Frontispiece engraving by James Peachey. From Daniel Claus's *A Primer for the Use of the Mohawk Children* (London: C. Buckton, 1786). Courtesy of the John Carter Brown Library, Brown University.

it is indistinguishable from the sort of one-room schoolhouse that was at the time common in rural areas throughout the United States and Canada. In the print, more than two dozen students are visible, and the artist's way of framing the image suggests that more lie just outside our field of vision. The scene is a familiar one, but the modern viewer is struck by little details that distinguish it from an Anglo-American classroom. The students, who are reading and reciting, are neatly dressed in European frock coats, knickers, and buckled shoes. Other details in their appearance mark them as Indians. The boys wear large earrings, and their heads are shaved so that only the distinctive Mohawk top-locks remain. Their male teacher sits in a chair at the head of the class, dressed like a middle-class Englishman from collar to shoe, but he also wears large earrings and has the same distinctly Mohawk hairstyle as his pupils.[30]

This striking combination of European architecture with mixed elements of indigenous and European dress was often remarked upon by visitors to the town. Elizabeth Simcoe, the wife of Upper Canada's lieutenant governor, preserved the richest visual record of life in the region during the 1790s—one that captures the hybridized cultures of the Grand River. Simcoe wrote a detailed diary of her experience and produced hundreds of sketches and watercolors of the landscapes and people of the Canadian Great Lakes region. Simcoe traveled far and wide on both sides of the Atlantic, so her artwork shows us how she understood indigenous Americans in a global context. At first glance, her images of the Grand River settlements are hardly distinguishable from her sketches of British Canada or even those of her native Herefordshire in England.[31] A 1793 watercolor of the Mohawk village shows it to be an attractive town on the bluff above the river, its one- and two-story homes bounded by tidy fences. Upstream stands the Mohawk council house with its high roof line, several chimneys, and a fluttering flag; a bit downstream stands a cluster of buildings and what appears to be a fortified block house, along with the Mohawk church, a handsome wooden structure with a graceful steeple.[32]

Other travelers also contributed to the surviving record of daily life in and around Brant's Ford. Just after the conclusion of the War of 1812, British officer and traveler Francis Hall passed through the Grand River settlements and attended church in the Mohawk Chapel. He described a congregation of between sixty and seventy people, the oldest among them dressed in traditional Mohawk garb, their bodies wrapped in cloaks and adorned with ornaments and medals. The younger parishioners wore European garments, but much like the children in the schoolhouse, they distinguished themselves from European neighbors by their hair and face paint. In the early days of the Grand River settlement, the Mohawk Chapel had no dedicated clergyman; it was visited on a circuit by the nearest priest. But by the time of Hall's visit, the church was fully staffed and occupied. The Mohawk priest Dr. Aaron Hill gave his sermons in English dress but with traditional red paint on his cheeks and forehead. Clearly, this church was attended and run by Mohawks. Though the Grand River had no college or seminary on the scale one associates with the native church in early Latin America, the Mohawk Chapel was at the center of a significant, informal intellectual community. Aaron Hill, who was closely connected to the Brant family, was a key figure in this social circle. He was an ordained priest with extensive pastoral responsibilities; he also collaborated with Elizabeth Brant (Joseph's daughter) to translate more of the Bible into Mohawk. Francis Hall met Brant and Hill during his visit to Burlington Bay and the Grand River. He was deeply impressed by both of them, remarking on their flawless command of the English language. Elizabeth he described as beautiful, elegant in manner, and dressed in a curious combination of European and Mohawk garments. He was quite taken by the effect.[33]

Inside the Mohawk Chapel, one could find liturgy and ritual that matched contemporary European notions of orthodox religious praxis.[34] Outside the church walls, North American Christianity was changing rapidly for Euro-Americans and Indians alike. During the first decades of the nineteenth century, a revival of native religion swept through the Great Lakes tribes. Just as Mohawk Bibles and traditional face paint could be found inside church-consecrated spaces, the ideas and images of Christianity were also spreading outside of the church and combining with local notions of indigenous renewal. These were the years when Handsome Lake, the Seneca mystic from New York, had his visions of a new Indian religion based on the rejection of European vice and the resurrection of ancestral ethics and ritual. His movement combined features of inherited Seneca religion with the phenomena of personal testimonials, temperance, and mass revival that were widespread among Protestant Euro-Americans during the Second Great Awakening. Though Handsome Lake himself lived in New York, his movement did not stop at the US-Canada border. The same was true of Tenskwatawa's movement, which began among the Shawnees but soon spread to native communities throughout the Mississippi and Great Lakes regions. On one hand, these native revivalist movements were modeled on Christian cosmology with a focus on virtue, vice, temptation, and the struggle between a benevolent universal god and the wiles of the devil. On the other hand, the movements were adamantly nativist and rejected the notion of European clergy as ritual specialists or arbiters of truth.[35]

Among the Haudenosaunee (both the Canadian settlers and the remaining populations in New York), strains of Christianity and traditional religion freely mixed. Historically, their midwinter religious rites had been among the most important, especially the White Dog Sacrifice. Some version of the same ritual existed throughout the Iroquois Confederacy: an unblemished white dog (or sometimes several) was carefully adorned, strangled, suspended from a pole for a period of time, and then finally burned. The ritual has been described in a variety of ways by early missionaries, later anthropologists, and the Haudenosaunee themselves. The sacrifice cleansed and protected the community, restored moral order, and defended it against disease, crop failure, and lightning.

For a time, it seemed that the practice of the White Dog Sacrifice had died out among the Haudenosaunee. But in 1798 it reappeared in the Grand River settlements, first in the Small Oneida community, and later throughout the Six Nations. Joseph Brant was initially uncertain about how to respond. He had invested years of effort in joining the Mohawks to the British Empire and the Church of England. Was the sacrifice an innocuous tradition or a real threat to his lifelong goal of cultural and political synthesis? Eventually, Brant struck a middle course. He gave his approval to the White Dog Sacrifice, allowing it and other aspects of native religion to coexist with Anglican Christianity. It was neither the first nor the last time that Mohawks would maintain community cohesion by artfully blending the old and the new.[36]

What was it like to be born into this world of hybridized political structures and syncretic religion? Perhaps the experience is best recaptured through the lives of elite Mohawks whose personal histories are better documented than others'. William Simcoe Kerr gives us a window on their world. In the year 1832, Simcoe Kerr was granted the title of Tekarihoken, arguably the most powerful hereditary position in the Mohawk tribe, and by extension, the most important title among the Haudenosaunee of the Grand River region. At the age of twelve, he had not yet done much to earn the distinction; it was a gift of high birth. Kerr's ancestry was an illustrious one, and the privileges and assets transmitted to him were the accumulated rewards accrued to his family after three generations of skillful diplomacy and strategic marriages.[37]

In the early nineteenth century, the Grand River lands lay on the fault line of the US-Canada border. The six Haudenosaunee tribes along with a group of Delaware Indians had been settled there among the region's original Mississauga inhabitants since the 1780s. The area was only a four-day march from Lundy's Lane, the battlefield near Niagara that claimed some of the greatest casualties in the War of 1812.[38] Grand River and nearby Burlington Bay could be risky places even in peace time. This zone at the head of Lake Ontario was a place where enterprising men dreamed of thriving towns and great personal fortunes. But the failed dreamers and schemers proved more numerous than those who actually succeeded over time. The Grand River flows through a narrow neck of land between Lake Eerie and Lake Ontario—a place of obvious opportunity that beckoned from the map in an age when western land speculation and the allure of profits from new canals and railroads created dizzying cycles of boom and bust. There are only so many ways to move goods by land and water through the Great Lakes region, and the Six Nations held a privileged position on the map. They occupied one of the only good overland routes connecting Detroit to the new western capital at York and ultimately to Ottawa and Montreal. This area was also crucial to controlling the routes linking New York and Western Canada. Any canal to be built between Lakes Eerie and Ontario (and there were many plans for such a canal in the 1820s) would have to come right through the Grand River region. With these abundant opportunities to profit from roads and canals, the area appeared a speculator's gold mine. But with such a heterogeneous collection of stakeholders in the US and Canada, it was a real trick to come out on top. Any business scheme to build new infrastructure was inherently political. Success required a combination of fortunate birth, social capital, and cultural competence across several very different environments. In many cases it also meant luck, timing, and pragmatic marriages between Indians and Europeans.[39]

Hybrid Dynasties in Anglo-Indian Canada

In the long history of the Haudenosaunee resettlement, two of the most powerful groups were the Johnson family and the Brant family. By the time of William Simcoe Kerr's political ascension, both the interests and the heredity of the two families had been intertwined for almost a century. Back in the 1740s, the young Anglo-Irishman William Johnson had established a trading post near the Mohawk village of Canajoharie in what is now New York State. He had a large family by two wives, the first an immigrant from Germany, the second Molly Brant. Johnson's gifts for intercultural diplomacy were significant. He learned the Mohawk language, built deep commercial ties with local Indian leaders, and joined his family to the Mohawk community through his informal marriage to Molly. He was soon the de facto representative of the British Empire to the Iroquois; and from 1756 onward, he was its de jure representative as superintendent for Indian affairs. Molly and William were able to exercise great influence as cultural intermediaries, both to advance their own interests and to serve the needs of their respective European and Indian clients. In 1761, they arranged an opportunity for Molly's younger brother, Joseph, that would have lasting cultural and political implications for the Mohawks. Young Joseph Brant was sent to More's Christian Charity School to study with Eleazar Wheelock. He would return years later, well versed in English language and custom, and with an aura of credibility among the colonists that rested on his reputation as a model Indian convert to Christianity.[40]

Governance among the Iroquois relied upon elegant structures that balanced the interests of nations, clans, and genders. Some positions of power were hereditary, others open to opportunity. Weighty matters often required deliberation by men's and women's councils. People from elite genealogies dominated statecraft, but succession was not controlled by the fixed rules that existed in English society. In times of war, male leadership was especially important, but it was women who ultimately made the decision on succession, selecting from among the viable claimants in a given family. Generally speaking, hereditary power was transmitted by women to men among Mohawks, while it was transmitted directly between men in European society. This made questions of land title and inheritance complex in frontier areas where intermarriage was common. Among Mohawks, access to natural resources was a matter of accustomed use and community allocation. There had been individual land rights in the precolonial era, but they existed amid practices of mobility, temporary land tenure, and community decision-making. Meanwhile among the English, land deeds and contracts trumped all else. In the uncertain world at the blurred boundaries of English and Mohawk cultures, family interests were best served by working in both systems. The most secure social position was one in which a powerful English family was joined to a powerful Indian one. Descent from an elite English father and an elite Indian mother would take advantage simultaneously of the succession rules in the matrilineal Indian sphere and in the patrilineal English one. Finally, the wisest person would seek to hold usufruct rights over land within the Mohawk tradition and at the same time hedge his bets by obtaining a redundant land title under English law.

These strategies taken together describe quite perfectly the story of the Brant-Johnson clan. Consider the ways in which Molly Brant and William Johnson preserved their valuable cross-cultural alliance for successive generations. Johnson had one line of descendants though his first common-law wife, Catherine Weissenberg, creating an entirely Euro-American branch of the family; and another line of descent through Molly Brant, creating an Anglo-Mohawk line. For his service as a commander in the Seven Years' War, Johnson was elevated to the nobility and awarded the title of baronet. By then, Johnson had advanced about as a far as a man could go by personal merit and initiative, becoming a successful businessman, the superintendent of Indian af-

fairs, and a military officer. He enjoyed the confidence of the colonial administration largely because of his influence with the Mohawks—an influence greatly
facilitated by his relationship to Molly Brant and her brother Joseph. Johnson's
elevation to baronet helped to ensure that his personal triumphs would lend
status to his male descendants in perpetuity. His son by Catherine Weissenberg
would inherit his title of nobility and would eventually succeed the father as
superintendent of Indian affairs. Molly Brant's hereditary position was also a
key to the family's influence. In fact, her position in the Turtle Clan made her
something of a kingmaker. Her relationship to Johnson combined the advantages of Mohawk elites with those of the rising English professional class. In
the next generation, her family would continue to embrace the same strategy.[41]

Molly and William's daughter Elizabeth Johnson carried matrilineal authority from her mother's clan, and her marriage to an enterprising colonial
Englishman gave her some of the same advantages that Molly had possessed.
The choice of Robert Kerr as a husband was a wise one. Kerr was a respectable
military surgeon who rose through the ranks of Canada's public and private organizations, consolidating property and influence along the way. He served in
the renowned military campaigns that defended Canada from the US invasion
in and around Niagara in the War of 1812. In professional life he was a doctor,
a military officer, and later a judge. Anglo-Canada had its own clan structures
in the form of complex voluntary associations with their own fictive kinship
networks that in some ways mirrored those of Mohawks. In this sphere, Kerr
wielded power though Masonic organizations, first as a deputy grand master
and later as the grand master of the Niagara lodge. He owned land and controlled vital infrastructure along the eastern shores of Lake Ontario, serving
for a time in the House Assembly and keeping a hand in commerce as superintendent of the Burlington Canal. Property came to this family on both sides.
Consequently, Robert and Elizabeth Johnson were able to live quite well. Like
many great dynastic unions, it was a marriage between cousins.[42]

The Kerrs were able to effect a dynastic union that would reconsolidate
the authority of two branches of the Brant and Johnson clan. Their son, William Johnson, married Elizabeth Brant, the daughter of Joseph and Catherine
Brant. The Johnson and Brant families had two great Mohawk matriarchs,
Molly Brant and Catherine Brant. And the power of both would be transmitted to the children of William Johnson Kerr and Elizabeth Brant. Catherine
outlived by many years not just her husband but also her in-laws. She knew

the value of a well-designed cross-cultural marriage. Her own mother was an important leader in the Turtle Clan and her father a prosperous fur trader from Ireland. Before her death in 1873, she exercised the traditional privilege of designating the next generation of male leadership. She chose William Simcoe Kerr, and in so doing neatly bound together the family's material assets and traditional authority in one package.[43]

Dreams of a Pan-Indian Nation

This melding of families with military and professional groups took place on both sides of the border. In the nineteenth-century United States, capital, property, and professional status had largely replaced heredity and nobility as the coins of the realm. No small number of Indian and mixed-race individuals had passed entirely into the Anglo-American community. At the same time, a few people traveled in the opposite direction. As in Canada and Latin America, some influential families combined Indian and European genealogies.[44] A striking family of this type was the one formed by Elizabeth Howell and the Ojibway intellectual George Copway.

In 1858, Elizabeth Howell Copway wrote to her husband in a storm of guilt and anxiety. She described her inner struggle as a volcano burning in her soul and as a crisis that left her on the brink of suicide. Repenting of her past errors and begging for forgiveness, she warned that ending her "life of utter agony and woe" was the only thought that thrilled "her desolate heart with momentary pleasure." The letter is penned in a frenetic hand, with compact words written over an earlier note. The effect is that of a tidy palimpsest, the two letters intersecting at ninety degrees, an earlier moment in her life erased by a later one. The first page of the correspondence is missing, and the terrible transgression for which she apologizes goes unnamed.[45]

Happily, Howell's life did not come to an end on that dark day in 1858. She would live on until 1904 and die at the venerable age of eighty-seven—but her life, and that of her husband, George, was dogged by disappointment. They had lost three children and had seen their wealth and social standing slip away from them. In their most fortunate hour, the Copways had been respected, famous, and politically influential. George Copway had been widely known as a clergyman, missionary, historian, newspaper publisher, and social reformer. He was once acknowledged as a chief of the Ojibway nation, and he had served as a diplomat between his community and the Canadian and US nations that surrounded the Ojibways to the north and the south.

To many of the Indians of the Great Lakes region, Elizabeth Copway was known as Wahbegoonequay (White Flower). The name was Ojibway, but the ones she gave to daughters came from far and wide: one was baptized Pocahontas after the famed Algonquian woman, another Minnehaha after the wife of Hiawatha. Despite the names, Elizabeth was not herself an Indian. She was born to Anglo-American parents and raised in Scarborough in Upper Canada, a place that is today within the bounds of greater Toronto. Her father, Captain Henry Hall, was a man of some social standing, but this was no guarantee of future prosperity. He raised her in a land where reversals of fortune were common and boundaries between cultures fluid.

When Elizabeth Copway baptized her daughter as Pocahontas, she must have reflected on the strange parallels between her own life and that of her daughter's more famous namesake. At a decisive moment in her youth, the young Algonquian Pocahontas married across cultures, crossed a boundary, and emerged as Lady Rebecca. The chronicles of the early Americas are filled with stories of elite Indian women who were bound by misfortune or by genuine affection to European men. But the biography of Elizabeth Howell (like that of Sarah Bird Northrup) is a new twist on an old tale—a European woman married to an influential Indian man. Her husband's career as a clergyman, journalist, and politician made him one of the most significant indigenous leaders in Anglo-America.

On January 25, 1849, when George Copway rose to address the Pennsylvania General Assembly, he began on a note of false modesty: "Gentlemen of the Legislature of Pennsylvania, my limited knowledge of your language will render it somewhat difficult for me to be understood this evening, as I speak a tongue which is not my own—which is not my native language. Permit me, however, to ask your indulgence while I endeavor to present to you the claims of the Indian." In truth, Copway was not a modest man. His speech sparkled with erudition, and it showed few signs of genuine humility. He was introduced as "a Chief of the Chippewa," and his claim to speak on behalf of the Chippewas and of other Western nations rested as much on his status as a gentleman and an intellectual as it did on his heredity or any formal office. In the lengthy address that followed, Copway presented a condensed history of America, an account of the changing Western economy, and a plan for Indian social uplift. He also presented his blueprint for a vast multiethnic Indian state that would in the future be admitted to the American union.[46]

Copway was a master orator, and he knew his audiences well.[47] When addressing Methodists, he spoke an evangelical language replete with soaring Biblical imagery and punctuated with redemptive tears. To churchmen and white politicians alike, he used the language of civilization and reform, soliciting aid for the projects of agriculture, literacy, and civic education among the Indians. Speaking to the Pennsylvania legislature, he struck just the right tone to win over a body of educated, skeptical men. His humor was self-referential and his manner disarming, but just beneath the surface, his speech was challenging Anglo-American attitudes and attacking US public policy. From the podium, and before the joint session of House and Senate, he shared an anecdote about his arrival in the capital: "Many have asked—'Who is that Indian? Where has he come for, and where was he born? And what is he about?' They have asked one another these questions when I have been endeavoring to explain my views in relation to the salvation of my poor countrymen. Thank Heaven, I am an Indian. . . . I heard one gentleman say to another—'Who is that?' 'Who is he?' Now if he is in this Hall at this present time, tell him I am a native American.'"[48] Copway's humor was a Trojan horse. He was both likeable and subversive. At the time, it was surely a surprise to hear an Ojibway call out a legislator in this way and take him to task for his attitude toward Indians. It was a risky approach but one that worked. The gallery burst out in laughter and applause. Copway went on to attack the history of bad faith by the United States toward Indian nations. Speaking in the aftermath of the great Indian removals of the 1830s and 1840s, he cautioned that all current US-Indian relations were burdened by the long history of treaty violations. He spoke directly to the assembled legislators, implicating them in this history and asking, "Have not the laws which have been secured to this people been violated by those who succeeded to the law-making power? Most assuredly they have."[49]

Copway's influence on the national and international discussions of the "Indian question" was significant. In the course of his public career, he published four books and traveled throughout the nation and the world in an attempt to popularize his views on religion, education, and public policy. The year after his address to the Pennsylvania legislature, Copway attended the World Peace Conference in Frankfurt, then returned to the United States where he began publishing his fascinating but short-lived New York newspaper *Copway's American Indian.*

George Copway often retold the troubling history of early European interactions with Native America in order to diagnose the current problems in US-Indian relations. This historical approach informed all of his attempts to chart a better future. For Copway, the age before Columbus was a prelapsarian paradise for the Indian: "The game of the forest he claimed as his own, the fish of the waters and the course of the river were also his. Proudly he roamed through the country where now stand your farms and your mighty cities. . . . He knew no boundaries, he knew no limits to his desire."[50] Describing the first English contacts in North America, Copway pointed to a path not taken— an alternate history that might have created a more just society. He recalled the lost possibilities inherent in the Massachusetts Thanksgiving story, and he reserved special praise for William Penn's early treaty with the Delaware Indians. He made a personal pilgrimage to the site in Philadelphia where the Delaware treaty was concluded, and he took a cutting from the elm tree under which it was supposedly signed. These were moments from the mythic past that pointed toward a better path for Anglo-Indian relations.

In the 1840 and 1850s, Copway saw a very different world than the one inhabited by William Penn: the natural resources necessary for Indians' traditional subsistence practices were fast disappearing, and Native American spaces were inundated by Anglo-American settlers.[51] Copway's response to the crisis was pragmatic. If the US conquest of the Great Plains was inevitable, then the best solution for the Indians of the West was to set aside their ethnic distinctions, negotiate a general settlement with the Anglo-Americans, and constitute themselves as a US state. If his plan succeeded, western Indians could avail themselves of the same legal mechanisms that had permitted Anglo-American squatters to transform territories into states. He proposed that a vast new territory—one which he sometimes called Kahgega—should include much of the land that is today western Iowa and North and South Dakota. In one form or another, Ojibway leaders had argued for some version of this settlement for a decade, but Copway's version of the proposal was sweeping. He called for a unification of the Ojibways with the Sioux, Winnebagos, Potawatomis, and Osages. His full proposal was described in a twenty-five-page pamphlet titled *Organization of a New Indian Territory East of the Missouri*

River, printed in New York and submitted to Congress in the 1849 session.[52] In fact, Copway's speech in Philadelphia was a condensed version, or a dress rehearsal, of the broader appeal he made thereafter to the national government. Unfortunately, rapidly changing conditions in Washington, DC, and on the American plains were fast overtaking Copway and forcing him to scale back his ambitions. Separated by just a few months, his Philadelphia speech and his draft legislation reflect a shift in proposed boundaries for the new territory of Kahgega, which he now delimited not by the Iowa River but by the Sioux River some two hundred miles to the west. Even with these more modest boundaries, it was to be a large territory, and one granted almost complete internal political autonomy. Its citizens would be drawn from all the displaced Indian nations of Michigan, Wisconsin, and Iowa.

The draft legislation detailed a constitutional system in which the inhabitants would be governed both by their own tribal councils and by a general council with legislative authority for the territory. Its executive authority was invested in a governor and lieutenant governor, each serving three-year terms. The United States government was to protect Kahgega's territorial integrity by establishing a garrison that would defend Indian lands against threats from white squatters. Copway described a system of secondary schools and seminaries, as well as a new agricultural system that would transform the prairies into productive farmland. The project was audacious and might at first have appeared impractical to Anglo-American readers, but Copway anticipated all objections. In his pamphlet, the draft legislation is followed by a series of letters from influential Americans endorsing his project—not just clergymen and philanthropists but also powerful politicians, including the current secretary of the interior.[53] Perhaps most interesting, in retrospect, is Copway's notion of Indian ethnicity and citizenship. His writings walk a narrow line, describing much of indigenous America as uncivilized while at the same time arguing for a future state governed by civilized Indians. How such a thing is possible becomes clearer once one begins to glimpse Copway's particular form of cultural elitism. In describing the civil functionaries of Kahgega, Copway frequently calls for the appointment of "educated Indians."

Early in his career, he may have had a more ethnically bounded notion of Indian identity. Copway had worked hard to translate the Gospel of Luke and the Book of Acts into Ojibway, and he had once represented himself primarily as a representative of that nation. But by 1849 his notion of Indianness seems to have changed. In his introduction to the Kahgega legislation, he argues for an educational system focused on English-language literacy, both because of its cultural capital in the growing United States and, presumably, because it could one day constitute a common language for all Indians.[54] Central to Copway's plan was the idea that distinct Indian nationalities would soon merge into one broader community. He cautioned that "not until they amalgamate, will they lose the hostile feelings they have for each other."[55] With respect to religion, Copway urged not just the abandonment of traditional native practices but also the end of denominational boundaries among Christian Indian converts. Whether speaking of faith, language, or clan, Copway's ultimate goal was to create what he termed a "great family of Indians."[56]

Crucial to all of Copway's plans was the leadership of the group of acculturated, Anglophone Indians to which he himself belonged.[57] His autobiography, which is laced with commentaries on history and politics, seems designed to illustrate the ancestral virtues of Indians, the tragedies of the conquest, and the ability of modern Indians to enter into European civilization. Copway builds his case partly on the basis of well-known Indian individuals and groups who had successfully crossed the cultural divide. Whenever Copway described the pathologies of impoverished and benighted Indians, he was quick to explain that he was not referring to the "educated and enlightened portion of the Indians that are now living in the different parts of the United States, as, for instance, the Indians of the state of New York, and those of Michigan, and the states of North and South Carolina, as well as Georgia." Clearly Copway distinguished not only between more and less educated members of a given tribe but also between entire Indian nations, some of which he considered "educated and enlightened," and some not. These "civilized" groups in the eastern half of the continent were profoundly connected to the Euro-American societies that surrounded them. He questioned whether "All these Indians . . . will go to the far West and there join their brethren and form one family," or stay among the European population. He also imagined different fates for individuals: "I do not mean that the more improved and educated portion of them, will remove from their present homes but only those who are not so advanced in civilization."[58] The natural leaders of Copway's Indian community—both inside Anglo-American states and in the newly formed territories—should be men like himself: "Chiefs" of their ancestral nations and civilized men of "liberal education."

Of course, Copway's dream never came to pass, but the fact that his proposal was so plausible to the members of educated society in the 1840s says a great deal about Anglo-American beliefs on status, ethnicity, and citizenship in his generation. This was the era of the Trail of Tears, of slavery in the American South, and of ongoing ethnic cleansing and settler colonialism in the West. And yet, for a significant sector of Anglo-American leaders, George Copway and the class of acculturated and formally educated Indians that he represented could be treated as professionals, intellectuals, and even peers. As paradoxical as these nineteenth-century US attitudes might appear, they are not entirely different from those of their sixteenth-century Spanish predecessors. For centuries, Native Americans had experienced a wide variety of fates at the hands of the colonizers. Europeans dispossessed indigenous peoples of their land, extorted labor and tribute, and even bought and sold them in a variety of legal and illegal slave-trading networks. They regarded many Indians as savages or perpetual minors; but others they saw as gentlemen, aristocrats, professionals, and scholars. In some ways, however, the nineteenth century really was different.

———

Across the Western Hemisphere, the age of independence shattered longstanding agreements between European leaders and indigenous elites. Indian republics as political institutions were erased, and nobility ceased to exist as a legal principle for colonizers and colonized alike. Empires built from constellations of client states were replaced with unitary nation-states whose new constitutions simplified civic identities, producing a world of citizens and noncitizens where a more subtle spectrum of political identities had once existed. The communities and individuals who survived this transition were forced to translate their old identities into terms intelligible to new liberal regimes. The George Copways and Henry Roe Clouds of the world forced their way into the structures of power not by touting their ancestry or the historic privileges of their communities but by representing themselves as educated scholars and professionals, whose markers of status were intelligible to the leadership of the new white republics on their own terms. Tragically, rising native elites were often forced to justify their positions by emphasizing their acculturation and modernity in contrast to humbler members of their own ethnic communities, who were consequently stigmatized as premodern and uncivilized. This also changed the political landscape for people of mixed ancestry throughout the Americas. Through much of colonial history, mestizos saw good reasons to shift in all directions among the standard categories of race and caste, seeking opportunities and avoiding liabilities as they claimed or shed different parts of their ancestry. But the nineteenth century was a different time. To be an Indian—no matter how distinguished in lineage, talent, or training—was now only rarely an asset.

Concluding
Thoughts

The colonial Americas was born from conquests and pandemics—in an age of profound social disruption that imposed terrible human costs but also offered unexpected opportunities. In the early days of transatlantic contact, travelers ventured deep into new and unfamiliar cultural spaces. Some did so out of ambition and some out of desperation. Others entered new lands by no choice of their own, transported as captives and slaves of foreign masters. Under these circumstances, swift and creative cultural improvisation was the key to survival. All European empires, however hegemonic, were inherently multicultural, and their stability required some degree of reciprocity between foreign and local leaders. It was a marriage of sorts, but an unequal one. In the sixteenth and seventeenth centuries, this troubled marriage bound Europeans and Native Americans together in a union of nations, families, institutions, and individuals. It merged languages, religions, customs, and aesthetics.

Initially the position of the conquerors was a tenuous one. The first Spaniards in the Andes and the Valley of Mexico were few in number and vulnerable at every moment. The same was true a century later in North America when a handful of Englishmen clung to the coasts of Virginia and Massachusetts, and a few Frenchmen to the banks of the Saint Lawrence. The Europeans' survival depended as much on their relationships with local leaders as it did on their own capabilities. Constructing these relationships meant bridging a cultural chasm that had separated the two halves of the planet since the last ice age.

Cultural diplomacy was a two-way street. Of necessity, Europeans and Native Americans were forced to learn each other's languages, conform to each other's diplomatic protocols, and navigate each other's cultural norms. Quechua and Nahua governments sent diplomats to Spain, and their nobles and intellectuals explored Europe both in the flesh and through the printed word. Scottish traders lived among Cherokees, and French fur trappers among Ojibways. Spanish conquerors arranged status marriages with Inca noblewomen; and Frenchmen mingled with native Canadians through commerce, military alliances, and strategic marriages on their northern and western trade routes.

In the long run, however, these conditions of reciprocal acculturation became rarer and rarer. A great demographic shift buried the surviving members of disease-ravaged native societies under an avalanche of European migrants. With each passing century, it was less necessary for Europeans to master native cultures and less possible for native people to avoid accommodation or acculturation to European languages, economics, and political systems.

The early colonial era married together the institutions and social elites of the conquered and conquerors, following a pattern common to European and American empires throughout history. Even before the arrival of Pizarro and Cortés, the Inca Empire had included Aymaras and Cañaris, and the Mexica Empire Totonacs and Otomis. The Spanish Empire that swallowed them both was an aggregation of nations (allied, conquered, and bound by marriage) from all over the Atlantic and Mediterranean Worlds. The early modern British Empire was no different. It was formed by conquest and colonization, and by intermarriage among English, Welsh, Scottish, and Irish subjects. The English were more reluctant than Iberians to integrate with Native Americans, but this did not prevent the formation of alliances, client states, and their own Anglo-indigenous "middle grounds." The New World's people were absorbed into European empires as individuals but also as whole communities and client kingdoms.

For native elites, these imperial structures offered certain advantages. Whether as leaders of allied nations, dependent states, or ethnically defined municipalities, some traditional leaders were able to protect their authority and wealth by preserving local institutions. But clientage was a double-edged sword: cooperation with European empires could also disrupt traditional hierarchies. Clever individuals from outside the ranks of native hereditary elites found new opportunities. By learning the conquerors' languages, military practices, legal systems, and religions, enterprising native people could outmaneuver their competitors. Thus was born a new class of hybrid social elites.

The conquest of the Americas began in an age before scientific racism. To the sixteenth-century European mind, the great divisions in the human community were between noble and common; civilized and barbarous; Christian, pagan, and infidel. But by the late eighteenth century, new beliefs about race began to overshadow these older notions. At the same time, the revolutionary political theories of the Enlightenment had paradoxical effects on colonial concepts of social hierarchy. On one hand, radical republicanism would seem to favor the cause of the colonized. On the other hand, liberalism and its individualistic assault on corporate communities, church authority, and the principle of nobility undermined the position of traditional native elites.

When creole revolutions swept the Americas, they dissolved Indian republics, Indian aristocracies, and collectively held Indian lands. In the long run, the same logic that ended encomienda and legal slavery also destroyed native dynasties and native lands: if all property was personal and all citizens legally identical, what grounds remained for asserting the historically distinctive identities of native communities and their leaders? There were also cultural and demographic reasons for the erosion of native privilege. Displacement, migration, and intermarriage made the boundaries of ethnicity harder to police and the connections between history, family, land, and governance harder to describe.

In theory, Mexico's constitutions of 1824 and 1857 brought Indians into the community of Mexican citizens. In practice, however, this imposition of universal liberal citizenship nullified generations of agreements that had safeguarded native lands, local government, and hereditary elites. Bolivia and Peru's first constitutions of 1823 and 1826 also dispensed with the notion of Indian republics and distinctive forms of Indian citizenship. All Andeans from that point forward were theoretically citizens of the same type, though in practice old systems of local governance and compulsory labor endured. The United States' constitution was far from clear in its description of Indians' status under the law. In preserving slavery, the United States had already made a sharp legal distinction between the larger population of permanent inhabitants and the smaller community of citizens, implicitly departing from the liberal ideal. The original constitution says little about the nature of citizenship, and the word "Indian"—which only appears twice in the document—arises only in reference to taxation, trade, and diplomacy. Consequently, the status of Indians in lands claimed by the United States but not yet incorporated into individual states was ambiguous. The Civil War and Reconstruction laid to rest some questions of citizenship (at least on paper), but others remained unresolved. Formally, former slaves and Euro-Americans were now citizens of the same type, but the place of Native Americans was less clear, falling awkwardly between the paradigms of international and domestic law. Political theory and moral philosophy, in the US as elsewhere in the world, gave way to ruthless pragmatism and the settler state's hunger for natural resources.

In the late nineteenth century, native lands and local political autonomy were under assault throughout North America. Mexico's Lerdo Law of 1856, Canada's Indian Act of 1876, and the United States' Dawes Act of 1887 all aimed to force native communities into a liberal political and economic regime. The explicit objective was assimilation, but the most concrete effects were the erosion of collective land rights and of native political autonomy. Ever since then, native people have faced a difficult choice: whether to fight for the restoration of historic lands and corporate legal communities or to compete in new national cultures and economies as individuals. Zapata's followers in the Mexican Revolution aimed for the former, and many defenders of treaty rights in the United States and Canada have done the same.

Indigenous politics has followed different paths depending on whether native people constituted a small or large proportion of national, regional, or local populations. In places like Bolivia, Paraguay, and highland Guatemala— where Aymara, Guarani, and Maya are everyday languages—the cultural connections between contemporary political identity and the preconquest past are obvious. Differences in population density, legal status, and institutional life have produced distinctly different conditions across the Americas. Consequently, native politics looks different in Chiapas, the Six Nations of the Grand River, or the Navajo Reservation than it does in Tampico, Montreal, or Chicago. Some nation-states have at least symbolically embraced native heritage, as one sees in Peru and Paraguay; and some communities have embraced the notion of intermarriage as a positive and unifying attribute, as is the case in Mexican national mythology and among many Canadian métis. Of course, radical transformations in the composition of the free nonnative population have also altered notions of nationhood and citizenship throughout the Americas. The existence of millions of Asian-Peruvians and Afro-Brazilians shows how insufficient a binary explanation of European and indigenous synthesis is in explaining the origin of American civic life. The twentieth and twenty-first centuries offer new kinds of cultural marriages and new kinds of intermediaries and leaders.

═══

In the end, what generalizations hold true for the long and troubled marriage that tied together the fates of Native and European Americans over the centuries? America's transcultural families rewrote the world's genealogical tree. Sometimes Europeans and Indians intermarried at the behest of leaders and political organizations; more often, though, they did so spontaneously, opportunistically, or in desperation when confronted with violence. The mingling of religions followed a similar path. Some conversions took place at sword point, but many more were the product of curiosity, inspiration, and ambition. It was a phenomenon too vast and complex to be controlled by any single institution. It is no surprise, then, that the religious life of the Americas, created by four centuries of cultural exchange, was not simply the Christianity of Europe boxed up and exported. Syncretism in all its forms—the blending of words, symbols, rituals, and ideas—was the rule, not the exception, in colonial history. Religion was often the handmaiden of transcultural intellectual life, spreading the written word and creating academic communities; but the intellectual production of Indian and mestizo writers soon extended far beyond the boundaries of religion, addressing history, philosophy, politics, and inquiries into the natural world. Though the written genres were often rooted in European print culture, the contents of native and mestizo writing also drew from longstanding traditions in native intellectual life.

The composite institutions of the Americas reflect the same crosscurrents of cultural exchange. Viceroyalties that stitched together European kingdoms and preconquest empires; cities made of semiautonomous Indian and European enclaves; and armies built from alliances between native and settler militias—in all of these phenomena, one sees the same forces at work. Viewed from the European perspective, this complex cross-cultural marriage made sense. The great Atlantic empires were composite kingdoms, forged over generations through a mix of conquest, arranged marriages, patronage, and economic partnerships. This was the political vocabulary of early modern empire. In the Americas, some participated in the imperial system as humble Indian militiaman or neighborhood sacristans, others as powerful native aristocrats or celebrated religious leaders. The colonial Americas never dispensed with heredity and ethnicity as basic organizing principles. On the contrary, ethnicity and hereditary were always present in public and private life—the basic building blocks of the social order. Heritage could be a heavy yoke or a great privilege. However, as the stories told in this book suggest, the assets and liabilities that came with birth could sometimes be renegotiated in the fullness of life.

NOTES

INTRODUCTION

Unless otherwise noted, all translated passages of non-English sources are my own.

1. Furtwangler, "Sacagawea's Son," 290–315; Colby, *Sacagawea's Child.*
2. Historians have reevaluated this narrative over the past several decades, changing our understanding of the relative power of native and colonizing peoples in North America. See White, *Middle Ground;* Kupperman, *Indians and English;* DeLay, *Indian Raids;* and Hämäläinen, *Comanche Empire.*
3. Consider the way the subject is summed up for high school students in the Kaplan guide to the US history advanced placement exam: "Europeans had extreme views on the native populations of the Americas: They perceived Indians as either 'noble savages' who welcomed them or as vicious and uncivilized brutes" (Dornbush, 83). On the origin of this notion, see Ellingson, *Myth of the Noble Savage.*
4. On Columbus's notions of civilization, see Borochoff, "Indians, Cannibals, and Barbarians," 17–38; on Spanish conceptions of civilization in New Spain, see Keen, *Aztec Image in Western Thought;* and on notions of civilization in English and French America, see Axtell, *Natives and Newcomers,* chap. 1, "Imagining the Other."
5. I refer here to Marxist approaches to social structure and to Hegelian approaches to self-awareness, freedom, and the exercise of power. See Hegel, *Phenomenology of Spirit;* and Lukács, *Studies in Marxist Dialectics.*
6. On mid-twentieth-century interpretations of empire arising from African experience, see Memmi, *Colonizer and the Colonized;* and Fanon, *Wretched of the Earth.* On the tradition of subaltern studies arising from India, see Guha and Spivak, *Selected Subaltern Studies.*
7. Sandos, "Borderlands Enter American History," 595–604; White, *Middle Ground;* Greene, *Peripheries and Center;* Stoler, "Politics of Comparison," 829–65; Pratt, "Contact Zone," 33–40.
8. Nash, "Mestizo America," 941–64. On the notion of hybridity, see Bhabha, *Location of Culture.*

1. Townsend, chap. 9 in *Malintzin's Choices*; Lanyon, chap. 2 in *Martín Cortés*; and Karttunen, "Rethinking Malinche."
2. Cline, "Hernando Cortés," 70–90.
3. Gibson, *Tlaxcala*, 164–65, describes this and subsequent missions of the Tlaxcalans. This one departed from Tlaxcala with Cortés in 1527 and returned in 1530; another departed in 1534 (the leader was either Diego Tlilquiyahuatzin or Diego Maxixcatzin, along with a Sebastián Yaotequihua and don Martín Cortés). They arrived in Spain in 1534 and returned to Mexico in late 1535, accompanied by Antonio de Mendoza. Diego Maxixcatzin returned on 22 April 1535 with royal heraldry and a promise of direct jurisdiction under the crown. On the Tlaxcalan use of heraldry and visual records, see Kranz, "Visual Persuasion"; and Herrera Valdez, "Escudo de Tlaxcala," 83–104.
4. For a description of the splendor and imagery of the Habsburg court, see Checa Cremades, "Monarchic Liturgies," 90–97.
5. The thirteen images have been digitized and widely disseminated. The original is held by the German National Museum in Nuremberg, Hs. 22474. Cline, "Hernando Cortés," 72–78; Satterfield, "Assimilation." Boone has questioned whether the famed Weiditz drawings are optical representations of the Mesoamerican visitors or are based on imagery in circulation from other parts of the Americas. "Seeking Indianness," 39–61.
6. Titian, *Portrait of Charles V* (1548), and *Carlos V en Mühlberg* (1547); Del Piombo, *Clement VII* (ca. 1531).
7. On Indian vassals petitioning in Europe, see Mira Caballos, "Indios nobles y caciques," 1–15.
8. Connell, *After Moctezuma*; Chipman, chaps. 3–4 in *Moctezuma's Children*; Karttunen, epilogue of *Between Two Worlds*.
9. Andrea Martínez Baracs, *Gobierno de indios*, 76–79. On royal grants of heraldry, see Dominguez Torres, "Emblazoning Identity," 98–105.
10. On the legal and physical construction of the new city of Tlaxcala, see Baber, "City of Tlaxcala" and "Colonial New Spain," 47.
11. The most extensive visual record of sixteenth-century Tlaxcala was produced by Muñoz Camargo in *Ciudad y provincia de Tlaxcala*. The urban drawings from the text have been carefully analyzed by Wake, "Codex Tlaxcala," 105–15; Edgerton, *Theaters of Conversion*, 183–86; Andrea Martínez Baracs, chaps. 4–5 in *Gobierno de indios*; Gibson, *Tlaxcala*, 41–54, 124–30; and Mullen, *Architecture and Its Sculpture*, 7–10. On Tlaxcalan pragmatism, see Hassig, "Xicoténcatl," 29–49.
12. On the documentary and archaeological record of this conflict, see Sheptak, chap. 2 in "Colonial Masca in Motion." Rolena Adorno has raised numerous questions about the historicity of Guerrero in relation to legends surrounding

him, in *Polemics of Possession*, chap. 9. The account of Gonzalo's death occurs in *Cartas de gobernadores, Andrés de Cereceda, de Puerto de Caballos*, 14 August 1536, AGI, Guatemala 39 R. 2 N. 6.

13. This has become a literary trope for revisiting Mexico's origins. Braham, "Feliz cautiverio," 1–17; Romero, "Texts, Pre-texts, Con-texts," 345–67.

14. Díaz del Castillo, chaps. 3 and 27 in *Historia verdadera*.

15. Cortés, *Letters from Mexico*, 13–19; Díaz del Castillo, chaps. 27–29.

16. Díaz del Castillo, chap. 29.

17. In the López de Gómara account, Aguilar asked: "'¿Señores, sois cristianos?' Respondieron que sí y que eran españoles. Alegróse tanto con tal respuesta, que lloró de placer. Preguntó si era miércoles, pues tenía unas horas durante las cuales rezaba cada día. Les rogó que diesen gracias a Dios; y él se hincó de rodillas en el suelo, alzó las manos y ojos al cielo, y con muchas lágrimas hizo oración a Dios." *Historia general*, 24–25.

18. On the significance of his Book of Hours, see Allen, "Book Marks."

19. The earliest version of the captivity story is in Cortés's first letter. *Letters from Mexico*, 17.

20. English translation from Díaz del Castillo, *Conquest of New Spain*, 31.

21. Landa Calderón, *Cosas de Yucatán*, 88–89.

22. Díaz del Castillo, *Conquest of New Spain*, 116.

23. My translation: "Gonzalo Herrero . . . is Nachancan's captain, and very respected for his victories that he won in the battles that he has with the neighboring peoples. I sent him the letter from your excellency, and in order to pray that he might come . . . but he did not want to, I think out of shame, having pierced his nose, pierced his ears, painted (or tattooed) his face and hands in the style of that land and people, and from lust for his wife and affection for his children." López de Gómara, *Historia general*, 25–26.

24. Landa Calderón, *Cosas de Yucatán*, 88–89.

25. Fernández de Oviedo y Valdés, *Historia general*, bk. 32, chap. 2, 232–33. This kind of cultural crossing is explored in English North America in Axtell, *Natives and Newcomers*, chap. 8, "The White Indians"; and in Peter Stern, "White Indians," 262–81.

26. Díaz del Castillo, *Conquest of New Spain*, 117–18.

27. All page citations are to Cabeza de Vaca, *Relación y comentarios* (1555). For a scholarly English translation of the original source, see Cabeza de Vaca, *Narrative of Cabeza de Vaca*, edited and translated by Adorno and Pautz. The most complete secondary work on his journey is Reséndez, *Land So Strange*.

28. Cabeza de Vaca, *Relación y comentarios*, 56v–62r, 47r–54v.

29. Cabeza de Vaca, 48v.

30. Cabeza de Vaca, 47r.

31. Cabeza de Vaca, 48v.

32. The following narrative of the life of Pocahontas is drawn primarily from Townsend, *Pocahontas*; and Jager, *Malinche, Pocahontas, and Sacagawea*.

33. On native appeals to the British crown, see Yirush, "'Chief Princes,'" 129–51.

34. Cuming, "Cherokee Indians," 1–17; Crane, *Southern Frontier*, 294–302. On the embassy to England, see Cuming, "Memoirs," 13–14. On early native diplomats visiting England, see Peyer, *Indian Missionary Writers*. On English knowledge of native polities, see Townsend, chap. 2 in *Pocahontas*. Vaughan catalogs a large number of visits of North American natives to Britain (both voluntary and involuntary) in *Transatlantic Encounters*.

35. Basire, "Seven Cherokees," British Museum, Y,1.110; Anon., "Three Cherokees," British Museum, 1982, U.3745.

36. Cuming, "Cherokee Indians," 1–17. That the British often saw the Cherokees as having a parallel civilization with analogous systems of governance and diplomacy is clear in the writings of travelers. Bartram, *Travels through North and South Carolina, Georgia, East and West Florida, the Cherokee Country [. . .]* (1791), pt. 4, chap. 2, "Of Government and Civil Society"; Timberlake, *Memoirs*, 70–81. This notion of parallel civic life, law, and governance had already been common in earlier English experience among the Powhatans. Fitzmaurice, "Powhatan Legal Claims."

37. "Articles of Friendship and Commerce [. . .] 1730. On pre- and postconquest development of Cherokee slavery, see Perdue, *Slavery and the Evolution of Cherokee Society*.

38. "Articles of Friendship and Commerce."

39. Timberlake, *Memoirs*.

40. Commonwealth of Virginia, *A treaty held with the Catawba and Cherokee Indians*.

41. White, *Middle Ground*, 50–85; Mangan, chap. 1 in *Transatlantic Obligations*; Guengerich, "Capac Women," 147–67. Pedro Carrasco, "Indian-Spanish Marriages," 87–103. McGrath, *Illicit Love*; Powers, *Women*. Sleeper-Smith, *Indian Women*.

42. *Portrait of Louis Riel*, Notman Studio, 1873, LAC, MIKAN no. 3228116.

43. Jennifer Reid, *Louis Riel*.

44. *Queen v. Louis Riel*, 311–43.

45. *Queen v. Louis Riel*, testimony of Charles Nolin, 194–204.

46. *Queen v. Louis Riel*, testimony of the accused, 318.

47. *Queen v. Louis Riel*, 320–21.

48. *Queen v. Louis Riel*, 312.

49. Note that in regional memory métis have become something of a race. The bibliography on Louis Riel compiled by the Provincial Library of Saskatchewan includes a preface describing the rebellion and trial as follows: "This is the most shameful chapter of Canadian history in which the federal government tried to exterminate the Métis race. . . . Louis Riel was a man with a strong sense of

Métis nationality and a devoted Roman Catholic." Parkash Arora, preface of *Louis Riel*. According to William McCartney Davidson, "The Métis closed the year 1871 in the greatest despondency and hopelessness. Never since they had become race-conscious was the present so depressing." *Louis David Riel*, 97.

50. Sleeper-Smith, *Indian Women*, 16–22; Van Kirk, *Many Tender Ties*, 28–52.

51. Bryce, *Hudson's Bay Company*, 202–50; Gordon Charles Davidson, *North West Company*, 119–35.

52. Hyde, *Empires, Nations, and Families*, 268–77. Hoig, chap. 9 in *Chouteaus*.

53. Lang, chap. 12 in "Chinookan Encounter."

54. Deur, *Ethnohistorical Overview*, 43–50; LaLande, *First over the Siskiyous*; Van Kirk, chap. 2 in *Many Tender Ties*; Binns, *Peter Skene Ogden*, 89–100.

55. Barman, *French Canadians*, 130–32, 88, 101–3. Hyde, *Empires, Nations, and Families*, 112–13, 508–9; Joshua L. Reid, *Sea Is My Country*, 101–3.

56. Boyd, "Lower Chinookan Disease," 229–49.

57. Van Kirk, chap. 10 in *Many Tender Ties*.

CHAPTER TWO

1. The following narrative of negotiations is drawn from Betanzos, chaps. 23–34 in *Narrative of the Incas* (1653); Cusi Yupanqui, *Inca Account*, intro., 122–32; Nowack, "Vilcabamba Inca"; Gose, *Invaders as Ancestors*, 85–91; Cattan, "Titu Cusi Yupanqui"; Regalado de Hurtado, *Titu Cusi Yupanqui*, 80–111.

2. "Las Armas de Paullo Inga," 9 May 1545.

3. The opportunistic flight and migration of tributary laborers is extensively documented in Wightman, *Indigenous Migration*.

4. Rodríguez de Figueroa, "Account of the route," 153–75.

5. Bauer, introduction to Cusi Yupanqui, *Inca Account*, 11–12.

6. Nowack, "Aquellas señoras." For my understanding of Andean elite marriages in relation to European incest and polygamy norms, I am indebted to Sara Guengerich.

7. For a detailed explanation of this dynastic diplomacy, see Nowack, "Vilcabamba Inca."

8. On Beatriz Clara Coya in relation to other women in aristocratic lines, see Guengerich, "Inca Women."

9. Cattan, "Titu Cusi Yupanqui," 13–28.

10. Nowack, "Vilcabamba Inca."

11. On the marriage and the resulting lineage and estate, see Rostworowski, "Repartimiento de doña Beatriz Coya," 153–267.

12. Campo de la Rynaga, *Memorial historico*. On the political position of curacas in this system, see Peter Stern, "Early Spanish-Indian Accommodation."

13. Lockhart, *Men of Cajamarca*.

14. Saravia Salazar, "Evolución de un cargo," 27–56.

15. "Visita y Padrón del Repartimiento de Cayautambo y Tauna de la encomienda de don Francisco Valverde, Reino de la Ciudad de Cusco," 7 February 1603, AGNP, Derecho Indígena y Encomiendas, legajo 4, cuaderno 46. For a similar case study on the defense of cacicazgos and encomienda, see Miguel Glave, "Curacazgo Andino," 11–39.

16. The interaction of Francisco Valverde de Montalvo and other magistrates with local indigenous leaders in shaping leadership claims is explored in Urton, chap. 2 in *History of a Myth*.

17. "Visita y Padrón," 7 February 1603, AGNP, Derecho Indígena y Encomiendas, legajo 4, cuaderno 46.

18. Fisher shows that this recovery did not take place until the mid- to late eighteenth century, in *Bourbon Peru*, 45–58.

19. Curacas from outside ethnic groups as well as mestizo and occasionally white curacas appear in the late colonial record, both as a result of intermarriage and as a result of political appointment. Godoy, *Kurakas sin sucesiones*, 68; Garrett, *Shadows of Empire*, 155–56; Ramírez, "Instability at the Top," 327–46. On multicultural politics and litigation, see Puente Luna, *Andean Cosmopolitans*. The precedent for legally sanctioned intermarriage and mestizo caciques came from the Caribbean. Gil, "Primeros mestizos indios."

20. "Petición Presentada por Dn. Francisco Javier Tico Chipana Indio Noble de Zepita y distinguido con la Real Medalla, sobre la sucesión y pertenencia del cacicazgo de la parcialidad de Urinsaya [. . .] Zepita," 4 November 1791, BNP, signatura C1705. The petitioner is her brother. Retaining power also required diversification in commercial activities. Adanaqué, "Caciques Chayhuac," 57–66. Indigenous elites in Peru not only routinely possessed tributary labor rights over native populations, but also sometimes held African slaves. Harth-Terré, "Esclavo negro," 297–340.

21. Burkholder, "Honor and Honors."

22. The structures of the Hispano-Inca nobility are explained in Zuidema, "Organización religiosa"; and Cahill, "Liminal Nobility." On diplomacy and elite intermarriage, see María Elena Martínez, "Indigenous Genealogies." On the preservation of preconquest panaca structures in the colonial period, see Amado Gonzalez, "Alferez real"; and Zuidema.

23. Garrett, "'In Spite of Her Sex,'" 547–81; Quichua Chaico, "María Sacama," 1–14; Nowack, "Aquellas señoras."

24. On convents for indigenous noblewomen, see Muriel, *Indias caciques*; and Guengerich, "Inca Women." Spores has called the period from 1550 to 1620 the "Golden Age of Cacicas" among New Spain's Mixtecs, and noted the persistence of this office until independence. "Mixteca Cacicas," 185–97. Graubart, chap. 5 in *Indigenous Women*. Terraciano, "Colonial Mixtec Community," 27–32; and chap. 4 in *Mixtecas of Colonial Oaxaca*.

25. Olasabal papers, 1823, AGNP, Donaciones y Adquisiciones, signatura D-10–12–181.

26. Olasabal papers.

27. Campo de la Rynaga, *Memorial historico*; Cutter, *Protector de Indios*; Novoa, *Protectors of Indians*.

28. "Autos sequidos ante el superior Gobierno, por don Francisco Galindo," 1763, AGNP, Cabildo de Provincias, legajo 3, expediente 136.

29. On indigenous church patrons, see Garrett, "Nobleza indígena cuzqueña."

30. All material on Montes drawn from Testamento de María Antonia Montes, 18 April 1801, AGNP, Testamentos de Indios, signatura T1. 4.494, expediente 4. On elite indigenous testaments in colonial Peru, see Nowack, "Testamentos," 51–77.

31. On beatas in Peru, see Burns, "Beatas."

32. Testamento de don Toribio Dávila, 1808, AGNP, Testamentos de Indios, signatura T1. 4.492.

33. On the scribal tradition of quipucamayocs under Spanish rule, see Rappaport, "Object and Alphabet." On the known elements of the quipus, see Urton, *Inka History in Knots*. On their legal and academic authority, see Ramos and Yannakakis, introduction to *Indigenous Intellectuals*; and Burns, "Making Indigenous Archives."

34. On the urban history of Lima, see Kagan, chap. 6 in *Urban Images*.

35. The following description of the beaterio and the image of its patroness are from Espinoza Soriano and Olmeda, "Beaterios," 131–47. On urban religous life in Lima during this period, see Osorio, chap. 5 in *Inventing Lima*.

36. Cofradía de Nuestra Señora de Copacabana, AAL, Cofradías, legajos 13 and 11, expedientes 7 and 10.

37. Espinoza Soriano and Olmeda, "Beaterios," 140–41.

CHAPTER THREE

1. Poole, *Our lady of Guadalupe*, 83–84.

2. González Gómez, "Antonio Valeriano," 3.

3. On the struggle of Valeriano to gain and regain office in this conflict between orders, see Connell, *After Moctezuma*, 70–89.

4. On indigenous collaboration in the creation of the codex, see Ricard, chap. 2 in *Spiritual Conquest of Mexico*.

5. Lockhart, *Nahuas after Conquest*, 350–52.

6. Chimalpahin Cuauhtlehuanitzin, *Codex Chimalpahin*, 2:177.

7. Benton, "Beyond the Burned Stake"; and Ruiz Medrano, "Don Carlos de Tezcoco." Tavárez, chap. 2 in *Invisible War*. The trial documents are available in published form in *Proceso inquisitorial*. Lee considers this event in the context

of widespread native ambivalence toward Christianity among literate Texcocan intellectuals. *Allure of Nezahualcoyotl*, 209–28.

8. On Tlatelolco elites in the sixteenth century, see Vargas Betancourt, "Caciques tlatelolcas."

9. For a profile of a sixteenth-century indigenous clergyman, see McDonough, chap. 1 in *Learned Ones*. On early plans for the native church, see Ricard, *Spiritual Conquest of Mexico*. On fluctuating church policy toward native ordination and native church intellectuals in New Spain, see Christensen, intro. to *Translated Christianities*.

10. On the remaining preconquest features of the urban landscape of Valeriano's moment, see Umberger, "Monarchía Indiana," 46–68; Mundy, *Death of Aztec Tenochtitlan*, 190–212; and Kagan, chap. 6 in *Urban Images*.

11. On Valeriano as politician and intermediary, see Mundy, 190–91. SilverMoon traces some of the notable alumni and estimates that approximately 1900 students attended Santa Cruz Tlatelolco in the course of the sixteenth century. "Imperial College," 76–79.

12. SilverMoon, 87–103.

13. On Nahua intellectual life during this period, see McDonough, *Learned Ones*. Christensen in *Nahua and Maya Catholicisms* describes the spread of alphabetic literacy in Mesoamerica—in the form of both official religious texts and native-authored documents completely unsanctioned or even unknown to the Spanish establishment. Tavárez, "Nahua Intellectuals," 203–35. Terraciano, "Three Texts in One," 51–72.

14. Townsend, *Malintzin's Choices*, 200.

15. Portillo Valdés, *Fuero indio*, 44. Gibson, "Diego Muñoz Camargo," 199–200.

16. Cuadriello, chap. 1 in *República de Tlaxcala*. Andrea Martínez Baracs, chap. 3 in *Gobierno de indios*.

17. On the document in relation to the royal questionnaire and Camargo's political rhetoric, see Mignolo, "Mandato y la ofrenda," 451–84.

18. The *Historia de Tlaxcala* is a composite work comprehending the *Descripción de la ciudad y provincia de Tlaxcala*, the *Tlaxcala Calendar*, and the *Tlaxcala Codex*. The entire work is held by the University of Glasgow: *Descripción de la ciudad y provincia de Tlaxcala* [. . .]. 1580–1585 (Special Collections, MS Hunter 242, U.3.15). A full facsimile, edited by René Acuña, is also available: *Descripción de la ciudad y provincia de Tlaxcala de las Indias y del Mar Océano para el buen gobierno y ennoblecimiento dellas* (Mexico City: UNAM, 1981). The only part of the source known in the mid-twentieth century was published as *Historia de Tlaxcala* (Mexico: Ateneo Nacional de Ciencas y Artes de Mexico, 1947).

19. On the earlier Tlaxcalan delegations of 1529, 1535, and 1562, see Baber, "Colonial New Spain." AGN, Civil, legajo 711, expediente 6.

20. From Gibson, "Diego Muñoz Camargo," 204. On the history of Tlaxcalan

delegations (though not the 1580 one) and the 1560 colonization proposal, see *Tlaxcalan Actas*.

21. Gibson, *Aztecs under Spanish Rule*, 167. On elite families and strategic intermarriage in Texcoco, see Douglas, "Our Fathers, Our Mothers," 117–31.

22. Gibson, "Diego Muñoz Camargo," 195–208. On petition practices, see Townsend, *Malintzin's Choices*, 200; and MacLean, "Historia de Tlaxcala," intro. to exhibit. On the tradition of native mapping in the context of imperial politics, see Mundy, chap. 1 in *Mapping of New Spain*; and Cline, "Relaciones Geográficas," 341–74.

23. Brading argues in *First America* that this patrimony was vital to the formation of creole national identities throughout Latin America. Villella shows in *Indigenous Elites* that indigenous and mestizo writers were key agents in this process of identity formation. Earle explores these phenomena across the Americas in *Return of the Native*. European representations of Inca elites freely blended images of European and indigenous authority. Fane, "Influential European Engraving," 31–39.

24. Lists of students in 1658, ARC, Colegio de Ciencias, legajo 45, expediente 2, folio 23v, 25r. On the impact of earthquakes, see ARC, Colegio de Ciencias, legajo 1, cuaderno 13, carta 11. On noble pedigrees, see "Relacion cronológica," 225–30.

25. On student dress, see ARC, Colegio de Ciencias, legajo 45, expediente 32, folio 33r.

26. The contents of the school's library have been reconstructed in Alaperrine-Bouyer, "Biblioteca," 163–79. On the professional attainments of Indian graduates, see Godoy, "Ascender al estado eclesiástico."

27. Alaperrine-Bouyer, "Enseñanza y pedagogía," 270–98. Escobari de Querejazu, chap. 5 in *Caciques, yanaconas y extravagantes*.

28. Charles, "Trained by Jesuits."

29. Correspondence of Juan de la Concepción, ARC, Colegio de Ciencias, legajo 1, cuaderno 13.

30. "Hospital de los Naturales," 55–56; "Indios para el servicio," 143–44.

31. On Indian education and the implications of literacy, see Dueñas, *Reshaping Justice*; and Ramos, "Indigenous Intellectuals."

32. The Native elite on horseback with European clothes was a standard part of Andean status culture after the horse replaced hammock bearers as a mark of prestige. Ramírez, "Cosmological Bases," 42–44.

33. Chocano Mena, "Contrastes y paralelismo," 112–37. On Toledo's theory of imperial succession and the hybrid state, see Mumford, chap. 7 in *Vertical Empire*.

34. On the culture of neo-Inca revival, see Cahill, "Nobleza asediada," 82–99.

35. *Mamusse wunneetupanatamwe Up-Biblum God* (1685). Dippold, "Wampanoag Word," 543–75.

36. "Charter of the President and Fellows of Harvard College [. . .] May 31, 1650."

37. This narrative of the Harvard Indian College is drawn from Szasz, chap. 4 in *Indian Education*; and Peyer, *Indian Missionary Writers*, 40–52.

38. William Wallace Tooker, *Cockenoe-de-Long Island*.

39. On James Printer and the production of the Algonquian Bible, see Lopenzina, chap. 2 in *Red Ink*. On praying towns, see Van Lonkhuyzen, "Praying Indians," 396–428; and Brenner, "Praying Town Indians," 135–52.

40. Szasz, *Indian Education*, 40–43

41. On Hiacoomes and Caleb Cheeshahteaumuck, see Monaghan, *Learning*, 55–60; and Silverman, "Creating Wampanoag Christianity," 141–74.

42. Szasz, *Indian Education*, 123–25.

43. On the social circle of Indian writers during this period, see Meserve, "Seventeenth-Century Indians," 264–76. On the spread of alphabetic literacy and Indian-controlled printing presses, see Round, *Removable Type*.

44. "Dartmouth College Charter [. . .] 1769," digitized and transcribed at the Dartmouth Library. On Wheelock's educational projects, see Axtell, chap. 7 in *Natives and Newcomers*.

45. "Some Correspondence between the Governors and Treasurers," xxvii, 88–89.

46. On the successes and limitations of Occom's projects, see Lopenzina, chap. 4 in *Red Ink*; and Occom's own autobiographical account, "Short Narrative of My Life" (1768), 43–49. The most complete study of Dartmouth and Indian education is Calloway, *Indian History*. On newly formed Indian communities in the West, see Cipolla, "Peopling the Place," 51–78.

47. Miller, *Shingwauk's Vision*; Reyner and Eder, *American Indian Education*; DeJong, *Promises of the Past*.

48. Demos, *Heathen School*; Gold, *Town of Cornwall*. The founding documents of the parent organization describe the Indians of North America as currently uncivilized, but also as having boundless aptitude. *First Ten Annual Reports* (1834).

49. Demos, chap. 6.

50. On the Boudinot-Gold courtship, wedding, and controversy, see McGrath, chap. 1 in *Illicit Love*. Later census records demonstrate that Anglo-Cherokee intermarriage was very common. McLoughlin and Conser, "Cherokees in Transition," 678–703. On the early Moravian mission, see McClinton, *Moravian Springplace Mission*. Demos, chap. 6. McLoughlin, *Cherokee Renascence*, 354–61.

51. Boudinot, *Cherokee Editor*; Dale and Litton, *Cherokee Cavaliers*. The correspondence of Gold and Boudinot is available in Strout Gaul, *To Marry an Indian*. Gabriel, *Elias Boudinot*. Boudinot was both a hero and a traitor to many in his generation, and he was ultimately executed for his role in the Cherokee removal. Schneider, "Cherokee Removal," 151–77.

52. Lopenzina argues in *Red Ink* that the Native writers used the written word to gain political capital in a colonial environment, but that their writings were constantly recontextualized by colonizers in ways that undermined the authors' aims.

53. Sequoya's journey to Mexico is recorded in "Narrative of Oo-Chee-Ah," 25–41.
54. For a contemporary description of the syllabary, see *Cherokee Phoenix*, 6–9.
55. On the development of standardized Cherokee writing and its political implications, see Cushman, "Cherokee Syllabary," 625–49; and McLoughlin, chap. 17 in *Cherokee Renascence*.
56. "Cherokee Philosopher" (29 July 1829). The paper was itself part of a Cherokee strategy to achieve recognition for being civilized and modern. Perdue, "Rising from the Ashes," 207–18.

CHAPTER FOUR

1. Emily Edwards, *Painted Walls*, 75–76. Pierce, "Crossroads," 30. On Gerson's use of Dürer as source material, see Moyssén, "Juan Gerson," 23–39.
2. On Gerson's identity, see Arredondo and Croix, *Juan Gerson*; and Gonzalbo, "Fulgor y muerte," 325–42. On the transition from preconquest literacies to postconquest scribal traditions, see Sampeck, "Colonial Mesoamerican Literacy," in a special issue of *Ethnohistory* (vol. 62, no. 3); and Restall, Sousa, and Terraciano, *Mesoamerican Voices*, 11–20. On prints as models for paintings and in arts pedagogy, see Donahue-Wallace, "Picturing Prints," 328–35.
3. Toussaint, chap. 6 in *Colonial Art in Mexico*.
4. Moyssén, "Juan Gerson," 7.
5. *Relaciones geográficas de la diócesis de Tlaxcala*. On Puebla, see Kinsbruner, chap. 5 in *Colonial Spanish-American City*.
6. Baird, *Churches of Mexico*, 114.
7. María Elena Martínez, "Indigenous Genealogies."
8. Brading, chap. 7 in *First America*; Gose, *Invaders as Ancestors*, 181–90.
9. Brading, 159.
10. On the position of mestizo scholar-clergy in Peru, see Marzal, "Blas Valera," 387–400.
11. Brokaw, "Poetics of Khipu Historiography," 111–47; Frye, intro. to *First New Chronicle*, by Guaman Poma de Ayala.
12. Mignolo, "Meninas," 40–47. Ralph Bauer notes Guaman Poma's integration of notions of cartography and historical narrative from both cultures. "'EnCountering,'" 274–312.
13. Cummins, "Let Me See!"
14. "Y que demás del servicio de vuestra Magestad que rezultará de ynprimirse la dicha historia, comensándose a selebrar y hazer ynmortal la memoria y nombre de los grandes señores antepasados nuestros aguelos como lo merecieron sus hazañas." Guaman Poma de Ayala, *Primer nueva corónica*, 5. "Herodotus of Halicarnassus here presents his research so that human events do not fade with time. May the great and wonderful deeds—some brought forth by the Hellenes, others by the barbarians—not go unsung." Herodotus, *Histories*, 3.

15. Guaman Poma de Ayala, *Primer nueva corónica*, 16–23, 38–39. On Guaman Poma's conception of time, see Rolena Adorno, *Guaman Poma*, chap. 1.

16. Guaman Poma de Ayala, 466–68.

17. Guaman Poma de Ayala, 342–43.

18. Guaman Poma de Ayala, 759; Burns, *Into the Archive*, 8–9.

19. Frye's translation, *First New Chronicle*, 160.

20. Guaman Poma de Ayala, *Primer nueva corónica*, 468–68.

21. Abercrombie, "Perpetuidad traducida."

22. Rolena Adorno, intro. to second ed., *Guaman Poma*.

23. Ossio, "Murúa's Two Manuscripts."

24. Guaman Poma de Ayala, *Primer nueva corónica*, 1009.

25. Dean, "Renewal," 171–82; Cummins, "Tale of Two Cities," 157–70. On indigenous artistic movements, see Wuffarden, "Native Artists." Cossio del Pomar, *Peruvian Colonial Art*. Benavente, "Pintores cuzqueños," 225–35.

26. Mesa and Gisbert, "Pintor virreinal," 212–24. Zendt, "Marcos Zapata's *Last Supper*," 9–11. García Sáiz, "Portraiture in Viceregal America," 77–78. Donahue-Wallace, *Art and Architecture*, 136–41.

27. In the Latin mass, "Accipite, et manducate: hoc est corpus meum," which references Matthew 26:26.

28. Mesa and Gisbert, "Pintor virreinal," 214–16.

29. Webster, chaps. 5 and 7 in *Lettered Artists*. Lepage, "Arte de la conversión," 47–77.

30. The following discussion of Tito Yupanqui and the *Virgin of Copacabana* appears in McEnroe, "Virgin of Copacabana," 109–17.

31. Stanfield-Mazzi, *Object and Apparition*, 79–84; Salles-Reese, *From Viracocha*. Dean, "Colonial Peruvian Visual Culture," 171–82; William B. Taylor, *Shrines and Miraculous Images*.

32. Del Río, "Sacerdotes del Tawantinsuyu," 9–69. Alcalá, "Beginnings," 157. Damian, "Artist and Patron," 25–53. My thanks to Susan Deans-Smith for a helpful conversation on artists' workshops.

33. Ramos Gavilán, *Historia del santuario*.

34. Ramos Gavilán, bk. 2, chap. 6, 234–38.

35. *Saint Augustine's Enchiridion*, 102–3.

36. Ramos Gavilán, *Historia del santuario*, bk. 1, chaps. 7–8.

37. Ramos Gavilán, bk. 1, chap. 9.

38. Ramos Gavilán, bk. 2, chap. 2, 205.

39. Ramos Gavilán, bk. 2, chap. 2, 206–7.

40. For example: "Dos milagros más verán / En tu obra peregrina / Donde en toda paz están / Una Paloma divina / En manos de un Gavilán / Y porque el otro veamos / Para gloria más crecida / En Autor, y libro hallamos / Al fruto, y árbol de vida / Colgado de vuestros Ramos." Ramos Gavilán, "Al Padre Fr. Alonso Ramos Gavilán autor deste Libro, el Padre Fr. Antonio de la Calancha," xxviii.

41. Salles-Reese and Mills excerpt the narrative. Salles-Reese omits the introduc-

tion from Ramos Gavilán, obscuring his intent. *From Viracocha*, 177–81; Mills, "Making an Image," 167–72. Ramos Gavilán, "Capítulo VI. Donde se pone la misma relación, que dexo escrita de su mano, y letra, el escultor desta santa imagen," 234–37.

42. Translation from Mills, "Making an Image," 169; unless noted, all other translations are mine and based on the Ignacio Río Prado edition.

43. Aristotle's *Metaphysics* opens: "All men by nature desire to know. An indication of this is the delight we take in our senses; for even apart from their usefulness they are loved for themselves; and above all others the sense of sight. For not only with a view to action, but even when we are not going to do anything, we prefer seeing (one might say) to everything else. The reason is that this, most of all the senses, makes us know and brings to light many differences between things" (bk. 1, pt. 1).

44. There are multiple cases of intertextuality in Ramos Gavilán's work, not all classical. Several miracle stories derive from European models. Gálvez Peña, "Milagro flamenco," 65–91.

45. Plato, *Republic*, bk. 7.

46. "In the beginning was the Word [logos], and the Word was with God, and the word was God. He was in the beginning with God. All things came into being through him. . . . What has come into being in him was life, and the life was the light of all people" (John 1:1–5, NRSV).

47. MacCormack, "Sun of the Incas," 30–60; Salles-Reese, chap. 2 in *From Viracocha*; Stanfield-Mazzi, *Object and Apparition*, 38–41.

48. Ramos Gavilán, *Historia del santuario*, bk. 1, chaps. 1, 18, 26.

49. This may be a literary device like the letters contained in *Utopia*. Salles-Reese considers it authentic, noting its distinct style and Quechua-influenced syntax (*From Viracocha*, 177). Regardless, the embedded story is deployed by Gavilán to express the objectives of his larger work. Alcalá notes that Ramos Gavilán's secondary narrative emphasizes the artist's determination and goal ("Beginnings," 154–57).

50. Zavala, "Utopía de Tomás Moro" and *Vasco de Quiroga*. Verástique, *Michoacán and Eden*, 113–17.

51. Translation from Mills, "Making an Image," 167.

52. Aristotle, *Poetics*, pt. 4, 55.

53. Levy, *Propaganda*, 15–64, 110–204.

54. Ramos Gavilán, *Historia del santuario*, bk. 2, chap. 6, 235.

55. Robert Pasnau, "Scholastic Aristotelianism," 666–85.

56. Ramos Gavilán, *Historia del santuario*, bk. 2, chap. 6, 236.

57. Plato, "Apology," 51–52.

58. Aristotle, *Metaphysics*, bk. 1, pt. 1.

59. This idea was embedded in the thinking of men like Ramos Gavilán through Aquinas's *Summa Theologica*, which applies its logic to Christian divinity.

60. Plato, *Republic*, bk. 7, 532–33.

61. "Twenty-Fifth Session," 235.

62. Mills, chap. 6 in *Idolatry and Its Enemies*.

63. Lisi, *Tercer Concilio Limense*: Session 2, chaps. 3, 6, 40, 42, 43; Session 5, chap. 4. Tineo, *Concilios limenses*, pt. 2, chap. 8. Brosseder, *Power of Huacas*.

64. Andrien, *Andean Worlds*, 171–84.

65. Arriaga, *Extirpation of Idolatry*; Shah, "Language, Discipline, and Power," 102–24. Indigenous perspectives on the extirpation campaigns are preserved in the Huarochirí Manuscript. See Durston, "Cristóbal Choquecasa."

66. Alaperrine-Bouyer, "Enseñanza y pedagogía," 270–98.

67. Cummins, "Indulgent Image." On the circulation of classical imagery, see Mac-Cormack, *Wings of Time*; and Lupher, *Romans*. On indigenous literacy, see Alperrine-Bouyer, "Enseñanza y pedagogía." On indigenous intellectuals, see Ramos and Yannakakis, *Indigenous Intellectuals*; and Brading, chaps. 12–16 in *First America*.

68. Construction of the church dated in Robert H. Jackson and Amador, *Visual Catalog*, 129–30.

69. Orozco considers Michoacán's Purépecha-Christian culture of the sixteenth century—along with that of the Nahua center—the likely points of origin for the shared artistic conventions of the Cristos de caña (*Cristos de caña*, 15–17). On the Michoacán environment from which these experiments may have arisen, see Verástique, *Michoacán and Eden*.

70. On maize, sacrifice, and rituals of renewal, see Florescano, *Quetzalcóatl*.

71. "Y en el Capítulo catorce se dice cómo nuestro Salvador Jesucristo se determinó a echar fuera a todos los que vendían en el templo de Jerusalem . . . no honra-ban la casa de Dios. . . . Está escrito que la casa de Dios casa de oración será llamada; pero vosotros habéis hecho casa de ladrones su casa." Carrillo y Gariel, *Cristo de Mexicaltzingo*, 65. In point of fact, the story of the cleansing of the temple does not occur in the fourteenth chapter of any of the Gospels, though the writer may have been speaking of the fourteenth *verse* of John's second chapter. In using the phrase "house of thieves," however, he would seem to be referring to one of the synoptic gospels that uses the same wording, rather than to John, which uses "house of trade."

72. Carrillo y Gariel, *Cristo de Mexicaltzingo*; Estrada Jasso, *Imágenes de caña*; Orozco, *Cristos de caña*, 266–71; Vallebueno Garcinava, "Señor de Mezquital," 76, 255–58.

73. Orozco, 182–85.

74. Treviño Villarreal, *Señor de Tlaxcala*, 18–30; Orozco, *Cristos de caña*, 182–85; McEnroe, *Colony to Nationhood*, 42–43; Butzer, chap. 6 in *Historia social*.

75. On procession and performance in early evangelization, see Ricard, chap. 11 in *Spiritual Conquest of Mexico*; Max Harris, *Aztecs, Moors, and Christians*; and

Ybarra, *Five Centuries*. On the structural function of cofradías in community life, see Flynn, *Sacred Charity*.

76. On Tlaxcalan colonization of the north, see Dávila Aguirre, *Colonización tlax-calteca*; Adams, *Colonias tlaxcaltecas*; Sego, *Aliados y adversarios*; Dávila del Bosque, *Cabildos tlaxcaltecas*; Adams, "Lion's Mouth," 324–46; Butzer, *Historia social*; Sheridan Prieto, "'Indios madrineros,'" 15–51; and McEnroe, chaps. 1–4 in *Colony to Nationhood*.

CHAPTER FIVE

1. Mogrovejo, *Libro de visitas*; Sáenz, *Arquetipos cristianos*, 102–25.
2. Estimate of distance based on *Libro de visitas*.
3. Mogrovejo, 443–46.
4. Lisi, *Tercer Concilio Limense*; Dueñas, *Reshaping Justice*, 166–72.
5. Visitors familiar with contemporary paintings of the Virgin from Spain and Italy may be struck by the fact that her complexion is neither more nor less dark than that of many sixteenth-century European images. By convention, though, she is widely described as dark and indigenous, and is today viewed in this light.
6. Beatty, "Pope in Mexico," 324–35. Burkhart, *Before Guadalupe*.
7. Poole, "History versus Juan Diego," 1–16; also see William B. Taylor, "Virgin of Guadalupe," 9–33. Brading, *Mexican Phoenix*.
8. On the relationship between texts and memory, see Luis Laso de la Vega, *The Story of the Virgin of Guadalupe: Luis Laso de Vega's Huei tlamahuiçoltica of 1649*.
9. William B. Taylor, "Virgin of Guadalupe," 14–15.
10. Rodrigo Martínez Baracs, *Secuencia Tlaxcalteca*; Nutini, "Syncretism and Ac-culturation," 301–21.
11. Alcalá, "Image of the Devout Indian," 227–49.
12. Lockhart, *Nahuas after Conquest*, 124; *Beyond the Codices*, 127.
13. Robert H. Jackson, *Conflict and Conversion*, 31–36; Andrea Martínez Baracs, chap. 3 in *Gobierno de indios*.
14. On the families, see Gibson, *Tlaxcala*, 10–12, 23–27, 34–37.
15. On the story of the martyrs as defining Tlaxcalan religious identity, see Cuadri-ello, *República de Tlaxcala*, 303–15.
16. Maza, "Fray Diego Valadés," 15–44.
17. Valadés, *Rhetorica christiana*, 88.
18. "Sic sedentes virgas in manibus tenentes sunt Iudices apud indigetes nosotros, quibus comissa est totius reipublicae gobiernatio" (Valadés, 111–12).
19. Maza, "Fray Diego Valadés," 16–18.
20. On elite Indian education and the activities of Pedro de Gante, see Ricard, chaps. 13–14 in *Spiritual Conquest of Mexico*.

21. On Tlaxcalan understandings of their self-governance under Spain, see Townsend, "Nahua Identity," 145–54.

22. Mills, William B. Taylor, and Graham, "Ideal Atrio," 150–52. On Diego Muñoz Camargo's representation of these spaces, see Mundy, *Mapping of New Spain*, 76–87.

23. On indigenous nuns in New Spain, see Córdova, "Clad in Flowers," 449–67.

24. Cruz, "Loa for el divino Narciso," 238–39; Arenal and Schlau, *Untold Sisters*, 337–43.

25. On women's motives for conversion, see Sleeper-Smith, chap. 2 ("Marie Rouensa and the Jesuits: Conversion, Gender, and Power") and chap. 4 ("Being Indian and Becoming Catholic") in *Indian Women*. On the Jesuit missionary program in New France, see Cushner, chap. 8 in *Why Have You Come Here?* Magnuson, chap. 3 in *Education in New France*.

26. Shoemaker, "Tortuous Path," 49–71.

27. Greer, *Mohawk Saint*, 114–17.

28. He refers to her as his "spiritual superior" (Greer, 5).

29. They learn about women's piety from Marie Skarichions who had been cared for by nuns at the hospital in Quebec City (Greer, 135).

30. Greer, 130–34.

31. Colonec, "Gracia triunfante."

32. Anderson, *Memoir of Catharine Brown* (composed 1824). On indigenous women's formal Protestant education in earlier generations, see Wyss, "Gender and Native Literacy," 387–412.

33. Catharine Brown Papers; Brown, *Cherokee Sister*.

34. Rubin, "First Fruits."

35. The scale of the crisis is made clear in Worcester v. Georgia (1832), in the court's ruling opinion, and by the Jackson administration's and Georgia government's subsequent noncompliance.

36. Anderson, *Memoir of Catharine Brown*, 24.

37. John and Sarah Brown letter addressed to "My Dear Son," 13 August 1822, Creek Path, Cherokee Nation, in the Catharine Brown Papers.

38. Vincent, "Slaveholding Indians," 1–16.

39. The Cherokees closely matched Anglo-American expectations about civilization; see "New Echota Cherokee Nation." The Cherokees' nineteenth-century political structures were closely modeled on US constitutional law. The Constitution of the Cherokee Nation was formulated by a convention of delegates at New Echota, July 1827. Young, "Cherokee Nation," 502–24.

40. On native retellings of their leadership in the conversion of Mexico, see Haskett, "Conquering the Spiritual Conquest."

CHAPTER SIX

1. Velasco Murillo et al., *City Indians*.
2. Mundy, chap. 4 in *Death of Aztec Tenochtitlan*.
3. Not only did traditional clothing persist among commoners, but Nahua elites continued to present themselves in traditional status clothing long after conquest. Olko, chap. 5 in *Insignia of Rank*.
4. Villella, "Indian Lords, Hispanic Gentlemen," 1–36.
5. The barrio was originally under the care of the Jesuit College of San Pablo, which educated Indians early in its history and mestizos in the late colonial period. Martín, *Conquista intelectual del Perú*, 44–70.
6. "Los Reyes 1568–1577," Fundación de la Ciudad India de Cercado de Santiago, LC, Harkness Collection, Registros Notariales 1558–1577, fols. 851–71. On Cercado in the context of Toledan policy, see Monsalve, "Curas abusivos," 164–72.
7. "Memorial presentado para la fundación del Colegio para los hijos de Caciques en la Ciudad de Cuzco" and "Provisión fundado el colegio para hijos de Caciques," ARC, Colegio de Ciencias, legajo 45; Dueñas, chap. 1 in *Reshaping Justice*. On the history of the Huamanga region during this period, see Steve Stern, *Peru's Indian Peoples*.
8. On Vilcahuara, see Cushner, *Lords of the Land*, 117.
9. Crahan, "Administration of don Melchor," 389–412.
10. A 1735 royal decree opened the positions of protector de indios and *procurador* to Indian office holders. In 1697, Charles II ordered the opening of church posts to noble Indians. Garrett, *Shadows of Empire*, 140–45. Legal confusion over the exact identities of mestizos and mulattos grew. Ares Queija, "Categorías del mestizaje," 193–218. On the blurring of ethnic boundaries in municipal politics, see Riley, "Public Works," 355–393.
11. Fray Calixto's whole document is reproduced in Túpak Inka, *Documentos originales*. The Latin version of the peitition sent to the Vatican is Cala's "Planctus indorum." "Representación verdadera y exclamación y lamentable que toda la nación Indiana hace a la majestad del señor rey de las Españas [...]," AGI, Audiencia de Lima, legajo 988.
12. Dueñas, "Social Justice," 296–304; and chap. 3 in *Reshaping Justice*. Kuethe and Andrien, *Spanish Atlantic World*, 174–76.
13. "Juan de Dios Chumbirayco, indio originario del pueblo de Cercado sobre que se le ampare en la posesión de no pagar los reales tributos," 1797–1798, AGNP, signatura C931.
14. "Expediente sobre la petición presentada por Eugenio Chumpitasí para que se recibe información sobre limpieza de sangre a fin de que su hijo ingrese al colegio de príncipe, 1799," BNP, MS signatura C1575. The question of how the principle of "limpieza de sangre" applied in the colonial indigenous and mestizo world is explored in Villella, "'Pure and Noble Indians,'" 633–63.

15. "Razón por menos de ropa blanca y color lavado calzado, papel, velas, medicina de los caciques del Colegio del Príncipe desde de 10 de mayo hasta del 10 de setiembre, 1795," BNP, MS signatura C3317. "Razón Poer Menor del Mantenimiento de los Caciques del Colegio de Príncipe en el Tercio corrido desde el 10 enero de 1793 hasta el 10 de enero 1796," BNP, MS signatura C3475.

16. "Expediente que trata sobre la pretencion que hace la parte del Colegio San Borja," ARC, Colegio de Ciencias, legajo 45, expediente 26.

17. AAL, Cofradías, 1689–1691, legajo 30-A.

18. On status and competition in church institutions, see Garrett, "Nobleza indígena cuzqueña."

19. AAL, Cofradías 1659, legajo 30, expediente 12.

20. AAL Cofradías, 1715–1755, legajo 40, expediente 45.

21. AAL Cofradías, 1756–1762, legajo 32-A.

22. "Carta de Capellán," 1783, AAL, Cofradías, legajo 10-B, expediente 75. See also Steve Stern, *Resistance, Rebellion, and Consciousness*, 65–66.

23. Dean, *Inka Bodies*.

24. On this community memory in Santa Ana, see Dean, "War Games," 133–49. On the Hispano-Inca ruling class in Cuzco, see Temple, "Don Carlos Inca," 134–79. On preconquest symbols in festivals, see Cahill, "The Inca Motif in Colonial Fiestas I" and "The Inca Motif in Colonial Fiestas II," chaps. 10–11 in *Habsburg Peru*.

25. Dean, *Inka Bodies*, 194. On commemorations of the city's complex ethnic origins, see Harris, "Saint Sebastian"; Garcilaso de la Vega, *Royal Commentaries*, 478–88; Cieza de León, *Discovery and Conquest of Peru*, 183–89; and Church and Von Hagen, "Chachapoyas," 916–22.

26. Mariátegui Oliva, *Pintura cuzqueña*, 27, 51.

27. An explanation of the ethnic composition of these districts and a list of the native caciques and principales of each is contained in a document of 8 August 1572, Cuzco, ARC, Colegio de Ciencias, legajo 14, cuaderno 1.

28. On confession and community in the early modern Catholic world, see Bossy, chap. 4 ("Sin and Penance") and chap. 5 ("The Social Miracle") in *Christianity in the West*. Church thinking on the spiritual process of confession and absolution found early expression in the Fourth Lateran Council of 1215; see "Fourth Lateran Council," 412–41.

29. A version of the following discussion of confession manuals has been published as part of McEnroe, "Confusion of Tongues," 207–14.

30. A significant number of manuals were written wholly, or in part, by Native Christians. Christensen, *Translated Christianities*; and chap. 5 in *Nahua and Maya Catholicisms*.

31. In addition to the two manuals addressed here, the same scripted form of instruction—and the same notion that penitents can be grouped by social or professional type—appears in Villaplana, *Centinela dogmatico-moral*.

32. On didactic performances in indigenous communities, see Burkhart, Sell, and Poole, *Aztecs on Stage*; Burkhart et al., *Nahuatl Theater*, vols. 1–4. In addition to performance, missionaries explored a variety of nonverbal and extraverbal means of communication for confession and instruction. Pardo, "Bárbaros y mudos," 25–53.

33. On confession as a mode of narrative, see Braswell, *Medieval Sinner*. Sell has described the narratives and dialogues of confessional manuals as "telenovelesque." Thus literature borrows from the praxis of confession while didactic confession manuals also draw from the techniques of literature. "Perhaps Our Lord," 181–205.

34. Gruzinski, "Individualization and Acculturation."

35. Schwaller, "Don Bartolomé de Alva"; Brian, "Conquest of Mexico." The principal work of Don Fernando Ixtlilxochitl may be found in *Native Conquistador*. Brian's *Native Archive* explains Ixtlilxochitl's relationship to Carlos Sigüenza y Góngora and argues for the existence of a cross-caste intellectual community. On both brothers and their intellectual community, see Schwaller, "Brothers."

36. Alva, *Confessionario* [sic] *mayor*, 71–72. A full digitized version of the original text is available at the Internet Archive.

37. Alva, 78–79.

38. Phelan, *Millennial Kingdom*.

39. *Advertencias*, 4 July 1796. On the application of European confession practices to communities in New Spain by regular clergy, see Melvin, *Mendicant Orders*, 122–29.

40. Clendinnen, *Ambivalent Conquests*.

41. This idea of typical flaws or criminal types has deeps roots and lasting effects in European and colonial history. Here I argue that the late colonial period in New Spain witnessed a shift away from a caste-based perspective on typical flaws. For a discussion of the later reemergence and modification of caste-based thinking in the era of scientific racism, see Goode, "Corrupting a Good Mix," 241–65.

42. For a discussion of Carlo Borromeo's 1574 *Advertenze* and the Tridentine-era shift toward understanding confession as a quasi-judicial process and as an instrument for social control and policing orthodoxy, see De Boer, *Conquest of the Soul*. On confession as social control, see Tentler, *Sin and Confession*. William B. Taylor, in chap. 9 of *Magistrates of the Sacred*, describes confession among other social controls such as instruction and exemplary punishment. The social-control function of confession expressed in the confession manuals is echoed in those of Inquisition proceedings, whether carried out by bishops or the Holy Office. See Chuchiak, *Inquisition in New Spain*; and Tavárez, *Invisible War*.

43. *Advertencias*, 32.

44. *Advertencias*, 29.

45. Because the early evangelization of the Americas and the European Reformation

were coeval, the Catholic world wrestled with the proper role of images in communicating the faith both across linguistic boundaries and in the face of Protestant charges of idolatry. The Council of Trent articulated the official church position after nearly a century of upheaval ("Session the Twenty-Fifth").

46. *Advertencias*, 36.
47. *Advertencias*, 38.
48. On *mestizaje* in the eighteenth century, see Carrera, *Imagining Identity*, 32–42. On the Afro-Mexican population of Valladolid, see Vinson III, *Free-Colored Militia*, 114–17. On the ethnic composition of the larger Bajío region, see Tutino, appendix C ("Bajío Population, 1600–1800") in *Making a New World*. On *mestizaje* in neighboring Guadalajara during the same period, see Van Young, chap. 2 ("Demographic Change—Rural and Urban") in *Hacienda and Market*.

CHAPTER SEVEN

1. On colonial- and precolonial-era slavery among the Creeks, see Braund, "Creek Indians," 601–36.
2. Varner, *El Inca*. On Garcilaso's self-representation, see Campos-Muñoz, "Vega's Self-Classicalization," 123–44.
3. On Garcilaso's erudition and his influences, see Brading, "Incas and the Renaissance," 1–23; Castro-Klarén and Fernández, *Inca Garcilaso*.
4. Garcilaso de la Vega, *Florida of the Inca*, xxxvii. Herodotus, *Histories*, bk. 1, line 1, 3. Garcilaso traveled to Spain as the legal representative of a group of Cuzco aristocrats who were described in the documents he carried as the lineal descendants of Inca emperors. "Poder de los descendientes," 67–68.
5. Vega, 281.
6. This theme of reconciliation and unification of Europe and the Americas runs throughout the writings of Garcilaso. Airaldi, "Garcilaso de la Vega," 233–36.
7. Powell, *Mexico's Miguel Caldera*. On his ethnic origins, see Ruiz Guadalajara, "Capitán Miguel Caldera," 23–58.
8. On the northern mining frontier, war, and settlement, see Altman, *War for Mexico's West*; Corbeil, *Motions Beneath*. On indigenous governance on mining frontiers, see Velasco Murillo, chaps. 3–4 in *Urban Indians*.
9. Naylor and Polzer, *Presidio and Militia*, 112n1.
10. Restall, *Maya Conquistador*, 29–50; McEnroe, *Colony to Nationhood*, 37–43; and "Indian Garrison Colonies."
11. On how Camargo's heritage and identity were viewed by fellow Nahua intellectuals, see Townsend, "Don Juan Buenaventura Zapata," 168–69; Stayton, "Terreros Collection," 69–74.
12. On the negotiations over Tlaxcala's status in the empire, see Portillo Valdés, chap. 1 in *Fuero Indio*.
13. Frye, *Indians into Mexicans*.

14. On Diego Muñoz Camargo's role in the settlement, see Andrea Martínez Baracs, "Colonizaciones tlaxcaltecas," 26–27; Corbeil, *Identities in Motion*, 283–311.

15. Much of the following research on co-colonization practices appears in McEnroe, "Indian Garrison Colonies."

16. Chávez Borjas, "Guancasco de Mexicapa," 38–45. The use of public performance to symbolize the civic integration of multiple caste communities in Mexico's postconquest era is explored in Curcio-Nagy, chap. 3 in *Great Festivals*. The same questions are considered about Peru in Urton, *History of a Myth*, 96–119.

17. Treviño Villarreal, *Señor de Tlaxcala*, 18–301; Becerra, "Etnografía del guancasco," 6–12; Katzew, "Construction of Festive Rites," 153–75.

18. Joya and Martínez, *Comayagua*, 70–71, 163–65.

19. On Nahua performance as historical reenactment, see Burkhart et al., *Nahuatl Theater*. On Honduran guancascos as a historical memory of war and peace, see Chapman, *Hijos*, 74–75; Burkhart, "Destruction of Jerusalem."

20. The experiences of Maya communities in the Yucatán and Guatemala during this period of conquest were highly varied. Furthermore, as Restall has shown in *Maya Conquistador*, historical memory sometimes reframed early conquest experiences to create narratives of survival and victory.

21. On San Miguel de Aguayo (now Bustamante, Nuevo León), see Butzer, *Historia social*. On the early history of Comayagua, see Chamberlain, chap. 5 in *Conquest and Colonization*; and Escalante Arce, chap. 4 in *Tlaxcaltecas*.

22. The first incarnation of this colonial capital—Ciudad de Santiago de los Caballeros—was founded in 1524 (at the site of Iximché) but soon abandoned during the regional rebellion. In 1527, the capital was reestablished at Almolonga only to be destroyed by a volcanic eruption and flood in 1541. The third iteration of Santiago de Guatemala (today's Antigua) was built in 1543, and endured until 1773 when two massive earthquakes forced the final transfer of the colonial capital to today's site. Lutz, chaps. 1–2 in *Santiago de Guatemala*.

23. Lempira's struggle has become a foundational myth for Honduras, though its historicity remains murky. On the myth of Lempira, see Earl, *Return of the Native*, 200–204. The Lencas (as a cultural and linguistic community, though not as a unitary polity) antedated conquest and persisted long after. Herranz, "Lenca."

24. On Tlaxcalan colonization of the North, see Dávila Aguirre, *Colonización tlaxcalteca*; Adams, *Colonias tlaxcaltecas*; Sego, *Aliados y adversarios*; Dávila del Bosque, *Cabildos tlaxcaltecas*; Adams, "Lion's Mouth," 324–46; Butzer, *Historia social*; Sheridan Prieto, "'Indios madrineros,'" 15–51; Martínez Saldaña, *Diáspora tlaxcalteca*; and McEnroe, chaps. 1–4 in *Colony to Nationhood*.

25. Matthew, chap. 3 in *Memories of Conquest*.

26. Paz, *Laberinto*, 78–79.

27. This chapter treats primarily the attempts by Indian elites to retain their historic ethnic identity and legal categorization. Lutz has demonstrated that

indigenous Guatemalans fleeing tribute demands frequently had as strong a motive to shed their ethnic identities as to retain them. *Santiago de Guatemala*, 45–78. In the case of Peru, Wightman in *Indigenous Migration* has shown the ways in which sustaining *and* escaping traditional categories could be advantageous to Indians depending on the historical moment.

28. The literature on interethnic negotiation, translation, and alliance is now extensive. Matthew and Oudijk, *Indian Conquistadors*; Metcalf, *Go-Betweens*; Townsend, *Malintzin's Choices*; Yannakakis, *Art of Being In-Between*; and Barr, *Peace Came*.

29. Wood, *Transcending Conquest*; Baber, "City of Tlaxcala"; Offutt, "Defending Corporate Identity," 351–75; Mundy, *Mapping of New Spain*.

30. Political coordination was facilitated by the spread of the Indian colonizers' language. Yannakakis notes that "nahuatl speakers became the primary face of Spanish colonization in the early years after conquest." "Making Law Intelligible," 83.

31. Acts of the Cabildo, 15 June 1560, and 16 November 1562, 106–8, 119–21; Gibson, chap. 6 in *Tlaxcala*; Andrea Martínez Baracs, chap. 6 in *Gobierno de indios*. For examples of declining Tlaxcalan status, see Corbeil, *Motions Beneath*; Robinson, *Mark of Rebels*; and Frye, *Indians into Mexicans*.

32. Reforms associated with the New Laws of 1542 provoked resistance from encomenderos throughout Spanish America. Zavala, "Encomienda como institución económica." The documentary record of these debates is well represented in Zavala, *Encomienda Indiana*. Poole, *Juan de Ovando*, 109–25.

33. The document has received considerable attention and has been published in translation by Restall and Asselbergs in *Conquered Conquistadors*. Cuadriello, *República de Tlaxcala*.

34. On visual records of indigenous co-conquest, see Wood, *Transcending Conquest*; Boone, *Stories in Black and Red*; and Kranz, "Tlaxcalan Conquest Pictorials." Also on pictorial accounts by Nahua conquistadors, see Restall and Asselbergs, chap. 4 in *Invading Guatemala*.

35. Early historical work on the question of privileges among Indian conquerors varied a great deal. Gibson emphasized the strengths and persistence of Tlaxcalan claims. More recently, Baber has revisited the issue in "Colonial New Spain." Sherman, largely on the basis of later sixteenth-century petitions, emphasized the decline in their allied status. "Tlaxcalans," 124–39.

36. "Letter from the King and Testimony by Tlaxcalan and Mexica Conquistadors in Guatemala," in Restall and Asselbergs, *Invading Guatemala*, from the original document of 1547, AGI, Guatemala 52, fols. 77–78r. This document is also treated by Matthew and Arce.

37. Andrea Martínez Baracs, *Gobierno de indios*, 270–73.

38. On demographic collapse, survival, and recovery, see Lovell, *Conquest and Survival*; Nobel David Cook, *Born to Die*; and Cook and Borah, *Indian Population*.

39. Ruiz Guadalajara, "Capitán Miguel Caldera," 23–58; Powell, *Mexico's Miguel Caldera*.

40. Cavazos Garza, *Francisco Barbadillo*.

41. Sheptak, Joyce, and Blaisdell-Sloan, "Pragmatic Choices."

42. León, Chapa, and Zamora, chaps. 2–3 in *Historia de Nuevo León*; Ríos, *Fray Margil de Jesús*; Alessio Robles, *Coahuila y Texas*, 332–47.

43. AGS, Secretaría de Guerra 7032, expediente 1, fols. 7, 11, 23; AGS, Secretaría de Guerra 6966, expediente 69, fol. 281.

44. Lovell et al., chap. 1 in *"Strange Lands"*; Restall and Asselbergs, chap. 1 in *Invading Guatemala*. Alvarado's representation of the mixture of indigenous and Spanish forces may be found in *Conquest of Guatemala*, 53–67. Chamberlain, in chap. 1 of *Conquest and Colonization*, gives the troop deployments as recorded in several sources. Cortés's fourth and fifth letters to the crown indicate similar proportions of Spaniards and Indians in the military forces in Guatemala and Honduras. *Letters from Mexico*, 338–447. Matthew provides an assessment of the ethnic composition of invasion forces in *Memories of Conquest*, 60–62. In virtually all cases, allied Indian troops vastly outnumbered Europeans.

45. On internal frontiers and diplomacy, see McEnroe, "Sites of Diplomacy," 179–202; and "Sleeping Army," 109–39. Sellers-García in *Distance and Documents* has described political authority in colonial Guatemala as defined more by routes than by spatially demarcated territories. Pohl calls some of these political-spatial webs "alliance corridors" and traces their history into the archaeological past. "Mexican Codices," 137–59; and *Politics of Symbolism*, 1–5. On Nahua traditions linking pre- and postconquest routes, see Levin Rojo, chap. 5 in *Return to Aztlan*.

46. AGCA, legajo 5357, signatura A3 512.

47. On various modes of elite indigenous self-representation in relation to the larger empire, see Haskett, "Paper Shields," 99–126; Garrett, *Shadows of Empire*; López Serrelangue, *Nobleza indígena*; and McEnroe, chap. 1 in *Colony to Nationhood*.

48. Sherman, "Conqueror's Wealth," 199–213.

49. "New Laws of the Indies," 93–102; Sarmiento Donate, bk. 6, chaps. 6–9, in *Leyes de indias*. Wake, in "Dawning Places," finds a burst of Nahua cartography and land titles produced in response to administrative threats from 1591 to 1620.

50. Elliott, *Richelieu and Olivares*, 73–141.

51. "Testimonio de los autos hechas."

52. Currency valuations for this period are notoriously difficult to assess, but this was certainly a substantial sum. Annual revenues for the Vatican were just over 1 million ducats annually for this period. Gross, *Rome*, 129.

53. Altman, *War for Mexico's West*.

54. The contents of the charters may be found in Gibson, app. 7 of *Tlaxcala*.

55. McEnroe, chap. 5 in *Colony to Nationhood*.

56. Archer, *Army in Bourbon Mexico*; Lynch, *Bourbon Spain*. On local systems, see Cuello, "Economic Impact," 301–24; Del Carmen Velásquez, *Tres estudios*; and Vizcaya Canales, *Albores de la independencia*.

57. AMM, Correspondencia, vol. 121, expediente 1, fol. 3.

58. Frontier violence in this region was a constant condition from the sixteenth to the nineteenth century. Powell, *Mexico's Miguel Caldera*; Moorhead, *Apache Frontier*; Griffen, *Apaches*; Weber, *Spanish Frontier*, 204–35. Spicer, *Cycles of Conquest*; Salmon, *Indian Revolts*.

59. On the appeal of the Jesuits, see Wilde, *Religión y poder*. In the wider Tupi-Guarani region of South America, a complex process of frontier violence was forcing native people to represent political membership in relation to territorial boundaries. Langfur, *Forbidden Lands*. Karasch in *Before Brasília* illustrates the extent to which free people of color carried out the colonization of the Brazilian interior.

60. Sarreal, *Guaraní and Their Missions*, 65–92; Robert L. Jackson, chap. 5 in *Demographic Change*; Abou, *Guaranís*, 65–87; McNaspy, *Lost Cities of Paraguay*. As Roller's *Amazonian Routes* shows, mission-town populations were volatile both as a result of crisis and as a result of opportunities.

61. "Letter of the Corregidor."

62. Herzog, "Guaranis and Jesuits," 50–52; Barcelos, "Transformed Worlds," 52–55; "Letter of the Corregidor."

63. Wright and Cunha, "Destruction, Resistance, and Transformation," 319–21; De Lucca, *Jesuits and Fortifications*, 164–69.

64. Ganson, *Guaraní*, 1–9; "Letter of Nicolás Ñeenguirú." On the role of native literacy, see Ganson, 98–108. On theory of literacy's strategic value in conquest and resistance, see Todorov, *Conquest of America*.

65. Ganson, 87–116; Sarreal, *Guaraní and Their Missions*, 140–68; Abou, *Guaranís*, 123–50.

66. Estigarribia, "A Grammar Sketch of Paraguayan Guaraní," in Estigarribia and Pinta, *Guaraní Linguistics*, 9. Crevels, "Language Endangerment," 177.

67. "Argentina: Andresito, lugarteniente Artigas, héroe nacional," 29 January 2015, *Agencia Italiana de Noticias: Noticiero en español*.

68. Alessio Robles, chap. 33 in *Coahuila y Texas*; Simmons, "Tlaxcalans," 101–10.

CHAPTER EIGHT

1. The land transactions and maps for this estate are included in the *Papers of Joseph Brant*. On the impressions of visitors, see Campbell, *Travels in the interior*, 185–211.

2. On outcomes for the Oneidas, see Alan Taylor, chap. 12 in *Divided Ground*.

3. Plank, "Deploying Tribes and Clans"; Pulsipher, "Gaining the Diplomatic Edge."

4. On the siege of Cuzco, see Walker, chap. 5 in *Tupac Amaru Rebellion*; and *Smoldering Ashes*, 40–48. On nonwhite royalists, see Echeverri, *Indian and Slave Royalists*.

5. In the patriotic narrative, Pumacahua has something of a conversion experience when he embraces independence. Juan José Vega, *Pumacahua*, 268–70. Analysis of the national myth in Glave, "1814 Revolution in Cuzco," 204–9.

6. Walker, *Tupac Amaru Rebellion*, 25–27; Gisbert, "Curacas de Collao," 54–58.

7. "Título de Coronel."

8. Walker, chap. 2 in *Smoldering Ashes*.

9. Cahill, "Noblesa asediada," 82–99.

10. Political agenda described in Walker, chap. 2 in *Smoldering Ashes*.

11. On Bastidas, see Walker, 41.

12. "List of the Principal Rebels," 15 May 1781, in Walker and Stavig, 127–29; original documentation from *Colección documental de la independencia del Perú*, vol. 2, bk. 2, 195.

13. Walker, intro. to *Smoldering Ashes*.

14. Aude Argouse, "¿Son todos caciques?" 163–84; Cahill, "Liminal Nobility," 177–82.

15. On the composition of the forces and their motives, see Van Young, chap. 2 in *The Other Rebellion*; and Ducey, *Nation of Villages*.

16. William B. Taylor in *Drinking, Homicide, and Rebellion* has shown how often local rebellion was understood as an element of the political system rather than as an attempt to destroy it.

17. On national and regional politics in relation to the Spanish constitutional crisis, see Anna, *Forging Mexico*; Van Young, "Nationalist Movement"; Rodríguez Ordóñez, *Independence of Spanish America*; Eastman, "Ya no hay Atlántico," 153–66; and Robinson, *Mark of Rebels*.

18. Brant and his followers are studied as part of the loyalist diaspora in Jasanoff, *Liberty's Exiles*.

19. O'Donnell, *Southern Indians*. Creeks also captured and purchased slaves. Snyder, "Conquered Enemies," 255–88.

20. Prucha, *Great Father*, 35–60.

21. On McArthur's campaign, see Alan Taylor, *Civil War of 1812*, 264–68.

22. "List of Pensioners," 302–3.

23. On the battles for control of the Grand River region, see Alan Taylor, *Civil War of 1812*, 290–307.

24. Johnson, "John Smoke Johnson," 102–13.

25. Alan Taylor, *Divided Ground*, 128–33.

26. Benn, chap. 2 in *Iroquois*.

27. Map of Brant County, LAC, MIKAN no. 4138486.

28. Brant Historical Society, *Glimpse of the Past*, 2–54.

29. Reville, *County of Brant*, 53–65.

30. Peachey, engraving; Kelsay, chap. 27 in *Joseph Brant*.

31. Simcoe, *Diary*.

32. Simcoe, "The Mohawk Village, Grand River, Near Brantford, Showing Indian Council House and Church, 1793," in *Diary*, 149.

33. Hall, *Travels*, 135–39. On hybrid dress among the Mohawks, see Shannon, "Dressing for Success," 13–42; and West, *Journal of a Mission*, 277–78.

34. Brant Historical Society, *Glimpse of the Past*, 4–5; Holden, *Brant Family*, 22–24.

35. Parker, *Code of Handsome Lake*. Voluntary associations also created an environment for ritual improvisation. Porter, *Native American Freemasonry*; Wallace, *Seneca*, 303–37.

36. Kelsay, *Joseph Brant*, 611–12; Blau, "Iroquois White Dog Sacrifice," 97–119; Elisabeth Tooker, "Iroquois White Dog Sacrifice," 129–40; Wallace, *Seneca*, 50–59.

37. On the transmission of the office of Tekarihoken, see Chadwick, *Brant Family*, 7; and "Introduction to the Finding Aid," Kerr Collection, LAC, MG 19, F 6. On strategic interethnic marriage in Canada, see Perry, *Colonial Relations*.

38. Alan Taylor, *Civil War of 1812*, 393–95.

39. Muir, *Brantford in the 1830s*, 1–16.

40. On visual representations of these cross-cultural alliances, see Reinhart, "Picture by Benjamin West," 283–305.

41. Alan Taylor, *Divided Ground*, 46–52. On clan membership, see Chadwick, *Brant Family*, 10.

42. Roland, "Portrait of Robert Kerr," 187–94.

43. Political succession was complicated by conflicting claims between Canadian Mohawks and those who had remained in the US. Howard Edwards to William John Simcoe Kerr, "Efforts of William John Simcoe Kerr to Reclaim Lands in New York," n.d., LAC, Joseph Brant and Family Fonds, C-6818/1101185/MG19F6. See also "William Johnson Kerr," in *Dictionary of Canadian Biography*.

44. On the evolution and persistence of Iroquois family organizations and political structures in nineteenth-century North America, see Morgan and Tooker, "Iroquois League," 141–54.

45. Elizabeth Copway to George Copway, n.d., George Copway Papers, 1818–1863, LC, MSS 5137, AC 9815.

46. "Address before the Legislature of Pennsylvania," in Copway [Kahgegagbow], *Life, Letters and Speeches*, 175–88.

47. On Copway's capacity for code-switching, personal reinvention, and mythmaking, see Bellin, *Demon of the Continent*, 187–99. Bellin also notes Copway's skill at harnessing the imagery of American Romanticism to his aims. Peyer, "George Copway, Canadian Ojibwa Methodist and Romantic Cosmopolite," in *Indian Missionary Writers*, 224–77.

48. Copway, *Life, Letters and Speeches*, 187–88.

49. Copway, 178.

50. Copway, 175.

51. He and a group of fellow petitioners noted in 1558: "The time is rapidly approaching when not only the last hunting grounds of the Indian will be contracted into narrow spaces of agricultural enclosure but when the game on which he now principally depends for his subsistence will be known like the mastodon only by a few scattered fossil relics. . . . Our people without education will always be like children." "George Copway to Hon W. R. Greenwood, Chairman of the Committee on Indian Affairs of the United States," n.d., LC, MSS 5137, AC 9815.

52. Copway, *New Indian Territory*.

53. Copway, *New Indian Territory*, 26–32

54. Copway, *New Indian Territory*, 9

55. Copway, *New Indian Territory*, 12–13.

56. Copway, *New Indian Territory*, 17.

57. The plausibility of Copway's plans is attested to by the career of Eleazar Williams, a half-Mohawk clergyman who transformed himself into a powerful political and spiritual leader of the Oneidas and an organizer of their relocation to Wisconsin. Oberg, *Professional Indian*.

58. "Address before the Legislature of Pennsylvania," in Copway, *Life, Letters and Speeches*, 177.

BIBLIOGRAPHY

ARCHIVES AND SPECIAL COLLECTIONS

AAL: Archivo Arzobispal, Lima
AAM: Archivo del Arzobispado de Monterrey, Nuevo León, Mexico
AGCA: Archivo General de Centro América, Guatemala City
AGENL: Archivo General del Estado de Nuevo León
AGI: Archivo General de Indias, Seville
AGN: Archivo General de la Nación, Mexico City
AGNP: Archivo General de la Nación del Perú, Lima
AGS: Archivo General de Simancas, Spain
AHN: Archivo Histórico Nacional de España, Madrid
AMM: Archivo Municipal de Monterrey, Nuevo León
ARC: Archivo Regional del Cusco
BC: Benson Collection, University of Texas, Austin
BL: Bancroft Library, Berkeley
BNE: Biblioteca Nacional de España, Madrid
BNP: Biblioteca Nacional de Perú, Lima
CBC: Centro Bartolomé de las Casas, Cuzco
INAH: Instituto Nacional de Antropología e Historia, Mexico City
JBC: John Carter Brown Library, Providence
LAC: Library and Archives Canada, Ottawa
LC: Library of Congress, Washington, DC
SMU: De Golyer Library, Southern Methodist University, Dallas

JOURNALS

American Anthropologist
American Ethnologist
American Historical Review
American Indian Quarterly
American Quarterly
The Americas
Anales del Instituto de Investigaciones Estéticas

The Art Bulletin
Bricolage
Bulletin de l'Institut Français d'Études Andines
Canadian Bulletin of Medical History
Colonial Latin American Review
Colonial Latin American Historical Review
Diálogos en Historia (Lima)
The Drama Review
Early American Literature
Eighteenth-Century Studies
English Literary History
Estudios de Cultura Náhuatl
Estudios de Historia Novohispana
Ethnohistory
Ethnology
European History Quarterly
Hispanic American Historical Review
Hispanic Review
Historia y Cultura (Lima)
Histórica (Lima)
Indiana
Investigaciones Sociales (Mexico City)
Journal of American History
Journal of Colonialism and Colonial Studies
Journal of Inter-American Studies
Journal of Southern History
Journal of the Southwest
Latin American Research Review
New England Quarterly
Notes in the History of Art
Potestas
Procesos
Revista Andina
Revista de Estudios Hispánicos
Revista de Indias
Revista del Archivo Histórico del Cuzco (at ARC)
Revista del Instituto Americano de Arte
Senri Ethnological Studies
Sixteenth Century Journal
Summa Humanitatis
Teatro Indígena
Temas Americanistas

Tiempos de América
Tlalocan
William and Mary Quarterly

ARCHIVAL PRIMARY SOURCES

Advertencias para los nuevos confesores. 4 July 1796. Colegio de Teología Moral de Carmelitas de Valladolid.

Anonymous. *Relacion, y verdadero romance, que declara la inconsiderada, y atrevida sublevacion, que intentaban hazer los indios mal acordados, y algunos mestizos en la ciudad de Lima: Se dà razon de las promptissimas, y bien ordenadas providencias, que se dieron para embarazo de tan odiosa execucion, y del justo castigo que se diò à los culpados.* Lima, 1750. JCB.

Anonymous. "The Three Cherokees, came over from the head of the River Savanna to London, 1762." George Brickham the Younger. British Museum. No. 1982, U.3745.

Basire, Isaac. "Seven Cherokees standing in a woodland setting." 1730. British Museum. No. Y,1.110.

Cabeza de Vaca, Alvar Núñez. *La relación y comentarios del gouernador Aluar Nuñez Cabeça de Vaca, de lo acaescido en las dos jornadas que hizo a las Indias.* 1555. Francisco Fernadedez de Cordova, Valladolid. JCB.

Campo de la Rynaga, Nicolás Matías del. *Memorial historico y iuridico, que refiere el origen del oficio de protector general de los Indios del Perú en su gentilidad, causas y vtilidades de su continuacion por nuestros gloriosos reyes de Castilla, nuevo lustre y autoridad que le comunicaron, haziendole vno de sus magistrados con toga, y motivos que persuaden su conservacion.* 1671. Mateo de Espinosa y Arteaga, Madrid. JCB.

Castelli, Juan José. *El Excmo. señor representante de la Junta Provisional Gubernativa del Rio de la Plata a los indios del vireynato del Perú: La proclama que con fecha 26 de octubre del año anterior os ha dirigido vuestro actual virey.* 1811. Real Imprenta de Niños Expósitos, Buenos-Ayres. JCB.

Catharine Brown Papers. The Congregational Library and Archive, Boston, MA. MS 0834. http://www.congregationallibrary.org/finding-aids/BrownCatharine 0834.

"The Charter of the President and Fellows of Harvard College, under the Seal of the Colony of Massachusetts Bay [...] May 31, 1650." Harvard University Archives. http://library.harvard.edu/university-archives/using-the-collections/online -resources/charter-of-1650.

Cotton, Josiah. "Vocabulary of the Massachusetts (or Natick) Indian Language." From 1609 manuscript. Collections of the Massachusetts Historical Society, 3rd ser., 3. Cambridge, MA, 1830.

"Dartmouth College Charter [...] 1769." Dartmouth Library. https://www .dartmouth.edu/~library/rauner/dartmouth/dc-charter.html.

Del Piombo, Sebastiano. *Clement VII.* Ca. 1531. Painting. Getty Museum, Los Angeles.

Map of the County of Brant drawn by C. L. Smith. Ontario: Page and Smith, 1875. Canadian County Atlas Digital Project, McGill University. https://digital.library .mcgill.ca/countyatlas/searchmapframes.php.

Mohawk antiphony. 1810. Quebec. JCB. Manuscripts.

Morachimo Capac, Vicente de. "Señor. Don Vicente de Mora Chimo, Capac, cazique principal de varios pueblos de indios en la jurisdiccion de la ciudad de Truxillo del Reyno del Perù: Procurador general de sus naturales, y nuevamente diputado general por los caziques mas principales de sus provincias [. . .]." 1729. Madrid. JCB.

Muñoz Camargo, Diego. *Descripción de la ciudad y provincia de Tlaxcala [. . .].* 1580– 1585. University of Glasgow Library. Special Collections. MS Hunter 242 (U.3.15).

Papers of Joseph Brant and his Descendants Accumulated and Preserved by the Kerr Family. 1774–1789. LAC. MG19-F6.

Para que se haga lista y padrón de los pueblos, e indios que ay, y a quien, y donde se reparten. Antonio Ricardo. 1603. Lima. JCB.

Plan showing lands purchased from the Indians, proposed settlements on Lake Huron, grant to Joseph Brant, etc. 1792. LAC. MIKAN no. 4138486.

"Proclama de un cura indio del obispado de Valladolid a todos los padres curas y vicarios indios, y a nuestros hijos los caziques gobernadores y demás indios de esta América." 1811. Mexico. *Noticias del Peru* 8. JCB.

Rocha, Diego Andrés. *Tratado único, y singular del origen de los indios occidentales del Pirú, México, Santa Fe, y Chile. Por el doctor don Diego Andres Rocha Oydor de la Real Audiencia de Lima.* Manuel de los Olivos and Joseph de Contreras. JCB. Lima: Manuel de los Olivos and Joseph Contreras, 1681.

Titian. *Carlos V en Mühlberg.* 1547. Painting. Museo del Prado, Madrid.

——— . *Portrait of Charles V.* 1548. Painting. Alte Pinakothek, Munich.

Weiditz, Christoph. *Trachtenbuch,* 1533/1540. Germanisches Nationalmuseum Nürnberg. Hs 22474. http://dlib.gnm.de/item/Hs22474/html.

PUBLISHED PRIMARY SOURCES

Acts of the Cabildo, 15 June 1560, and 16 November 1562. In *The Tlaxcalan Actas: A Compendium of the Records of the Cabildo of Tlaxcala 1545–1627,* edited by James Lockhart, Frances Berdan, and Arthur J. O. Anderson. Salt Lake City: University of Utah Press, 1986.

Alva, Bartolomé de. *Confessionario mayor, y menor en lengua mexicana. Y platicas contra las supresticiones de idolatria [. . .]* 1634. Mexico: Francisco Salbago, 1634. JCB. Internet Archive. https://archive.org/details/confessionariomao0alva.

——— . *A Guide to Confession Large and Small in the Mexican Language,* 1634.

Edited by Barry D. Sell and John Frederick Schwaller. Norman: University of Oklahoma Press, 1999.

Alvarado, Pedro de. *An Account of the Conquest of Guatemala in 1524 by Pedro de Alvarado*. Edited by Sedley J. Mackie with facsimile of Spanish original from 1525. New York: Cortes Society, 1924.

Anderson, Rufus. *Memoir of Catharine Brown*. Philadelphia: American Sunday School Union, 1831.

Aristotle. *Metaphysics*. In *Complete Works of Aristotle*, edited by Jonathan Barnes. Princeton, NJ: Princeton University Press, 1984.

———. *Poetics*. Translated by S. H. Butcher. New York: Hill and Wang, 1961.

"Las Armas de Paullo Inga." *Revista del Archivo Histórico del Cuzco* ii. ARC.

"Articles of Friendship and Commerce proposed by the Lords Commissioners for Trade and Plantations, to the Deputies of the Cherokee Nation in South Carolina by his Majesty's Order, on Monday Sept. 7, 1730." In *The Historical Register Containing an Impartial Relation of all Transactions, Foreign and Domestic* [. . .] *Vol XVI, for the year 1730* [. . .], no. 16, West Indies, Carolina. London, 1731.

Augustine of Hippo. *Saint Augustine's Enchiridion*. Translated by Ernest Evans. London: Society for Promoting Christian Knowledge, 1953.

Bartram, William. *Travels through North and South Carolina, Georgia, East and West Florida, the Cherokee Country, the Extensive Territories of the Muscogulges, or Creek Confederacy, and the Country of the Chactaws* [. . .]. Philadelphia, James and Johnson, 1791.

Betanzos, Juan de. *Narrative of the Incas*. 1653. Edited and translated by Roland Hamilton and Dana Buchanan. Austin: University of Texas Press, 1996.

Beyond the Codices: The Nahua View of Colonial Mexico. Edited and translated by Arthur J. O. Anderson, Frances Berdan, and James Lockhart. Berkeley: University of California Press, 1976.

Biglow, William. *History of the Town of Natick, Mass: From the Days of the Apostolic Eliot to the Present Time*. Boston: Marsh, Capen, and Lyon, 1830.

Boudinot, Elias. *Cherokee Editor: The Writings of Elias*. Edited by Theda Perdue. Athens: University of Georgia Press, 1996.

Brown, Catharine. *Cherokee Sister: The Collected Writings of Catharine Brown, 1818–1823*. Edited by Theresa Strouth Gall. Lincoln: University of Nebraska Press, 2014.

Cabeza de Vaca, Álvar Núñez. *The Narrative of Cabeza de Vaca*. 1542. Edited and translated by Rolena Adorno and Patrick Charles Pautz. Lincoln: University of Nebraska Press, 1999.

———. *La relación y comentarios del gouernador Alvar Nuñez Cabeça de Vaca, de lo acaescido en las dos jornadas que hizo a las Indias*. Valladolid: Francisco Fernández de Córdova, 1555.

Cala, Isidoro de. "El Planctus indorum christianorum en America peruntina." In *Una*

Denuncia profética desde el Perú a mediados del siglo XVIII. Edited by José María Navarro. Lima: Pontífica Universidad Católica del Perú, 2000.

Campbell, Patrick. *Travels in the interior inhabited parts of North America: In the years 1791 and 1792 [. . .].* Edinburgh, 1793.

Canons and Decrees of the Sacred and Oecumenical Council of Trent. Edited and translated by J. Waterworth. London: Dolman, 1848.

Chimalpahin Cuauhtlehuanitzin, Domingo Francisco de San Antón Muñón. *Codex Chimalpahin.* Edited and translated by Arthur J. O. Anderson and Susan Schroeder. Norman: University of Oklahoma Press, 1997.

Cieza de León, Pedro. *The Discovery and Conquest of Peru.* Edited and translated by Alexandra Parma Cook and Noble David Cook. Durham, NC: Duke University Press, 1998.

Colección documental de la independencia del Perú. Lima: Comisión Nacional del Sesquicentenario de la Independencia del Perú, 1971–.

Colonec [sic: Cholonec], Francisco. *La gracia triunfante en la vida de Catharina Tegakovita. India Iroquesa, y en las de otras assi de su Nacion, como de esta Nueva-España.* Translated from French to Spanish by Padre Juan de Urtassum. Mexico City, 1724.

Commonwealth of Virginia. *A treaty held with the Catawba and Cherokee Indians at the Catawba-Town and Broad-River in the Months of February and March 1756: By Virtue of a Commission granted by the Honorable Robert Dinwiddie, Esquire, His majesty's Lieutenant-Governor and Commander in Chief of the Colony and Dominion of Virginia, to the Honorable Peter Randolph and William Byrd, Esquires, Members of His Majesty's Council of the said Colony.* Williamsburg, VA: Hunter, 1756. Reprint, Boston, 1928.

Copway, George [Kahgegagbow]. *Life, Letters and Speeches.* Edited by LaVonne Brown Ruoff and Donald B. Smith. Lincoln: University of Nebraska Press, 1997. Originally published in 1850 as *The Life, Letters and Speeches of Ka-Ge-Ga-Gah-Bowh, or George Copway, Chief of the Ojibway Nation* by S. W. Benedict (New York).

——— [The Indian Chief Kah-Ge-Gah-Bouh, or Geo. Copway]. *Organization of a New Indian Territory East of the Missouri River: Arguments and Reasons Submitted to the Honorable the Members of the [. . .] 31st Congress of the United States.* New York: S. W. Benedict, 1850.

Cortés, Hernan. *Letters from Mexico.* Edited and translated by Anthony R. Pagden. New York: Grossman, 1971.

The Council of Trent: Canons and Decrees. Edited by J. Waterworth. Chicago: 1848.

Cruz, Juana Inés de la. "Loa for el divino Narciso." In *Sor Juana Inés de la Cruz: Poems, Protest, and a Dream,* bilingual edition, edited by Margaret Sayers Peden. New York: Penguin, 1997.

Cuming, Alexander. "The Account of the Cherokee Indians, and of Sir Alexander Cuming's Journey amongst them." In *The Historical Register Containing an*

Impartial Relation of all Transactions, Foreign and Domestic [. . .] 16, no. 61 ("West
Indies, Carolina," 1731). London, 1731.

———. "Memoirs of the Life of Sir Alexander Cuming of Culter (1764)." In
Cherokee Voices: Early Accounts of Cherokee Life in the East, by Vicki Rozema.
Winston/Salem, NC: John F. Blair, 2002.

Cusi Yupanqui, Titu. *An Inca Account of the Conquest of Peru.* Ralph Bauer. Boulder:
University Press of Colorado, 2005.

Dale, Edward Everett, and Gaston Litton. *Cherokee Cavaliers: Forty Years of Cherokee
History as Told in the Correspondence of the Ridge-Watie-Boudinot Family.* Norman:
University of Oklahoma Press, 1995.

Díaz del Castillo, Bernal. *Historia verdadera de la conquista de la Nueva España.* 1568.
Madrid: Biblioteca Homo Legens, 2009.

———. *The History of the Conquest of New Spain.* Edited by Davíd Carrasco. Essays
by Rolena Adorno, Davíd Carrasco, Sandra Cypress, and Karen Viera Powers.
Albuquerque, NM: University of New Mexico Press, 2008.

Fernández de Oviedo y Valdés, Gonzalo. *Historia general y natural de las Indias.* 16th
century. Edited by José Amador de los Rios. Madrid: Real Academia de Historia, 1851.

First Ten Annual Reports of the American Board of Commissioners for Foreign Missions.
Boston: Crocker and Brewster, 1834.

"Fourth Lateran Council." In *Medieval Handbooks of Penance: A Translation of the
Principal Libri Poenitentiales,* edited by John T. McNeill and Helena M. Gamer,
413–14. New York: Columbia, 1990.

Gold, Theodore Sedgewick. *Historical Records of the Town of Cornwall, Litchfield
County, Connecticut.* 2nd ed. Hartford, CT: Case, Lockwood and Brainard, 1902.

Gookin, Daniel. *Historical Collections of the Indians in New England: Of their Several
Nations, Numbers, Customs, Manners, Religion and Government, before the English
Planted There.* Boston: Belknap and Hall, 1792.

Guaman Poma de Ayala, Felipe. *The First New Chronicle and Good Government.*
Translated and with an introduction by David Frye. Cambridge: Hackett, 2006.

———. *El primer nueva corónica y buen gobierno.* Edited by John V. Murra and
Rolena Adorno. Translated by Jorge L. Orioste. Madrid: Siglo Veintiuno, 1980.

Hall, Lieutenant Francis. *Travels in Canada and The United States, 1816 and 1817.*
Boston: Wells and Lilly, 1818.

Herodotus. *The Histories.* Translated by Aubrey de Sélincourt and John Marincola.
New York: Penguin, 2003.

"Hospital de los Naturales, Cuzco, 1699." *Revista del Archivo Histórico del Cuzco*
11:55–56. ARC.

"Indios para el servicio del hospital de naturales." *Revista del Archivo Histórico del
Cuzco* 11:143–44. ARC.

Landa Calderón, Diego de. *Relación de las cosas de Yucatán.* Edited by María del
Carmen León Cázares. Mexico City: Consejo Nacional para la Cultura y las
Artes, 1994.

León, Alonso de, Juan Bautista Chapa, and Fernando Sánchez de Zamora. *Historia de Nuevo León: Con noticias sobre Coahuila, Tamaulipas, Texas y Nuevo México, escrita en el siglo XVII por el Cap. Alonso de León, Juan Bautista Chapa y el Gral. Fernando Sánchez de Zamora.* Notes by Cavazos Garza. Monterrey, Mexico: Ayuntamiento de Monterrey, 1980.

"Letter from the King and Testimony by Tlaxcalan and Mexica Conquistadors in Guatemala." 1547. In *Invading Guatemala: Spanish, Nahua, and Maya Accounts of the Conquest Wars,* by Mattew Restall and Florine Asselbergs. University Park: Pennsylvania State University Press, 2007. From Guatemala 52, fols. 77–78r, AGI.

"Letter of Nicolás Ñeenguirú, Corregidor of Mission Concepción, to the Governor of Buenos Aires, José de Andonaegui, July 20, 1753." In *The Guaraní under Spanish Rule in Río de la Plata,* by Barbara Ganson. Stanford, CA: Stanford University Press, 2003.

"Letter of the Corregidor Miguel Guaiho of Mission San Juan Bautista, 1753?" In app. of *The Guaraní under Spanish Rule in Río de la Plata,* by Barbara Ganson. Stanford, CA: Stanford University Press, 2003.

Lisi, Francisco Leonardo. *El Tercer Concilio Limense y la aculturación de los indígenas sudamericanos: Estudio crítico con edición, traducción y comentario de las actas del Concilio Provincial celebrado en Lima entre 1582 y 1583.* Salamanca, Spain: Universidad de Salamanca, 1990.

"List of Pensioners." In *History of the County of Brant,* by F. Douglas Reville, 302–3. Brantford, Ontario: Brant Historical Society, 1920.

"List of the Principal Rebels That Are Held in This Jail (Barracks) of Cuzco, and of Those Who Have Died in the Fighting That Has Taken Place between the Sacrilegious Troops of the Traitor and Our Forces." In *The Tupac Amaru and Catarista Rebellions: An Anthology of Sources,* edited and translated by Ward Stavig and Ella Schmidt. Indianapolis: Hackett, 2008.

López de Gómara, Francisco. *Historia general de las Indias.* Vol. 2. 1553. Edited by Pilar Guibelalde and Emiliano M. Aguilera. Barcelona: Obras Maestras, 1954.

Mamusse wunneetupanatamwe Up-Biblum God: Naneeswe Nukkone Testament kah wonk Wusku Testament. Cambridge, MA: Samuel Green, 1685. JCB.

Mogrovejo, Toribio Alfonso de. *Libro de visitas de Santo Toribio de Mogrovejo (1593–1605).* Edited by José Antonio Benito. Lima: Pontificia Universidad Católica, 2000.

Muñoz Camargo, Diego. *Descripción de la ciudad y provincia de Tlaxcala de las Indias y del Mar Océano para el buen gobierno y ennoblecimiento dellas.* Edited by René Acuña. Mexico City: UNAM, 1981.

——. *Historia de Tlaxcala.* México: Ateneo Nacional de Ciencias y Artes de Mexico, 1947.

"The Narrative of Oo-Chee-Ah." *Chronicles of Oklahoma* 12, no. 1 (March 1934): 25–41.

"New Echota Cherokee Nation, May 8, 1830." In *New Echota Letters: Contributions of Samuel A. Worcester to the Cherokee Phoenix*, edited by Jack Frederick Kilpatrick and Anna Gritts Kilpatrick. Dallas: Southern Methodist University Press, 1968.

"New Laws of the Indies." In *An Account, Much Abbreviated, of the Destruction of the Indies: And Related Texts*, edited by Franklin W. Knight, 93–102. Indianapolis: Hackett, 2003.

Occom, Samson. "A Short Narrative of My Life." 1768. In *American Indian Nonfiction: An Anthology of Writings, 1760s–1930s*, edited by Bernd Peyer, 43–48. Norman: University of Oklahoma Press, 2007.

Peachey, James. Engraving. *A Primer for the Use of the Mohawk Children*, by Daniel Claus, frontispiece. London: C. Buckton, 1786.

Plato. "Apology." In *The Last Days of Socrates*, translated by Hugh Tredennick. New York: Penguin, 1969.

———. *Republic*. Translated by C. D. C. Reeve. Cambridge: Hackett, 2004.

"Poder de los descendientes de los Incas del Cusco al Inca Garcilaso de la Vega." *Revista del Archivo Histórico del Cuzco* 11:67–68. ARC.

Proceso inquisitorial del cacique de Tetzcoco don Carlos Ometochtzin. Mexico City: Patrimonio Cultural y Artístico del Estado de México, 1980.

The Queen v. Louis Riel. Transcript, testimony of the accused. 31 July–1 August 1885. Toronto: University of Toronto Press, 1974.

Ramos Gavilán, Alonso. *Historia del santuario de Nuestra Señora de Copacabana*. Transcribed by Ignacio Prado Pastor. Lima: Gerónimo de Contreras, 1621. Reprint, Lima: P. L. Villanueva, 1988.

"Relacion cronológica de los casiques e indios nobles que han tenido sus hijos en el Colegio Real de San Francisco Borja." *Revista del Archivo Histórico del Cuzco*, no. 1 (1950), 225–30. ARC.

Relaciones geográficas de la diócesis de Tlaxcala: Manuscritos de la Real Academia de Historia de Madrid y del Archivo de Indias en Sevilla. Papeles de Nueva Espana, second ser., Geografía y Estadística 5, 1580–1582. Sevilla: Impresores de la Real Casa, 1905.

Rodríguez de Figueroa, Diego. "Account of the route and journey made by Diego Rodríguez [de Figueroa] from the city of Cuzco to the land of war of Manco Inca [. . .]." 1565. In *Voices from Vilcabamba: Accounts Chronicling the Fall of the Inca Empire*, edited by Brian S. Bauer, Madeleine Halac-Higashimori, and Gabriel E. Cantarutti. Boulder: University Press of Colorado, 2016.

Sarmiento Donate, Alberto, ed. *De las leyes de Indias: Antología de la recopilación de 1681*. Mexico City: Secretaría de Educación Pública, 1988.

Simcoe, Elizabeth. *Diary of Mrs. John Graves Simcoe, Wife of the Lieutenant-Governor of the Province of Upper Canada, 1792–6*. With notes and a biography by J. Ross Robertson. Toronto: William Briggs, 1911.

Some Correspondence between the Governors and Treasurers of the New England

Company in London and the Commissioners of the United Colonies in America [. . .]
between the Years 1657 and 1712. London: Eliot Stock, 1897.

Strout Gaul, Theresa. *To Marry an Indian: The Marriage of Harriett Gold and Elias
Boudinot in Letters, 1823–1839*. Chapel Hill: University of North Carolina Press,
2005.

"Testimonio de los autos hechas en el distrito de la Audiencia de Guatemala para
el cumplimento de la cédula de Su Majestad ordenado se le sirva con 250,000
ducados para la unión de las armas, 1629." In *Cartas de cabildos hispanoamericanos:
Audiencia de Guatemala*, edited by Javier Ortiz de la Tabla Ducasse, Bibiano
Torres Ramírez, and Enriqueta Vila Vilar. Guatemala 43. Seville: Consejo
Superior de Investigaciones Científicas, 1984.

Thomas, Thorowgood. *Jews in America, or Probabilities that those Indians are Judaical,
made more probable by Some Additions to the former Conjectures*. London: Henry
Brome, 1660.

Timberlake, Henry. *The Memoirs of Lieut. Henry Timberlake, (Who accompanied the
Three Cherokee Indians to England in the Year 1762)*. London: Ridley, Nicoll, and
Henderson, 1765.

Tineo, Primitivo. *Los concilios limenses en la evangelización latinoamericana*.
Pamplona: Universidad de Navarra, 1990.

"Título de Coronel de Milicias a don Mateo Pumacahua." 23 August 1783. AGI
Pensiones 1053, San Ildefonso. Reproduced in *Revista del Archivo Histórico del
Cuzco* 11. ARC.

*The Tlaxcalan Actas: A Compendium of the Records of the Cabildo of Tlaxcala (1545–
1627)*. Edited by James Lockhart, Frances Berdan, and Arthur J. O. Anderson. Salt
Lake City: University of Utah Press, 1986.

Torres Rubio, Diego de. *Arte, y vocabulario de la lengua quichua general de los indios de
el Perú* [. . .]. Lima: Imprenta de la Plazuela de San Christoval, 1754.

Túpak Inka, Fray Calixto. *Documentos originales y, en su mayoría, totalmente
desconocidos, auténticos, de este apóstol indio, valiente defensor de su raza, desde el año
de 1746 a 1760*. Edited by Fernando A. Loayza. Lima: Pequeños Grandes Libros
de Historia Americana, 1948.

Valadés, Diego de. *Rhetorica christiana*. Bilingual Latin-Spanish edition. Translated
by Tarsicio Herrera Zapién. Facsimile of 1579 edition. Mexico: UNAM, 1989.

Vega, Garcilaso de la. *The Florida of the Inca*. Translated by John Varner and Jeanette
Varner. Austin: University of Texas Press, 1951.

——— . *Royal Commentaries of the Incas and General History of Peru*. Translated by
Harold V. Livermore. Austin: University of Texas Press, 1966.

Vega, Luis Laso de la. *The Story of the Virgin of Guadalupe: Luis Laso de la Vega's
"Huei tlamahuiçoltica" of 1649*. Edited and translated by Lisa Sousa, Stafford
Poole, and James Lockhart. Stanford, CA: Stanford University Press, 1998.

Villaplana, Hermenegildo. *Centinela dogmatico-moral con oportunos avisos al confessor,
y penitente*. Mexico City: Biblioteca Mexicana, 1767.

West, John. *A Journal of a Mission to the Indians of the British Provinces of New Brunswick and Nova Scotia and the Mohawks on the Ouse, or Grand River, Upper Canada.* London: L. B. Seeley and Son, 1828.

Williams, Roger. *Correspondence of Roger Williams.* Providence: Brown / New England Historical Society, 1988.

———. *A Key into the Language of America: Or, An help to the Language of the Natives in that part of America, called New-England.* London: Gregory Dexter, 1643.

———. *Letters and Papers of Roger Williams, 1629–1682.* Boston: New England Historical Society, 1924.

Worcester, Samuel A. *New Echota Letters: Contributions of Samuel A. Worcester to the Cherokee Phoenix,* edited by Jack Frederick Kilpatrick and Anna Gritts Kilpatrick. Dallas: Southern Methodist University Press, 1968.

Yáñez, José. *Leales y generosos caciquez gobernadores, alcaldes, justicias principales, y demás naturales del reyno.* Guatemala, 1609.

SECONDARY SOURCES

Abercrombie, Thomas A. "La perpetuidad traducida: Del 'debate' al Taki Onqoy y una rebelión comunera peruana," In *Incas e indios cristianos: Élites indígenas e identidades cristianas en los Andes coloniales,* edited by Jean-Jacques Decoster. Cuzco: Centro de Estudios Regionales Bartolomé de las Casas, 2002.

Abou, Sélim. *The Jesuit 'Republic' of the Guaranís (1609–1768) and its Heritage.* Translated by Lawrence J. Johnson. New York: UNESCO/Crossroads, 1997.

Adams, David B. "At the Lion's Mouth: San Miguel de Aguayo in the Defense of Nuevo León, 1686–1820." *Colonial Latin American Historical Review* 9, no. 3 (2000): 324–46.

———. *Las colonias tlaxcaltecas de Coahuila y Nuevo León en la Nueva España: Un aspecto de la colonización del norte de México.* Saltillo: Archivo Municipal de Saltillo, 1991.

Adanaqué, Raúl. "Los caciques Chayhuac de Mansiche (Trujillo, siglos XVI–XVIII)." *Diálogos en Historia* (Lima) 1 (1999): 57–66.

Adorno, Rolena. *Guaman Poma: Writing and Resistance in Colonial Peru.* 2nd ed. Austin: University of Texas Press, 2000.

———. *Polemics of Possession in Spanish American Narrative.* Bridgeport: Yale University Press, 2008.

Airaldi, Gabriela. "El inca Garcilaso de la Vega entre economía y política." In *Entre dos mundos: Fronteras culturales y agentes mediadores,* edited by Berta Ares Queija and Serge Gruzinski. Seville: CSIC, 1997.

Alaperrine-Bouyer, Monique. "La biblioteca del colegio de yngas nobles: San Borja del Cuzco." *Histórica* (Lima) 29, no. 2 (1005): 163–79.

———. "Enseñanza y pedagogía de los jesuitas en los colegios para los hijos de caciques (siglo xvii)." In *Los jesuitas y la modernidad en Iberoamérica: 1549–1573*, edited by Manuel Marzal and Luis Bacigalupo. Lima: Instituto Frances de Estudios Andinos, 2007.

Alcalá, Luisa Elena. "Beginnings: Art, Time, and Tito Yupanqui's Virgin of Copacabana." In *The Arts of South America 1492–1850*, edited by Donna Pierce. Denver: Denver Art Museum, 2010.

———. "The Image of the Devout Indian: The Codification of a Colonial Idea." In *Contested Visions in the Spanish Colonial World*, edited by Ilona Katzew. Los Angeles: LACMA; Mexico: Museo Nacional de Historia, 2012.

Alessio Robles, Vito. *Coahuila y Texas en la epoca colonia*. 2nd ed. 1938. Mexico, D.F.: Biblioteca Porrúa, 1978.

Allen, Heather. "Book Marks: Jerónimo de Aguilar and the Book of Hours." In *Objects of Culture in the Literature of Imperial Spain*, edited by Mary E. Barnard and Frederick A. De Armas. Toronto: University of Toronto Press, 2013.

Altman, Ida. *The War for Mexico's West: Indians and Spaniards in New Galicia, 1524–1550*. Albuquerque: University of New Mexico Press, 2010.

Amado Gonzalez, Donato. "El alférez real de los incas: Resistencia, cambios y continuidad de la Identidad indígena." In *Élites indígenas en los Andes: Nobles, caciques y cabildantes bajo el yugo colonial*, edited by David Cahill and Blanca Tovías. Quito: Abya-Yala, 2003.

Andrien, Kenneth J. *Andean Worlds*. Albuquerque: University of New Mexico Press, 2001.

Anna, Timothy E. *Forging Mexico, 1821–1835*. Lincoln: University of Nebraska Press, 1998.

Arenal, Electra, and Stacey Schlau. *Untold Sisters: Hispanic Nuns in their Own Works*. Translated by Amanda Powell. Albuquerque: University of New Mexico Press, 1989.

Ares Queija, Berta. "Las categorías del mestizaje: Desafíos a los constreñimientos de un modelo social en el Perú colonial temprano." *Histórica* 28, no. 1 (2004): 193–218.

Argouse, Aude. "¿Son todos caciques? Curacas, principales e indios urbanos en Cajamarca (siglo XVII). *Bulletin de l'Institut Français d'Études Andines* 37, no. 1 (2008): 163–84.

Arriaga, Pablo José de. *The Extirpation of Idolatry in Peru*. Edited and translated by Clark Keating. Lexington: University of Kentucky Press, 1968.

Asselbergs, Florine. *Conquered Conquistadors: The Lienzo de Quauhquechollan, a Nahua Vision of the Conquest of Guatemala*. Boulder: University Press of Colorado, 2008.

Axtell, James. *Natives and Newcomers: The Cultural Origins of North America*. New York: Oxford University Press, 2011.

Baber, R. Jovita. "Empire, Indians, and the Negotiation for the Status of the City of Tlaxcala, 1521–1550." In *Negotiation within Domination: New Spain's Indian Pueblos*

Confront the Spanish State, edited by Ethelia Ruiz Medrano and Susan Kellogg. Boulder: University Press of Colorado, 2010.

———. "Law, Land, and Legal Rhetoric in Colonial New Spain." In *Native Claims: Indigenous Law and Empire, 1500–1920*, edited by Saliha Belmessous. Oxford, UK: Oxford University Press, 2012.

Baird, Joseph Armstrong. *The Churches of Mexico, 1530–1810*. Berkeley: University of California Press, 1962.

Barcelos, Artur. "Transformed Worlds: Missionaries and Indigenous Peoples in South America." *ReVista* 14, no. 3 (Spring 2015): 52–55.

Barman, Jean. *French Canadians, Furs, and Indigenous Women in the Making of the Pacific Northwest*. Vancouver: University of British Columbia Press, 2014.

Barr, Juliana. *Peace Came in the Form of a Woman: Indians and Spaniards in the Texas Borderlands*. Chapel Hill: University of North Carolina Press, 2007.

Bauer, Brian S., Madeleine Halac-Higashimori, and Gabriel E. Cantarutti, eds. *Voices from Vilcabamba: Accounts Chronicling the Fall of the Inca Empire*. Boulder: University Press of Colorado, 2016.

Bauer, Ralph. "'EnCountering' Colonial Latin American Indian Chronicles: Felipe Guaman Poma de Ayala's History of the 'New' World." *American Indian Quarterly* 25, no. 2 (2001): 274–312.

Beatty, Andrew. "The Pope in Mexico: Syncretism in Public Ritual." *American Anthropologist* 108, no. 2 (2006): 324–35.

Becerra, Rebeca. "Etnografía del guancasco entre la villa de San Antonio, departamento de Comayagua y Yarumela, departamento de La Paz, Honduras." *Bricolage* 4, no. 12 (2006): 6–12.

Bellin, Joshua David. *The Demon of the Continent: Indians and the Shaping of American Literature*. Philadelphia: University of Pennsylvania Press, 2001.

Belmessous, Saliha, ed. *Native Claims: Indigenous Law and Empire, 1500–1920*. Oxford, UK: Oxford University Press, 2012.

Benavente, Teófilo. "Los pintores cuzqueños de la colonia." *Revista del Instituto Americano de Arte* 11 (1963): 225–35.

Benn, Carl. *The Iroquois in the War of 1812*. Toronto: University of Toronto Press, 1998.

Benton, Bradley. "Beyond the Burned Stake: The Rule of don Antonio Pimentel Tlahuitoltzin in Texcoco, 1540–45." In *Texcoco: Prehispanic and Colonial Perspectives*, edited by Jongsoo Lee and Galen Brokaw. Boulder: University Press of Colorado, 2014.

Bhabha, Homi K. *The Location of Culture*. New York: Routledge, 2004.

Binns, Archie. *Peter Skene Ogden: Fur Trader*. Portland, OR: Binfords and Mort, 1967.

Blau, Harold. "The Iroquois White Dog Sacrifice: Its Evolution and Symbolism." *Ethnohistory* 11, no. 2 (1964): 97–119.

Boone, Elizabeth Hill. "Seeking Indianness: Christoph Weiditz, the Aztecs, and Feathered Amerindians." *CLAHR* 26, no. 1 (2017): 39–61.

————. *Stories in Black and Red: Pictorial Histories of the Aztecs and Mixtecs*. Austin: University of Texas Press, 2000.

Borochoff, David A. "Indians, Cannibals, and Barbarians: Hernán Cortés and Early Modern Cultural Relativism." *Ethnohistory* 62, no. 1 (2015): 17–38.

Bossy, John. *Christianity in the West, 1400–1700*. Oxford, UK: Oxford University Press, 1985.

Boyd, Robert T. "Lower Chinookan Disease and Demography." In *Chinookan Peoples of the Lower Columbia*, edited by Robert T. Boyd, Kenneth M. Ames, and Tony A. Johnson. Seattle: University of Washington Press, 2013.

Brading, David A. *The First America: The Spanish Monarchy, Creole Patriots, and the Liberal State, 1492–1867*. New York: Cambridge University Press, 1993.

————. "The Incas and the Renaissance: The Royal Commentaries of Inca Garcilaso de la Vega." *Journal of Latin American Studies* 18, no. 1 (1986): 1–23.

————. *Mexican Phoenix: Our Lady of Guadalupe: Image and Tradition across Five Centuries*. Cambridge: Cambridge University Press, 2001.

Braham, Persophone. "El feliz cautiverio de Gonzalo Guerrero." *Hispanic Review* 74, no. 1 (2006): 1–17.

Brant Historical Society. *A Glimpse of the Past: A Centennial History of Brantford and Brant County*. Brantford, Ontario: Brant Historical Society, 1966.

Braswell, Mary Flowers. *The Medieval Sinner: Characterization and Confession in Literature of the English Middle Ages*. Rutherford, NJ: Fairleigh Dickenson University Press, 1983.

Braund, Kathryn E. Holland. "The Creek Indians, Blacks, and Slavery." *Journal of Southern History* 57, no. 4 (1991): 601–36.

Brenner, Elise M. "To Pray or to Be Prey: That Is the Question; Strategies for Cultural Autonomy of Massachusetts Praying Town Indians." *Ethnohistory* 27, no. 2 (1980): 135–52.

Brian, Amber. *Alva Ixtlilxochitl's Native Archive and the Circulation of Knowledge in Colonial Mexico*. Nashville: Vanderbilt, 2016.

————. "Don Fernando de Alva Ixtlilxochitl's Narratives of the Conquest of Mexico: Colonial Subjectivity and the Circulation of Native Knowledge." In *The Conquest All Over Again: Nahuas and Zapotecs Thinking, Writing, and Painting Spanish Colonialism*. Edited by Susan Schroeder. Portland, OR: Sussex Academic Press, 2010.

Brokaw, Galen. "The Poetics of Khipu Historiography: Felipe Guaman Poma de Ayala's *Nueva corónica* and the *Relación de los quipucamayos*." *Latin American Research Review* 38, no. 3 (2003): 111–47.

Brosseder, Claudia. *The Power of Huacas*. Austin: University of Texas Press, 2014.

Bryce, George. *The Remarkable History of the Hudson's Bay Company*. New York: Burt Franklin, 1968.

Burkhart, Louise M. *Before Guadalupe: The Virgin Mary in Early Colonial Nahuatl*

Literature. Austin: University of Texas Press for the Institute of Mesoamerican Studies, SUNY Press, Albany, 2001.

———. "The Destruction of Jerusalem as Colonial Nahuatl Historical Drama." In *The Conquest All Over Again: Nahuas and Zapotecs Thinking, Writing, and Painting Spanish Colonialism*, edited by Susan Schroeder. Eastbourn, UK: Sussex Academic Press, 2010.

Burkhart, Louise M., Barry D. Sell, and Stafford Poole. *Aztecs on Stage: Religious Theater in Colonial Mexico*, edited by Louise M. Burkhart. Norman: University of Oklahoma Press, 2011.

Burkhart, Louise M., Barry D. Sell, Stafford Poole, Gregory Spira, Elizabeth R. Wright, eds. and trans. *Nahuatl Theater*. Vols. 1–4. Norman: University of Oklahoma Press, 2004–2009.

Burkholder, Mark A. "Honor and Honors in Colonial Spanish America." In *The Faces of Honor, Sex, Shame, and Violence in Colonial Latin America*, edited by Lyman L. Johnson and Sonya Lipsett-Rivera. Albuquerque: University of New Mexico Press, 1998.

Burns, Kathryn J. "Beatas, 'decencia' y poder: La formación de una elite indígena en el Cuzco colonial." In *Incas e indios cristianos: Élites indígenas e identidades cristianas en los Andes coloniales*, edited by Jean-Jacques Decoster. Cuzco: Centro de Estudios Regionales Bartolomé de las Casas, 2002.

———. *Into the Archive: Writing and Power in Colonial Peru*. Durham, NC: Duke University Press, 2010.

———. "Making Indigenous Archives: The Quilcaycamayoc of Colonial Cuzco." In *Indigenous Intellectuals: Knowledge, Power, and Colonial Culture in Mexico and the Andes*, edited by Gabriela Ramos and Yanna Yannakakis. Durham, NC: Duke University Press, 2014.

Butzer, Elisabeth. *Historia social de una comunidad tlaxcalteca: San Miguel de Aguayo (Bustamante, N.L.) 1686–1820*. Translated by Jerónimo Valdés Garza. Saltillo, Mexico: Archivo Municipal de Saltillo, 2001.

Cahill, David. "The Inca Motif in Colonial Fiestas." In *Habsburg Peru: Images, Imagination and Memory*, edited by Peter T. Bradley and David Cahill. Liverpool, UK: Liverpool University Press, 2000.

———. "A Liminal Nobility: The Incas in the Middle Ground of Late Colonial Peru." In *New World, First Nations: Native Peoples of Mesoamerica and the Andes under Colonial Rule*, edited by David Cahill and Blanca Tovías. Brighton, UK: Sussex Academic Press, 2006.

———. "Una nobleza asediada: Los nobles incas del Cusco en el ocaso colonial." In *Élites indígenas en los Andes: Nobles, caciques, y cabildantes bajo el yugo colonial*, edited by David Cahill and Blanca Tovías, 82–99. Quito: Abya-Yala, 2003.

Cahill, David, and Blanca Tovías, eds. *Élites indígenas en los Andes: Nobles, caciques, y cabildantes bajo el yugo colonial*. Quito: Abya-Yala, 2003.

Calloway, Colin. *The Indian History of an American Institution: Native Americans and Dartmouth*. Hanover, NH: Dartmouth College Press, 2010.

Camelo Arredondo, Rosa, and J. Gurría la Croix. *Juan Gerson: tlacuilo de Tecamachalco*. Mexico: INAH, 1964.

Campos-Muñoz, Germán. "Cuzco, 'Urbs et Orbis': Rome and Garcilaso de la Vega's Self-Classicalization." *Hispanic Review* 81, no. 2 (2013): 123–44.

Cañizares-Esguerra, Jorge. *How to Write the History of the New World: Histories, Epistemologies, and Identities in the Eighteenth-Century Atlantic World*. Stanford, CA: Stanford University Press, 2001.

Carrasco, David. "Indian Spanish Marriages in the First Century of the Colony." In *Indian Women in Early Mexico*, edited by Susan Schroeder, Stephanie Wood, and Robert Haskett. Norman: University of Oklahoma Press, 1997.

Carrasco, Pedro. "Indian-Spanish Marriages in the First Century of the Colony." In *Indian Women in Early Mexico*, edited by Susan Schroeder, Stephanie Wood, and Robert Haskett. Norman: University of Oklahoma Press, 1997.

Carrera, Magali M. *Imagining Identity in New Spain: Race, Lineage, and the Colonial Body in Portraiture and Casta Paintings*. Austin: University of Texas Press, 2012.

Carrillo y Gariel, Abelardo. *El Cristo de Mexicaltzingo: Técnica de las esculturas en caña*. Mexico City: Instituto Nacional de Antropología e Historia, 1949.

Castro-Klarén, Sara, and Christian Fernández, eds. *Inca Garcilaso and Contemporary World-Making*. Pittsburgh: University of Pittsburg Press, 2016.

Cattan, Marguerite. "En los umbrales de la instrucción de Titu Cusi Yupanqui." *Histórica* (Lima) 35, no. 2 (2011): 7–44.

Cavazos Garza, Israel. *El lic. Francisco Barbadillo: Fundador de Guadalupe, Nuevo León*. Monterrey, Mexico, 1980.

Chadwick, Edward Marion. *A Genealogy of the Brant Family*. Toronto: Rolph, Smith and Co., 1894.

Chamberlain, Robert S. *The Conquest and Colonization of Honduras*. New York: Octagon Books, 1966.

Chapman, Anne. *Los hijos del copal y la candela*. Vol. 1. Mexico City: UNAM, 1985.

Charles, John. "Trained by Jesuits: Indigenous Letrados in Seventeenth Century Peru." In *Indigenous Intellectuals: Knowledge, Power, and Colonial Culture in Mexico and the Andes*, edited by Gabriela Ramos and Yanna Yannakakis. Durham, NC: Duke University Press, 2014.

Chávez Borjas, Manuel. "El guancasco de Mexicapa: Comunidad campesina del occidente de Honduras." *Teatro Indígena* 33 (1992), 38–45.

Checa Cremades, Fernando. "Monarchic Liturgies and the 'Hidden King': The Function and Meaning of Spanish Royal Portraiture in the Sixteenth and Seventeenth Centuries." In *Iconography, Propaganda, and Legitimation*, edited by Allan Ellenius. Oxford, UK, Oxford University Press, 1998.

Chipman, Donald E. *Moctezuma's Children: Aztec Royalty under Spanish Rule, 1520–1700*. Austin: University of Texas Press, 2005.

Chocano Mena, Magdalena. "Contrastes y paralelismo: Provinciales; La autoridad indígena entre Lucanas y Conchos." In *Élites indígenas en los Andes: Nobles, caciques, y cabildantes bajo el yugo colonial*, edited by David Cahill and Blanca Tovías. Quito: Abya-Yala, 2003.

Christensen, Mark Z. *Nahua and Maya Catholicisms: Texts and Religion in Colonial Central Mexico and Yucatan*. Stanford/Berkeley: Stanford University Press / Academy of American Franciscan History, 2013.

———. *Translated Christianities: Nahuatl and Maya Religious Texts*. University Park: Pennsylvania State University Press, 2014.

Christon I. Archer, *The Army in Bourbon Mexico, 1760–1810*. Albuquerque: University of New Mexico Press, 1977.

Chuchiak, John. *The Inquisition in New Spain, 1536–1820*. Baltimore: Johns Hopkins, 2012.

Church, Warren B., and Adriana Von Hagen. "Chachapoyas: Cultural Development at an Andean Cloud Forest Crossroads." In *Handbook of South American Archaeology*, edited by Helaine Silverman and William H. Isbell. New York: Springer, 2009.

Cipolla, Craig N. "Peopling the Place, Placing the People: An Archaeology of Brothertown Discourse." *Ethnohistory* 59, no. 1 (Winter 2012): 51–78.

Clendinnen, Inga. *Ambivalent Conquests: Maya and Spaniard in Yucatan, 1517–1570*. 2nd ed. Cambridge, 2003.

Cline, Howard F. "Hernando Cortés and the Aztec Indians in Spain." *The Quarterly Journal of the Library of Congress* 26, no. 2 (1969): 70–90.

———. "The Relaciones Geográficas of the Spanish Indies, 1577–1586." *Hispanic American Historical Review* 44, no. 3 (1964): 341–74.

Colby, Susan M. *Sacagawea's Child: The Life and Times of Jean-Baptiste Charbonneau*. Norman: University of Oklahoma Press, 2004.

Connell, William F. *After Moctezuma: Indigenous Politics and Self-Government in Mexico City, 1524–1730*. Norman: University of Oklahoma Press, 2011.

Cook, Nobel David. *Born to Die: Disease and New World Conquest, 1492–1650*. Cambridge, UK: Cambridge University Press, 1998.

Cook, Sherburne, and Woodrow Borah. *The Indian Population of Central Mexico, 1530–1610*. Berkeley: University of California Press, 1960

Corbeil, Laurent. *Identities in Motion: The Formation of a Plural Indio Society in Early San Luis Potosí, New Spain, 1591–1630*. PhD diss., McGill-Queen's University Press, 2014.

———. *The Motions Beneath: Indigenous Migrants on the Urban Frontier of New Spain*. New York: Cambridge, 2018.

Córdova, James M. "Clad in Flowers: Indigenous Arts and Knowledge in Colonial Mexican Convents." *The Art Bulletin* 93, no. 4 (2011): 449–67.

Cossio del Pomar, Felipe. *Peruvian Colonial Art: The Cusco School of Painting*. Translated by Genaro Arbaiza. Mexico City: Editorial Libros de México, 1964.

Crahan, Margaret E. "The Administration of don Melchor de Navarra y Rocafull, Duque de la Palata: Viceroy of Peru, 1681–1689." *The Americas* 27, no. 4 (1971): 389–412.

Crane, Vernor W. *The Southern Frontier, 1670–1732.* Durham, NC: Duke University Press, 1928.

Crevels, Mily. "Language Endangerment in South America." In *The Indigenous Languages of South America: A Comprehensive Guide,* edited by Lyle Campbell and Verónica Grondona. Berlin/Boston: Walter de Gruyter, 2012.

Cuadriello, Jaime. *Las glorias de la república de Tlaxcala: O la conciencia como imagen sublime.* Mexico, D.F.: UNAM, 2004.

Cuello, José. "The Economic Impact of the Bourbon Reforms and the Late Colonial Crisis of Empire at the Local Level: The Case of Saltillo, 1777–1817." *The Americas* 44, no. 3 (1988): 301–24.

Cummins, Thomas. "The Indulgent Image." In *Contested Visions in the Spanish Colonial World,* edited by Ilona Katzew. Los Angeles: LACMA; Mexico: Museo Nacional de Historia, 2012.

———. "Let Me See! Reading Is for Them: Colonial Andean Images and Objects, 'como es costumbre tener los caciques Señores.'" In *Native Traditions in the Postconquest World,* edited by Elizabeth Hill Boone and Tom Cummins. Washington, DC: Dubarton Oaks Research Library, 1998.

———. "A Tale of Two Cities: Cusco, Lima, and the Construction of Colonial Representation." In *Converging Cultures: Arts and Identity in Spanish America,* edited by Diana Fane. New York: Brooklyn Museum and Harry N. Abrahams, 1996.

Curcio-Nagy, Linda. *The Great Festivals of Colonial Mexico City: Performance, Power, and Identity.* Albuquerque: University of New Mexico Press, 2004.

Cushman, Ellen. "Cherokee Syllabary from Script to Print." *Ethnohistory* 57, no. 4 (2010): 625–49.

Cushner, Nicholas P. *Lords of the Land: Sugar, Wine, and Jesuit Estates of Coastal Peru, 1600–1767.* Albany, NY: SUNY Press, 1980.

———. *Why Have You Come Here? The Jesuits and the First Evangelization of Native America.* Oxford, UK: Oxford University Press, 2006.

Cutter, Charles R. *The Protector de Indios in Colonial New Mexico, 1659–1821.* Albuquerque: University of New Mexico Press, 1986.

Damian, Carol. "Artist and Patron in Colonial Cuzco: Workshops, Contracts, and a Petition for Independence. *CLAHR* 4, no. 1 (1995): 25–53.

Davidson, Gordon Charles. *The North West Company.* New York: Russell and Russell; Berkeley: University of California Press, 1967.

Davidson, William McCartney. *Louis David Riel, 1844–1885: A Biography.* 1928. Calgary, Alberta, 1955.

Dávila Aguirre, José de Jesús. *La colonización tlaxcalteca y su influencia en el noreste de la Nueva España.* Coahuila, Mexico: Colegio Coahuilense de Investigaciones Históricas, 1977.

Dávila del Bosque, Ildefonso. *Los cabildos tlaxcaltecas: Ayuntamientos del pueblo de San Esteban de la Nueva Tlaxcala desde su establecimiento hasta su fusión con la villa del Saltillo.* Saltillo: Archivo Municipal, 2000.

Dean, Carolyn. *Inka Bodies and the Body of Christ: Corpus Christi in Colonial Cuzco, Peru.* Durham, NC: Duke University Press, 1999

———. "The Renewal of Old World Images and the Creation of Colonial Peruvian Visual Culture." In *Converging Cultures: Arts and Identity in Spanish America,* edited by Diana Fane. New York: Brooklyn Museum and Harry N. Abrahams, 1996.

———. "War Games: Indigenous Militaristic Theater in Colonial Peru." In *Contested Visions in the Spanish Colonial World,* edited by Ilona Katzew. Los Angeles: LACMA; Mexico: Museo Nacional de Historia, 2012.

De Boer, Wietse. *The Conquest of the Soul: Confession, Discipline, and Public Order in Counter-Reformation Milan.* Boston: Brill, 2001.

DeJong, David H. *Promises of the Past: A History of Indian Education in the United States.* Golden, CO: Fulcrum Press, 1993.

DeLay, Brian. *War of a Thousand Deserts: Indian Raids and the U.S.-Mexican War.* New Haven: Yale University Press, 2009.

Del Carmen Velásquez, María. *Tres estudios sobre las provincias internas de Nueva España.* Mexico City: Colegio de México, 1979.

Del Río, Mercedes. "De sacerdotes del Tawantinsuyu a cofrades coloniales: Nuevas evidencias sobre los Acustupa y Viracocha Inga de Copacabana." *Revista Andina* 49 (2009): 9–69.

De Lucca, Dennis. *Jesuits and Fortifications: The Contribution of the Jesuits to Military Architecture in the Baroque Age.* Leiden: Brill, 2012.

Demos, John. *The Heathen School: A Story of Hope and Betrayal in the Age of the Early Republic.* New York: Alfred A. Knopf, 2014.

Deur, Douglas. *An Ethnohistorical Overview of Groups with Ties to Vancouver National Historic Site.* Seattle: Pacific Northwest Cooperative Ecosystem Studies Unit, National Park Service, 2012.

Dippold, Steffi. "The Wampanoag Word: John Eliot's *Indian Grammar,* the Vernacular Rebellion, and the Elegancies of Native Speech." *Early American Literature* 48, no. 3 (2013): 543–75.

Dominguez Torres, Monica. "Emblazoning Identity: Indigenous Heraldry in Colonial Mexico and Peru." In *Contested Visions in the Spanish Colonial World,* edited by Ilona Katzew. Los Angeles: LACMA; Mexico: Museo Nacional de Historia, 2012.

Donahue-Wallace, Kelly. *Art and Architecture of Viceregal Latin America, 1521–1821.* Albuquerque: University of New Mexico Press, 2008.

———. "Picturing Prints in Early Modern New Spain." *The Americas* 64, no. 3 (2008): 328–35.

Dornbush, Krista. *AP US History, 2017–2018.* New York: Kaplan, 2017.

Douglas, Eduardo de Jesús. "Our Fathers, Our Mothers: Painting an Indian Genealogy in New Spain." In *Contested Visions in the Spanish Colonial World*, edited by Ilona Katzew. Los Angeles: LACMA; Mexico: Museo Nacional de Historia, 2012.

Ducey, Michael T. *A Nation of Villages: Riot and Rebellion in the Mexican Huasteca, 1750–1850*. Tucson: University of Arizona Press, 2004.

Dueñas, Alcira. *Indians, Mestizos, and the "Lettered City": Reshaping Justice, Social Hierarchy, and Political Culture in Colonial Peru*. Boulder: University Press of Colorado, 2010.

———. "Social Justice and Reforms in Late Colonial Peru: An Andean Critique of Spanish Colonialism." In *Struggles for Social Rights in Latin America*, edited by Susan Eva Eckstein and Timothy P. Wickham-Crowley, 296–304.

Durston, Alan. "Cristóbal Choquecasa and the Making of the Huarochirí Manuscript." In *Indigenous Intellectuals: Knowledge, Power, and Colonial Culture in Mexico and the Andes*, edited by Gabriela Ramos and Yanna Yannakakis. Durham, NC: Duke University Press, 2014.

Earle, Rebecca. *The Return of the Native: Indians and Myth-Making in Spanish America, 1810–1930*. Durham and London: Duke University Press, 2007.

Eastman, Scott. "Ya no hay Atlántico, ya no hay dos continentes: Regionalismo e identidad nacional durante la Guerra de Independencia en Nueva España." *Tiempos de América* 12 (2005): 153–66.

Echeverri, Marcela. *Indian and Slave Royalists in the Age of Revolution: Reform Revolution and Royalism in the Northern Andes, 1780–1825*. New York: Cambridge, 2016.

Edgerton, Samuel Y. *Theaters of Conversion: Religious Architecture and Indian Artisans in Colonial Mexico*. Albuquerque: University of New Mexico Press, 2001.

Edwards, Emily. *Painted Walls for Mexico from Prehistoric Times until Today*. Austin: University of Texas Press, 1996.

Ellingson, Terr. *The Myth of the Noble Savage*. Berkeley: University of California Press, 2001.

Elliott, John H. *Richelieu and Olivares*. Cambridge, UK: Cambridge University Press, 1984.

Escalante Arce, Pedro. *Los tlaxcaltecas en Centro América*. San Salvador: Biblioteca de Historia Salvadoreña, 2001.

Escalante Gonzalbo, Pablo. "Fulgor y muerte de Juan Gerson, o las oscilaciones de los pintores de Tecamachalco." In *El proceso creativo: XXVI Coloquio Internacional de Historia del Arte*, 325–42. Mexico: Universidad Nacional Autónoma de México, 2006.

Escobari de Querejazu, Laura. *Caciques, yanaconas y extravagantes: La sociedad colonial en Charcas, siglos XVI –XVIII*. La Paz: Institut Français d'Études Andines, 2001.

Espinoza Soriano, Valdemar, and Mery Baltasar Olmeda. "Los beaterios en la Lima colonial: Un caso de un beaterio para mujeres indígenas nobles." *Investigaciones Sociales* 14, no. 24: 131–47.

Estigarribia, Bruno, and Justin Pinta, eds. *Guaraní Linguistics in the Twenty-First Century.* Leiden: Brill, 2017.

Estrada Jasso, Andrés. *Imágenes de caña de maíz: Estudio, catálogo y bibliografía.* 2nd. ed. San Luis Potosí: Universidad Autónoma de San Luis Potosí, 1996.

Fane, Diana. "Notes on an Influential European Engraving." *Notes in the History of Art* 28, no. 3 (2009): 31–39.

Fanon, Frantz. *The Wretched of the Earth.* New York: Grove Press, 1965.

Fisher, John R. *Bourbon Peru, 1750–1824.* Liverpool, UK: Liverpool University Press, 2003.

Fitzmaurice, Andrew. "Powhatan Legal Claims." In *Native Claims: Indigenous Law and Empire, 1500–1920,* edited by Saliha Belmessous. Oxford, UK: Oxford University Press, 2012.

Florescano, Enrique. *Quetzalcóatl y los mitos fundadores de Mesoamérica.* Mexico, D.F.: Taurus, 2004.

Flynn, Maureen. *Sacred Charity: Confraternities and Social Welfare in Spain, 1400–1700.* Ithaca, NY: Cornell, 1989.

Frye, David. *Indians into Mexicans: History and Identity in a Mexican Town.* Austin: University of Texas Press, 1996.

Furtwangler, Albert. "Sacagawea's Son as a Symbol." *Oregon Historical Quarterly* 102, no. 3 (Fall 2001): 290–315.

Gabriel, Ralph Henry. *Elias Boudinot: Cherokee and His America.* Norman: University of Oklahoma Press, 1941.

Gálvez Peña, Carlos. "Un milagro flamenco en los Andes. In *Palabra e imagen en Hispanoamérica,* edited by Cecile Michaud. Lima: Pontificia Universidad Católica del Perú, 2015.

Ganson, Barbara. *The Guaraní under Spanish Rule in Río de la Plata.* Stanford, CA: Stanford University Press, 2003.

García Sáiz, Maria Concepción. "Portraiture in Viceregal America." In *Retratos: 2,000 Years of Latin American Portraits,* edited by Marion Oettinger. New Haven: Yale University Press, 2004.

Garrett, David T. "La iglesia y el poder social de la nobleza indígena cuzqueña, siglo XVIII. In *Incas e indios cristianos: Élites indígenas e identidades cristianas en los Andes coloniales,* edited by Jean-Jacques Decoster. Cuzco: Centro de Estudios Regionales Bartolomé de las Casas, 2002.

———. "'In Spite of Her Sex': The Cacica and the Politics of the Pueblo in the Late Colonial Andes." *The Americas* 64, no. 4 (2008): 547–81.

———. *Shadows of Empire: The Indian Nobility of Cusco, 1750–1825.* Cambridge, UK: Cambridge University Press, 2005.

Gaustad, Edwin S. *Roger Williams.* New York: Oxford University Press, 2005.

Gibson, Charles. *The Aztecs under Spanish Rule.* Stanford, CA: Stanford, 1964.

———. "The Identity of Diego Muñoz Camargo." *The Hispanic American Historical Review* 30, no. 2 (1950): 199–200.

———. *Tlaxcala in the Sixteenth Century.* New Haven: Yale University Press, 1952.

Gil, Jean. "Los primeros mestizos indios en España: Una voz ausente." In *Entre dos mundos: Fronteras culturales y agentes mediadores,* edited by Berta Ares Queija and Serge Gruzinski. Seville: CSIC, 1997.

Gisbert, Teresa. "Los curacas de Collao y la conformación de la cultura mestiza andina." *Senri Ethnological Studies* 33 (1992): 54–58.

González Gómez, José Antonio. "El caso de Antonio Valeriano y el *Nican mopohua*: Entre la historia y la tradición." Conference paper, Encuentro Interdisciplinario de Antropología e Historia del Guadalupanismo, Escuela Nacional de Antropología e Historia, Mexico City, September 2003.

Goode, Joshua. "Corrupting a Good Mix: Race and Crime in Late Nineteenth- and Early Twentieth-Century Spain." *European History Quarterly* 35, no. 2 (2005): 241–65.

Gose, Peter. *Invaders as Ancestors: On the Intercultural Making and Unmaking of Spanish Colonialism in the Andes.* Toronto: University of Toronto Press, 2008.

Graubart, Karen. *With Our Labor and Sweat: Indigenous Women and the Formation of Colonial Society in Peru, 1550–1700.* Stanford, CA: Stanford, 2007.

Greene, Jack P. *Peripheries and Center: Constitutional Development in the Extended Politics of the British Empire and the United States, 1607–1788.*

Greer, Allan. *Mohawk Saint: Catherine Tekakwitha and the Jesuits.* Oxford, UK: Oxford University Press, 2005.

Griffen, William B. *Apaches at War and Peace: The Janos Presidio, 1750–1858.* Norman: University of Oklahoma Press, 1988.

Gross, Hanns. *Rome in the Age of Enlightenment: The Post Tridentine Syndrome and the Ancien Regime.* Cambridge, 1990.

Gruzinski, Serge. "Individualization and Acculturation: Confession among the Nahuas of Mexico from the Sixteenth to the Eighteenth Century." In *The Church in Colonial Latin America,* edited by John Frederick Schwaller. Lanham, MD: Roman and Littlefield, 2000.

Guengerich, Sara Vicuña. "Capac Women and the Politics of Marriage in Early Colonial Peru." *Colonial Latin American Review* 24, no. 2 (2015): 147–67.

———. "Inca Women under Spanish Rule: Probanzas and Informaciones of the Colonial Andean Elite." In *Women's Negotiations and Textual Agency in Latin America, 1500–1799,* edited by Mónica Díaz and Rocío Quispe-Agnoli. New York: Routledge, 2016.

Guha, Ranajit, and Gayatri Chrakravorty Spivak. *Selected Subaltern Studies.* With a foreword by Edward Said. Oxford, UK: Oxford University Press, 1988.

Hämäläinen, Pekka. *Comanche Empire.* New Haven: Yale University Press, 2009.

Harris, Max. *Aztecs, Moors, and Christians: Festivals of Reconquest in Mexico and Spain.* Austin: University of Texas Press, 2000.

————. "Saint Sebastian and the Blue-Eyed Blacks: Corpus Christi in Cusco, Peru." *The Drama Review* 47, no. 1 (2003): 149–65.

Harth-Terré, Emilio. "El esclavo negro en la sociedad indoperuana." *Journal of Inter-American Studies* 3, no. 3 (1961): 297–340.

Haskett, Robert. "Conquering the Spiritual Conquest in Cuernavaca." In *The Conquest All Over Again: Nahuas and Zapotecs Thinking, Writing, and Painting Spanish Colonialism*, edited by Susan Schroeder. Eastbourn, UK: Sussex Academic Press, 2010.

————. "Paper Shields: The Ideology of Coats of Arms in Colonial Mexican Primordial Titles." *Ethnohistory* 43, no. 1 (1996): 99–126.

Hassig, Ross. "Xicoténcatl: Rethinking an Indigenous Mexican Hero." *Estudios de Cultura Náhuatl* 32 (2001): 29–49.

Hegel, G. W. F. *The Phenomenology of Spirit.* Translated by A. V. Miller. New York: Oxford University Press, 1977.

Herranz, Atanasio. "Lenca." In *The Oxford Encyclopedia of Mesoamerican Cultures: The Civilizations of Mexico and Central America.* Edited by Davíd Carrasco. Oxford, UK: Oxford University Press, 2001.

Herrera Valdez, Luis Fernando. "Origen y significado del escudo de Tlaxcala." *Potestas* 8 (2017): 83–104.

Herzog, Tamar. "Guaranis and Jesuits: Bordering the Spanish and Portuguese Empires." *ReVista: Harvard Review of Latin America* 14, no. 3 (Spring 2015): 50–52.

Hoig, Stan. *The Chouteaus: First Family of the Fur Trade.* Albuquerque: University of New Mexico Press, 2008.

Holden, John Rose. *The Brant Family: A Primitive Civilization.* Hamilton, Ontario: Wentworth Historical Society, 1904.

Hyde, Anne F. *Empires, Nations, and Families: A History of the North American West, 1800–1860.* Lincoln: University of Nebraska Press, 2011.

Ixtlilxochitl, Don Fernando. *Native Conquistador: Alva Ixtlilxochitl's Account of the Conquest of New Spain.* Edited and translated by Amber Brian, Bradley Benton, and Pablo García Loaeza. University Park: Pennsylvania State University Press, 2015.

Jackson, Robert H. *Conflict and Conversion in Sixteenth Century Central Mexico: The Augustinian War on and beyond the Chichimeca Frontier.* Boston: Brill, 2013.

Jackson, Robert H., and Fernando Esparragoza Amador. *A Visual Catalog of Sixteenth Century Central Mexican Doctrinas.* Cambridge, UK: Cambridge Scholars, 2016.

Jackson, Robert L. *Demographic Change and Ethnic Survival among the Sedentary Populations on the Jesuit Mission Frontiers of Spanish Latin America, 1609–1803: The Formation and Persistence of Mission Communities in a Comparative Context.* Leiden: Brill, 2015.

Jager, Rebecca. *Malinche, Pocahontas, and Sacagawea: Indian Women as Cultural*

Intermediaries and National Symbols. Norman: University of Oklahoma Press, 2015.

Jasanoff, Maya. *Liberty's Exiles: American Loyalists in the Revolutionary World.* New York: Random House, 2011.

Johnson, Evelyn H. C. "John Smoke Johnson: Sakayengwaraton—Disappearing of the Indian Mist." In *Ontario Historical Society: Papers and Records,* 9:102–13. Toronto: Ontario Historical Society, 1910.

Joya, Olga Marina, and Paúl Martínez. *Comayagua: Guía de arquitectura.* Seville: Junta de Andalucía, 2011.

Kagan, Richard L. *Urban Images of the Hispanic World, 1493–1793.* New Haven: Yale University Press, 2000.

Kamen, Henry. *Empire: How Spain Became a World Power, 1492–1763.* New York: Harper Collins, 2004.

———. *Philip of Spain.* New Haven: Yale University Press, 1997.

Karasch, Mary. *Before Brasília: Frontier Life in Central Brazil.* Albuquerque: University of New Mexico Press, 2016.

Karttunen, Frances. *Between Two Worlds: Interpreters, Guides, and Survivors.* New Brunswick, NJ: Rutgers University Press, 1994.

———. "Rethinking Malinche." In *Indian Women of Early Mexico,* edited by Susan Schroeder, Stephanie Wood, and Robert Haskett. Norman: University of Oklahoma, 1997.

Katzew, Ilona, ed. *Contested Visions in the Spanish Colonial World.* Los Angeles: LACMA; Mexico: Museo Nacional de Historia, 2012.

———. "'Remedo de la ya muerta América': The Construction of Festive Rites in Colonial Mexico." In *Contested Visions in the Spanish Colonial World,* edited by Ilona Katzew. Los Angeles: LACMA; Mexico: Museo Nacional de Historia, 2012.

Keen, Benjamin. *The Aztec Image in Western Thought.* New Brunswick, NJ: Rutgers University Press, 1990.

Kelsay, Isabel Thompson. *Joseph Brant: A Man of Two Worlds.* Syracuse, NY: Syracuse University Press, 1984.

Kinsbruner, Jay. *The Colonial Spanish-American City: Urban Life in the Age of Atlantic Capitalism.* Austin: University of Texas Press, 2005.

Kranz, Travis Barton. "The Tlaxcalan Conquest Pictorials: The Role of Images in Influencing Colonial Policy in Sixteenth-Century Mexico." PhD diss., UCLA, 2001.

———. "Visual Persuasion: Sixteenth-Century Tlaxcalan Pictorials in Response to the Conquest of Mexico." In *The Conquest All Over Again: Nahuas and Zapotecs Thinking, Writing, and Painting Spanish Colonialism,* edited by Susan Schroeder. Eastbourn, UK: Sussex Academic Press, 2010.

Kuethe, Allan J., and Kenneth J. Andrien. *The Spanish Atlantic World in the Eighteenth Century: War and the Bourbon Reforms, 1713–1796.* New York: Cambridge University Press, 2014.

Kupperman, Karen Ordahl. *Indians and English Facing off in Early America*. Ithaca, NY: Cornell University Press, 2000.

LaLande, Jeff. *First over the Siskiyous: Peter Skene Ogden's 1826–1827 Journey through the Oregon-California Borderlands*. Portland: Oregon Historical Society Press, 1987.

Lane, Kris E. *Quito 1599: City and Colony in Transition*. Albuquerque: University of New Mexico Press, 2002.

Langfur, Hal. *The Forbidden Lands: Colonial Identity, Frontier Violence, and the Persistence of Brazil's Eastern Indians, 1750–1830*. Stanford, CA: Stanford University Press, 2006.

Lang, William L. "The Chinookan Encounter with Euro-Americans in the Lower Columbia River Valley." In *The Chinookan Peoples of the Lower Columbia*, edited by Robert T. Boyd, Kenneth Ames, and Tony A. Johnson. Seattle: University of Washington Press, 2016.

Lanyon, Anna. *The New World of Martín Cortés*. Sidney: Allen and Unwin, 2003.

Lee, Jongsoo. *The Allure of Nezahualcoyotl: Pre-Hispanic History, Religion, and Nahua Poetics*. Albuquerque: University of New Mexico Press, 2009.

Lepage, Andrea. "El arte de la conversión: Modelos educativos del Colegio de San Andrés de Quito." *Procesos* 25, no. 1 (2007): 47–77.

Levin Rojo, Danna A. *Return to Aztlan: Indians, Spaniards, and the Invention of Nuevo México*. Norman: University of Oklahoma Press, 2014.

Levy, Evonne. *Propaganda and the Jesuit Baroque*. Oakland: University of California Press, 2004.

Lockhart, James. *The Men of Cajamarca: A Social and Biographical Study of the First Conquerors of Peru*. Austin: University of Texas Press, 1972.

———. *The Nahuas after Conquest: A Social and Cultural History of the Indians of Central Mexico, Sixteenth through Eighteenth Centuries*. Stanford, CA: Stanford University Press, 1992.

Lopenzina, Drew. *Red Ink: Native Americans Picking Up the Pen in the Colonial Period*. Albany: SUNY Press, 2012.

López Serrelangue, Delfina Esmeralda. *La nobleza indígena de Pátzcuaro en la época virreinal*. Mexico City: UNAM, 1965.

Lovell, W. George. *Conquest and Survival in Colonial Guatemala: A Historical Geography of the Cuchumatán Highlands, 1500–1821*. Buffalo: McGill-Queen's University Press, 1985.

Lovell, W. George, Christopher H. Lutz, Wendy Kramer, and William R. Swezey. *"Strange Lands and Different Peoples": Spaniards and Indians in Colonial Guatemala*. Norman: University of Oklahoma Press, 2013.

Lukács, Georg. *Studies in Marxist Dialectics*. Translated by Rodney Livingstone. Cambridge, MA: MIT Press, 1990.

Lupher, David. *Romans in the New World*. Ann Arbor: University of Michigan Press, 2003.

Lutz, Christopher H. *Santiago de Guatemala, 1541–1773: City, Caste, and the Colonial Experience*. Norman: University of Oklahoma Press, 1994.

Lynch, John. *Bourbon Spain, 1700–1808*. Oxford, UK: Basil Blackwell, 1989.

MacCormack, Sabine. "From the Sun of the Incas to the Virgin of Copacabana." *Representations* 8 (1984): 30–60.

———. *On the Wings of Time*. Princeton, NJ: Princeton University Press, 2007.

MacLean, Robert. "Historia de Tlaxcala." Introduction to exhibit, Special Collections Department, University of Glasgow Library, January 2003.

Magnuson, Roger. *Education in New France*. Montreal: McGill-Queen's University Press, 1992.

Mangan, Jane E. *Transatlantic Obligations: Creating the Bonds of Family in Conquest-Era Peru and Spain*. New York: Oxford University Press, 2016.

Mariátegui Oliva, Ricardo. *Pintura cuzqueña del siglo XVII: Los maravillosos lienzos del corpus existentes en la iglesia de Santa Ana del Cuzco*. Lima: Alma Mater, 1951.

Martínez Baracs, Andrea. "Colonizaciones tlaxcaltecas." *Historia Mexicana* 43, no. 2 (1993): 195–250.

———. *Un gobierno de indios: Tlaxcala, 1519–1750*. Mexico City: CIESAS, 2008.

Martínez Baracs, Rodrigo. *La secuencia Tlaxcalteca, orígenes del culto de Nuestra Señora de Ocotlán*. Mexico City: INAH, 2000.

Martínez, María Elena. "Indigenous Genealogies: Lineage, History, and the Colonial Pact in Central Mexico and Peru." In *Indigenous Intellectuals: Knowledge, Power, and Colonial Culture in Mexico and the Andes*, edited by Gabriela Ramos and Yanna Yannakakis. Durham, NC: Duke University Press, 2014.

Martínez Saldaña, Tomás. *La diáspora tlaxcalteca: Colonización agrícola del norte mexicano*. Tlaxcala, Mexico: Gobierno del Estado de Tlaxcala, 1998.

Martín, Luis. *La conquista intelectual del Perú*. Barcelona: Editorial Casiopea, 2001.

Marzal, Manuel. "Blas Valera y la verdadera historia incaica." In *Guamán Poma y Blas Valera*, edited by Francisco Canti. Rome: Institution Italiano-Latinoamericano, 2001.

Marzal, Manuel, and Luis Bacigalupo, eds. *Los Jesuitas y la modernidad en Iberoamérica, 1549–1573*. Lima: Instituto Frances de Estudios Andinos, 2001.

Matthew, Laura E. *Memories of Conquest: Becoming Mexicano in Colonial Guatemala*. Chapel Hill: University of North Carolina Press, 2012.

Matthew, Laura E., and Michel R. Oudijk. *Indian Conquistadors: Indigenous Allies in the Conquest of Mesoamerica*. Norman: University of Oklahoma Press, 2007.

Maza, Francisco de la. "Fray Diego Valadés: Escritor y grabador franciscano del siglo XVI." *Anales del Instituto de Investigaciones Estéticas* (Mexico City) 13 (1945): 15–44.

McCartney Davidson, William. *Louis David Riel, 1844–1885: A Biography*. 1928. Calgary, Alberta, 1955.

McClinton, Rowena. *The Moravian Springplace Mission to the Cherokees*. Lincoln: University of Nebraska Press, 2010.

McDonough, Kelly S. *The Learned Ones: Nahua Intellectuals in Postconquest Mexico.* Tucson: University of Arizona Press, 2014.

McEnroe, Sean F. "A Confusion of Tongues or the Want of Schooling: A Carmelite Vision of Humble Penitents." In *Imagining Histories of Colonial Latin America: Essays on Synoptic Methods and Practices,* edited by Sylvia Sellers-García and Karen Melvin. Albuquerque: University of New Mexico Press, 2017.

———. *From Colony to Nationhood in Mexico: Laying the Foundations, 1560–1840.* Cambridge, UK: Cambridge University Press, 2012.

———. "The Indian Garrison Colonies of New Spain and Central America." Chap. 6 in *Borderlands of the Iberian World,* edited by Cynthia Radding and Danna Levin Rojo. New York: Oxford University Press, 2019.

———. "Plato, Aristotle, and the Virgin of Copacabana." In *Imagining Histories of Colonial Latin America: Essays on Synoptic Methods and Practices,* edited by Sylvia Sellers-García and Karen Melvin. Albuquerque: University of New Mexico, 2017.

———. "Sites of Diplomacy, Violence, and Refuge: Topography and Negotiation in the Mountains of New Spain." *The Americas* 69, no. 2 (2012): 179–202.

———. "A Sleeping Army: Diplomatic and Civic Structures on the Nahua-Chichimec Frontier." *Ethnohistory* 59, no. 1 (2012): 109–39.

McGrath, Ann. *Illicit Love: Interracial Sex and Marriage in the United States and Australia.* Lincoln: University of Nebraska Press, 2015.

McLoughlin, William G. *Cherokee Renascence in the New Republic.* Princeton, NJ: Princeton University Press, 1986.

McLoughlin, William G., and Walter H. Conser, Jr. "The Cherokees in Transition: A Statistical Analysis of the Federal Cherokee Census of 1835." *Journal of American History* 64, no. 3 (1977): 678–703.

McNaspy, C. J. *Lost Cities of Paraguay: Art and Architecture of the Jesuit Reductions, 1607–1767.* Chicago: Loyola Press, 1982

Melvin, Karen. *Building Colonial Cities of God: Mendicant Orders and Urban Culture in New Spain.* Stanford, CA: Stanford University Press, 2012.

Memmi, Albert. *The Colonizer and the Colonized.* Expanded edition. Boston: Beacon Press, 1991.

Mesa, José, and Teresa Gisbert. "El pintor virreinal Marcos Zapata y su círculo." *Revista del Instituto Americano de Arte* 11, no. 11 (1963): 212–24.

Meserve, Walter. "English Works of Seventeenth-Century Indians." *American Quarterly* 8, no. 3 (1956): 264–76.

Metcalf, Alida. *Go-Betweens and the Colonization of Brazil, 1500–1600.* Austin: University of Texas Press, 2005.

Mignolo, Walter D. "El mandato y la ofrenda: La descripción de la ciudad y provincia de Tlaxcala de Diego Muñoz Camargo y las relaciones de indias." *Nueva Revista de Filología Hispánica* 35, no. 2 (1983): 451–84.

———. "Las Meninas: A Decolonial Response." *The Art Bulletin* 92 (2010): 40–47.

Miguel Glave, Luis. "Historical and Cultural Perspective on the 1814 Revolution in

Cuzco." In *New World, First Nations: Native Peoples of Mesoamerica and the Andes under Colonial Rule*, edited by David Cahill and Blanca Tovías. Brighton, UK: Sussex Academic Press, 2006.

————. "Un curacazgo andino y la sociedad campesina del siglo XVII: La historia de Bartolomé Tupa Hallicalla, curaca de Asillo." *Allpanchis* 33 (1989): 11–39.

Miller, J. R. *Shingwauk's Vision: A History of Native Residential Schools*. Toronto: University of Toronto Press, 1999.

Mills, Kenneth. *Idolatry and Its Enemies*. Princeton, NJ: Princeton University Press, 1997.

Mills, Kenneth, and Sandra Lauderdale Graham. "Making an Image and a Shrine." In *Colonial Latin America: A Documentary Reader*, edited by Kenneth Mills, William B. Taylor, and Sandra Lauderdale Graham. Lanham, MD: Roman and Littlefield, 2004.

Mills, Kenneth, William B. Taylor, and Sandra Lauderdale Graham. "Fray Diego Valadés's Ideal Atrio and Its Activies." In *Colonial Latin America: A Documentary Reader*, edited by Kenneth Mills, William B. Taylor, and Sandra Lauderdale Graham. Lanham, MD: Roman and Littlefield, 2004.

Mira Caballos, Esteban. "Indios nobles y caciques en la corte real española, siglo XVI." *Temas Americanistas*, no. 15 (2003): 1–15.

Monaghan, E. Jennifer. *Learning to Read and Write in Colonial America*. Amherst: University of Massachusetts Press, 2005.

Monsalve, Martín. "Curacas, pleitistas, y curas abusivos: Conflicto, prestigio, y poder en los Andes coloniales, siglo XVII." In *Incas e indios cristianos: Élites indígenas e identidades cristianas en los Andes coloniales*, edited by Jean-Jacques Decoster. Cuzco: Centro de Estudios Regionales Bartolomé de las Casas, 2002.

Moorhead, Max L. *The Apache Frontier in Northern New Spain, 1769–1791*. Norman: University of Oklahoma Press, 1968.

Morgan, Lewis H., and Elisabeth Tooker. "The Structure of the Iroquois League: Lewis H. Morgan's Research and Observations." *Ethnohistory* 30, no. 3 (1983): 141–54.

Moyssén, Xavier. "Tecamachalco y el pintor indígena Juan Gerson." *Anales del Instituto de Investigaciones Estéticas* (Mexico City) 9, no. 33 (1959): 23–39.

Muir, Gary. *Bits and Pieces of Brantford's History: Brantford in the 1830s*. Brantford, Ontario: Brantford Public Library, 1977.

Mullen, Robert. *Architecture and Its Sculpture in Viceregal Mexico*. Austin: University of Texas Press, 2002.

Mumford, Jeremy Ravi. *The Vertical Empire: The General Resettlement of Indians in the Colonial Andes*. Durham, NC: Duke University Press, 2012.

Mundy, Barbara E. *The Death of Aztec Tenochtitlan, the Life of Mexico City*. Austin: University of Texas Press, 2015.

————. *The Mapping of New Spain: Indigenous Cartography and the Maps of the Relaciones Geográficas*. Chicago: University of Chicago Press, 1996.

Muriel, Josefina. *Las indias caciques de Corpus Christi*. Mexico City: UNAM, 1963.

Nash, Gary B. "The Hidden History of Mestizo America." *Journal of American History* 82, no. 3 (1995): 941–64.

Naylor, Thomas H., and Charles W. Polzer. *The Presidio and Militia on the Northern Frontier of New Spain: A Documentary History*. Vol. 1. Tucson: University of Arizona Press, 1986.

Novoa, Mauricio. *The Protectors of Indians in the Royal Audiencia of Lima: History, Careers and Legal Culture, 1575–1775*. Boston: Brill, 2016.

Nowack, Kerstin. "Aquellas señoras del linaje real de los incas: Vivir y sobrevivir como una mujer inca noble en el Perú colonial temprano." In *Élites indígenas en los Andes: Nobles, caciques y cabildantes bajo el yugo colonial*, edited by David Cahill and Blanca Tovías. Quito: Abya-Yala, 2003.

———. "Las mercedes que pedía para su salida: The Vilcabamba Inca and the Spanish State, 1539–1572." In *New World, First Nations: Native Peoples of Mesoamerica and the Andes under Colonial Rule*, edited by David Cahill and Blanca Tovías. Brighton, UK: Sussex Academic Press, 2006.

———. "Testamentos de la elite indígena en el Perú del siglo XVI." *Indiana* (Berlin) 23 (2006): 51–77.

Nutini, Hugo G. "Syncretism and Acculturation: The Historical Development of the Cult of the Patron Saint in Tlaxcala, Mexico (1519–1670)." *Ethnology* 15, no. 3 (1976): 301–21.

Oberg, Michael Leroy. *Professional Indian: The American Odyssey of Eleazar Williams*. Philadelphia: University of Pennsylvania Press, 2015.

O'Donnell, James. *Southern Indians in the American Revolution*. Knoxville: University of Tennessee Press, 1973.

Offutt, Leslie. "Defending Corporate Identity on Spain's Northeastern Frontier: San Esteban de Nueva Tlaxcala, 1780–1810." *Americas* 64, no. 3 (2007): 351–75.

Olko, Justyna. *Insignia of Rank in the Nahua World: From the Fifteenth to Seventeenth Century*. Boulder: University Press of Colorado, 2014.

O'Phelan Godoy, Scarlett. "Ascender al estado eclesiástico: La ordinación de indios en Lima a medianos del siglo XVIII." In *Incas e indios cristianos: Élites indígenas e identidades cristianas en los Andes coloniales*, edited by Jean-Jacques Decoster. Cuzco: Centro de Estudios Regionales Bartolomé de las Casas, 2002.

———. *Kurakas sin sucesiones: Del cacique al alcalde de indios*. Cuzco: Centro de Estudios Rurales Andinos Bartolomé de las Casas, 1997.

Orozco, Luis Enrique. *Los Cristos de caña de maíz y otras venerables imágenes de Nuestro Señor Jesucristo*. Vol. 1. Guadalajara, Jalisco: Arzobispado de Guadalajara, 1970.

Osorio, Alejandra B. *Inventing Lima: Baroque Modernity in Peru's South Sea Metropolis*. New York: Palgrave Macmillan, 2008.

Ossio, Juan M. "Murúa's Two Manuscripts: A Comparison." In *The Getty Murúa: Essays on the Making of Martín de Murúa's "Historia General del Piru,"* edited by

Thomas B. F. Cummins and Barbara Anderson. Los Angeles: Getty Research Institute, 2008.

Pardo, Osvaldo. "Bárbaros y mudos: Comunicación verbal y gestual en la confesión de los nahuas." *Colonial Latin American Review* 5, no. 1 (1996): 25–53.

Parkash Arora, Ved. *Louis Riel: A Bibliography*. Regina: Saskatchewan, 1972.

Parker, Arthur C. *The Code of Handsome Lake*. Albany: New York State Museum, 1913.

Pasnau, Robert. "The Distinctive Character of Scholastic Aristotelianism." In *The Oxford Handbook of Aristotle*. Oxford, UK: Oxford University Press, 2012.

Paz, Octavio. *El laberinto de la soledad*. Mexico: Fondo de Cultura Económica, 2000.

Perdue, Theda. "Rising from the Ashes: The Cherokee Phoenix as an Ethnohistorical Source." *Ethnohistory* 24, no. 2 (1977): 207–18.

———. *Slavery and the Evolution of Cherokee Society, 1540–1866*. Knoxville: University of Tennessee Press, 1979.

Perry, Adele. *Colonial Relations: The Douglas-Connolly Family and the Nineteenth-Century Imperial World*. Cambridge, UK: Cambridge University Press, 2015.

Peyer, Bernd C. *The Tutor'd Mind: Indian Missionary Writers in Antebellum America*. Amherst: University of Massachusetts Press, 1997.

Phelan, John Leddy. *The Millennial Kingdom of the Franciscans in the New World*. 2nd ed. Berkeley: University of California Press, 1970.

Pierce, Donna. "At the Crossroads: Cultural Confluence and Daily Life in Mexico." In *Painting a New World: Mexican Art and Life, 1521–1821*, edited by Donna Pierce, Rogelio Ruiz Gomar, and Clara Bargellini. Austin: University of Texas Press, 2004.

Plank, Geoffrey. "Deploying Tribes and Clans: Mohawks in Nova Scotia and Scottish Highlanders in Georgia." Chap. 9 in *Empires and Indigenes: Intercultural Alliance, Imperial Expansion, and Warfare in the Early Modern World*, edited by Wayne E. Lee. New York: New York University Press, 2011.

Pohl, John. "Mexican Codices, Maps, and Lienzos as Social Contracts." In *Writing without Words: Alternative Literacies in Mesoamerica and the Andes*. Durham, NC: Duke University Press, 1994.

———. *The Politics of Symbolism in the Mixtec Codices*. Nashville, TN: Vanderbilt, 1994.

Poole, Stafford. "History versus Juan Diego." *Americas* 62, no. 1 (2005): 1–16.

———. *Juan de Ovando: Governing the Spanish Empire in the Reign of Philip II*. Norman: University of Oklahoma Press, 2004.

———. *Our lady of Guadalupe: The Origins and Sources of a Mexican National Symbol*. Tucson: University of Arizona Press, 1995.

Porter, Joy. *Native American Freemasonry: Associationalism and Performance in America*. Lincoln: University of Nebraska Press, 2011.

Portillo Valdés, José. *Fuero indio: Tlaxcala y la identidad territorial entre la monarquía imperial y la república nacional, 1787–1824*. Mexico City: Colegio de México, 2014.

Powell, Philip Wayne. *Mexico's Miguel Caldera: The Taming of America's First Frontier, 1548–1597.* Tucson: University of Arizona Press, 1977.

Powers, Karen Viera. *Women in the Crucible of Conquest: The Gendered Genesis of Spanish American Society.* Albuquerque: University of New Mexico Press, 2005.

Pratt, Mary Louise. "Arts of the Contact Zone." *The Profession* (1991): 33–40.

Prucha, Francis Paul. *The Great Father: The United States Government and the American Indians.* Lincoln: University of Nebraska Press, 1984.

Puente Luna, José Carlos de la. *Andean Cosmopolitans: Seeking Justice and Reward at the Spanish Royal Court.* Austin: University of Texas Press, 2018.

Pulsipher, Jenny Hale. "Gaining the Diplomatic Edge: Kinship, Trade, Ritual, and Religion in Amerindian Alliances in Early North America." Chap. 2 in *Empires and Indigenes: Intercultural Alliance, Imperial Expansion, and Warfare in the Early Modern World*, edited by Wayne E. Lee. New York: New York University Press, 2011.

Quichua Chaico, David. "María Sacama, curaca de los andamarkas, 1600–1641." *Summa Humanitatis* 6, no. 1 (2012): 1–14.

Ramírez, Susan E. "The Cosmological Bases of Local Power in the Andes." In *New World, First Nations: Native Peoples of Mesoamerica and the Andes under Colonial Rule*, edited by David Cahill and Blanca Tovías. Brighton, UK: Sussex Academic Press, 2006.

———. "Instability at the Top: A Social History of the Landed Elite in Colonial Peru." *CLAHR* 3, no. 3 (1994): 327–46.

Ramos, Gabriela. "Indigenous Intellectuals in Andean Colonial Cities." In *Indigenous Intellectuals: Knowledge, Power, and Colonial Culture in Mexico and the Andes*, edited by Gabriela Ramos and Yanna Yannakakis. Durham, NC: Duke University Press, 2014.

Ramos, Gabriela, and Yanna Yannakakis, eds. *Indigenous Intellectuals: Knowledge, Power, and Colonial Culture in Mexico and the Andes.* Durham, NC: Duke University Press, 2014.

Rappaport, Joanne. "Object and Alphabet: Andean Indians and Documents in the Colonial Period." In *Writing Without Words: Alternative Literacies in Mesoamerica and the Andes.* Durham, NC: Duke University Press, 1994.

Rappaport, Joanne, and Tom Cummins. *Beyond the Lettered City: Indigenous Literacies in the Andes.* Durham, NC: Duke University Press, 2012.

Regalado de Hurtado, Liliana. *El inca Titu Cusi Yupanqui y su tiempo: Los incas de Vilcabamba y los primeros cuarenta años del dominio español.* Lima: Pontificia Universidad Católica del Perú, 1997.

Reid, Jennifer. *Louis Riel and the Creation of Modern Canada: Mythic Discourse and the Postcolonial State.* Albuquerque: University of New Mexico Press, 2009.

Reid, Joshua L. *The Sea Is My Country: The Maritime World of the Makahs, an Indigenous Borderlands People.* New Haven: Yale University Press, 2015.

Reinhart, Leslie. "British and Indian Identities in a Picture by Benjamin West." *Eighteenth-Century Studies* 31, no. 3 (1998): 283–305.

Reséndez, Andrés. *A Land So Strange: The Epic Journey of Cabeza de Vaca*. New York: Basic Books, 2007.

Restall, Matthew. *Maya Conquistador*. Boston: Beacon, 1998.

Restall, Matthew, and Florine Asselbergs. *Invading Guatemala: Spanish, Nahua, and Maya Accounts of the Conquest Wars*. University Park: Pennsylvania State University Press, 2007.

Restall, Matthew, Lisa Sousa, and Kevin Terraciano, eds. *Mesoamerican Voices: Native Language Writings from Colonial Mexico, Yucatan, and Guatemala*. New York: Cambridge University Press, 2005.

Reville, F. Douglas. *History of the County of Brant*. Brantford, Ontario: Brant Historical Society, 1920.

Reyner, John, and Jeanne Eder. *American Indian Education: A History*. Norman: University of Oklahoma Press, 2004.

Ricard, Robert. *The Spiritual Conquest of Mexico: An Essay on the Apostolate and the Evangelizing Methods of the Mendicant Orders in New Spain: 1523–1572*. Translated by Lesley Byrd Simpson. Berkeley: University of California Press, 1966.

Riley, James D. "Public Works and Local Elites: The Politics of Taxation in Tlaxcala, 1780–1810." *The Americas* 58, no. 3 (2001): 355–393.

Ríos, Eduardo Enrique. *Fray Margil de Jesús: Apóstol de América*. 2nd. ed. Mexico: Editorial Jus, 1955.

Robinson, Barry. *The Mark of Rebels: Indios Fronterizos and Mexican Independence*. Tuscaloosa: University of Alabama Press, 2016.

Robles, Vito Alessio. *Coahuila y Texas en la época colonial*. 2d ed. Mexico City: Editorial Porrúa, 1978.

Rodríguez Oródñez, Jaime. *The Independence of Spanish America*. New York: Cambridge, 1998.

Roland, Charles G. "The Portrait of Robert Kerr." *Canadian Bulletin of Medical History* 12 (1995): 187–94.

Roller, Heather Flynn. *Amazonian Routes: Indigenous Mobility and Colonial Communities in Northern Brazil*. Stanford, CA: Stanford University Press, 2014.

Romero, Rolando J. "Texts, Pre-texts, Con-texts: Gonzalo Guerrero in the Chronicles of Indies." *Revista de Estudios Hispánicos* 26, no. 3 (October 1992): 345–67.

Rostworowski, María. "El repartimiento de doña Beatriz Coya en el valle de Yucay." *Historia y Cultura* (Lima) 4 (1970): 153–267.

Round, Philip H. *Removable Type: Histories of the Book in Indian Country, 1663–1880*. Chapel Hill: University of North Carolina Press, 2010.

Rubin, Julius. "The First Fruits of the Cherokee Nation: Catharine Brown and Sister Margaret Ann." Chap. 5 in *Perishing Heathens: Stories of Protestant Missionaries and Christian Indians in Antebellum America*. Lincoln: University of Nebraska Press, 2017.

Ruiz Guadalajara, Juan Carlos. "El capitán Miguel Caldera y la frontera chichimeca:

Entre el mestizo historiográfico y el soldado del rey." *Revista de Indias* 70, no. 248 (2010): 23–58.

Ruiz Medrano, Ethelia. "Don Carlos de Tezcoco and the Universal Rights of Emperor Carlos V." In *Texcoco: Prehispanic and Colonial Perspectives*, edited by Jongsoo Lee and Galen Brokaw. Boulder: University Press of Colorado, 2014.

Ruiz Medrano, Ethelia, and Susan Kellogg. *Negotiation within Domination: New Spain's Indian Pueblos Confront the Spanish State*. Boulder: University Press of Colorado, 2010.

Sáenz, Alfredo. *Arquetipos cristianos*. Pamplona: Gratis Date, 2005.

Salles-Reese, Verónica. *From Viracocha to the Virgin of Copacabana*. Austin: University of Texas Press, 1997.

Salmon, Roberto Mario. *Indian Revolts in Northern New Spain (1680–1786)*. Lanham, MD: University Press of America, 1991.

Sampeck, Kathryn. "Colonial Mesoamerican Literacy: Method, Form, and Consequence." *Ethnohistory* 62, no. 3 (2015): 409–20.

Sandos, James A. "From 'Boltonlands' to 'Weberlands': The Borderlands Enter American History." *American Quarterly* 46, no. 4 (1994): 595–604.

Saravia Salazar, Javier Iván. "La evolución de un cargo: La protectoría de indios en el virreinato peruano." *Desde el Sur* (Lima) 4, no. 1 (2012): 27–56.

Sarreal, Julia J. S. *The Guaraní and Their Missions: A Socioeconomic History*. Stanford, CA: Stanford University Press, 2014.

Satterfield, Andrea McKenzie. "The Assimilation of the Marvelous Other: Reading Christoph Weiditz's *Trachtenbuch* (1529) as an Ethnographic Document." MA thesis, University of South Florida, 2007.

Schneider, Bethany. "Boudinot, Emerson, and Ross on Cherokee Removal." *English Literary History* 75, no. 1 (2008): 151–77.

Schroeder, Susan, ed. *The Conquest All Over Again: Nahuas and Zapotecs Thinking, Writing, and Painting Spanish Colonialism*. Eastbourn, UK: Sussex Academic Press, 2010.

Schroeder, Susan, Stephanie Wood, and Robert Haskett, eds. *Indian Women of Early Mexico*. Norman: University of Oklahoma Press, 1997.

Schwaller, John Frederick. "The Brothers Fernando de Alva Ixtlilxochitl and Bartolomé de Alva." In *Indigenous Intellectuals: Knowledge, Power, and Colonial Culture in Mexico and the Andes*, edited by Gabriela Ramos and Yanna Yannakakis. Durham, NC: Duke University Press, 2014.

———. "Don Bartolomé de Alva, Nahuatl Scholar of the Seventeenth Century." In *A Guide to Confession Large and Small in the Mexican Language, 1634*, edited by Barry D. Sell, John Frederick Schwaller, and Lu Ann Homza. Norman: University of Oklahoma Press, 1999.

Sego, Eugene B. *Aliados y adversarios: Los colonos tlaxcaltecas en la frontera septentrional de Nueva España*. San Luís Potosí: Colegio del Estado de Tlaxcala, 1998.

Sell, Barry D. "Perhaps Our Lord, God, Has Forgotten Me: Intruding into the

Colonial Nahua (Aztec) Confessional." In *The Conquest All Over Again: Nahuas and Zapotecs Thinking, Writing, and Painting Spanish Colonialism*. Portland, OR: Sussex Academic Press, 2010.

Sellers-García, Sylvia. *Distance and Documents at the Spanish Empire's Periphery*. Stanford, CA: Stanford University Press, 2013.

Shah, Priya. "Language, Discipline, and Power." *Voces Novae* 4, no. 1 (2013): 102–24.

Shannon, Timothy J. "Dressing for Success on the Mohawk Frontier: Hendrick, William Johnson, and the Indian Fashion." *The William and Mary Quarterly* 53, no. 1 (1996): 13–42.

Sheptak, Russell. "Colonial Masca in Motion: Tactics of Persistence of a Honduran Indigenous Community." PhD diss., University of Leiden, 2013.

Sheptak, Russell, Rosemary A. Joyce, and Kira Blaisdell-Sloan. "Pragmatic Choices, Colonial Lives: Resistance, Ambivalence, and Appropriation in Northern Honduras." In *Enduring Conquests: Rethinking the Archeology of Resistance to Spanish Colonialism in the Americas*, edited by Matthew Liebmann and Melissa S. Murphy. Santa Fe: School for Advanced Research, 2010.

Sheridan Prieto, Cecilia. "'Indios madrineros': Colonizadores tlaxcaltecas en el noreste novohispano." *Estudios de Historia Novohispana* 24 (2001): 15–51.

Sherman, William L. "A Conqueror's Wealth: Notes on the Estate of Don Pedro de Alvarado." *The Americas* 26, no. 2 (1969): 199–213.

———. "Tlaxcalans in Post-Conquest Guatemala." *Tlalocan* 6 (1970): 124–39.

Shoemaker, Nancy. "Kateri Tekakwitha's Tortuous Path to Sainthood." In *Negotiators of Change: Historical Perspectives on Native American Women*. New York: Routledge, 1995.

Silverman, David J. "Indians, Missionaries, and Religious Translation: Creating Wampanoag Christianity in Seventeenth-Century Martha's Vineyard." *William and Mary Quarterly*, 3rd ser., 62, no. 2 (2005): 141–74.

SilverMoon. "The Imperial College of Tlatelolco and the Emergence of a New Nahua Intellectual Elite." PhD diss., Duke University, 2007.

Simmons, Marc. "Tlaxcalans in the Spanish Borderlands." *New Mexico Historical Review* 39, no. 2 (1964): 101–10.

Sleeper-Smith, Susan. *Indian Women and French Men: Rethinking Cultural Encounter in the Western Great Lakes*. Amherst: University of Massachusetts Press, 2001.

Sleeper-Smith, Susan, Juliana Barr, Jean M. O'Brien, and Nancy Shoemaker, eds. *Why You Can't Teach United States History without American Indians*. Chapel Hill: University of North Carolina Press, 2005.

Snyder, Christina. "Conquered Enemies, Adopted Kin, and Owned People: The Creek Indians and Their Captives." *Journal of Southern History* 73, no. 2 (2007): 255–88.

Spicer, Edward H. *Cycles of Conquest: the Impact of Spain, Mexico, and the United States on the Indians of the Southwest, 1533–1960*. Tucson: University of Arizona Press, 1962.

Spores, Ronald. "The Mixteca Cacicas: Status, Wealth, and the Political Accommodation of Native Elite Women in Early Colonial Oaxaca." In *Indian Women in Early Mexico*, edited by Susan Schroeder, Stephanie Wood, and Robert Haskett. Norman: University of Oklahoma Press, 1997.

Stanfield-Mazzi, Maya. *Object and Apparition.* Tucson: University of Arizona Press, 2013.

Stayton, Kevin. "The Algara Romero de Terreros Collection: Mexican Colonial Family in an Aristocratic Era." In *Converging Cultures: Arts and Identity in Spanish America*. New York: Brooklyn Museum and Harry N. Abrahams, 1996.

Stern, Peter. "The White Indians of the Borderlands." *Journal of the Southwest* 33, no. 3 (1991): 262–81.

Stern, Steve. "Early Spanish-Indian Accommodation in the Andes." In *The Indian in Latin American History: Resistance, Resilience, and Accommodation*, edited by John E. Kicza. Lanhan, MD: Roman and Littlefield, 2000.

———. *Peru's Indian Peoples and the Challenge of the Spanish Conquest: Huamanga to 1640.* 2nd ed. Madison: University of Wisconsin Press, 1993.

———. *Resistance, Rebellion, and Consciousness in the Andean Peasant World, 18th–20th Centuries.* Madison: University of Wisconsin Press, 1983.

Stoler, Ann Laura. "The Politics of Comparison in North American History and (Post) Colonial Studies." *Journal of American History* 88, no. 3 (2001): 829–65.

Szasz, Margaret. *Indian Education in the American Colonies, 1607–1783.* Lincoln: University of Nebraska Press, 1988.

Tavárez, David. *The Invisible War: Indigenous Devotions, Discipline, and Dissent in Colonial Mexico.* Stanford, CA: Stanford, 2011.

———. "Nahua Intellectuals, Franciscan Scholars, and the *Devotio Moderna* in Colonial Mexico." *The Americas* 70, no. 2 (2013): 203–35.

Taylor, Alan. *The Civil War of 1812: American Citizens, British Subjects, Irish Rebels, & Indian Allies.* New York: Vintage, 2011.

———. *The Divided Ground: Indians, Settlers, and the Northern Borderland of the American Revolution.* New York: Vintage, 2006.

Taylor, William B. *Drinking, Homicide, and Rebellion in Colonial Mexican Villages.* Stanford, CA: Stanford University Press, 1979.

———. *Magistrates of the Sacred: Priests and Parishioners in Eighteenth-Century Mexico.* Stanford, CA: Stanford University Press, 1996.

———. "Religious Prints and their Uses." Paper presented at Harvard University, 4 October 2014.

———. *Shrines and Miraculous Images.* Albuquerque: University of New Mexico Press, 2010.

———. "The Virgin of Guadalupe in New Spain: An Inquiry into the Social History of Marian Devotion." *American Ethnologist* 14, no. 1 (1987): 9–33.

Temple, Ella Dunbar. "Don Carlos Inca." *Revista Histórica* 17 (1948): 134–79.

Tentler, Thomas N. *Sin and Confession on the Eve of the Reformation.* Princeton, NJ: Princeton University Press, 1977.

Terraciano, Kevin. "The Colonial Mixtec Community." *HAHR* 80, no. 1 (2000): 27–32.

———. *The Mixtecs of Colonial Oaxaca: Ñudzahui History, Sixteenth through Eighteenth Centuries.* Stanford, CA: Stanford, 2001.

———. "Three Texts in One: Book XII of the Florentine Codex." *Ethnohistory* 57, no. 1 (2010): 51–72.

Todorov, Svetan. *The Conquest of America: The Question of the Other.* Translated by Richard Howard. New York: Harper, 1982.

Tooker, Elisabeth. "The Iroquois White Dog Sacrifice in the Latter Part of the Eighteenth Century." *Ethnohistory* 12, no. 2 (1965): 129–40.

Tooker, William Wallace. *John Eliot's First Indian Teacher and Interpreter Cockenoe-de-Long Island and the Story of His Career from the Early Records.* London: Henry Stevens, Son and Stiles, 1896.

Toussaint, Manuel. *Colonial Art in Mexico.* Edited and translated by Elizabeth Wilder Weissman. Austin: University of Texas Press, 1967.

Townsend, Camilla. "Don Juan Buenaventura Zapata y Mendoza and the Notion of a Nahua Identity." In *The Conquest All Over Again: Nahuas and Zapotecs Thinking, Writing, and Painting Spanish Colonialism*, edited by Susan Schroeder. Eastbourn, UK: Sussex, 2010.

———. *Malintzin's Choices: An Indian Woman in the Conquest of Mexico.* Albuquerque: University of New Mexico Press, 2006.

———. *Pocahontas and the Powhatan Dilemma.* New York: Hill and Wang, 2004.

Treviño Villarreal, Hector Jaime. *El Señor de Tlaxcala.* Monterrey, Mexico: Archivo General del Estado de Nuevo León, 1986.

Tutino, John. *Making a New World: Founding Capitalism in the Bajío and Spanish North America.* Durham, NC: Duke University Press, 2011.

Umberger, Emily. "The Monarchía Indiana in Seventeenth-Century New Spain." In *Converging Cultures: Arts and Identity in Spanish America*, edited by Diana Fane. New York: Brooklyn Museum and Harry N. Abrahams, 1996.

Urton, Gary. *The History of a Myth: Pacaritambo and the Origin of the Incas.* Austin: University of Texas Press, 1990.

———. *Inka History in Knots: Reading Khipus as Primary Sources.* Austin: University of Texas Press, 2017.

Vallebueno Garcinava, Miguel. "El señor de Mezquital: Un Cristo de caña del siglo XVI en Durango." *Anales del Instituto de Investigaciones Estéticas* 22, no. 76 (2000): 255–58.

Van Kirk, Sylvia. *Many Tender Ties: Women in Fur-Trade Society, 1670–1870.* Norman: University of Oklahoma Press, 1980.

Van Lonkhuyzen, Harold W. "A Reappraisal of the Praying Indians: Acculturation, Conversion, and Identity at Natick, Massachusetts, 1646–1730." *New England Quarterly* 63, no. 3 (1990): 396–428.

Van Young, Eric. *Hacienda and Market in Eighteenth-Century Mexico: The Rural*

Economy of the Guadalajara Region, 1675–1820. Berkeley: University of California Press, 1981.

———. "Nationalist Movement without Nationalism: The Limits of Imagined Community in Mexico, 1810–1821." In *New World, First Nations: Native Peoples of Mesoamerica and the Andes under Colonial Rule,* edited by David Cahill and Blanca Tovías. Brighton, UK: Sussex Academic Press, 2006.

———. *The Other Rebellion: Popular Violence, Ideology, and the Mexican Struggle for Independence, 1810–1821.* Stanford, CA: Stanford University Press, 2001.

Vargas Betancourt, Margarita. "Caciques tlatelolcas y tenencia de la tierra en el siglo XVI: Don Juan Quauiconoc y don Juan de Austria, en los casos de doña Leonor y doña María Coatonal." *Nuevo Mundo Mundos Nuevos* (January 2011). http://journals.openedition.org/nuevomundo/60635; https://doi.org/10.4000/nuevomundo.60635.

Varner, John Grier. *El Inca: The Life and Times of Garcilaso de la Vega.* Austin: University of Texas Press, 1969.

Vaughan, Alden. *Transatlantic Encounters: American Indians in Britain, 1500–1776.* New York: Cambridge University Press, 2006.

Vega, Juan José. *Pumacahua: De cacique represor a prócer patriota.* Lima: Universidad Nacional de Educación, 1985.

Velasco Murillo, Dana. *Urban Indians in a Silver City: Zacatecas Mexico, 1546–1810.* Stanford, CA: Stanford University Press, 2016.

Velasco Murillo, Dana, Mark Lentz, and Margarita R. Ochoa, eds. *City Indians in Spain's American Empire: Urban Indigenous Society in Colonial Mesoamerica and Andean South America, 1530–1810.* Brighton, UK: Sussex Academic Press, 2013.

Verástique, Bernardino. *Michoacán and Eden.* Austin: University of Texas Press, 2000.

Villella, Peter B. "Indian Lords, Hispanic Gentlemen: The Salazars of Colonial Tlaxcala." *The Americas* 69, no. 1 (2012): 1–36.

———. *Indigenous Elites and Creole Identity in Colonial Mexico, 1500–1800.* New York: Cambridge University Press, 2016.

———. "'Pure and Noble Indians, Untainted by Inferior Idolatrous Races': Native Elites and the Discourse of Blood Purity In Late Colonial Mexico." *HAHR* 91, no. 4 (2011): 633–63.

Vincent, Bernard. "Slaveholding Indians: The Case of the Cherokee Nation." *Deportate, Esuli, Profughe* (Venice), no. 5/6 (2006): 1–14.

Vinson III, Ben. *Bearing Arms for His Majesty: The Free-Colored Militia in Colonial Mexico.* Stanford, CA: Stanford University Press, 2002.

Vizcaya Canales, Isidro. *En los albores de la independencia: Las provincias internas de oriente durante la insurgencia de Don Miguel Hidalgo.* Monterrey, Mexico: ITESM, 1976.

Wake, Eleanor. "Codex Tlaxcala: New Insights and New Questions on the Physical Construction of Tlaxcala." *Estudios de Cultura Nahuatl* 33: 105–15.

————. "The Dawning Places: Celestially Defined Land Maps, Títulos Primordiales, and Indigenous Statements of Territorial Possession in Early Colonial Mexico." Chap. 9 in *Indigenous Intellectuals: Knowledge, Power, and Colonial Culture in Mexico and the Andes*, edited by Gabriela Ramos and Yanna Yannakakis. Durham, NC: Duke University Press, 2014.

Walker, Charles F. *Smoldering Ashes: Cuzco and the Creation of Republican Peru, 1780–1840*. Durham, NC: Duke University Press, 1999.

————. *The Tupac Amaru Rebellion*. Cambridge: Harvard University Press, 2014.

Wallace, Anthony F. C. *The Death and Rebirth of Seneca*. New York: Vintage, 1972.

Weber, David J. *Bárbaros: Spaniards and Their Savages in the Age of Enlightenment*. New Haven: Yale University Press, 2005.

————. *The Spanish Frontier in North America*. New Haven: Yale University Press, 1992.

Webster, Susan Verdi. *Lettered Artists and the Languages of Empire: Painters and the Profession in Early Colonial Quito*. Austin: University of Texas Press, 2017.

White, Richard. *The Middle Ground: Indians, Empires, and Republics in the Great Lakes Region, 1650–1815*. New York: Cambridge University Press, 1991.

Wightman, Ann M. *Indigenous Migration and Social Change: The Forasteros of Cuzco, 1570–1720*. Durham, NC: Duke University Press, 1990.

Wilde, Guillermo. *Religión y poder en las misiones de guaraníes*. Buenos Aires, Editorial SB, 2009.

"William Johnson Kerr." *Dictionary of Canadian Biography*. Vol. 7. Toronto: University of Toronto Press, 1966.

Wood, Stephanie. *Transcending Conquest: Nahua Views of Spanish Colonial Mexico*. Norman: University of Oklahoma Press, 2003.

Wright, Robin M., and Manuela Carneiro da Cunha. "Destruction, Resistance, and Transformation—Southern, Coastal, and Northern Brazil, 1580–1890." In *The Cambridge History of Native Peoples of the Americas*, vol. 3, pt. 2, edited by Frank Salomon and Stuart B. Schwartz. Cambridge, UK: Cambridge, 1999.

Wuffarden, Luis Eduardo. "From Apprentices to 'Famous Brushes': Native Artists in Colonial Peru." In *Contested Visions in the Spanish Colonial World*, edited by Ilona Katzew. Los Angeles: LACMA, 2012.

Wyss, Hilary E. *English Letters and Indian Literacies: Reading, Writing, and New England Missionary Schools, 1750–1830*. Philadelphia: University of Pennsylvania Press, 2012.

————. "Mary Occom and Sarah Simon: Gender and Native Literacy in Colonial New England." *New England Quarterly* 79, no. 3 (2006): 387–412.

Yannakakis, Yanna. *The Art of Being In-Between: Native Intermediaries, Indian Identity, and Local Rule in Colonial Oaxaca*. Durham, NC: Duke University Press, 2009.

————. "Making Law Intelligible." In *Indigenous Intellectuals: Knowledge, Power, and Colonial Culture in Mexico and the Andes*, edited by Gabriela Ramos and Yanna Yannakakis. Durham, NC: Duke University Press, 2014.

Ybarra, Patricia. *Five Centuries of Theater, History, and Identity in Tlaxcala, Mexico.* Austin: University of Texas Press, 2009.

Yirush, Craig. "'Chief Princes and Owners of All': Native American Appeals to the Crown in the Early-Modern British Atlantic." In *Native Claims: Indigenous Law and Empire, 1500–1920,* edited by Saliha Belmessous. Oxford, UK: Oxford University Press, 2012.

Young, Mary. "Cherokee Nation: Mirror of the Republic." *American Quarterly* 33, no. 5 (1981): 502–24.

Zavala, Silvio Arturo. "La encomienda como institución económica." Chap. 8 in *Ensayos sobre la colonización española en América.* Mexico, D.F.: Editorial Porrúa, 1978.

———. *La encomienda indiana.* 3rd. ed. Mexico City: Editorial Porrúa, 1992.

———. *Recuerdos de Vasco de Quiroga.* Mexico City: Porrúa, 1965.

———. *La utopía de Tomás Moro en la Nueva España.* Mexico City: Biblioteca Histórica Mexicana, 1937.

Zendt, Christina. "Marcos Zapata's *Last Supper*: A Feast of European Religion and Andean Culture." *Gastronomica* 10, no. 4 (2010): 9–11.

Zuidema, Tom. "La organización religiosa del sistema de panacas y memoria en el Cuzco incaico." In *Incas e indios cristianos: Élites indígenas e identidades cristianas en los Andes coloniales,* edited by Jean-Jacques Decoster. Cuzco: Centro de Estudios Regionales Bartolomé de las Casas, 2002.

INDEX

Page numbers in *italic* text indicate illustrations.

Rolfe, Thomas (son of Pocahontas), 29
Rosario de los Negros de Santo
    Domingo cofradía, 148

Sacaco, Diego, 45
Sacaco, Felipe, 45
sachems, 74, 76, 214
Sahagún, Bernardino de, 59, 61
Saint Augustine, 100
Saint Christopher, 151
Saint Francis of Assisi, 52, 96, 124
Saint Sebastian, 151, 171
saints, veneration of, 52, 96, 98, 104–10,
    113–17, 126–28, 148, 151, 170–71, 189
Salamanca, Spain, 14
Salazar family of Tlaxcala, 138
Salish people, 32
salt trade, 67–68
Salteaux people, 30
Saltillo, Mexico, 109, 110, 173, 178
San Antonio, Texas, 179
San Esteban de Nueva Tlaxcala, 109, 110,
    173, 178
San Francisco Borja, Colegio de, 68–72,
    138, 142, 143
San Gabriel reducción (Guarani), 189
San Joachim cofradía (Lima), 148
San José de los Naturales, Colegio de,
    62, 122
San José, Fray Calixto de, 143
San Juan Batista reducción (Guarani),
    188
San Juan de los Naturales (church), 61
San Juan Moyotlan (Mexico-
    Tenochtitlan), 60
San Lazaro barrio (Lima), 55, 149
San Lorenzo barrio (Lima), 141
San Luis Potosí, 165, 170, 173, 178
San Mateo de Mexicaltzingo, 107
San Miguel de Aguayo de la Nueva
    Tlaxcala, 109–10, 172–73, 178, 179, 185.
    See also Bustamante

San Miguel de Analco, Santa Fe, 190
San Miguel de Mexquitic de la Nueva
    Tlaxcala, 169
San Miguel, Guanajuato, 166
San Pablo Zoquipan (Mexico-
    Tenochtitlan), 60
San Pablo, College of (Lima), 70
San Pedro, College of (Lima), 70
San Sebastián. *See* Saint Sebastian
San Sebastian Atzacoalco (Mexico-
    Tenochtitlan), 60
Santa Ana barrio (Cuzco) 150–51
Santa Ana parish (Lima) 51, 52, 54, 148
Santa Cruz de la Trinidad confraternity
    (Lima), 149
Santa Fe, New Mexico, 190
Santa Felipa, 52
Santa Lucia, 170–71
Santa Maria Cuepopan (Mexico-
    Tenochtitlan), 60
Santiago de Guatemala, 172
Santiago del Cercado, Lima, 52–6,
    138–147
Santiago del Surco cofradía, 148
Santiago el Apóstol Church (Cuzco), 139
Santiago, Order of, 4, 151
Santo Domingo cofradía (Lima), 148
Santos, 98. *See also* images, sacred;
    saints, veneration of
Saskatchewan, 25–28
Sayre Topa, 35–40
Sayre Topa, Beatriz, 36
Scali Cosken, 22
Scayagusta, 22
scribes, xxi, xxiii, 34, 39, 88, 92, 54, 62,
    84, 86, 90, 93, 108
Sea Venture, 17
Selkirk venture, 29–30
Semana Santa. *See* Holy Week
Seminoles, 159–61
Senecas, 197, 213, 217
Señor de la Capilla, Saltillo, 109